Forbidden

Forbidden

Receiving Pope Francis's Condemnation
of Nuclear Weapons

Drew Christiansen, SJ, and **Carole Sargent,** Editors

Georgetown University Press / Washington, DC

© 2023 Jesuits USA East Province. All rights reserved. No part of this book may be reproduced or utilized in any form or by any means, electronic or mechanical, including photocopying and recording, or by any information storage and retrieval system, without permission in writing from the publisher.

The publisher is not responsible for third-party websites or their content. URL links were active at time of publication.

Library of Congress Cataloging-in-Publication Data

Names: Christiansen, Drew, editor. | Sargent, Carole, editor.
Title: Forbidden : receiving Pope Francis's condemnation of nuclear weapons / Drew Christiansen, SJ and Carole Sargent, editors.
Other titles: Forbidden (Georgetown Univesity Press)
Description: Washington, DC : Georgetown University Press, 2023. | Includes bibliographical references and index.
Identifiers: LCCN 2022001994 (print) | LCCN 2022001995 (ebook) | ISBN 9781647122898 (hardcover) | ISBN 9781647122904 (ebook)
Subjects: LCSH: Francis, Pope, 1936– | Nuclear weapons—Moral and ethical aspects. | Nuclear weapons—Religious aspects—Catholic Church. | Nuclear disarmament—Moral and ethical aspects. | Nuclear disarmament—Religious aspects—Catholic Church. | Deterrence (Strategy)—Religious aspects—Catholic Church. | Peace—Religious aspects—Catholic Church. | Just war doctrine.
Classification: LCC JZ5665 .F665 2022 (print) | LCC JZ5665 (ebook) | DDC 327.1/747—dc23/eng/20221005
LC record available at https://lccn.loc.gov/2022001994
LC ebook record available at https://lccn.loc.gov/2022001995

∞ This book is printed on acid-free paper meeting the requirements of the American National Standard for Permanence in Paper for Printed Library Materials.

24 23   9 8 7 6 5 4 3 2 First printing

Printed in the United States of America

Cover design by Jim Keller
Interior design by BookComp, Inc.

Dedicated to the Holy Father, Pope Francis

———————

Rev. Drew Christiansen, SJ, 1945–2022,
in memoriam

Contents

Preface	xi
Acknowledgments	xv
Introduction	1
Drew Christiansen, SJ	

PART I. How We Got Here

1 From Deterrence to Abolition: The Evolution of Roman Catholic Nuclear Ethics *William Werpehowski*	31
2 Just War Lessons We Should Remember *Tobias Winright*	37
3 Philosophical Debate on Nuclear Deterrence *Gregory M. Reichberg*	47
4 The Moral Ecology of Deterrence and Abolition *William Barbieri*	59

PART II. Witnesses

5 Nuclear Realists *David Cortright*	69
6 The Testimony of Witnesses *Daniel Hall*	76
7 Swords into Plowshares *Carole Sargent*	90

PART III. Toward a World without Nuclear Weapons

8 National Attitudes toward Nuclear Deterrence — 105
James E. Goodby

9 6 + 6 = 9: Law and Nuclear Weapons — 119
David A. Koplow

10 Abolition in the Context of General Disarmament — 128
Pierce S. Corden

11 New Models: Building Capacities for Nuclear Cooperation — 136
Richard A. Love

12 Nuclear Abolition and Global Human Needs — 146
Lawrence J. Korb

PART IV. Evolution of Just War

13 Nuclear Disarmament: Ethical Challenges at or Near Zero — 153
Gerard F. Powers

14 Just Peace and Nuclear Disarmament — 172
Maryann Cusimano Love

15 Peacebuilding and Nuclear Deterrence — 180
Daniel Philpott

16 Prophetic Indictment or Deliberative Discussion? — 193
Bernard G. Prusak

PART V. Conscience Formation

17 Formation of Conscience Regarding the Development, Possession, and Use of Nuclear Weapons — 205
Margaret R. Pfeil

18 Catholic Conscience and Nuclear Weapons — 220
Joseph J. Fahey

19 The Conundrum of Deterrence: A Practical Christian Response — 229
Lisa Sowle Cahill

| 20 | Pastoral Accompaniment: Pope Francis's Approach to the Human Vocation
Drew Christiansen, SJ | 238 |

PART VI. Moral Education

21	Reviving Disarmament Education *Kelsey Davenport*	251
22	The Nuclear History Boot Camp *David Holloway*	263
23	Propaganda for Peace: Memes, Mass Moralizing, and a World Free of Nuclear Weapons *Theodore G. Dedon*	269
24	A World without Nuclear Weapons: Imagine It One Step at a Time *John Paul Lederach*	278

PART VII. Responsible Actors

25	The Ethics of Nuclear Stewards *Maryann Cusimano Love*	287
26	In the Chain of Command *Drew Christiansen, SJ*	297
27	Profiting from the Bomb *Susi Snyder*	314
28	The Condemnation of the Possession, Threat of Use, and Use of Nuclear Weapons: Reflections for Scientists and Technologists *Pierce S. Corden*	318
29	Morality Matters: A Parliamentarian Reflects on Nuclear Disarmament *David Lammy*	328
30	The Ethics of Manufacturing Nuclear Weapons *Ramón Luzárraga*	334

31 The Responsibilities of "Enabled" Citizens for Integral
   Disarmament and Sustainable Human Development   338
   James P. O'Sullivan

   PART VIII. The Role of Lay Catholic Movements

32 Organizing the Church for a World without
   Nuclear Weapons   351
   Kevin Ahern

Index   359
About the Contributors   381

Preface

Seek peace and pursue it.
Psalm 34:14

In choosing Francis as his papal name, Jorge Mario Bergoglio identified an agenda he hoped to take from the poor man of Assisi: to embrace the poor, care for the planet, and foster peace among the peoples of Earth.[1] From the beginning his devotion to the poor, refugees, migrants, and the homeless was evident. The depth of his commitment to the environment came to public view in his encyclical *Laudato si'* (On Care of Our Common Home) and in the seven-year program the Vatican has undertaken to implement it.

Though less dramatic, Pope Francis's commitment to peace has blazed new paths, especially in relations with the Muslim world.[2] He joined in a compact of tolerance with Muslim leaders in the Persian Gulf and visited Iraq to affirm its people as they attempted to rebuild their country after twenty years of war. In an achievement that eluded his predecessors, Pope Francis concluded an agreement with China on the appointment of bishops.[3] Less well known has been his support for nuclear disarmament.

In 2017, the Holy See was among the first states to sign and ratify the United Nations Treaty on the Prohibition of Nuclear Weapons. At a Vatican symposium that November, Pope Francis condemned the possession, threat to use, and use of nuclear weapons.[4] In the wake of the condemnation, skeptics asked, what does he expect? Should officers resign their commissions? Should missile personnel become selective conscientious objectors?[5] Can states abandon their nuclear arsenals? After all, once invented, the weapons' defenders object, nuclear explosives cannot be uninvented.

Forbidden: Receiving Pope Francis's Condemnation of Nuclear Weapons addresses the question of what we should do in response to the papal condemnation. The book attempts to provide background and guidance for those—including citizens of nuclear-armed states and their allies—for whom the papal condemnation presents challenging vocational and civic choices. These include political leaders, military professionals, weapons scientists, and defense intellectuals.

The book is also intended as a resource for pastoral workers who are asked to accompany women and men in making these moral choices: pastors, preachers, pastoral counselors, spiritual directors, and teachers who share Catholic social teaching with the community of faith and the broader public.

The question is "What *shall* I do?"—or "What *shall* we do together?"—rather than the expected and speciously more exacting question "What *must* I do?" The reasons are threefold. First, Pope Francis's teaching, in keeping with the Second Vatican Council, is an invitation to action to change the world, specifically to participate in the nuclear disarmament movement. It is not a matter of keeping oneself from having "dirty hands." Rather, it is a call to respond to an urgent sign of the times, one that has been on the Catholic social policy agenda from the time of Pope Saint John XXIII sixty years ago.

Second, nuclear disarmament is a personal call. God prompts individuals and sometimes groups in a personal way, asking them to find ways appropriate to their own situations and personal gifts to contribute to the elimination of nuclear weapons.

Third, eliminating nuclear weapons is a duty incumbent upon us all, especially if we are citizens of nuclear weapons–armed states or an alliance in which nuclear weapons are central to national defense policy. No doubt, there is a strong element of duty in the papal condemnation. But "oughts" do not exhaust the experience of conscience. Pope Francis's moral pedagogy focuses on the greater good, on what God calls us to do for the sake of the common good, in this case abolishing nuclear weapons and the threat of nuclear war. The pope's condemnation places less emphasis on minimal obligations than on traditional approaches to what I must do to avoid grave sin. This is a morality for adults who take responsibility, in keeping with the Second Vatican Council, for their own lives, the direction of their own societies, and especially use of the technologies they have developed.[6]

This book will be of interest to a wide range of audiences, but not every essay will be of equal interest to every group. The introduction provides a guide to assist readers in identifying sections of the book that will possibly be of greater interest to them. In addition, it provides thumbnail sketches of each essay.

For those who would like to do further reading on the evolution of the Catholic Church's teaching on nuclear weapons, I recommend Mathias Nebel and Gregory M. Reichberg, eds., *Nuclear Deterrence: An Ethical Perspective* (Geneva: Caritas in Veritate Foundation, 2015), and my own coedited book, *A World Free from Nuclear Weapons: The Vatican Conference on Disarmament* (Georgetown University Press, 2020). The latter includes the address in which Pope Francis first voiced his condemnation.[7]

Nuclear disarmament is the work of the whole Church in the company of international civil society. For that reason, this collection may also serve as a *vademecum* (handbook) for those in the global public square, especially small discernment circles in parishes, in professional associations, and among civic action groups as well as ecumenical, interreligious, and cross-sectoral alliances.[8]

It is our hope that these essays will help clarify the moral burden we all bear for the elimination of nuclear weapons, assist in discerning the pathways that readers can take to contribute to that task, and aid the human family in its advance toward a world free from nuclear weapons.

May God, who has begun this good work in us,
bring it to completion.

Drew Christiansen, SJ

Notes

1. For Saint Francis's tripartite mission, see Leonardo Boff, *Saint Francis: A Model for Human Liberation* (Maryknoll, NY: Orbis, 1984).
2. On Pope Francis's mission for peace, see Victor Gaetan, *God's Diplomats: Pope Francis, Vatican Diplomacy, and America's Armageddon* (Lanham, MD: Rowman & Littlefield, 2021), esp. chaps. 6–12. On his Muslim initiatives, see Gaetan, *God's Diplomats*, chap. 10.
3. On the China accord, see Gaetan, *God's Diplomats*, chap. 12.

4. For the text of the papal condemnation, see Christiansen and Sargent, eds., *A World Free from Nuclear Weapons: The Vatican Conference on Disarmament* (Washington, DC: Georgetown University Press, 2020), 3–5.
5. Decades before the papal condemnation, the US bishops twice pointed to those working in the nuclear services as people who might consider selective conscientious objection. See their 1968 pastoral letter, published as American Bishops, *Human Life in Our Day: A Collective Pastoral Letter of the American Bishops* (Mahwah, NJ: Paulist Press, 1968), and their 1971 statement "Declaration on Conscientious Objection and Selective Conscientious Objection, October 21, 1971," United States Conference of Catholic Bishops, https://www.usccb.org/resources/declaration-conscientious-objection-and-seletive-conscientious-objection-october-21-1971.
6. See Second Vatican Council (1965), *Gaudium et spes: The Pastoral Constitution on the Church in the Modern World*, nos. 4 and 9, and Pope Paul VI, *Octogesima adveniens: A Call to Action*, no. 4. *Gaudium et spes* no. 9 concludes "man [humanity] is becoming aware that it is his responsibility to guide aright the forces which he has unleashed and which can enslave him or minister to him. That is why he is putting questions to himself."
7. Other significant statements include his addresses in Nagasaki and Hiroshima in November 2019 and his recent encyclical *Fratelli tutti*, no. 262.
8. See *Octogesima adveniens*, nos. 4 and 50.

Acknowledgments

The coeditors open these acknowledgments with thanks to Cardinal Silvano Tomasi, who first made the proposal to Father Christiansen for a volume of pastoral and moral counsel on Pope Francis's condemnation of nuclear weapons and has been a source of support and wise advice throughout the project.

Likewise, we are grateful to Cardinal Peter Turkson, the former prefect of the Dicastery for Integral Human Development, and to the staff of the dicastery, above all Dr. Alessio Pecorario, for the steady support they gave this project.

We owe a debt of gratitude to all our contributors for their essays, of course, but especially for their patience in responding to our requests for revision. We are grateful too for the participation of several of the authors in the Berkley Center's January 2020 conference "The Pope and the Bomb" and particularly to the event coordinator, Ruth Gopin.

We thank Al Bertrand, the director of Georgetown University Press, and his editorial board for having the vision to publish this volume and to their staff for all their work in preparing, producing, and promoting it.

Note from Fr. Christiansen: Finally, I would like to extend my thanks and praise to my coeditor, Dr. Carole Sargent, for her extraordinary work in managing the manuscript files and preparing them for publication, especially in the last months when I was taken ill, and for the exceptional work she did in the book's advanced promotion. She took this work on as a true mission.

Note from Carole Sargent: My abundant gratitude goes to Dr. (Fr.) Christiansen for welcoming me to this project because I study Catholic sisters active in disarmament issues. He first gave me the privilege of going to the Vatican in 2017 and then the honor of coediting. Thanks also to Katherine Marshall of the Berkley Center, who changed my life when she introduced us in 2017; to Gerard Powers at Notre Dame; to David Koplow at Georgetown Law; and to Theodore Dedon, who initially worked with us on this book.

Drew Christiansen, SJ
Carole Sargent

The authors and editors wish to express our deep gratitude to lead editor Fr. Drew Christiansen, SJ, who left us just as this book was in its final stages. It would not have been possible without him, for he conceived the project, assembled the authors, inspired their contributions, and completed his own important chapters and introduction.

Father Drew was a pioneering scholar and advocate for nuclear disarmament and global peace, a beloved teacher, mentor and colleague to many, and an innovative and diplomatic bridge-builder who advanced the global vision of a world free of nuclear weapons.

This book, a companion volume to *A World Free from Nuclear Weapons: The Vatican Conference on Disarmament* (Georgetown University Press, 2020), is just one of his many contributions to peacebuilding.

Ad maiorem Dei gloriam inque hominum salutem. For the greater glory of God, and the salvation of humanity.

Introduction

DREW CHRISTIANSEN, SJ

It was the pope's last testament, conceived as his physician informed him of the cancer that would take his life. The previous month the Cuban Missile Crisis had brought the world to the brink of nuclear war, and President John F. Kennedy had enlisted his service as an intermediary in efforts to avert it. Soviet leader Nikita Khrushchev welcomed the pope's initiatives and voiced his esteem for the mediation. Weeks before his death Angelo Roncalli, Pope (now Saint) John XXIII, in the encyclical *Pacem in terris* (Peace on Earth), shared with the world the vision of peace that had taken root in him during the missile crisis.

Most of the letter was devoted to sketching a world where human rights are guaranteed for all and governments' central responsibility would be to secure them. The Italian journalist Giancarlo Zizola called the vision Pope John's "utopia."[1] Concluding the encyclical, the pope articulated for the first time a new principle of international life, "the universal common good," a solution to a global problem that can only be attained with transnational collaboration.[2] In our own day, climate change would be a premier example of such an issue, as would marine resources, migration and refugee policy, and pandemic response programs. In the wake of the missile crisis, however, nuclear disarmament was the element of the universal common good that the pope believed most needed attention. "Nuclear weapons," he declared, "must be banned."[3]

Pope John acknowledged that the nuclear powers had to undertake disarmament "simultaneously" and "with an effective system of mutual control." He realized, moreover, that there would be a sequence of stages to implementing the policy: halting the arms race, reducing the size of nuclear arsenals, and finally eliminating nuclear weapons altogether. He underscored the final goal, writing "this is the main thing—ultimately to abolish them entirely."

The dying pope was not the only one to take the lesson of abolition from the experience of the Cuban Missile Crisis. Just two months after the release of *Pacem in terris*, in a commencement address at American University, President Kennedy laid out his own "Strategy of Peace," announcing that he would address "the most important topic on earth: world peace. . . . [N]ot merely peace in our time but peace for all time."[4]

In view of the prospect of total war, President Kennedy reported that the United States and the Soviet Union were talking in Geneva about limiting the nuclear arms race and reducing the risk of accidental war. He then set a marker for the next big step on the path to disarmament, the cessation of nuclear testing beginning with tests in the atmosphere. "While we proceed to safeguard our national interests," he concluded, "let us also safeguard human interests. And the elimination of war and arms is clearly in the interest of both." Peace with disarmament, Kennedy believed, is "the rational end of rational men." Already in his address to the United Nations (UN) General Assembly in 1961, he had proposed, with the agreement of the Soviet Union, a program of general and complete disarmament, made legally binding in 1970 in Article VI of the Nuclear Non-Proliferation Treaty.

The Holy See Embraces Abolition

Pope John XXIII and John Kennedy both died in 1963. In succeeding years, arms control rather than disarmament grew apace. During the Cold War, both sides learned to live under the mushroom cloud. Although *Pacem in terris* had decried the climate of fear induced by deterrence, two decades later first Pope John Paul II and soon after the US Catholic bishops warranted the possession of the weapons provided they were used solely to deter. Now Pope Francis has condemned nuclear armaments as weapons of mass destruction, dismissing deterrence as a strategy for a counterfeit peace.

In 2017 the Holy See was highly active on nuclear issues. In March that year, Pope Francis helped open the UN's "Conference to Negotiate a Legally Binding Instrument to Prohibit Nuclear Weapons, Leading towards Their Total Elimination." The conference voted to accept the

Holy See as a full state member, and on July 7 the Holy See cast its first UN ballot in favor of the new ban treaty. I served as a member of the Holy See delegation to that conference. In September at a meeting of the UN General Assembly, Archbishop Richard Paul Gallagher, a foreign minister as the Vatican secretary of state for relations with states, signed the treaty on behalf of the Holy See and presented Pope Francis's ratification to the full assembly.

In November, the Dicastery for Promoting Integral Human Development, the Vatican department dealing with social policy that is led by Cardinal Peter Turkson of Ghana, hosted the international symposium "Prospects for a World Free of Nuclear Weapons and for Integral Disarmament." The invitees included Nobel Peace Prize laureates, diplomats, peace activists, and other civil-society representatives. It was there that Pope Francis delivered his condemnation. "The threat of their use," the pope declared, "as well as their very possession is to be firmly condemned." The papers of that conference are collected in the book *A World Free from Nuclear Weapons: The Vatican Conference on Disarmament*.[5]

The purpose of this companion volume is to explain in depth the context of Pope Francis's condemnation of nuclear weapons and explore its implications for those charged with responsibility for national defense and international security. The day after the pope's address Archbishop Silvano Tomasi, the pope's adviser on these matters, asked me to gather moral and pastoral theologians to elaborate on the pope's teaching. The archbishop's hope was to provide commentary that would prove helpful to those pastoral workers who would advise defense professionals on the difficult questions the condemnation would pose for the conduct of their duties. These pastoral workers would include bishops, members of bishops' conferences, parish priests, pastoral counselors, professors, educators, and catechists.

Traditional moral theology has held that to become part of the Catholic tradition, the teachings of popes and bishops need to be "received" by the faithful. This collection contributes to the reception of the Holy Father's teaching. As Saint John Henry Newman noted, the Catholic Church is at its best when bishops and people are one in matters of doctrine. Part of that process is simply its propagation in the media. Not having been sufficiently noted or debated in the media, Pope Francis's condemnation of nuclear weapons still needs to become known in many quarters. Of course, additional statements by the Holy Father and declarations by the diplomatic corps of the Holy See have begun to increase awareness of the teaching. Yet, even in the academy it has received relatively little notice, obscured by controversies and more recently the coronavirus pandemic. This book contributes further to reception of the teaching in the following three communities with a special interest in the Church's teaching on issues of war and peace:

> Universities and colleges, especially in Catholic institutions of higher learning, as well as those specializing in the teaching of diplomats, military personnel and policymakers;
> Pastoral workers who are on the front lines of the transmission and interpretation of the Church's teaching to the faithful; and
> Men and women in the military and national security sector on whom the burden of the condemnation falls most heavily.

What Shall I Do? Responding to the Condemnation

To many Catholics, the first issues that come to mind when they learn that Pope Francis has condemned nuclear weapons are where this stands in the hierarchy of the Church's teaching and how authoritative and definitive it is. They then can consider what the condemnation demands of those most directly engaged with nuclear weapons, including military officers and defense professionals. Must they resign their commissions or immediately withdraw from engagement with nuclear policy? None of these allow a simple answer.

The Authority of the Teaching

Within living memory theologians graded papal statements as to their importance, with conciliar decrees and papal encyclicals standing at the very top and proceeding downward through apostolic letters, *motu proprios* (Latin for "on his own impulse," referring to legal decisions), messages, addresses, talks, and homilies. At the same time, theologians assigned "theological notes" to indicate the degree of authority that attached to any given document: solemnly defined dogmas, doctrines, certain teachings, theological opinions, and so on. But the system of theological notes has also fallen out of use, and for several years Pope Francis's preferred mode of teaching has been the apostolic exhortation concluding a synod. Apostolic exhortations underscore the collegiality of the pope's teaching with that of the world's bishops meeting in synod, and—by citation of bishop and bishops conference statements—the universality of the teaching.

Sometimes, as with both Pius XII and John Paul II, almost everything a pope said seemed to take on the air of authority, particularly for those who seek papal warrant for actions they believe everyone must do or avoid doing. Since the 1990s, moreover, inclusion in the catechism of the Catholic Church took on special weight even though its declared purpose is to guide the writers of religious education texts on the basics of Catholic teaching. All these indicators of authoritative Catholic teaching presumed a kind of deductive logic, as found in natural law reasoning and traditional just war analysis. Such moral systems apply principles and refine them over time in relation to specific cases, thus the term "casuistry," or case-related ethics, often used to describe them.

Beginning with the Second Vatican Council, in matters of social teaching at least, a new inductive method, "reading the signs of the times," came into use.[6] The signs of the times method weights historical conditions more heavily and draws on other sources of guidance, especially scriptural models and precedents, as well as established moral principles to inform its reasoning. This method is employed not just to guide personal life choices but also explicitly to direct collaborative programs of social change.

Unlike the deductive moral methods, signs of the times is also pluralistic in the outcomes it foresees. It allows for a variety of applications rooted in the same moral understanding of the situation. As Pope Paul VI wrote, "In concrete situations, and taking account of solidarity in each person's life, one must recognize a legitimate variety of possible options. The same Christian faith can lead to different commitments."[7] When it comes to responding to the signs of the times, there is thus no one right action because a morality of principles often seems to presume. Rather, there is an array of possible right actions. Just as Christian communities should discern the activities they may undertake in response to the signs of the times, so too are individuals responsible for discerning their own course of action in light of the pope's condemnation of nuclear weapons and their assessment of the current geostrategic situation and recent nuclear policy developments.

Pope Francis's Moral Pedagogy

Pope Francis's own moral pedagogy points to the signs of the times as the framework in which to understand his condemnation of nuclear weapons. With respect to pastoral care (confessional practice and spiritual direction), he famously asked a reporter who was pressing him on the moral standing of a gay man, "Who am I to judge?"[8] The pope is opposed to moralism and legalism into which an ethics of principles can readily slip. A legalistic approach to morality, he believes, misses the heart of the Gospel message, which is God's forgiving love. Furthermore, in a breakthrough of great importance to pastoral practice and spirituality, Pope Francis believes that the Holy Spirit is at work even in apparently sinful souls, prompting them to draw near to God and to do good. Moralism tends to suppress these divinely inspired impulses and lock us into identities as (unforgiven) sinners, immune to the liberating power of grace. By contrast, people who are moved to do good by God's grace will, based on Francis's reading, soon repent of their past sins as they respond to God's love and grace.

Francis also follows Pope Paul VI in consciously delimiting the scope of his moral judgments. In *Evangelii gaudium* (The Joy of the Gospel) Pope Francis wrote that "it is not the task of the Pope to offer a detailed and complete analysis of contemporary reality, but I do exhort all the communities to an 'ever watchful scrutiny of the signs of the times.' This is in fact a grave responsibility, since 'certain present realities, unless effectively dealt with, are capable of setting off processes of dehumanization which would then be hard to reverse.'"[9]

Likewise, in *Amoris laetitia* (The Joy of Love), Pope Francis acknowledges that the approach he takes to the pastoral care of those in difficult marriages is his own and that there are other positions he respects. With Jesuit Saint Peter Faber as his model, Francis is reluctant to impose his view and prefers to make his appeal by gentle example.

Francis understands that the teacher is not a commander. As Nicholas Lash writes, "The teacher looks for understanding, the commander for obedience. . . . [I]f a pupil's response to a piece of teaching is yes, the student is saying something like 'I see' or 'I understand.'"[10] Furthermore, Francis's pedagogy is a form of what Etienne Gilson called "Christian Socratism," prodding Christians to discern conscientiously their own moral vocations as they attempt to imitate Christ rather than ordering them to take up or abandon a particular course of action on command.[11]

In Francis's view, the Church is a teaching-learning community. Everyone is called to listen, and the distinction between the teachers and the learners is relative. Through baptism and confirmation, all the faithful are anointed with the Spirit so that the whole Christian community is infallible when it discerns together and witnesses as one. The authoritative teaching of the bishops, moreover, is rooted in the *sensus fidei* (sense of faith) possessed by the whole Church.[12] This is especially true in discerning the moral demands of the signs of the times. As Francis explains, "even the flock has a 'nose' for discerning the new paths that the Lord is opening up to the church."[13]

When we ask therefore what the authoritative status of the condemnation is or whether Pope Francis is commanding officers to resign their commissions, we are probably asking inappropriate questions. Francis's expectation is that like him we should be learners, inquiring for ourselves and making our own judgments about the moral demands of our times. We should be discerning the signs of the times, responding to the promptings of the Spirit and ready to give ourselves to working for the greater good, the *magis*, as God calls us.

Ultimately, however, the issue is not what everyone should do but instead—given the gravity of the situation, the urgency of the moment, and the light and strength we receive in the Spirit—what we discover we *personally* are called to do as Jesus's disciples and as responsible human persons taking an active role in the shaping of history. Preferably, we should undertake this discernment within a community of faith or in moral dialogue with other men and women of conscience. As the Second Vatican Council taught, humanity has a solemn "responsibility to guide aright the forces which [we have] unleashed."[14] Among the devices humans have invented, nuclear weapons have the most destructive capacity and so require the firmest human direction.

A Change of Outlook

In my introduction to this book's 2020 companion, *A World Free from Nuclear Weapons: The Vatican Conference on Disarmament*, I described how Vatican diplomacy and Pope Francis himself came to embrace the cause of nuclear abolition.[15] This volume opens with several essays that help explain how many people have begun to change their minds on this difficult topic as well as how the Catholic Church came to change its teaching. In the first place, there are essays that explain how, as geostrategic conditions and doctrines changed, the paradigm of "strictly conditioned moral acceptance of deterrence" articulated in the influential 1983 US Catholic bishops' pastoral letter "The Challenge of Peace" ultimately failed. The paradigm crumbled in the face of new realities such as the multipolarity of nuclear-armed states, the centrality of nuclear weapons to overall defense strategies of the nuclear powers and their allies, and the emergence of new technologies such as cyber weapons.

Paradigm failures open intellectual space for new ways of thinking. Just as with new perplexities and new discoveries, chemistry shifted from the oxidation-reduction model to atomic theory, so the moral justification of deterrence policies gave way to fresh perspectives such as moral ecology. William Barbieri utilizes this recent theory in his essay "The Moral Ecology of Deterrence and Abolition," where he explicitly founds moral judgments in evolving climates of opinion. Moral ecology, as other authors show, describes how following 9/11 former US secretary of state George P. Shultz and his colleagues William Perry, Sam Nunn, and Henry Kissinger became proponents of nuclear abolition.

A second way moral theories evolve happens when older styles of thinking find new relevance. A classic example from mid-twentieth-century theology is the movement called *ressourcement*, the retrieval of patristic theology and its adaptation to twentieth-century problems that contributed to the renewal of theology at Vatican II. In Catholic moral theology, the revival of biblical studies has retrieved new resources even for such late modern issues as nuclear weapons. A variety of biblical metaphors, from Armageddon to Babel to the Kingdom of God, have informed religious and secular responses to nuclear weapons. The largely unfulfilled mandate of Vatican II for the renewal of moral theology through scripture has nonetheless also provided new perspectives on nuclear weapons and deterrence.

Finally, in new circumstances moral theories can yield different conclusions. Thus, while just war thinking lies behind many defenses of deterrence, it has increasingly come to ground "nuclear pacifism," the rejection of nuclear weapons on just war grounds, especially the disproportionate destruction and the magnitude of inexcusable civilian deaths that Vatican II condemns when its documents refer to total war. In nuclear warfare, the just war tradition meets its limits as the prospect of nuclear war challenges its coherence and credibility. But seen another way, refusing to justify nuclear war affirms the fundamental purpose of just war analysis: to prevent and limit the use of force. Just war pacifists recognize any rationalizations of nuclear war for the abuse of moral rationality they are. Catholic advocates of nuclear abolition may not be pacifists, but on nuclear weapons policy they become so on just war grounds, not in spite of them.

For readers who want to cut to the chase in this volume, I recommend reading part I, "How We Got Here." It lays out the change in thinking that led to Pope Francis's condemnation. Then I recommend part VII, "Responsible Actors," and part VIII, "The Role of Lay Catholic Movements," where the more practical implications of the Church's teaching are discussed.

Pastoral workers will want to read part V, "Conscience Formation," and part VI, "Moral Education." Military personnel and military educators will be interested in part III, "Toward a World without Nuclear Weapons," to learn the various factors that have contributed to building the pressure for abolition; part IV, "Evolution of Just War," on the progression of just war thinking on nuclear weapons; and part II, "Witnesses," which documents the witness of various advocates of nuclear abolition including onetime policymakers. Peace educators will find parts II, III, IV, VI, and VIII pertinent to their interests.

Part I: How We Got Here

The opening set of essays represents each of the three forms of new thinking: paradigm failure, the application of new modes of thought, and revival or reconception of traditional theological methods.

William Werpehowski expounds the development of the Catholic stance on nuclear weapons in its best-known form, the strictly conditioned acceptance of deterrence in the US bishops' 1983 pastoral letter "The Challenge of Peace." He demonstrates how that "strictly conditioned" position grew implausible for internal theological reasons and also due to changes in empirical conditions and policy positions assumed in the bishops' provisional acceptance of deterrence in 1983. As a result, Werpehowski believes, advocating abolition of nuclear weapons became essential to collective security, so nuclear abolition came to the forefront of the Church's global social agenda.

In "Just War Lessons We Should Remember," Tobias Winright argues that strict just war thinking leads to "nuclear pacifism," that is, the outright rejection of nuclear war and deterrence. While still a realist advocate of just war in conventional conflicts, Winright draws the line at nuclear weapons. He reminds readers that already in 1983, the US bishops warned their readers that "some important elements of contemporary nuclear strategies move beyond the limits of moral justification."

In the first decades of nuclear casuistry, debate of the moral legitimacy of deterrence focused on whether it was legitimate to threaten to do something that is morally forbidden. Pope Francis's condemnation of deterrence—the possession of nuclear weapons and the threat to use them to deter nuclear adversaries—has once again raised the question of the morality surrounding a threat. Gregory M. Reichberg, in "Philosophical Debate on Nuclear Deterrence," reviews philosophers' discussions of the morality of nuclear threats. He agrees with Michael Walzer's statement that since "nuclear war is and will remain morally unacceptable, and there is no case for its rehabilitation. . . . [W]e must seek out ways to prevent it." For those who find theologians' dismissal of nuclear deterrence overly strict, Reichberg provides a rigorous defense of the prohibition.

William Barbieri takes us beyond the familiar terrain of just war analysis into the new field of moral ecology to argue that Pope Francis's embrace of nuclear abolition emerges from a shift of intellectual climate. Deterrence and abolition, Barbieri argues, are outgrowths of two different intellectual landscapes, moral ecologies with their own characteristic styles of argument. Barbieri employs the notion of "integral ecology" in Pope Francis's encyclical on the environment, *Laudato si'*, to illustrate how "the problem[s] of nuclear deterrence are recast as matters of holistic moral equilibrium rather than contests of competing rational principles." Indeed, Pope Francis's use of integral ecology is one instance of his ecological and holistic style of thinking. From the perspective of moral ecology, Barbieri argues, nuclear deterrence "is an unsustainable, (integrally) ecologically harmful, and hence indefensible practice."

Moral ecology illustrates how moral reasoning about deterrence changes with a shift in intellectual outlooks.

Part II: Witnesses

Today's nuclear abolition efforts launched with the Humanitarian Consequences Movement in 2013 and the adoption of the Treaty on the

Prohibition of Nuclear Weapons in 2017. These, however, represent only the most recent developments in the latest wave of antinuclear campaigns, and today's abolitionists have significant precursors.

Part II profiles the early leaders of twenty-first-century nuclear abolitionism. David Cortright, historian of the peace movement in the 1970s and 1980s, was executive director of the National Committee for a Sane Nuclear Policy, commonly known as SANE. His chapter surveys a roster of former government and military officials who, having been the guardians of nuclear deterrent, became its critics and opponents. "Collectively they have many decades of experience creating and implementing national security policy. It is because of that experience that they consider it necessary to get rid of these weapons."

The most prominent among them was a group headed by former secretary of state George P. Shultz that included former defense secretary William Perry, retired US senator Sam Nunn, and former secretary of defense Henry Kissinger. Dubbed by *Time* magazine as "the four horsemen of the nuclear apocalypse," their 2007 appeal in the *Wall Street Journal* garnered support from many other nuclear experts.[16] Already in 1999 Paul Nitze, "one of America's most seasoned and experienced nuclear diplomats and a principal author of the Cold War containment policy," declared that "it is the presence of nuclear weapons that threatens our existence."[17] In 1996, sixty-one retired generals and admirals from seventeen countries, led by former NATO supreme Allied commander, Europe, Gen. Andrew Goodpaster, urged "the complete elimination of nuclear weapons from all nations." These expert witnesses, Cortright notes, bring specialized knowledge to the task of eliminating nuclear weapons that suggest "concrete steps and realistic options" to follow in reaching nuclear zero.

Another set of witnesses with unique stories to tell are the survivors of the atomic bombings at Hiroshima and Nagasaki and the downwinders (those affected by airborne radioactive fallout and contaminants) and refugees from nuclear test explosions in several countries and island territories. Daniel Hall, director of public affairs at Soka Gakkai International–USA, explains how their "often graphic testimonies disrupt the notion that discussions about nuclear weapons policy are only salient when confined to the sanitized realm of abstract military doctrines." Their narratives, he believes, show why it makes sense to place humanitarian concerns at the heart of nuclear disarmament policies. In the Treaty on the Prohibition of Nuclear Weapons, the survivors' view that "the only guarantee that [nuclear weapons] will not be used again is through complete elimination" has taken legal form.

Finally, Georgetown University's Carole Sargent, the author of a book on the Plowshares movement, *Transform Now Plowshares: Megan Rice, Gregory Boertje-Obed, and Michael Walli,* discusses the origins, development, and workings of the largely Catholic pacifist protest group noted for its direct actions at nuclear facilities in the United States and in several other countries.[18] Consisting of both laypeople and present and former priests and sisters, Plowshares is noted for actions at nuclear production and storage facilities, such as the Y-12 weapons facility in Oak Ridge, Tennessee, and the recent Kings Bay Plowshares 7 action protesting the Trident submarine in Georgia, with a destructive power on just one vessel of multiple Hiroshimas. They draw their inspiration from Servant of God Dorothy Day, Thomas Merton, Philip and Daniel Berrigan, and Óscar Romero, among others, but there is considerable influence from the witness of the Historic Peace Churches as well. These actions are not impromptu affairs; they take a year or more to discern and plan. Sargent also explains how religious congregations adapt to make space for the conscientious decisions of members, and how Plowshares actions impact American jurisprudence, particularly around jury nullification and the necessity defense.

Part III: Toward a World without Nuclear Weapons

The third section examines the conditions under which transition to a nuclear-free world can take place. To present readers with a starting point for assessing new arms control and disarmament initiatives, Ambassador (ret.) James E. Goodby, a veteran arms negotiator and the author or editor of numerous books on nuclear abolition, reports on the current positions of the nuclear powers with respect to their commitments for nuclear disarmament. "Tragically," writes Goodby, the nuclear-armed states have not heard or understood Pope Francis's proposition that too much is at stake to go on believing that nuclear weapons bring security.

Goodby provides readers with a primer on the arsenals and deterrence postures of today's nine nuclear states. He gives special attention to the complexities of deterrence in a multipolar world. Under these conditions, he concludes that nuclear weapons inject uncertainty into interstate relations, making their use more likely than during the Cold

War. Both the United States and Russia have declared their willingness to employ nuclear weapons even when others had not used them, and, Goodby adds, they have taken steps to make "their nuclear forces more effective and usable." While NATO has declared that its nuclear weapons will be used only as a "last resort," this does not exclude using them "first, if necessary, to defend against an overwhelming attack with nonnuclear weapons." In this already volatile environment, North Korea is a wild card.

International humanitarian law is one of the disciplines that contributed to the Treaty on the Prohibition of Nuclear Weapons. Over the last forty years, several treaties have been adopted to constrain the inhumanity of war and the illicit trade in arms. These include the Landmine Treaty, the Cluster Munitions Treaty, and the Arms Trade Treaty. Scholars of international law contributed to the drafting of the Treaty on the Prohibition of Nuclear Weapons, applying the emergent prohibition against "unnecessary suffering" and identification of "the legal gap"—that is, the absence until the treaty of a prohibition on the most destructive of all weapons of mass destruction, whereas treaties had proscribed chemical and biological weapons for some time—as arguments for abolition.

In "6 + 6 = 9: Law and Nuclear Weapons," David A. Koplow reviews the treaties and constitutional provisions relevant to nuclear weapons, engaging the frustrations we face in trying to eliminate those arms. The failure to honor the rule of law embodied in the Nuclear Non-Proliferation Treaty and the US Constitution, he argues, "has contributed . . . to perhaps the most devastating threat that the human species has ever faced." Frustration arises because Article VI of the treaty requires parties "to pursue negotiations in good faith on effective measures relating to cessation of the nuclear arms race at an early date and to nuclear disarmament." The two largest nuclear powers have not undertaken genuine disarmament talks, Koplow notes, since the signing of the New START treaty in 2010, and a new arms race is ongoing among the three global nuclear powers (the United States, Russia, and China) and even with regional powers, such as North Korea—thus the frustration of advocates of disarmament.

The Nuclear Non-Proliferation Treaty's one-sentence-long Article VI, requiring negotiation leading to disarmament, ends with the phrase "in the context of general and complete disarmament," an aspiration that goes back to the Kellogg-Briand Pact of 1928 and to a proposal of President John F. Kennedy, with the agreement of the Soviet Union, in an address to the UN General Assembly in 1961. Pierce S. Corden, a veteran arms controller and disarmament expert, reviews the history of this proposed linkage of nuclear and conventional disarmament, noting that only once at the end of the Cold War, in the Treaty on Conventional Armed Forces in Europe (1991), did conventional disarmament become a serious concern for negotiations among nuclear powers. Progress toward disarmament, Corden points out, will require not only the nuclear weapon states who are party to the Nuclear Non-Proliferation Treaty (the United States, Russia, China, the United Kingdom, and France), but also those nuclear weapon states that remain outside the treaty (India, Pakistan, North Korea, and presumably Israel). The disarmament of all will require elimination of not just nuclear weapons but also chemical and biological stockpiles as well as conventional weapons. Corden goes on to review recent statements by the UN, the Holy See, and especially Pope Francis.

During the Cold War and especially in the post–Cold War era following the collapse of the Soviet Union, the two nuclear superpowers—the Russian Federation and the United States—had a network of relationships for monitoring and verifying compliance with arms control agreements and for reducing tensions in times of conflict. Backstopping today's faltering arms control regime, Richard A. Love reviews a little-known alternative tool that may take on new importance: the Proliferation Security Initiative. The initiative, Love explains, "is a growing coalition of like-minded countries that plan, exercise, and execute interdiction operations aimed at disrupting the traffic in materials and technologies involving missiles and weapons of mass destruction and missiles" inaugurated during the George W. Bush administration.

The Proliferation Security Initiative embraced "a new concept in proliferation prevention in which taking action operationally was encouraged . . . [and] cooperation and information sharing would be promoted. States would demonstrate resolve by openly testing interdiction concepts at sea, on land, and even in the air domain through exercises." The associated states participate after agreeing to a set of principles on interdiction of shipments of weapons of mass destruction by states and nonstate actors. From an original 11, participating and supporting states have grown to 105. The initiative's most successful achievement was the breakup of the A. Q. Khan network that operated a black market in nuclear technology and expertise out of Pakistan.

A major church concern with respect to nuclear weapons is their impact on domestic spending, particularly the diminishment they cause in meeting the needs of the poor. The Second Vatican Council complained that "while extravagant sums are being spent for the furnishing of new weapons, an adequate remedy cannot be provided for the multiple miseries afflicting the whole modern world."[19] The council added that weapons spending "ensnares the poor to an intolerable degree."[20] Recently Pope Francis has renewed Saint Pope Paul VI's 1968 call for a global fund drawn from savings taken from the elimination of nuclear weapons to invest in poverty programs. "With the money spent on weapons and other military expenditures," he wrote in *Fratelli tutti*, "let us establish a global fund that can finally put an end to hunger and favour development in the most impoverished countries."[21] Through poverty alleviation and development, he believes, citizens of less-developed countries "will not resort to violent or illusory solutions, or have to leave their countries in order to seek a more dignified life."[22]

Lawrence J. Korb, a former assistant US secretary of defense who managed 70 percent of the defense budget in the early years of the Reagan administration, shares the pope's conviction. In "Nuclear Abolition and Global Human Needs," Korb makes the case for cutting nuclear weapons spending and reallocating the savings to the world's priorities. The nuclear powers, he reports, spend $100 billion a year on their forces, more than twice Africa's development needs. Seventy-five percent of that spending comes from the superpowers: the United States and the Russian Federation. "Diverting about half the money spent in nuclear weapons," Korb contends, "would help the global community meet the UN's 2030 Sustainable Development Goals."

Part IV: Evolution of Just War

The fourth set of essays takes a further look at adaptations of just war analysis and especially a novel school of thought called just peace theory as intellectual assets for states taking steps toward nuclear zero. Realistically, of course, relying on negotiations among potential adversaries, the world will not reach nuclear zero for some time. Gerard F. Powers, who leads the Catholic Peacebuilding Network's Project on Revitalizing

Catholic Engagement on Nuclear Disarmament, contends that just war thinking will remain a useful intellectual asset as states move toward nuclear abolition and even in assessing the new issues that will arise as the world approaches or achieves nuclear abolition. His essay will be an important point of reference for policymakers and negotiators working to effect the various stages en route to nuclear zero.

Just peace theory first emerged in the 1990s as a collaboration between just war analysts and theological advocates of nonviolence in an effort to augment the preventative aspects of traditional just war analysis usually encapsulated in the norm of last resort. Concretely, just peace theory expands the menu of options that policymakers may employ to secure conditions of peace, thereby diminishing recourse to the use of force in international affairs. Maryann Cusimano Love and Daniel Philpott are among the leading Catholic contributors to this school of thinking.

From peacemaking experience around the world, Cusimano Love draws a series of principles proven in zones of conflict to prevent war, manage conflict, and build sustainable peace. She applies them to a reduction of nuclear rivalries, progress toward disarmament, and securing a world free from nuclear weapons. Of special note is the principle of participation. While nuclear arms negotiation has typically been an elite exercise, Cusimano Love explains that during the interval of good feelings following the Cold War, several nuclear management programs and disarmament negotiations made considerable gains. "Expanding participation beyond bilateral approaches is necessary," she argues, "for principled as well as practical reasons, particularly at a time when bilateral relations are strained."

Daniel Philpott's book *Just and Unjust Peace*, one of the most sophisticated treatises in the field, articulates an ethic of reconciliation as a framework for postconflict justice.[23] Especially valuable is his analysis of the wounds of the victims of war, particularly those inflicted by political authorities when they deny government offenses and tolerate counter-narratives from those who perpetrate atrocities. In "Peacebuilding and Nuclear Deterrence," Philpott applies his theory to our movement toward a nuclear-free world, providing remedies for potential issues of the post-1945 era. These may include responsibility toward the victims of nuclear tests, the threat to kill citizens of adversary states, the corrosive effects of the atmosphere of mistrust in politics and international affairs, and the cost of weapons development to the poor and the common good.

From the perspective of peacebuilding, Philpott asserts, "The US bombings of Hiroshima and Nagasaki demand certain peacebuilding measures—namely truth telling, acknowledgment, and forgiveness—but the problem that nuclear weapons have posed for peace since remains to be settled." Accordingly, Philpott proposes apology for the 1945 bombings by the American perpetrators as the principal peacebuilding work we can undertake, along with its reciprocal forgiveness from Japanese victims. He is not sure, however, that the world is ready for apology, acknowledgment, and forgiveness around the evils of the Cold War, the post–Cold War, or the renewed arms race of the present day. As to peacebuilding measures in connection with deterrence, Philpott demurs. Only when there is "widespread consensus on the evil" of nuclear weapons "can [we] hope that nuclear-armed states will renounce their deterrence posture and their attendant threats." As we have seen earlier, for many the paradigm of nuclear deterrence on just war grounds collapsed under the weight of historical experience. Bernard G. Prusak is another ethicist who regards Pope Francis's condemnation as prophetic speech rather than careful moral deliberation. The chapter offers a series of thought experiments to support the legitimacy in principle of deterrence and nuclear deterrence though not necessarily particular policies or practices.[24] In the end, Prusak concludes, "even prophets should not restrict themselves to prophetic denunciation. Just saying 'no' will not do."

Part V: Conscience Formation

For centuries, conscience has been the cornerstone of Catholic teaching on the moral life. As the Second Vatican Council observed, "Always summoning [the human person] to love good and avoid evil, the voice of conscience when necessary speaks to [the human] heart: do this, shun that. . . . Conscience is the most secret core and sanctuary of [the human person]. There [a person] is alone with God, whose voice echoes in [one's] depths."[25] In their 1993 pastoral statement *The Harvest of Justice Is Sown in Peace*, the US bishops stressed the centrality of conscience in taking positions on peace and war and once more defended the right of selective conscientious objection to service, renewing their endorsement of it in the strategic nuclear forces due to potential involvement in indiscriminate killing. Pope Francis's condemnation of nuclear weapons and even of nuclear deterrence poses difficult questions for all Catholics and our fellow citizens, not just for the military but also for politicians, policymakers, and legislators as well as for ordinary citizens of states dependent on nuclear weapons for their defense. So, these responsibilities extend beyond states that possess nuclear weapons to include allied countries that rely on extended deterrence for their national security.

The essays collected in this section will address more generally the topic of the formation of conscience. While conscience is always the ultimate arbiter of a person's moral responsibilities, guilt or innocence, the tradition insists that conscience needs to be rightly formed, that is, informed and attuned to respond to the moral dimensions of situations in life. Being informed entails learning the basic, updated facts about nuclear weapons and policy and also learning about the state of arms control and disarmament and the Catholic Church's current teaching. The preceding sections of this book have attempted to provide that information.

Conscience formation builds on that body of knowledge to lead Catholics and men and women of goodwill to considered judgments of their own as part of a life of Christian and public virtue. These include judgments about their own specific role responsibilities as public officials, military personnel, scientists, citizens, and so on.

Drawing on the traditions of Catholic moral theology, Margaret R. Pfeil and Joseph J. Fahey offer accounts of the development of conscience with a view to discerning their responsibilities toward nuclear policy and nuclear abolition. Pfeil's essay opens with reports of the struggles between atomic scientists and the military to illustrate the obstacles that organizations can place in the way of conscientious actions on the part of individuals and even groups in opposing immoral technological and policy developments. She also explores some of the issues that ought to be part of the moral assessment of nuclear weapons and concludes with an inventory of questions that conscientious men and women should pose when making their judgments and in choosing their options for personal and community action.

A founder and former general secretary of Pax Christi USA, Fahey has made a career of teaching, lecturing, and writing on conscience and war. His essay "Catholic Conscience and Nuclear Weapons" examines the shift in Catholic social teaching after World War II toward nonviolence and nuclear abolition in the context of Christian peace witness across the centuries. He then applies the traditional moral teaching on complicity with evil to those involved in the nuclear weapons industry. Fahey concludes with an appeal for a Church-wide pastoral plan that will "ensure the safety of our fragile planet for generations to come."

Lisa Sowle Cahill picks up the topic of complicity with evil with a sober acknowledgment. Those working in the nuclear establishment, she observes, "enter a de facto ongoing situation in which these immoral policies are a point of departure and set conditions for and parameters of available paths to deterrence." Accordingly, she reasons, the Church's pursuit of nuclear disarmament "must employ nuclear policy as a medium." Those who want a world free of nuclear weapons and "work for change within nuclear-dependent political and bureaucratic systems shoulder the burden of nuclear injustice to some extent."

In that context, Cahill regards the casuistry of complicity in evil as a tool for helping those in the nuclear establishment assess their responsibilities. That line of casuistic reasoning, however, is insufficient to provide alternatives to the problematic policy of deterrence. What is necessary, she believes, are deep changes in culture and worldview identified in Pope Francis's encyclical letter on ecology, *Laudato si'* (On Care of Our Common Home). Following Francis's lead, Cahill looks to a coalition of "religious traditions, humanitarian organizations, governmental representatives at multiple levels, and political movements" that joined together in the Humanitarian Consequences Movement and brought about the Treaty on the Prohibition of Nuclear Weapons.

Finally, my own essay on pastoral accompaniment draws on the pastoral strategies that Pope Francis has expounded in his apostolic exhortations *Evangelii gaudium* and *Amoris laetitia*. He elaborates a pastoral approach more akin to spiritual direction than to confessional practice, the context in which casuistry focuses on assessing degrees of guilt. In this model, all Christians are learners ready to ponder how to apply the Gospel in their lives and are disposed to discern under the inspiration of the Spirit how to accomplish the greater good with respect to the problems confronting them and their societies. The responsibility belongs primarily to members of the nuclear establishment, politicians, and citizens of nuclear states and their allies. The role of pastoral workers—ministers, confessors, professors, spiritual directors, and pastoral counselors—is to accompany individuals, faith groups, and small communities in discerning the signs of the times and choosing the options before them to engage in the process of nuclear disarmament leading to abolition.

Pastoral accompaniment consists of multiple tasks: education, moral discussion including sometimes serving as a sounding board, prayer, discernment of spirits, and a conscientious reading of the needs of the age, leading to a commitment to a specific course of action. Accompaniment builds on the belief that the Spirit is at work in everyone. The Spirit urges us to not just avoid but also resist grave evil, especially to achieve the greater good.

Part VI: Moral Education

Conscience formation addresses personal moral development as part of the pastoral care of the Church and is for the faithful and their growth as disciples of Jesus. It is a multidimensional process involving study, prayer, spiritual direction, discernment, and so on, leading to discovery of a specific moral vocation. Moral education envisages a less intimate set of activities and practices for the wider public and particular subgroups (e.g., activists, potential arms negotiators). Moral education places more emphasis on the communication of information and specific intellectual skills, such as those required in negotiation and policy formation, though as with the Nuclear History Boot Camp described by David Holloway, it may involve practical exercises as well as intellectual content. In terms of the broad purposes of this book, namely reception of Pope Francis's teaching on the elimination of nuclear weapons, the essays in this section are intended to promote wider exposure, beyond communities of faith, to the issues of nuclear elimination among the general public and in educational systems from high school to postgraduate education.

Kelsey Davenport, director for nonproliferation policy at the Arms Control Association, opens with an examination of the apathy that much of the public exhibits toward nuclear disarmament. She contends that overcoming this indifference "requires tailoring disarmament education resources to demonstrate that the nuclear threat is still proximate and pairing information with impactful steps that individuals can take to advance the goal of eliminating nuclear weapons." She reviews a number of techniques that educators use to make the nuclear threat "visible and relatable." These include storytelling across a range of media, interactive learning, and actionable steps toward the aspirational goal of nuclear abolition, such as the programs of Physicians for Social Responsibility to elicit nuclear disarmament resolutions from city councils and state legislatures.

For the last decade, Stanford professor emeritus David Holloway has been a faculty member for the Nuclear History Boot Camp, sponsored by the Woodrow Wilson International Center for Scholars, based in Washington, DC, and hosted by Roma Tre University for ten days each summer in the municipality of Allumiere near Rome. The fellows studying in the program include historians, anthropologists, political scientists, and other social scientists. In addition to the history of nuclear weapons, policy, and deployment, participants study the health and environmental impacts of nuclear weapons and movements to prevent nuclear war and abolish nuclear weapons. The encounter of scholars across national boundaries, Holloway proposes, contributes to the solidarity that Pope Francis has said forms "the basis for peaceful co-existence between members of the human family."[26]

For the millennial generation and through Generation Z and Generation Alpha, social media is a preferred medium for learning. In "Propaganda for Peace: Memes, Mass Moralizing, and a World Free of Nuclear Weapons," Theodore G. Dedon reviews the potential of social media for raising consciousness about the nuclear threat and organizing for nuclear abolition. He discusses how to mobilize memes to build propaganda for peace, opening imaginations and stimulating appetites for a postnuclear peace.

John Paul Lederach is one of the world's foremost conflict transformation specialists. He has worked with Mennonite and Catholic peacebuilding programs and in zones of conflict from Mindanao in the Philippines to Cartagena, Colombia, where he has played a key role in that country's peace process. His book *Moral Imagination: The Art and Soul of Building Peace* explains how the active peacemaker identifies turning points and possibilities to envisage the realization of states of affairs that do not yet exist.[27] His contribution, "A World without Nuclear Weapons: Imagine It One Step at a Time," applies his model to the cause of nuclear abolition. Working at the grass roots he discovered "grandmothers' imagination," the perception of grandparents contemplating their grandchildren within a web of life that involves even enemies. From there, they could envision next steps to reduce the violence in their localities, such as securing a marketplace. When it comes to nuclear disarmament, as in any peacebuilding process, Lederach believes that progress comes after listening attentively to many conversations and in "taking a step together on something you find relevant, compelling, and within reach."

Part VII: Responsible Actors

For many readers, these essays will be the most interesting because they address the basic issue, in light of Pope Francis's condemnation of nuclear weapons, of what we as individuals must do. The essays in this section examine the responsibilities not just of the missile personnel and the military chain of command but also less examined roles such as those of industrialists and legislators as well as informed citizens. These responsibilities go beyond the tasks associated with a particular job to the ethical responsibilities toward the wider society and future generations inherent in any specific post or profession. Some professions such as medicine and law have well-elaborated codes of conduct. The military, especially its officer corps, has codes of conduct, but those codes do not address nuclear warfare or even strategic bombing. Nuclear scientists have a basic code but, remarkably, no code that addresses nuclear weapons. So, role responsibilities here refer to not just job-related obligations but also natural duties that go beyond those prescribed in existing codes.

Some of those duties, such as those described in Maryann Cusimano Love's essay on "nuclear stewards," are incumbent on everyone (e.g., not cheating on exams and refraining from drinking or taking drugs on the job). Others, however, derive from our membership in one human family and our duties to future generations. The notion of "professional" has always entailed a sense of independent judgment not just by reason of specialized knowledge but also in terms of the ability to take a wider view of human affairs. In some ways, professional duties resemble John Paul Lederach's "grandmothers' imagination," which sees family relations as part of the web of life. Thus, to be professionals, members of the nuclear establishment need to see themselves as citizens of not just their own country but the world. They have responsibilities to this generation and to succeeding generations too. It is interesting that George Shultz and the Four Horsemen made the move from advocates of deterrence to proponents of abolition when they were in retirement, out of office, where it was possible for them to take the long view as they came to recognize what they called "the power of the ought."[28]

Pope Francis's condemnation challenges high-level government officials and anyone holding a position in the nuclear establishment to reconsider what their responsibility to the human family is and what the planetary future demands of them. These essays provide those professionals and officeholders with tools to (re)assess their role responsibilities, as the Second Vatican Council wrote, "with an entirely new attitude."[29]

In "The Ethics of Nuclear Stewards," Maryann Cusimano Love looks at the everyday ethics of the missile personnel in light of scandals in recent years resulting from lapses in ordinary moral integrity. As she explains, the military is charged with safeguarding nuclear arsenals until they can be dismantled. In the post–Cold War era, however, there has been an erosion of the security of nuclear weapons and delivery vehicles. When you are dealing with nuclear weapons, she submits, "moral lapses are nuclear hazards." Furthermore, cooperative post–Cold War programs to reduce nuclear accidents and increase nuclear security have been the victims of new superpower tensions. For that reason, Cusimano Love recommends, "expanding participation in nuclear threat reduction and security programs is needed to develop an expanding cadre of ethical nuclear stewards."

With the essay "In the Chain of Command," I examine the responsibility of senior military officers and defense personnel. The essay begins with the military duty to refuse illegal orders and the application of that principle to nuclear war, including commanding generals practicing refusal in annual exercises. I comment that "resistance to illegal orders not only protects the innocent from attack but also upholds the honor of the military and the integrity of the military justice system."

The weight of the duty to refuse is greatly amplified by current policy developments, today's multipolar geostrategic environment, the unraveling of the fabric of arms control and disarmament, and the new arms race we call "modernization." The essay goes on to discuss discernment of one's stance toward nuclear weapons as a function of belonging to a teaching-learning Church.

Susi Snyder of the Nobel Peace Prize laureate group ICAN, and its past president, shows how we can hold Boeing, Lockheed Martin, Northrop Grumman, and their ilk responsible for targeted weapons, drones, and space warfare systems. Citing Pope Francis on the immorality of supporting an industry "drenched in blood," she calls on citizens to demand reputational accountability, as with the tobacco industry, to trace their money to its source and disrupt it, to enforce the TPNW, and to consider ethical shareholding strategies.[30]

One set of agents whose work has evoked little moral analysis and criticism is weapons scientists.[31] Despite the US bishops' rather laudatory comment in "The Challenge of Peace," the Church has offered scarce criticism of the bishops' profession. The code of conduct for American nuclear scientists does not touch on their role in weapons development. Pierce Corden, a physicist who has spent a lifetime in arms control, reflects in his second essay in the present volume on the impact of the evolving position of the Holy See and particularly Pope Francis's condemnation on scientists and technicians working for weapons labs and associated industries.

Consistent with the ethics of complicity in evil, explained by Lisa Sowle Cahill above, Corden surveys a wide range of weapons-science projects for their compatibility with the Church's condemnation of the possession, threat, and use of nuclear weapons. He explains how some programs, such as warhead modernization and dual-use delivery vehicles, are clearly problematic. Some, such as protection for command-and-control systems, represent ambiguous undertakings, requiring careful moral analysis and deliberation. Finally, other projects, such as designing sensors to prevent theft of nuclear materials and systems to monitor and verify reduction or elimination of nuclear arsenals, may even be desirable contributions to a world free of nuclear weapons. Corden repeatedly observes that in addition to Catholic social teaching, scientists and engineers should weigh government policy and policy trends in their deliberations.

At the political level, legislators constitute a special group. Unlike members of the military, elected officials are not in the chain of command. They do, however, have considerable authority in funding and even promoting nuclear weapons development, the capacity to limit executive branch policies, and the responsibility for oversight of nuclear weapons policy. David Lammy, a Labour member of Parliament for Tottenham, writes as a legislator who believes that morality has a place in policy formation, and his morality, he writes, is informed by his Christian faith. Local faith communities, he argues, can "move national governments and international institutions to embrace nuclear disarmament with renewed vigor." He resonates particularly with Pope Francis's contention that money spent on nuclear weapons is money squandered.

On that basis, Lammy opposed the renewal of Britain's Trident nuclear submarine program.

The least parliamentarians can do, Lammy believes, is ask hard questions of their governments. In addition, they can work with civil society organizations to educate the public on the dangers of nuclear weapons. Disarmament, he asserts, should be at the center of a genuinely realistic multilateral security policy.

One field that remains opaque to the outside public is the manufacture of nuclear weapons. Prior to the 1990s, most of the coverage of manufacturers concerned itself with lobbying. In "The Ethics of Manufacturing Nuclear Weapons," Ramón Luzárraga traces the brief history of discussions among manufacturers about the ethics of the business of making nuclear weapons, with emphasis on the initiatives during the 1990s of the Honeywell Corporation.

During the nuclear debates of the 1980s, the Church made clear that public opinion had a role in shaping government policy. In publishing their pastoral letter "The Challenge of Peace," the US bishops articulated their intention "to form public opinion with a clear determination to resist the resort to nuclear war as an instrument of national policy."[32] Particularly in democratic societies such as the United States but analogously in the United Kingdom, France, India, and Israel, they hoped "to encourage a public attitude which sets stringent limits on the kind of action our own government and other governments will take on nuclear policy." Just as forty years ago Pope John Paul II and the bishops counseled the faithful "to say 'no' to nuclear war," today Pope Francis looks to all Christians as well as men and women of goodwill to say "no" to nuclear weapons including their use for deterrence.[33] For that reason, the duty to oppose nuclear weapons also falls on citizens of allied countries living beneath the US nuclear umbrella under the policy of extended deterrence, NATO members but also Japan and South Korea. In authoritarian nuclear powers such as China and North Korea, while the capacity to protest policies may not be available to the average citizen, members of some elite groups (e.g., scientists, lawyers, and military commanders), insofar as they enjoy political influence as well as requisite expertise, may be able to move government policy toward disarmament and ultimately abolition.

In his essay "The Responsibilities of 'Enabled' Citizens for Integral Disarmament and Sustainable Human Development," James P. O'Sullivan focuses on the duties of citizens at large, especially those whose political participation is enabled by virtue of the free exercise of civil rights. As the Second Vatican Council declared, organized political communities should "afford all their citizens the chance to participate freely and actively in establishing the constitutional bases of a political community, governing the state, and choosing leaders."[34] The council also enjoined citizens "always [to] look simultaneously" to their own country and "to the welfare of the whole human family, which is held together by manifold bonds linking races, peoples, and nations." In that wider context, O'Sullivan maintains that citizens bear duties to promote the (universal) common good in the form of integral disarmament and integral development. In a twist on the casuistry of complicity, moreover, he argues that responsibility varies with complicity as well as capability. He also places emphasis on citizens actively engaging through civil society organizations to build momentum for policy change. "Civil society" is a composite term for what we once described as nongovernmental organizations such as the International Committee of the Red Cross, Pax Christi, and the International Campaign to Abolish Nuclear Weapons.

Catholic social teaching envisages the full flourishing of every person as the goal of collective action. In this tradition, the adjective "integral" means "multidimensional," embracing both material and spiritual conditions of human well-being. In the field of disarmament, integral disarmament refers to both the elimination of weapons, from small arms to nuclear weapons, and the disarmament of hearts in the interest of peace as the common good of the one human family.

Part VIII: The Role of Lay Catholic Movements

Finally, we come to the response of the wider Church to Pope Francis's teaching, particularly to the response of the organized Catholic laity. Kevin Ahern was for many years a leader in Pax Romana and the International Movement of Catholic Students. During the pontificate of Pope Benedict, Ahern represented lay ecclesial movements in talks with the Roman Curia on their reorganization. In his essay "Organizing the Church for a World without Nuclear Weapons," Ahern explains how lay movements might "better actualize [the Church's] potential" to promote nuclear abolition in service to the Church's social mission.

Ahern, author of the book *Structures of Grace: Catholic Organizations Serving the Global Common Good*, builds on John Paul Lederach's peacebuilding pyramid to explain how lay movements can exercise their religious soft power to form individual consciences and influence public policy debate across three echelons of deliberation and social action from grassroots base communities to top-level decision makers.[35] But he gives special attention to midlevel actors, members of religious congregations, nongovernmental organizations, educational institutions, and social movements in doing the heavy lifting needed to bring about social transformation.

"The full actualization of this potential for disarmament," Ahern observes, "will demand scaling up existing structures, leadership, and coordinated efforts that bring together a range of actors within and outside Catholicism." A precedent for this kind of mobilization, he suggests, may be found in the debt relief campaign that Saint Pope John Paul II organized for Jubilee 2000. Another such model would be the seven-year-long program the Holy See is currently undertaking to implement sustainable ecology in the spirit of *Laudato si'.* If the Church can mobilize in the same way for the elimination of nuclear weapons, it will be the most significant contribution by the Church to peace since 1963, when Saint John XXIII, in *Pacem in terris*, made the case for their abolition the centerpiece of his agenda for peace in the nuclear age.

Notes

1. Giancarlo Zizola, *The Utopia of Pope John XXIII* (Maryknoll, NY: Orbis, 1979).
2. John XXIII, *Pacem in terris*, 100.
3. *Pacem in terris*, 112.
4. John F. Kennedy, "Commencement Address at American University," June 10, 1963.
5. Drew Christiansen, SJ, and Carole Sargent, eds., *A World Free from Nuclear Weapons: The Vatican Conference on Disarmament* (Washington, DC: Georgetown University Press, 2020).
6. Second Vatican Council (1965), *Gaudium et spes: Pastoral Constitution on the Church in the Modern World*, no. 4.
7. Pope Paul VI, *Octogesima adveniens*, 50.
8. Tracey Connor, "'Who Am I to Judge?' The Pope's Most Powerful Phrase in 2013," NBC News, December 22, 2013.
9. Pope Francis, *Evangelii gaudium*, 51.
10. Nicholas Lash, "Teaching or Commanding? When Bishops Instruct the Faithful," *America*, December 13, 2010.

11. Etienne Gilson, "Self-Knowledge and Christian Socratism," in *The Spirit of Mediaeval Philosophy* (New York: Sheed and Ward, 1936), 209–28.
12. *"Sensus Fidei* in the Life of the Church," International Theological Commission, 2014.
13. Pope Francis, address to the XIV Ordinary General Assembly of the Synod of Bishops, October 17, 2015.
14. *Gaudium et spes*, no. 9.
15. Christiansen and Sargent, "Introduction," in *A World Free from Nuclear Weapons*, xiii–xxii.
16. Eben Harrell, "The Four Horsemen of the Nuclear Apocalypse," *Time*, March 10, 2011.
17. Paul H. Nitze, "A Threat Mostly to Ourselves," *New York Times*, October 28, 1999.
18. Carole Sargent, *Transform Now Plowshares: Megan Rice, Gregory Boertje-Obed, and Michael Walli* (Collegeville, MN: Liturgical Press, 2022).
19. *Gaudium et spes*, no. 81.
20. *Gaudium et spes*, no. 81.
21. Pope Francis, *Fratelli tutti*, 262.
22. *Fratelli tutti*, 262.
23. Daniel Philpott, *Just and Unjust Peace: An Ethic of Political Reconciliation* (New York: Oxford University Press, 2012).
24. Cathleen Kaveny, *Prophecy without Contempt: Religious Discourse in the Public Square* (Cambridge, MA: Harvard University Press, 2016).
25. *Gaudium et spes*, no. 16.
26. Address of His Holiness Pope Francis to Participants in the International Symposium "Prospects for a World Free of Nuclear Weapons and for Integral Disarmament," November 10, 2017.
27. John Paul Lederach, *Moral Imagination: The Art and Soul of Building Peace* (New York: Oxford University Press, 2010).
28. George P. Shultz, "The Power of the Ought," lecture at the Hoover Institution, October 9, 2009. The quote is originally attributed to Ambassador Max Kampelman, one of Reagan's chief negotiators.
29. *Gaudium et spes*, no. 80.
30. This paragraph was written by co-editor Carole Sargent.
31. See also Drew Christiansen, "The Social and Moral Responsibility of Knowledge Workers," in Christiansen and Sargent, eds., *A World Free from Nuclear Weapons*, 120–34.
32. National Conference of Catholic Bishops of the United States, *The Challenge of Peace: God's Promise and Our Response* (Washington, DC: United States Catholic Conference, 1984), para. 139.
33. *The Challenge of Peace*, 132, 139–41.
34. *Gaudium et spes*, no. 75.
35. Kevin Ahern, *Structures of Grace: Catholic Organizations Serving the Global Common Good* (Maryknoll, NY: Orbis, 2015).

PART I

How We Got Here

1

From Deterrence to Abolition

The Evolution of Roman Catholic Nuclear Ethics

WILLIAM WERPEHOWSKI

The traditional Roman Catholic doctrine relating human moral life to warfare fulfills, as John Courtney Murray puts it, a "triple function": "to condemn war as evil, to limit the evils it entails, and to humanize its conduct as far as possible."[1] The historical development of a Catholic stance on nuclear deterrence may be similarly described.

Deterrence and Just War's Triple Function

The possession and deployment of nuclear weapons are regularly condemned on two general grounds. They and their deterrent use place human persons, created for and destined to universal familial fellowship under God, "in the grip of constant fear" and escalating mistrust.[2] Additionally, the race for nuclear arms that invariably accompanies deterrence is "an utterly treacherous trap for humanity," since it "ensnares the poor to an intolerable degree" in that their dignity and needs are abandoned.[3]

The concern to constrain the evils that nuclear deterrence may entail has focused on how the use of these weapons may be, if you will, *licitly threatened*. The categorical declaration in *Gaudium et spes* applies: "Any act of war aimed indiscriminately at the destruction of entire cities or extensive areas along with their populations is a crime against God and man himself, and merits unequivocal and unhesitating condemnation."[4] An act of war aimed at the innocent as such is murder (i.e., unjust killing). An act that threatens as much for the sake of staving off nuclear attack is murderous and unjust and merits condemnation as well. Identifying a nuclear deterrent that conceivably aligns with just war norms that protect the innocent from direct attack with proportionate means is, then, like just war theory itself, a way to establish and sustain *moral limits*.

What would it mean to humanize nuclear deterrence as far as possible? It would mean substantially and effectively serving human purposes that are authentically human, such as genuine peace, stable security, and a justice that honors God's creation across the board. The going work of humanization in this case would be to show that deterrence may result in peace of a sort under certain carefully circumscribed conditions that encompass a commitment to reduce and ultimately abolish nuclear weaponry.

In the following section of this essay, I elaborate on each feature of the triple function in the relevant case. In the concluding part, I sketch the warrants in play today for holding that the Catholic moral case for nuclear deterrence fails. That failure leaves in its wake a moral call for nuclear abolition.

Nonviolence, Intention, and Political Purpose

The damage that nuclear arms and deterrence does, I suggest, has been significantly *magnified* in Catholic moral conscience over the last fifty years or so due to the increasing emphasis of two themes. One is that faithful discipleship encourages and demands service to and solidarity with those of our fellows who are marginalized or even excluded from participation in social life. They are owed a special effort, in virtue of their equality with all human beings under God, to be empowered for active and responsible life in community. Solidarity also includes trying to see the world from the point of view of the poor rather than from perches of privilege and comfort. The second theme is that Catholic living is nonviolent. Even with its principled commitment to the possibly justifiable recourse to armed force internationally, the Church has moved more and more in a direction that suspects violence of any sort, asserts a fundamental moral presumption against war, encourages dialogue with pacifist interlocutors of one or another stripe, and wills nonviolence of spirit in all that we do.

Thus, moral attention is more intensely directed to the close and perhaps inseparable connection between the suffering of the poor and violence in the specific instances of preparing for, waging, and indeed deterring war through nuclear weapons. There is heightened awareness of the need to plumb "the relationship between disarmament and development," as Pope John Paul II observed in his 1982 message to the General Assembly of the United Nations.[5] "By means of creating consciences sensitive to the absurdity of war, "we advance the value of creating the material and spiritual conditions which will lessen the glaring inequalities and which will restore to everyone that minimum of space for the freedom of the spirit."

Roman Catholic attempts to limit the evil that the international nuclear weapons system brings have importantly included analysis, in terms of traditional *jus in bello* criteria of noncombatant immunity and proportionate means, of the real connections between nuclear possession, deterrent threat, and possible use. The US bishops' 1983 pastoral letter "The Challenge of Peace" offered three clear judgments about American nuclear policy: both nuclear use *and* nuclear threats directed at noncombatants are absolutely impermissible, nuclear "first use" against "counterforce" legitimate military targets are invariably disproportionate, and a second strike against an adversary's nuclear forces is almost sure to be disproportionate as well.[6]

The first conclusion is an implication of the condemnation from *Gaudium et spes* quoted above. Again, murderous acts and threats to murder are both morally criminal, for it is wrong to threaten (and just so credibly threaten for the sake of deterrence) what it is wrong to do. "It is not morally acceptable to intend to kill the innocent as part of a strategy of deterring nuclear war."[7] The conclusion about first use is based on strong rejection of the great dangers of nuclear escalation following any such use. The bishops express "extreme skepticism about the prospects for controlling a nuclear exchange, however limited the first use might be."[8] The last judgment follows from what Fr. Bryan Hehir, principal adviser to the bishops at the time, called a "centimeter of ambiguity" regarding the legitimacy of second-strike retaliation in response to a nuclear attack.[9] Given that ambiguity about use, a parallel counterforce deterrent threat might conceivably be permissible but only if certain conditions are met. So, in practice and in fact, deterrence against nuclear attack by others must be the sole reason to possess nuclear weapons; "proposals that go beyond this to planning for prolonged periods of repeated nuclear strikes and counterstrike or 'prevailing' in nuclear war, are not acceptable. They encourage notions that nuclear war can be engaged in with tolerable human and moral consequences."[10] Another condition is closely related; that is, if deterrence is the goal, then "sufficiency to deter is an adequate strategy; the quest for nuclear superiority must be rejected."[11]

Thus far, everything the bishops offer is reasonably rooted, in principle and prudentially, in *jus in bello* norms. Within Murray's rubric, we are moving at this point from limiting the evils that nuclear policies entail toward larger human purpose, because just as war may justifiably be waged for the end of peace, nuclear deterrence may be justifiably employed for the end of that "peace of a sort" that includes preventing nuclear attack justly.

The bishops' final condition for morally accepting deterrence lands squarely in Murray's third feature or function of traditional just war theory. American deterrence is "humanized" insofar as it serves "as a step on the way to progressive disarmament. Each proposed addition to our strategic system or change in strategic doctrine must be assessed precisely in light of whether it will render steps toward 'progressive disarmament' more or less likely." In 1993 the bishops reaffirmed this condition plus the other two as providing "a useful guide for evaluating the continued moral status of nuclear weapons in a post–Cold War world." They also pointed to a distinctive moral challenge in that world, that is, "the threat of global nuclear war has been replaced by a threat of global nuclear proliferation."[12] The Treaty on the Non-Proliferation of Nuclear Weapons of 1968 endorsed a threefold bargain in which non–nuclear weapon states were never to acquire nuclear weapons in exchange for nuclear weapon states actively pursuing disarmament while sharing with all the benefits of peaceful nuclear technology. Notably, the disarmament envisioned by the treaty aims at the abolition of nuclear weapons in their entirety. Hence, the moral assessment of deterrence as a practical step toward progressive disarmament in a post–Cold War world must include determining whether nuclear states are in fact discouraging proliferation by leading the way in disarmament toward ultimate abolition.

The Moral Case Fails

During the time of Pope Francis, the Vatican has in effect argued that the moral justification for nuclear deterrence as we find it above does not succeed. The evils associated with deterrence are found to be graver and deeper than hitherto acknowledged. There remains the climate of fear, the ordering of life through violence rather than nonviolence, and the assault on the poor. Add to these how the deterrence regime today, no longer under the control of Cold War superpowers, carries increasing risks of nuclear accident and nuclear terrorism. The regime itself has become a basis for national security rather than a moment in forging an alternative and as such drives the development of new and modernized nuclear weapons. Plans to fight and prevail in nuclear conflict are still on the table in some quarters, and arsenals are bigger than needed for deterrence proper. Indeed, there is today a morally distorting ideology of deterrence that overstates its present and historical effectiveness and dodges or masks these very problems. Finally, in the absence of nuclear weapon states taking serious and vigorous initiatives to disarm and instead building national security and power prerogatives on deterrence, the current class structure of the international system gives non–nuclear weapon states an incentive to acquire nuclear arms. Needless to say, the presence of these evils generally belies the three moral conditions of exclusive deterrent purpose, sufficiency rather than superiority, and progress toward disarmament.

With regard to the attempt to limit the evils of deterrence, Pope Francis and the Vatican insist that earlier accounts of what those limits are in just war theory need to be complemented, if not in some sense corrected or surpassed. Merely to focus on noncombatant immunity and proportionate means as they (properly) bear on the evil of mass killing encourages a complacency regarding the unnecessary suffering and broader humanitarian costs of nuclear war, possession, testing, and deterrence. We need to count the reality and risk of the intolerable suffering of nuclear survivors, the perils of radiation sickness and the spread of disease, starvation, contamination of water, and the inability of ecosystems to restore themselves. Included in what I have called the ideology of deterrence is a sleight of hand in which the appeal to what deterrence intends (here, the prevention of war) obscures the way it actually rests on a "fight the war" ground. It "involves a whole series of acts that are predisposed to use: strategic designs, targeting plans, training drills, readiness checks, alerts, screening for conscientious objectors among operators, and so on."[13] The US Catholic bishops and the just war tradition they apply are not guilty of this dishonest deflection, although appeal to a centimeter of ambiguity for the sake of logical consistency may in fact contribute to it. "But since what is intended is mass destruction—with extensive and lasting collateral damage, inhumane suffering, and the risk of escalation—the system of nuclear deterrence can no longer be deemed a policy that stands firmly on moral ground."[14]

The two ways to humanize the conduct of deterrence therefore come to a dead end. "Peace of a sort" "is a misnomer that tends to cloud collective vision."[15] And the class structure of nations I mentioned earlier is hostile to the progressive disarmament that moral acceptance of deterrence commends.

The practice of nuclear deterrence today is an obstacle to peace. If, however, the only moral basis for the possession of nuclear weapons is morally acceptable deterrence and if deterrence is not morally acceptable today, then there is no moral basis for possession. If possession is not justified, then the goal of nuclear abolition is morally required. "The time has come to embrace the abolition of nuclear weapons as an essential foundation of collective security."[16]

Notes

1. John Courtney Murray, *We Hold These Truths: Catholic Reflections on the American Proposition* (New York: Sheed and Ward, 1960), 270.
2. Pope John XXIII, *Pacem in terris*, no. 111.
3. Second Vatican Council (1965), *Gaudium et spes: Pastoral Constitution on the Church in the Modern World*, no. 81.
4. *Gaudium et spes*, 80.
5. John Paul II, Message to the Second Special Session of the United Nations General Assembly Devoted to Disarmament (June 1982).
6. National Conference of Catholic Bishops of the United States, *The Challenge of Peace: God's Promise and Our Response* (Washington, DC: United States Catholic Conference), February 1, 1984, no. 165.
7. *The Challenge of Peace*, no. 178.
8. *The Challenge of Peace*, no. 153.
9. J. Bryan Hehir, "The Context of the Moral-Strategic Debate and the Contribution of the U.S. Catholic Bishops," in *Peace in a Nuclear Age: The Bishops' Pastoral Letter in Perspective*, ed. Charles Reid Jr. (Washington, DC: Catholic University Press, 1986), 150.
10. *The Challenge of Peace*, no. 545.
11. *The Challenge of Peace*, no. 532.
12. Patrick W. Carey, ed., *Pastoral Letters of the United States Catholic Bishops*, Vol. 6 (Washington, DC: National Conference of Catholic Bishops, 1998), 571.
13. "Nuclear Disarmament: Time for Abolition," in Mathias Nebel and Gregory M. Reichberg, eds., *Nuclear Deterrence: An Ethical Perspective* (Chambésy: Caritas in Veritate Foundation, 2015), 90.
14. "Nuclear Disarmament: Time for Abolition."
15. "Nuclear Disarmament: Time for Abolition," 93.
16. "Nuclear Disarmament: Time for Abolition," 90.

2

Just War Lessons We Should Remember

TOBIAS WINRIGHT

Although I did not read it until some years after it was published, I was a senior in high school in 1983 when the US Catholic bishops issued their pastoral letter, *The Challenge of Peace: God's Promise and Our Response*. Its "central" focus on the "global threat of nuclear war" was timely for me, for angst about all-out annihilation was palpable among youths and young adults.[1] Indeed, I remember some of my peers asking, "Why plan for the future when everything's going to be blown to bits by nuclear war anyway?"

That year, more so than a magisterial document, movies preoccupied our minds on the subject, including *The Day After* and *War Games*, with even more during both the immediately previous and subsequent years. Likewise, a lot of popular music during the 1980s referred to the Cold War and the nuclear nightmare, such as The Fixx's "Red Skies" (1982), Nena's "99 Luftballons" (1983), U2's "Seconds" (1983), Men at Work's "It's a Mistake" (1983), The Call's "The Walls Came Down" (1983), and Genesis's memorable "Land of Confusion" (1986).[2]

My existential interest in this issue carried over into my academic study of political science as an undergraduate, especially in courses I took on international relations. In one of my exams an essay question asked, "In the event of a Soviet conventional attack on Western Europe, what will be the implications of NATO fighting a limited nuclear war, assuming it decides to adopt such a strategy?" At the time, although I worried that "even in a limited nuclear war, the casualties would be too high for military and civilians," I concluded that being prepared to execute such a strategy as deterrence, along with improved conventional military capacities, should "maintain stability in the world."

Because my undergraduate academic mentor, Regis Factor, was a Roman Catholic political theorist who believed that ethics should play an important role in foreign policy, he also introduced me to just war theory, to Vatican II's *Gaudium et spes*, and to the US bishops' 1983 pastoral letter, including attention to the latter's stance on nuclear weapons.[3] Although I did not then find the bishops' position completely convincing, their moral reasoning and the principles they used from just war theory interested me since I was—also during my undergraduate years—a law enforcement officer and in the Reserve Officers' Training Corps considering a career in the US Army. At the same time, after seeing the 1982 movie *Gandhi*, I read and wrestled with his writings and life; indeed, his principled and pragmatic nonviolence inspired and challenged me. In addition, I began to pore over the work of Stanley Hauerwas (under whom I would later study in graduate school) defending Christian pacifism and critiquing just war theory.[4] Nevertheless, it was due to just war thinking and principles that I stopped short of joining the military; I did not want to be possibly involved in an unjust war. Upon graduating, I left law enforcement because I was uncomfortable with the brutality and excessive force I sometimes witnessed as well as the informal reprimand I received for questioning what I perceived to be unlawful orders from a supervising sergeant. The just war tradition helped guide me on ethics and the use of force back then, and it continues to do so.

My assignment for this present volume on nuclear ethics is to highlight some lessons from the just war tradition that we ought to keep in mind. Just war theory has come under severe criticism in recent years. In the "Appeal to the Catholic Church to Re-Commit to the Centrality of Gospel Nonviolence," issued in April 2016, some eighty activists and scholars, whose gathering at the Vatican was cosponsored by Pax Christi International and the Pontifical Council for Justice and Peace, exhorted the Catholic Church to "no longer use or teach 'just war theory.'"[5] Indeed, one of its participants, Mairead Corrigan-Maguire, an Irish Nobel Peace Prize winner whose work on peace in Northern Ireland I have admired and taught, later repeated this call for the Catholic Church to renounce just war theory and to pursue only nonviolence in her speech on November 11, 2017, at the symposium "Prospects for a World Free from Nuclear Weapons and for Integral Disarmament," held at the Vatican and sponsored by the Dicastery for Promoting Integral Human Development.[6] Indeed, the peace laureate asserted, "we need to throw out the 'just war' theory, a phony piece of morality."[7]

I have published elsewhere why I think that this most recent (it's not the first) appeal to repudiate just war theory is mistaken.[8] A couple of caveats before proceeding: first, it is important to distinguish between theory and tradition and then to note that there are rival versions of just war theory within the just war tradition, and, second, the tradition is a living, developing one.[9] As such, I agree with and have attempted to contribute to efforts "to develop a peacebuilding ethic to match the sophistication of the just war ethic,"[10] one that integrates the latter within the former under the umbrella of "integral peacemaking," and which is more constructive and positive than the dicastery's wording of "integral disarmament."[11]

I argue that the present position of Pope Francis and the Catholic Church on nuclear weapons is in keeping with the logic of strict Catholic just war thinking and principles. In his exhortation to just war thinkers to "be honest" about just war theory, the Christian pacifist John Howard Yoder asked, "Can the criteria function in such a way that in a particular case a specified cause, or a specified means, or a specified strategy or tactical move could be *excluded*? Can the response ever be 'no'?"[12] In my view, present Catholic just war theory yields a "no" about each of these specified considerations concerning nuclear weapons, even if those who employed its reasoning and principles until recently accepted a strategy of nuclear deterrence as an "interim ethic."[13] Evidence of such "honest" (I prefer instead the term "strict" in order to avoid implying that some just war thinkers are being "dishonest") just war reasoning and principles may be found in Pope Francis's address to the participants in the international symposium "Prospects for a World Free of Nuclear Weapons and for Integral Disarmament."[14]

I wish to highlight three points that Pope Francis makes. First, he laments how "the escalation of the arms race continues unabated and the price of modernizing and developing weaponry, not only nuclear weapons, represents a considerable expense for nations." Its costs have diverted from and deprived efforts to reduce poverty, promote human rights, and build educational, ecological, and health care projects. Not only has it come at the expense of economic development, but it has also impeded "integral human development," which encompasses the flourishing of "human beings in the indissoluble unity of soul and body" in both their "individual and ... social dimensions." Accordingly, the price is too burdensome and broad-based. In other words, these negative effects of the nuclear arms race are disproportionate to any goods possibly sought from it, and these bad consequences also indiscriminately impact innocent people.[15]

Second, Pope Francis is "genuinely concerned by the catastrophic humanitarian and environmental effects of any employment of nuclear devices."[16] Nuclear weapons are weapons of mass destruction such as land mines, cluster munitions, and chemical and biological weapons. Like these other weapons of mass destruction, which are "all expressly prohibited by international conventions," so too "nuclear weapons are not only immoral, but must also be considered an illegal means of warfare." They threaten, moreover, not only people but the planet not only immediately but also indefinitely. Indeed, they are also weapons of long-term destruction.[17] The effects of both mass and long-term destruction are indiscriminate and excessive, so much so that even the "risk of an accidental detonation as a result of error of any kind" factors negatively into the equation.[18] Moreover, the "mentality of fear that affects not only the parties in conflict but the entire human race" is, again, both indiscriminate and disproportionate. For these reasons, Pope Francis has "firmly condemned," for the very first time in Catholic teaching, not only the use of nuclear weapons but also "the threat of their use, as well as their very possession."

Third, in the pope's view, nuclear weapons and deterrence have not been successful in providing real security but instead "create nothing but a false sense of security" and thereby "cannot constitute the basis for peaceful coexistence between members of the human family."[19] Nor have "the instruments of international law ... prevented new states from joining those already in possession of nuclear weapons." Plus, there are heightened concerns now given "the challenges of contemporary geopolitics, like terrorism or asymmetric warfare." In short, it seems more likely, or probable, that nuclear weapons and deterrence have been and will continue to be unsuccessful in achieving their aims of security.

These three major points highlighted by Pope Francis cohere with traditional just war reasoning and principles, especially the *jus in bello* criteria of discrimination and proportionality but also the *jus ad bellum* criteria of probability of success and proportionality.[20] They are neither pacifist nor strictly nonviolent in their moral presuppositions and methodology. No pacifist or nonviolent reasons, in principle, are invoked. After all, as the US bishops acknowledge in *The Challenge of Peace*, it "is clear that those in the Church who interpret the gospel teaching as forbidding all use of violence would oppose any use of nuclear weapons under any conditions."[21] Period. Although pacifism and nonviolence rightly have come to be officially lauded as a valid approach for Catholics, as acknowledged in *Gaudium et spes*, *The Challenge of Peace*, and other magisterial documents, that approach to the ethics of war and peace is not evident in Pope Francis's address on nuclear weapons.[22] Of course, admittedly, pacifists, even as they criticize just war thinking and principles, sometimes use that very sort of reasoning and criteria to do so or to make negative judgments about specific wars.[23]

Regardless, Pope Francis's reasoning in his address coincides with what the US Catholic bishops observed as to how, for "the tradition which acknowledges some legitimate use of force, some important elements of contemporary nuclear strategies move beyond the limits of moral justification."[24] Pacifists should be okay with this too. As Yoder wrote, "Wherever any new opening for the moral criticism of the use of violence arises, it is in some way a use of the just war logic, and should be welcomed as at least an opening for possible moral judgment."[25] In *The Challenge of Peace*, the bishops held that US and Soviet strategies at the time failed the tests of the *jus in bello* criteria of discrimination and proportionality.[26] Indeed, the bishops ruled out counterpopulation warfare and "the deliberate initiation of nuclear warfare, on however restricted a scale."[27] On the use of limited or "tactical nuclear weapons," the bishops expressed their "extreme skepticism about the prospects for controlling a nuclear exchange, however limited the first use might be."[28] As we have seen, these *in bello* concerns have been echoed by Pope Francis. In addition, the bishops invoked the *jus ad bellum* criterion of a reasonable hope of success in bringing about justice and peace, and they questioned "whether such a reasonable hope can exist once nuclear weapons have been exchanged."[29] Similarly, David Hollenbach wrote that the "*ad bellum* criterion of reasonable hope of success becomes the relevant moral norm in this debate," leading him to conclude that "the hope that any use of strategic weapons can be kept limited exceeds the bounds of reasonable judgment."[30] Importantly, Pope Francis extends this consideration of probability of success to the question of deterrence, which the bishops accepted "for a time."[31] In all of this, as the bishops put it, the "'no' to nuclear war must, in the end, be definitive and decisive,"[32] a clear example of the "honest" just war reasoning Yoder rightly respected even though that "no" was accompanied for a few decades with a conditional and temporary "yes" on deterrence.[33]

According to Yoder, this more "honest" approach to just war, which draws lines identifying where a "no" is obliged, was already evident among those Catholic just war thinkers who condemned obliteration and area bombing during World War II. "It is this notion that there must be a limit somewhere which in the 1950s came to be called nuclear pacifism, even though in its logic it is a form of just-war thinking."[34] But again, there were and continue to be rival versions of just war thinking, including among Catholic writers. Ted Grimsrud refers to those who, like Hollenbach and the US Catholic bishops, are "nuclear pacifists," who think that no nuclear war can ever be justified or justly conducted on just war grounds, as opposed to those who are just war "realists," such as William O'Brien and John Courtney Murray, SJ, who maintain that just war principles can indeed govern and regulate even nuclear war.[35]

A noteworthy example of a strict interpretation and application of just war reasoning was a 1961 collection of essays by several Catholic writers, *Nuclear Weapons and Christian Conscience*, edited by Walter Stein, who also contributed a couple of essays to it.[36] Hardly pacifistic—indeed, in her contribution G.E.M. Anscombe was scathing of pacifism—these authors stringently employed just war reasoning to condemn nuclear weapons, both their use in war and their use in deterrence.[37] In contrast to both pacifism and amoral cynicism, they believed that it is still possible to differentiate between justified killing and murder, between combatants and noncombatants, between limited and total war. Thus, just war reasoning and principles remain in force even as they rule out the possibility of either justifying embarking upon nuclear war or its just conduct.[38] In the end, for them, nuclear war was immoral because it is mass murder and because even "the policy of 'deterrence' involves a conditional willingness to unleash such a war . . . [and] is therefore not only wicked in what it risks, but in terms of implicit *intention*."[39] For Stein, the "distinction between 'using' and 'possessing' these weapons" upon which those who "defend the stock-piling of nuclear weapons tend to base" their stance collapses.[40] In the end, the approach to just war reasoning represented by Stein et al. holds "that there are *limits*—creaturely limits, in war as in every other sphere of human action; that these limits bind, and sustain, us even in the face of the most urgent 'necessity.'"[41]

To return to where I began this essay, during my initial study of just war thinking and questions regarding nuclear arms, I was more of a "realist"; however, over the decades I have become a strict just war proponent who, accordingly, is a nuclear pacifist. I think that the Catholic Church, while open to the possibility of the "realist" approach at first and while temporarily granting conditional acceptance of deterrence, has now, with the papacy of Francis, also embraced nuclear pacifism in accordance with a stricter approach to just war reasoning. These just war lessons now decrease that interim acceptance of nuclear weapons and deterrence to zero, just like they have yielded a firm "no" to the morality of nuclear war.

Notes

1. National Conference of Catholic Bishops, *The Challenge of Peace: God's Promise and Our Response* (Washington, DC: United States Catholic Conference, 1983), no. 5.
2. See Ryan Leas, "38 Essential '80s Songs about Nuclear Anxiety," *Stereogum*, January 23, 2018.
3. I wrote about Regis Factor's impact on my life in "Way beyond 'the Way,' but It Paved the Way: On C. S. Lewis's *The Abolition of Man*," in *Take and Read*, ed. Dianne Bergant and Mike Daley (Berkeley, CA: Apocryphile Press, 2017), 19–23.
4. The first books I read by Stanley Hauerwas were *Against the Nations: War and Survival in a Liberal Society* (Notre Dame, IN: University of Notre Dame Press, 1985) and *Should War Be Eliminated? Philosophical and Theological Investigations* (Milwaukee, WI: Marquette University Press, 1984).
5. "Appeal to the Catholic Church to Re-Commit to the Centrality of Gospel Nonviolence," Catholic Nonviolence Initiative, May 17, 2016, https://nonviolencejustpeace.net/2016/05/17/an-appeal-to-the-catholic-church-to-re-commit-to-the-centrality-of-gospel-nonviolence/.
6. Claire Giangravè, "Vatican Nuclear Summit Blends Realpolitik and 'Reaching for the Moon,'" *Crux: Taking the Catholic Pulse*, November 11, 2017. I too attended this summit; see Tobias Winright, "What Do Pope Francis' Statements on Nuclear Weapons Mean for Catholics in the Military?," *Sojourners*, November 15, 2017.
7. "Nobel Laureate Mairead Maguire: Concept of 'Just Wars' Must Be Thrown Out," *Belfast Telegraph*, November 11, 2017.

8. Tobias Winright, "Why I Shall Continue to Use and Teach Just War Theory," *Expositions: Interdisciplinary Studies in the Humanities* 12, no. 1 (2018): 142–61; and Tobias Winright, "Just War and Imagination Are Not Mutually Exclusive," *Horizons* 45, no. 1 (June 2018): 114–19.
9. Tobias Winright, "Hawks and Doves: Rival Versions of Just War Theory," *Christian Century* 123, no. 25 (December 12, 2006): 32–35; and Tobias Winright, "Two Rival Versions of Just War Theory and the Presumption against Harm in Policing," *Annual of the Society of Christian Ethics* 18 (1998): 221–39.
10. Gerard Powers, "The Nuclear Ethics Gap: Finding Our Way on the Road to Disarmament," *America*, May 17, 2010.
11. I initially called for "integral peacemaking" in "Your 'Just Peace' Reading List," *National Catholic Reporter*, December 21, 2016.
12. John Howard Yoder, *When War Is Unjust: Being Honest in Just-War Thinking*, rev. ed. (Maryknoll, NY: Orbis Books, 1996), 3. After I studied under Hauerwas at Duke Divinity School, I became Yoder's student and graduate assistant at the University of Notre Dame. In recent years Yoder's violence toward women has come to light, causing many Christian ethicists to question his writings, especially on nonviolence. Although I continue to wrestle with what to do with his work, I think that his call to just war Christians to be stricter is right. See Tobias Winright, "I Was John Howard Yoder's Graduate Assistant. Should I Still Use His Work?," *Sojourners*, October 23, 2015.
13. Laurie Johnston, "Nuclear Deterrence: When an Interim Ethic Reaches Its Expiration Date," Political Theology Network, May 9, 2014.
14. Address of His Holiness Pope Francis to Participants in the International Symposium "Prospects for a World Free of Nuclear Weapons and for Integral Disarmament," November 10, 2017.
15. Address of His Holiness Pope Francis to Participants in the International Symposium.
16. Address of His Holiness Pope Francis to Participants in the International Symposium.
17. Mark J. Allman, *Who Would Jesus Kill? War, Peace, and the Christian Tradition* (Winona, MN: Anselm Academic, 2008), 230.
18. Address of His Holiness Pope Francis to Participants in the International Symposium "Prospects for a World Free of Nuclear Weapons and for Integral Disarmament."
19. Address of His Holiness Pope Francis to Participants in the International Symposium.
20. On proportionality in these two categories, see Allman, *Who Would Jesus Kill?*, 199, 204, where he distinguishes between macroproportionality (*jus ad bellum*) and microproportionality (*jus in bello*).
21. National Conference of Catholic Bishops, *The Challenge of Peace*, no. 143. For a similar observation, see David Hollenbach, *Nuclear Ethics: A*

Christian Moral Argument (Mahwah, NJ: Paulist Press, 1983), 47: "For the pacifist the answer to this question is clear and unambiguous. Since all use of lethal force is judged to be incompatible with the gospel, then a fortiori the use of nuclear weapons must be rejected."

22. Second Vatican Council (1965), *Gaudium et spes*. "[W]e cannot fail to praise those who renounce the use of violence in the vindication of their rights and who resort to methods of defense which are otherwise available to weaker parties too, provided this can be done without injury to the rights and duties of others or of the community itself" (para. 78). See also National Conference of Catholic Bishops, *The Challenge of Peace*, no. 119. Moreover, given how "political transitions in places as diverse as the Philippines and Eastern Europe demonstrate the power of nonviolent action, even against dictatorial and totalitarian regimes," the US Catholic bishops write, "[o]ne must ask, in light of recent history, whether nonviolence should be restricted to personal commitments or whether it also should have a place in the public order with the tradition of justified and limited war." United States Conference of Catholic Bishops, *The Harvest of Justice Is Sown in Peace*, https://www.usccb.org/resources/harvest-justice-sown-peace.
23. Peter Steinfels notes that "the pacifist Catholic Worker regularly discussed just-war principles either to criticize them or to demonstrate how they ruled out any contemporary war." See Peter Steinfels, "The War against Just War: Enough Already," *Commonweal* 144, no. 11 (June 16, 2017). See also Michael Baxter, "Just War and Pacifism: A 'Pacifist' Perspective in Seven Points," *Houston Catholic Worker*, June 1, 2004.
24. National Conference of Catholic Bishops, *The Challenge of Peace*, no. 144.
25. John Howard Yoder, *The Original Revolution: Essays on Christian Pacifism* (Scottdale, PA: Herald Press, 1971), 132.
26. National Conference of Catholic Bishops, *The Challenge of Peace*, no. 144.
27. National Conference of Catholic Bishops, nos. 147–50.
28. National Conference of Catholic Bishops, no. 153.
29. National Conference of Catholic Bishops, no. 159.
30. Hollenbach, *Nuclear Ethics*, 53.
31. National Conference of Catholic Bishops, *The Challenge of Peace*, no. 154.
32. National Conference of Catholic Bishops, no. 138.
33. Yoder, *When War Is Unjust*, 63.
34. Yoder, 44.
35. Ted Grimsrud, "Just War Thought: A Pacifist Analysis," Peace Theology: Engaging Faith and Pacifism, January 2009 (originally written in 1986). Grimsrud's interpretation of Murray differs from Yoder's. See Yoder, *When War Is Unjust*, 61–64.
36. Walter Stein, ed., *Nuclear Weapons and Christian Conscience* (London: Merlin, 1961).
37. G.E.M. Anscombe, "War and Murder," in *Nuclear Weapons and Christian Conscience*, 45–62. For example, "Now pacifism teaches people to make no

distinction between the shedding of innocent blood and the shedding of any human blood. And in this way pacifism has corrupted enormous numbers of people who will not act according to its tenets. They become convinced that a number of things are wicked which are not; hence, seeing no way of avoiding 'wickedness', they set no limits to it" (56). She regarded the Allies' policy of obliteration bombing of cities and civilians as evidence of this problem. Her treatment of the problem of "double-think about double effect" (57–59), I think, is valuable, and I drew from it in Tobias Winright, "The Morality of Cluster Bombing," *Studies in Christian Ethics* 22, no. 3 (August 2009): 357–81.
38. Walter Stein, "Introductory: The Defence of the West," in *Nuclear Weapons and Christian Conscience*, 23–29.
39. Stein, 23.
40. Stein, 32. On that distinction, regarding the US bishops' "careful border-walking on nuclear deterrence" in *The Challenge of Peace*, Yoder added, "The term use is deceptive. Threatening is also use. . . . A mugger uses his pistol when he points it at my head, even if he does not fire." Yoder, *When War Is Unjust*, 45n32. I think there's something to be said for this point. As a former law enforcement officer, my mere presence—with my firearm in its holster—is technically a form of coercive force. On the other hand, to use another example, I suppose it is possible that some homeowners put a "Beware of the dog" sign on their fence, even though they may not actually own a dog, as a deterrent to possible burglars. This latter is much more of a bluff than if the homeowner actually were to have a dog that he or she would never command to attack an intruder (although a dog might do so nevertheless). Because other contributors to this volume concentrate on the question of deterrence, I will say no more here except that strict just war thinkers will take this matter very seriously.
41. Stein, *Nuclear Weapons and Christian Conscience*, 40.

3

Philosophical Debate on Nuclear Deterrence

GREGORY M. REICHBERG

In their public pronouncements, states typically emphasize that they have acquired nuclear weapons not so much for their battlefield utility but rather because their possession provides a secure method to deter armed aggression. This takes us into the normative assessment of nuclear deterrence, a topic that was hotly debated by philosophers in the last two decades of the twentieth century.

The idea that nuclear weapons have been sought after so as to exercise influence and that this constitutes their principal utility goes to the heart of why states have expended enormous amounts of money to include these weapons in their arsenals. From this perspective, the use to which these weapons are put has little to do with their detonation. Their use is verbal/expressive—the issuance of a threat—and the effect is psychological rather than physically destructive. A nuclear weapon state can issue threats of a potency not available to their nonnuclear weapons counterparts. The fact that no destruction is directly caused by a nuclear threat makes such threats seem relatively benign, certainly when compared with actual detonation of such a weapon. And if a nuclear threat can stop a would-be aggressor without the least bloodshed, this would seem highly advantageous and even a morally good course of action. Much death and destruction would thereby be forestalled. For this reason, the possession of nuclear weapons has often been presented (paradoxically, given their destructive potential) as a pathway to peace.[1]

Thus understood, to deter by possession of a weapon is to threaten use of that weapon in the event a prohibited act is performed. A threat is a special kind of speech act whereby one person (P) tells another (Q) that she will intentionally bring about some harm x unless Q does (or refrains from doing) the action y. A deterrent threat, as already noted, promises infliction of harm if the forbidden action is carried out. A compellent threat, by contrast, promises harm if the commanded act is not done.[2]

Under the standard conception of deterrence that emerged during the Cold War, nuclear threats had a strictly deterrent character. Indeed, after Hiroshima and Nagasaki, the view quickly gained widespread currency that compellent nuclear threats were blackmail writ large and were devoid of moral legitimacy. By contrast, deterrent threats made by means of nuclear weapons were viewed largely in a positive light. The country possessing such a weapon communicated to its nuclear peers that should it become the target of a nuclear first strike or even invasion by conventional means, it might unleash a retaliatory nuclear attack in response. The whole point was to prevent a nuclear first strike (or invasion by conventional forces) and to render impotent any attempt at nuclear blackmail. This was considered a good thing insofar as it appeared to fulfill a fundamental duty of political leadership, namely to protect the citizenry from harm. It was with this in mind that the teaching magisterium of the Catholic Church has in the past expressed its support for the system of nuclear deterrence, albeit as a provisional measure on the way to full collective disarmament.[3] Nonetheless, over the last few years and in light of the scant progress made toward such disarmament, the magisterium has withdrawn this provisional acceptance and instead emphasized how the possession of nuclear weapons, even solely for purposes of deterrence, must be considered immoral.[4]

Since the point of the deterrent threat was to deter the other by instilling in it fear of a massive reprisal against what the other valued most—namely its civilian population—during that period nuclear deterrent threats were typically made against urban population centers. This was termed "deterrence by punishment." The harm to be inflicted would have no direct military function. It would not be defensive in the narrow sense of the term, because the underlying supposition was that the adversary had already completed its nuclear attack (hence there would no longer be a question of repelling it), and the second strike would come ex post facto as retaliation.[5] In the words of US secretary of defense Robert McNamara, "assured destruction is the very essence of the whole deterrence concept."[6]

Theorists of nuclear deterrence have emphasized how it is a joint product of capability and credibility. While obviously essential, simply having the weapons (capability) is never enough, as their possession will function as a deterrent only if the potential target as well as allies who benefit from extended deterrence believe that a violation—a nuclear first strike or conventional military aggression—will be met with a nuclear response. Nuclear threats will have this credibility only when the issuer state is able to convey its intent to fulfill them should a violation occur. Deterrence is moreover about a certain kind of relationship, including a set of shared assumptions about what each side can expect from the other, what it values and most wishes to avoid, and so forth. In the Soviet-US relationship stability was eventually achieved, but with the growth of nuclear proliferation, the achievement of deterrent stability has become ever more challenging.[7]

Having provided this brief outline of nuclear deterrence, how are we to assess its morality?

Since deterrence is about threatening rather than carrying out armed attack, the former must constitute the crux of our analysis. At the outset it can be noted how, for purposes of ethical analysis, there is not a pure and simple identity between the threat and the actual performance of the threatened action.[8] In the sphere of state-to-state relations, threats of armed force are viewed with more leniency than actual employment of the corresponding force. Thus, whereas preventive war has typically been condemned (by inter alia the Catholic theorists of just war), preventive issuance of threats has been viewed under a somewhat more positive light.[9] Indeed, nuclear deterrent threats are issued with the preventive aim in mind; it is precisely this aim coupled with the absence of any actual destruction that has given them an aura of moral legitimacy.[10] Is this legitimacy deserved?

Simplifying a complex philosophical literature, we can say that strategies to demonstrate a moral foundation for nuclear deterrent threats are of two basic kinds.

One strategy (articulated with considerable sophistication by the philosopher Gregory S. Kavka) is to establish a wide gulf between a threat, on the one side, and concrete implementation of the threat, on the other.[11] Such an analysis would seek to explain why moral evaluation of the threat cannot simply track the evaluation of the corresponding act once carried out. Those who follow this approach openly concede that nuclear retaliation on an urban population center would be grossly immoral. Simultaneously, however, they affirm that to threaten such retaliation could be morally allowable and even good, precisely insofar as it is the most effective way to deter a first strike. Ruling out bluffs and deliberate indecisiveness (holding off the decision whether to retaliate until after an attack has already occurred) as inefficacious to sustain the credibility needed for deterrence, advocates of this position emphasize the distinctiveness of deterrent intentions, that is, those conditional intentions whose existence is based on the agent's desire to thereby deter others from actualizing the antecedent condition of the intention.[12] Such intentions

> are, by nature, self-stultifying: if a deterrent intention fulfills the agent's purpose, it ensures that the intended (and possibly) evil act is not performed, by preventing the circumstances of performance from arising.... Normally, an agent will form the intention to do something because she either desires doing that thing as an end in itself, or as a means to other ends.... But, in the case of deterrent intentions, the ground of the desire to form the intention is entirely distinct from any desire to carry it out.... Thus, while the object of her deterrent intention might be an evil act, it does not follow that, in desiring to adopt that intention, she desires to do evil, either as an end or a means.[13]

Against this approach the objection can be raised that the one forming this deterrent intention voluntarily assumes the risk of carrying out the immoral act (in the worst-case scenario massive nuclear retaliation against urban centers).[14] Even though this outcome is in no way desired (to the contrary, the conditional intentional was formed precisely to avoid it), nonetheless to place oneself in a position where failure would in all likelihood entail this result is itself morally objectionable. Indeed, the very logic of deterrence entails that the more effective the deterrence, the more immoral its threats will be. Inversely, the more restrictive a deterrence policy becomes, the less effectively it will deter. Moreover, the credibility of these threats will depend on a demonstrated will and a readiness to carry them out.[15]

The philosopher David Gauthier has argued that the person who forms a deterrent intention does so to secure certain benefits that outweigh the costs that would be nevertheless incurred in the event of a failure (namely having to carry out the deterrent threat). The appraisal of these costs is factored into the formation of the conditional intention.[16] In his words, "if it is rational to form this conditional, deterrent intention, then, should deterrence fail and the condition be realized, it is rational to act on it. The utility cost of acting on the deterrent intention enters, with appropriate probability weighting, into determining whether it is rational to form the intention."[17] For Gauthier, to say that an action (in this case the mental act of forming an intention and expressing it as a threat) is rational is equivalent to saying it is moral. His aim, in mounting the argument outlined above, was to provide an ethical justification for robust nuclear deterrence, namely deterrence that would be fully credible hence well suited to succeed. In so doing, he proceeded on the basis of a thoroughgoing consequentialism. For those, by contrast, who acknowledge that certain actions should never be performed whatever the perceived benefits—in other words, those who recognize a deontological core to ethics—Gauthier's argument can be turned around. Agreeing with him that the conditional, deterrent intention implies an acceptance of massive retaliation in the event the deterrent threat fails, we must opt for the opposing path, namely to reject the formation of such an intention in the first place. On this understanding, the gap between threat and action is not nearly so wide as Kavka and other apologists of nuclear deterrence had assumed. If we condemn massive nuclear retaliation as inherently immoral—under the principle that the innocent should never be directly targeted with lethal harm—the willingness to accept such a cost as the condition of forming the conditional intention of retaliation (even if solely to avoid it) must be condemned as well.

Gauthier himself seems to have become aware of this implication, as ten years later he wrote:

> However advantageous in prospect a threat may be, the possibility of sincerely issuing it, and so of adopting a policy requiring or permitting its issuance, must depend on the expected costs, should one be called on to execute it, being offset by the overall expected benefits of the policy, so that on balance adopting the policy is more

advantageous than adopting no policy. A rational agent cannot sincerely and wittingly issue an apocalyptic threat. Rational deterrence is limited in ways that I have previously failed to recognize.[18]

Awareness that issuing a threat with "apocalyptic" consequences is wholly unsustainable on moral grounds has led some ethicists to propose an alternative strategy toward justifying nuclear deterrence. Closely associated with Paul Ramsey, a Methodist theologian who taught at Princeton University, on this account nuclear weapons were considered on two levels: their actual use on the battlefield and their threatened use within a strategy of deterrence. Regarding the first, Ramsey maintained that such use would be morally licit only when directed against the military forces of an invading enemy, but against civilian population centers it would be entirely ruled out. With respect to the second level, Ramsey paints a considerably more nuanced picture. While an enemy's cities should never be directly threatened with nuclear retaliation, the prospect of massive side-effect harm to its civilian population, stemming from a direct nuclear attack on its military forces, would nevertheless provide it with a powerful disincentive against ever initiating such an exchange in the first place.[19] Ramsey summed this up when he wrote that "a threat of something disproportionate is not always a disproportionate threat."[20]

Like Kavka's strategy, Ramsey's approach acknowledges a gap between the moral assessment of a threat and the parallel assessment of the threat's actualization. In particular, the proportionality criterion would apply differently in the two cases precisely because the immediate harm resulting from each would be different (fear on the one hand, death and bodily suffering on the other). The gap is nonetheless narrower for Ramsey than for Kavka, since the former recuses any deliberate targeting of civilian population centers (so-called countervalue targeting). He recognizes, however, that restricting nuclear targeting to military objectives (so-called counterforce targeting) may be insufficient to deter an enemy's nuclear first strike (or invasion with conventional weaponry). Hence, Ramsey proposes that the adversary state's fear can be heightened by letting it know that a nuclear attack intentionally directed solely at military targets will foreseeably result in widespread collateral damage to civilians. Applying the doctrine of double effect, Ramsey maintains that so long as this collateral damage is in no way directly intended or threatened, it may be licit to make good use of the prospect of the said damages (i.e., the target state's awareness that it would ensue), namely as a way to deter aggression.

"Double effect" is the heading under which the ethical quandaries surrounding side-effect harm have traditionally been discussed in Catholic philosophy. This term is shorthand for the two different kinds of effects that can emerge from our actions. On the one hand, there is the very state of affairs that our actions are meant to produce. This goal we will succeed at achieving more or less well depending on our skill. On the other hand, there are the side effects that result from this deliberate intervention in the world. The idea that we are answerable for these side effects, yet in a manner different than the accountability that obtains vis-à-vis our intentional projects, has been dubbed the "doctrine of double effect."[21]

Does Ramsey's proposal succeed in providing a morally acceptable justification for nuclear deterrence? First of all, despite his disclaimers to the contrary, it must be admitted that whosoever threatens to carry out an action that is likely (or certain) to have damaging side effects must be willing, as indicated above, to accept this outcome should the threat be actualized. Under the scenario considered, the outcome would not be directly intended by the one doing the threatening, yet that person would still bear responsibility for bringing it about. As Thomas Aquinas and other Catholic theorists of double effect have maintained, a person who foresees (or should foresee) that a certain side effect will arise from her or his actions is not automatically to be exculpated of moral blame for producing that harm simply because it was not directly intended. Rather, the agent must apply the rule of proportionality: the good aimed at must outweigh the harmful side effects that will inevitably follow. During the Cold War it was thus argued by Michael Quinlan and others that the good of stopping a full-scale Soviet invasion of Western Europe could justify the use of tactical nuclear weapons, a use that would inevitably cause much side-effect harm to civilians.[22] This sort of reasoning could be sustained (it must be acknowledged) under a Catholic reading of the principle of double effect.

However, and this is an important caveat, such double-effect reasoning could be made applicable to side-effect harms caused by nuclear weapons solely under condition that the intended effect of this military action—striking military targets—could itself be considered permissible.

The second of the two prongs of the double-effect equation may be deemed morally permissible only when the first prong—the action deliberately carried out as a means to the presumably good end—is itself justifiable. If this would not be the case, it follows as a necessary consequence that double-effect reasoning will no longer be germane, and proportionality calculations to justify the allowance of related side-effect harms will be inoperative as well. If it is true that the employment of nuclear weapons against military targets—especially the sustained employment of these weapons in a theater of war—cannot meet the baseline standards of discrimination, proportionality, and avoidance of cruel or superfluous harm to combatants, it follows that the resulting side-effect harm to noncombatants cannot be justified either.[23]

Justifications of nuclear deterrence based on double-effect reasoning will necessarily fail whenever it can be shown that the direct (intended) effect of nuclear attack must itself be deemed immoral. This (as was explained above in the section on nuclear use) would almost certainly be the case for all but the most minimal (and implausible) employments of nuclear weapons on the battlefield. Indeed, Ramsey's argumentation depends on the threat of nuclear attacks against military targets of sufficiently wide scope that the side effects can be expected to be significantly daunting. Michael Walzer, the preeminent just war theorist of our time, criticized this line of reasoning when he concluded that "nuclear war is and will remain morally unacceptable, and there is no case for its rehabilitation. Because it is unacceptable, we must seek out ways to prevent it, and because deterrence is a bad way, we must seek out others."[24] In other words, if it is true that effective nuclear deterrence entails immorality (this has been our argument above), we should urgently press for the abandonment of this strategy in favor of general nuclear disarmament.

Abandonment of nuclear deterrence has now been given legal form in the Treaty on the Prohibition of Nuclear Weapons (which entered into force on January 22, 2021).[25] By virtue of its Article 1(d), state parties to the treaty assume an obligation to refrain from threatening any use of nuclear weapons. This amounts to a renunciation of nuclear deterrent threats as a procedure that may lawfully be undertaken by parties to the treaty under the implied supposition that such threats are morally unjustifiable. Some two months after the treaty opened for signature at the United Nations (September 20, 2017), Pope Francis echoed this adverse moral judgment on nuclear deterrence when he affirmed (November 10,

2017) that we should not "fail to be genuinely concerned by the catastrophic humanitarian and environmental effects of any employment of nuclear devices. If we also take into account the risk of an accidental detonation as a result of error of any kind, the threat of their use and indeed their very possession are to be firmly condemned."[26]

This statement is highly significant. For the first time ever a pope condemned possession of nuclear weapons not just for use (a long-standing papal view) but also for reasons of deterrence.[27]

Notes

1. For a seminal articulation of this view, see John Lewis Gaddis, "The Long Peace: Elements of Stability in the Postwar International System," *International Security* 10, no. 4 (1986): 99–142. For a critique, see Ward Wilson, "Myth 5, Nuclear Weapons Keep Us Safe," in *Five Myths about Nuclear Weapons* (New York: First Mariner Books, 2014), 87–103. Going even further in criticizing the contention that nuclear weapons are a pathway to peace, some authors have "maintained that blind faith in nuclear deterrence risks unleashing a massive conventional war. . . . Scholars call this the 'stability-instability paradox.'" Hal Brands and Michael Beckley, "Washington Is Preparing for the Wrong War with China," *Foreign Affairs*, December 16, 2021.
2. See Thomas Schelling, "The Distinction between Deterrence and 'Compellence'," in *Arms and Influence* (New Haven, CT: Yale University Press, 1966), 69–78.
3. The US Catholic bishops, in their 1983 pastoral letter *The Challenge of Peace* (nos. 186 and 188), affirmed a "moral acceptance" of nuclear weapons, albeit one that is "strictly conditioned" by a set of restrictions ("no targeting of civilian population centers, no prolonged periods of repeated nuclear strikes, and that it be provisional, i.e. a step on the way toward progressive disarmament"). The French bishops seemed more torn by competing negative and positive assessments: "Faced with a choice between two evils, both of them all but unavoidable, capitulations or counter-threats, one chooses the lesser *without pretending that one is choosing a moral good*" (my emphasis), while in the next breath they lay out the conditions that will make nuclear deterrence "morally acceptable." *Gagner la paix*, §30.
4. See "Nuclear Disarmament: Time for Abolition. Contribution of the Holy See to the Vienna Conference, 8 December 2014," reproduced in *Nuclear Deterrence: An Ethical Perspective*, ed. Mathias Nebel and Gregory M. Reichberg, 87–97 (Geneva: Caritas in Veritate Foundation, 2015). This position paper by the Holy See prepared the way for Pope Francis's statement of November 10, 2017 (to the international symposium Prospects of

a World Free from Nuclear Weapons and for Integral Disarmament), when, speaking of nuclear weapons, he said that "the threat of their use ... is to be firmly condemned." In this connection it can be noted that the present chapter represents a revised and shortened version of an essay 'The Morality of Nuclear Deterrence: A Reassessment' that appeared the Caritas in Veritate publication (9-31) referenced above. The author thanks the Caritas in Veritate Foundation for allowing this material to be reproduced here.

5. For this reason, the idea that extended deterrence functions as a nuclear "umbrella" is a misnomer, since it misleadingly suggests that countries under the umbrella "are protected by some kind of missile defense shield—rather than the threat of retaliation." Scott D. Sagan, "Shared Responsibilities for Nuclear Disarmament," *Daedalus* 138, no. 4 (2009): 162.

6. Robert S. McNamara, *The Essence of Security* (New York: Harper and Row, 1968), 52.

7. In this connection, Hedley Bull astutely noted that "the theory [of nuclear deterrence] assumes ... that both sides in a relationship of mutual deterrence share a conception of rational action. It is easy to conceive of situations of nuclear confrontation in the future in which states, divided not only politically and ideologically but also culturally, do not share a conception of rational action to the extent to which the super-powers have done in the past." Hedley Bull, "Future Conditions of Strategic Deterrence," in *The Future of Nuclear Deterrence*, Part I, Adelphi Paper 160 (London: International Institute for Strategic Studies, 1975), 21. For a more recent discussion of the risks associated with deterrence under conditions of multipolarity, see Scott D. Sagan's contribution to his debate with Kenneth L. Waltz, *The Spread of Nuclear Weapons: An Enduring Debate*, 3rd ed. (New York: Norton, 2012).

8. See Gregory M. Reichberg and Henrik Syse, "Threats and Coercive Diplomacy: An Ethical Analysis," *Ethics and International Affairs* 32, no. 2 (2018): 179–202.

9. Gregory M. Reichberg, "Preventive War," in *Thomas Aquinas on War and Peace*, 201–2 (Cambridge: Cambridge University Press, 2017).

10. Along these lines the French bishops' conference wrote that "threat is not use. Does the immorality of use render the threat immoral? This is not evident." *Gagner la paix*, November 8, 1983, §29. Earlier they had noted that "the threat of force is not the use of force. It is the basis of deterrence, and this is often forgotten when the same moral qualification is attributed to the threat as to the use of force (§36).

11. Gregory S. Kavka, *Moral Paradoxes of Nuclear Deterrence* (Cambridge: Cambridge University Press, 1987).

12. Kavka, 48–54.

13. Kavka, 20–21.

14. As the French bishops put the point, "the danger of the logic of deterrence is immediately evident. In order not to allow a possible aggressor to have illusions about the credibility of our defenses, we must show ourselves ready to use our weapons if deterrence should fail." *Gagner la paix*, no. 27.

15. During the Cold War it was common to hedge on this readiness by cultivating a posture of deliberate ambiguity, especially vis-à-vis extended deterrence commitments. It was thought that the possibility of nuclear retaliation (and the attendant risk of escalation) would be sufficient to deter enemy attack. This posture was also thought to be beneficial insofar as it assuaged the conscience of the state issuing the threat, which told itself that it was not quite committed to a nuclear retaliation that would target whole cities. Objections were raised, however, that this ambiguity decreased the credibility of deterrence and for that very reason could prove destabilizing, provoking the very attack it was meant to prevent. The instability resulting from the maintenance of ambiguity will likely grow in the context of a multipolar world. See Keith B. Payne, *The Great American Gamble: Deterrence Theory and Practice from the Cold War to the Twenty-First Century* (Fairfax, VA: National Institute Press, 2008), 234–39. Hence this does not seem a suitable strategy to lessen the moral qualms that arise from nuclear deterrence.
16. David Gauthier, "Deterrence, Maximization, and Rationality," *Ethics* 94, no. 3 (1984): 474–95.
17. Gauthier, 486.
18. David Gauthier, "Assure and Threaten," *Ethics* 104, no. 4 (1994): 719.
19. Paul Ramsey, "The Limits of Nuclear War," in *The Just War: Force and Political Responsibility* (New York: Scribner, 1968). For a recent defense of Ramsey's argumentation against objections raised by Michael Walzer in *Just and Unjust Wars* (New York: Basic Books, 1977), 278–83, see F. M. Kamm, "Nuclear Deterrence and Reliance on Harm," in *The Moral Target*, 228–49 (Oxford: Oxford University Press, 2012).
20. Ramsey, *The Just War*, 303.
21. See Gregory M. Reichberg, "Restrictive versus Permissive Double Effect: Interpreting Aquinas," *Proceedings of the American Catholic Philosophical Association* 91 (2017): 211–23.
22. Michael Quinlan, *Thinking about Nuclear Weapons: Principles, Problems, Prospects* (Oxford: Oxford University Press, 2009).
23. For elaboration, see the essays in Gro Nystuen, Stuart Casey-Maslen, and Annie Golden Bersagel, eds., *Nuclear Weapons under International Law* (Cambridge: Cambridge University Press, 2014).
24. Walzer, *Just and Unjust Wars*, 283. Walzer's critique of nuclear deterrence was developed in the context of Catholic moral theology by John Finnis, Joseph M. Boyle Jr., and Germain Grisez, *Nuclear Deterrence, Morality, and Realism* (Oxford: Oxford University Press, 1987).
25. See Kjølv Egeland, "Arms, Influence and the Treaty on the Prohibition of Nuclear Weapons," *Survival* 61, no. 3 (2019): 57–80.
26. Address of His Holiness Pope Francis to participants in the International Symposium "Prospects for a World Free of Nuclear Weapons and for Integral Disarmament," November 10, 2017.
27. In this connection, see the recent intervention (October 13, 2021) at the United Nations by Archbishop Gabriele Caccia, apostolic nuncio and

permanent observer of the Holy See to the United Nations: "Pope Francis has emphasized, 'the use of atomic energy for purposes of war is immoral, just as the possessing of nuclear weapons is immoral' since the intrinsic intentionality of having nuclear weapons is the threat to use them. "Archbishop Caccia on Nuclear Weapons, WMDs and Disarmament," October 13, 2021, Permanent Observer Mission of the Holy See to the United Nations, https://holyseemission.org/contents//statements/6167527bd8e72.php.

4

The Moral Ecology of Deterrence and Abolition

WILLIAM BARBIERI

The papacy of Pope Francis has been eventful with respect to the Catholic Church's engagement with nuclear weapons and the ethics of war and peace. In 2013 and 2014, representatives of the Holy See participated in conferences in Norway, Mexico, and Austria building a case for disarmament on the empirical findings concerning the predictable humanitarian impact of even limited nuclear war. In 2016, the Pontifical Council for Justice and Peace hosted a landmark conference on nonviolence that symbolized the shifting balance between the Church's traditional commitment to just war reasoning and the more recent emphasis on nonviolent means ushered in by Pope John Paul II. In 2017, the Vatican played an uncharacteristically active role in formulating the United Nations Treaty on the Prohibition of Nuclear Weapons and then became one of the first states to ratify it. Later that year at another conference hosted by the Holy See, Francis took the additional step of formalizing the judgment of the Vatican that nuclear deterrence is no longer morally defensible as a security policy. This message was prominently repeated in his 2020 encyclical *Fratelli tutti*.

These developments constitute important changes in themselves, but their full significance can be appreciated only if they are seen in the context of deeper shifts being enacted with respect to the basic paradigm through which the Catholic Church's moral teaching engages the world. In this respect, the 2015 encyclical *Laudato si'* marks a transition to a new fundamental orientation resituating Catholic social ethics within the broader framework of what Pope Francis calls "integral ecology." This paradigm not only broadens the scope of concern for Catholic moral teaching and action but also introduces a new methodological approach, one that understands morality in terms of interlocking nexuses of ecological relations connecting humans and the rest of creation. I refer to this as the paradigm of moral ecology.

The paradigm of moral ecology has implications across the spectrum of issues to which Catholic ethics attends, from sexual ethics to political economy, and the ethics of war and peace is no exception. Considered from the standpoint of integral ecology, questions about the morality of weapons systems and resorts to the use of force become more firmly embedded in broader examinations of authentic human development and environmental sustainability. At the same time, ethical quandaries such as the problem of nuclear deterrence are recast as matters of holistic moral equilibrium rather than contests of competing rational principles. Understanding the character and significance of the methodological shift in Catholic teaching inaugurated in *Laudato si'* requires taking a closer look at Francis's conception of integral ecology. This ethical vision, as it turns out, provides a firm foundation for the emergent just peace perspective that has helped inform the Church's ethical case for the abolition of nuclear weapons. At the same time, it contains elements of an ecologically informed moral theory that can help reformulate the Church's response to the problem of nuclear deterrence.

Laudato si' and Integral Ecology

There is a sense in which *Laudato si'*, Pope Francis's teaching "On Care for Our Common Home," can be considered one in a line of influential Catholic social encyclicals including landmark statements such as *Centesimus annus* (1991), *Pacem in terris* (1963), and *Quadragesimo anno* (1931) and stretching back to 1891's *Rerum novarum.* But it might be more accurate to say that Francis explodes, or at least radically expands, the very notion of a social encyclical when he states in *Laudato si'* that "we are faced not with two separate crises, one environmental and the other social, but rather with one complex crisis which is both social and environmental."[1] The core thesis of his document is that the Church's response to the variety of concerns traditionally gathered under the notion of "the social question" cannot be addressed separately from our response to the litany of issues associated with the problem of environmental degradation, hence the need for an "integral ecology," an ethical approach that thoroughly integrates concern for persons with care for creation. Indeed, Francis argues that two millennia of Christian spirituality can be seen as leading up to an "ecological conversion" rooted in the recognition that "to be protectors of God's handiwork is essential to a life of virtue; it is not an optional or secondary aspect of our Christian experience."[2]

Integral ecology takes the perception of the functional interdependence of the natural world and the world of human relations and parlays it into a conception of "universal communion" uniting human persons with all other creatures and the rest of nature. Within this context, Francis goes on to identify an interlocking set of subsystems—ecologies—that must be taken into account in trying to promote the health and flourishing of the whole. These ecological systems—each of which has a distinctive value associated with it—can be thought of as occupying levels in a pyramidal structure:

> The largest, most fundamental system is what Francis calls "environmental ecology." This includes the physical, chemical, and biological substrates undergirding life on the planet as well as ecosystems in particular that, Francis notes, "have an intrinsic value independent of their usefulness."[3]
>
> Existing atop this system and interacting with it we find a series of nested human ecological systems. Francis refers to the first of these as "economic ecology." By this he means the foundational set of relations in which human agency impinges on the materials of the natural world in order to support human projects. Economic ecology is the field within which human development occurs, and its primary directive is the imperative of sustainability.
>
> The next subsystem described in *Laudato si'* is that of "social ecology." This concerns the functioning of the various institutions and organs patterning human life, from the family up to the state and international organizations. The mark of a healthy social ecology is justice in its various forms and nuances.
>
> Within the broad frame of society Francis next identifies the domain of "cultural ecology," which revolves around interactions within and among peoples. The building up of civilization, the nurturing of distinctive ways of life, and the flourishing of the arts and

other forms of human expression are all concerns of cultural ecology, with pluralism an important watchword in this field.

An additional subsystem of integral ecology is characterized interchangeably in *Laudato si'* as the "ecology of daily life" and "human ecology" and has to do primarily with the shape of the built environment, the physical settings and home conditions that shape everyday coexistence. At issue here is the fostering of habitable spaces that enable the preservation of human dignity.

The five subsystems of integral ecology Francis names—environmental, economic, social, cultural, and human ecology—together exhibit two important features. The first is that they are systems of value, revolving around basic goods (respectively, intrinsic value, sustainability, justice, pluralism, and human dignity) and hence involving moral relationships. The second is that they are interlocking and interdependent such that distortions or pathologies in one system carry over into disturbances of the other systems. These two features taken together enable us to characterize Francis's account as a "moral ecology." I will return to the implications of this point below.

Just Peace and Abolitionism

It is hardly surprising that the model of integral ecology Francis presents in *Laudato si'* has a good deal to say about peace. The document reflects a keen awareness that social conflict, organized violence, and war are strongly correlated with ecological degradation: just as environmental abuses can contribute to the causes of human strife, so too can modern warfare wreak havoc on natural systems. Moreover, violence can be a medium that transfers distortions from one ecological subsystem—say, cultural ecology—to others, be they larger systems such as environmental ecology or smaller ones such as human ecology. By the same token, however, nonviolence, peacebuilding, and reconciliation techniques tend to produce positive effects that can redound through the various levels of integral ecology to help promote harmonious, flourishing human relationships. In keeping with this insight, Francis would have been justified in revising Paul VI's well-known adage in *Populorum progressio* (1967) to state that ecology, more than development, is the new name for peace.

The conception of peace animating the pope's account of integral ecology at once resonates with and deepens the model of just peace presented at the Vatican conference in 2016. Just peace is a normative framework that recontextualizes and, to some extent, transforms traditional just war and pacifist perspectives by considering the morality of conflict within the broader, longer-term horizon of peacebuilding and reconciliation. In light of the notion of integral ecology, central values of the just peace approach disclose additional dimensions. Thus, for example, the common good as a criterion for just peace is revealed to have an ecological dimension that recasts it as not only the international or global but also the cosmic common good.[4] The criteria of right relationship and restoration take on additional meanings linked to human relations to the natural world. And sustainability becomes a standard referring to not only just and peaceful human relations but also ecological stability and restraint. The just peace ethic, in short, is incomplete if it is not integrated into an environmental sensibility.

Laudato si' models in some of its individual sections how the concerns of a just peace approach are applied within the ethics of integral ecology. Francis speaks, for example, of the importance of inner peace, noting that it is integrally related to both care for ecology (#225) and social peace (#159). He goes on to contrast the virtues of peaceful patterns of integral development with the effects of neoliberal strategies of globalization marked by consumerism and overconsumption, practices, he suggests, that violate the commandment "Thou shall not kill" (#95). On the topic of war, Francis points to the interdependence of ecological imbalance and armed conflict (#57) and highlights how poverty exacerbates both (#48). And in several places he alludes to the risks and costs of nuclear weapons (#57, #104, #175). It is in this context that he invokes the ideal, cited in Benedict XVI but traceable back to John XXIII in *Pacem in terris*, of "integral disarmament," a conception that not only encompasses nuclear arsenals but also stretches to people's "very souls." Integral disarmament is a notion entirely in keeping with the holistic sensibility of the just peace approach.

Although the Vatican made common cause with a number of NGOs of various stripes in organizing a series of conferences in 2013 and 2014 devoted to assessing the "humanitarian impact" of the use of nuclear weapons, it is clear that the Catholic Church's commitment to abolitionism is not concerned only with human costs but ultimately entails comparable concern for the ecological impact of nuclear war as well. In short, the Catholic approach to nuclear weapons revolves around three interlocking normative conceptions. The idea of integral disarmament situates the abolitionist cause within a program of moral conversion. More broadly, the program of integral development emphasizes the economic and social costs and distortions produced by maintaining and modernizing nuclear weapons. Finally, and most fundamentally, the standpoint of integral ecology shows the maintenance of nuclear weapons to be at odds with not only the priorities of authentic human development but also the human obligation to care for creation.

Moral Ecology and Deterrence

From a Catholic standpoint, as Pope Francis has stated, the ethics of nuclear deterrence is situated within the problematic of integral disarmament.[5] As we have seen, integral disarmament is a topic within the broader field of integral development; which is in turn a component of the primary, overarching framework of integral ecology. Integral ecology is premised on the inseparability and interdependence of human aspirations, such as authentic human development, on the one hand and the flourishing of the natural world, understood as God's creation, on the other. Ethically speaking, integral ecology can be understood to employ an emergent moral paradigm, one that understands and reasons about normative questions based on the model of ecological relationships. I call this the paradigm of moral ecology. In light of this development, the question arises as to how to think about deterrence from the point of view of this new moral theory.

What does it mean to think in terms of moral ecology? While space limits preclude a detailed characterization of this paradigm, we can note a few of its defining features.[6] Moral ecology, to begin with, conceives of ethical relations as constituting systems (and interrelated subsystems) in which actors (agents) interact with each other and their surroundings. As Francis repeatedly remarks in *Laudato si'*, "Everything is interconnected." The resulting patterns of action have moral valences associated with the extent to which they conduce to the health, wellbeing, or flourishing of a given system and its components. Moral ecology does not simply rely on an analogy to natural relationships in the form of physical or biological ecosystems; rather, it is itself, in a sense,

a naturalistic, teleological conception. As such, it operates as both a descriptive and normative moral theory. However, far from relying on a theory of strict, exceptionless moral rules derived from a static conception of human nature, it also admits of a good deal of diversity, acknowledging that while there are universal features to human conduct, these will interact with different environments and historical conditions in a range of different ways. Moral ecology also makes much of the way in which distortions in one subsystem can undermine the equilibrium of other affiliated subsystems. As applied in *Laudato si'*, the perspective of moral ecology presumes that there are mutually reinforcing practices that either contribute to or detract from the harmonious and sustainable functioning of environmental, economic, social, ethnological, and habitational systems.

In line with its descriptive and normative facets, Pope Francis's moral ecology produces two related perspectives on the issue of nuclear deterrence. Descriptively, it illuminates how changing conditions have occasioned an official judgment that the grounds for a conditional acceptance of a policy of nuclear deterrence have expired. Gerard Powers puts this well when he notes that changing "signs of the nuclear times" have produced an environment in which nuclear deterrence is no longer morally tolerable; by this he means that a record of missed opportunities and an altered geopolitical landscape have revised the prudential judgment originally arrived at by the Holy See.[7] Normatively, the context of moral ecology informs the evaluation of deterrence policies in light of the ideal of integral disarmament. This entails assessing the prospect of the continued possession of nuclear weapons not only with reference to the likelihood that their future use may be avoided but also with a view to the effects of maintaining nuclear arsenals on interlocking environmental, economic, cultural, and existential ecosystems. Placing nuclear deterrence in this holistic, comprehensive framework heightens the perception that it is an unsustainable, (integrally) ecologically harmful, and hence indefensible practice.

In conclusion, it is well worth noting that the Catholic Church's revised position on nuclear deterrence is only one topic in which an underlying tectonic shift toward integral moral-ecological reasoning is coming to light. The Church's increasing emphasis on nonviolence and the recent revision of the teaching on capital punishment are just two more instances in which a process of recontextualizing understandings of human dignity within the framework of integral ecology is taking place. Policies of nuclear deterrence look different and are more difficult to accept as justifiable for a Church that is going through a process of greening and coming to terms with the signs of the times in the Anthropocene. In the midst of this shift, working out the implications of the new paradigm of moral ecology is one of the foremost tasks for not only the ethics of war and peace but also Catholic ethics in general.

Notes

1. Pope Francis, *Laudato si'*, no. 139.
2. *Laudato si'*, no. 217.
3. *Laudato si'*, no. 140.
4. On this notion, see Daniel Scheid, *The Cosmic Common Good: Religious Grounds for Ecological Ethics* (New York: Oxford University Press, 2016).
5. Address of His Holiness Pope Francis to participants in the International Symposium, "Prospects for a World Free of Nuclear Weapons and for Integral Disarmament," November 10, 2017.
6. For more on the idea of ecology as a moral framework, see Daniel R. Finn, *The Moral Ecology of Markets: Assessing Claims about Markets and Justice* (Cambridge: Cambridge University Press, 2006); Svend Brinkmann, "The Topography of Moral Ecology," *Theory and Psychology* 14, no. 1 (2004): 57–80; Allen D. Hertzke, "The Theory of Moral Ecology," *Review of Politics* 60, no. 4 (1998): 629–59; Stephen C. Yanchar, "Identity, Interpretation, and the Moral Ecology of Learning," *Theory and Psychology* 26, no. 4 (2016): 496–515; and Lauren Baker et al., "Mainstreaming Morality: An Examination of Moral Ecologies as a Form of Resistance," *Journal for the Study of Religion, Nature, and Culture* 11, no. 1 (2017): 23–55.
7. Gerard Powers, "Papal Condemnation of Nuclear Deterrence and What Is Next," *Arms Control Today*, May 1, 2018.

PART II

Witnesses

5

Nuclear Realists

DAVID CORTRIGHT

Those of us who advocate for a world without nuclear weapons are often dismissed as naive and pusillanimous, utopian dreamers unhinged from political reality. You can't put the nuclear genie back in the bottle, we are told. Our enemies have these weapons, so we must maintain and upgrade ours. Even if we wanted to get rid of the bomb, we cannot and should not. Our survival and security depend on maintaining nuclear deterrence.

In this essay I challenge these assumptions. I do so by pointing to the public witness of many senior former government officials and military leaders who have come to the realization that these weapons are dangerous and unnecessary and that they can and must be eliminated. These nuclear abolitionists are hard-core realists. Collectively they have many decades of experience creating and implementing national security policy. It is because of that experience that they consider it necessary to get rid of these weapons. They have crafted specific proposals and policy initiatives to show that it is possible in a realistic, step-by-step fashion to move toward nuclear zero. I highlight these voices and some of their proposals to emphasize the feasibility of disarmament and the pathways for achieving that goal.

The Reykjavik Precedent

The most visible and significant advocates for denuclearization have been former secretary of state George Shultz, former defense secretary Bill Perry, former Senate Armed Services Committee chair Sam

Nunn, and former secretary of state and national security adviser Henry Kissinger. In January 2007 these leaders published an extraordinary article in the *Wall Street Journal* declaring their support for the elimination of nuclear weapons and calling for US leadership in "reversing reliance on nuclear weapons globally . . . and ultimately ending them as a threat to the world."[1]

This call for a world without nuclear weapons by eminent former national security officials turned heads in Washington and capitals around the globe. Especially remarkable was the apparent conversion of Kissinger, arch political realist and architect of US Cold War nuclear policies.[2] The *Wall Street Journal* statement gave unprecedented legitimacy to the goal of nuclear disarmament. Joining the four authors in the appeal were seventeen former ambassadors and national security officials from both Republican and Democratic administrations, including senior Central Intelligence Agency official John McLaughlin, Adm. William Crowe (US Navy ret.), and former ambassadors Jack Matlock, James Goodby, and Thomas Graham Jr.

The *Wall Street Journal* article grew out of an October 2006 consultation at Stanford University's Hoover Institution, the home base for Shultz and Perry. The consultation commemorated the twentieth anniversary of the Reagan-Gorbachev summit at Reykjavik, Iceland, in 1986, when the United States and the Soviet Union came close to an agreement for the elimination of all nuclear weapons. During that extraordinary session at Reykjavik, Ronald Reagan and Mikhail Gorbachev discussed sweeping proposals for disarmament. When Gorbachev proposed eliminating all nuclear weapons, Reagan said that would be fine with him. Gorbachev replied, "We can do that. We can eliminate them." Shultz, who was sitting next to Reagan, chimed in, "Let's do it." Reagan proposed the preparation of a detailed agreement on eliminating nuclear weapons that the two leaders could sign at a summit in Washington. Gorbachev agreed.[3]

The proposed nuclear abolition agreement fell apart over differences on strategic missile defenses, but the negotiations at Reykjavik were partially successful and laid the groundwork for the historic Intermediate-Range Nuclear Forces Treaty (1987) eliminating theater nuclear forces in Europe. This was followed by the START treaties (1991 and 1993) that dramatically reduced nuclear stockpiles and helped to end the Cold War. The goal of abolition remained elusive, but negotiations for disarmament had significant benefits in reducing nuclear tensions and paving the way for arms reduction.

Many of Reagan's advisers in Reykjavik were shocked by his willingness to negotiate away nuclear weapons, but Shultz stood by the president and supported his disarmament vision. So did Max Kampelman, Reagan's senior disarmament negotiator. As historian Paul Lettow has documented, Reagan was never comfortable with the dilemmas of nuclear deterrence and spoke on numerous occasions of his desire to eliminate nuclear weapons. He was a conservative and a staunch anticommunist, but he was also a nuclear abolitionist.[4] It was this vision of a nuclear weapons–free future that Shultz and his colleagues at the Hoover Institution consultation articulated in the 2007 article and promoted in the following years through numerous conferences and publications examining the requirements for a world without nuclear weapons.

The Hoover Institution initiative was followed in 2009 by similar statements from other high-level groups of former officials and prominent leaders in the United Kingdom, Russia, Germany, France, Norway, Poland, Australia, and other countries.[5] Many of these national initiatives, following the model of the original Shultz statement, were nonpartisan and cross-party in character, Democrats joining Republicans in the United States and conservatives, liberals, and social democrats speaking together in Europe and beyond.

Throughout the nuclear age, prestigious governmental commissions have developed detailed proposals for how to reduce and eliminate nuclear weapons. One of the most authoritative of these was the 1996 Canberra Commission. Chaired by Australian foreign minister Gareth Evans, the commission consisted of seventeen members, including several former military commanders and defense officials. Among the major players were Gen. George Lee Butler, former commander in chief of the US Strategic Command; retired field marshal Lord Carver, former chief of the British General Staff; Robert McNamara, former US secretary of defense; and Michel Rocard, former prime minister of France.

The Canberra Commission emphasized that nuclear explosives are too destructive and indiscriminate to achieve military objectives on the battlefield. They are not usable in combat. The existence of nuclear arsenals does not deter war and has not prevented military interventions by the major powers. The only realistic purpose of nuclear weapons, the commission argued, is to deter their use by others. If nations agree to their elimination, that mission disappears along with the need for such weapons.

The Canberra Commission's report emphasized the gravity of the nuclear danger and the urgency of "immediate and determined efforts" to rid the world of nuclear weapons. The proposition that nuclear weapons can be retained in perpetuity and never be used, accidentally or by design, "defies credibility," the report stated.[6] The same point was made in an article a few years earlier by McNamara. It can be predicted with confidence, he wrote, that "the combination of human fallibility and nuclear arms will inevitably lead to nuclear destruction."[7]

A similar argument was voiced in 1999 by Paul Nitze, one of America's most seasoned and experienced nuclear diplomats and a principal author of Cold War containment policy.[8] "It is the very presence of these weapons that threatens our existence," Nitze wrote. The simplest and most direct solution to the danger of nuclear weapons is their complete elimination. "I see no compelling reason why we should not unilaterally get rid of our nuclear weapons."[9]

Butler played a crucial role in building support for the recommendations of the Canberra Commission. In December 1996 he joined with retired general and former NATO supreme commander Andrew Goodpaster to release a statement signed by sixty-one retired generals and admirals from seventeen countries urging "the complete elimination of nuclear weapons from all nations."[10] The statement asserted that "the continuing existence of nuclear weapons . . . constitutes a peril to global peace and security and to the safety and survival of the people we are dedicated to protect."[11] For the next several years Butler devoted himself to public education and advocacy on behalf of nuclear arms reduction and elimination.

This support for denuclearization among senior military commanders and policymakers lends credibility to the cause of disarmament and reinforces religious and moral appeals for nuclear abolition. In addition, this support brings realism to the nuclear debate by identifying concrete steps and realistic options, recommended by the most knowledgeable and experienced nuclear experts, for moving toward nuclear zero.

Disarmament Step-by-Step

The first step is to negotiate mutual reductions in US and Russian nuclear arsenals down to the level of minimum deterrence, which is the lowest number of weapons needed to deter a potential nuclear attack, usually calculated to be about two hundred weapons. When the United States and Russia reduce down to this level they could negotiate with other nuclear states for further mutual reductions.

Another necessary step would be the separation of nuclear warheads from delivery vehicles. Retired US Navy admiral and Central Intelligence Agency director Stansfield Turner called this idea "nuclear escrow," placing bombs and delivery systems in separate locations under rigorous inspection.[12] This would provide a form of shadow deterrence to reassure states as they transition to postnuclear security policies. It would also lower the risk of accidental launch or first strike.

Other measures to reduce the nuclear danger would include eliminating the last remaining tactical nuclear weapons (thousands of these devices have been retired and dismantled since the end of the Cold War) and strengthening the security of all global nuclear production sites (the Nuclear Security Initiative launched during the Obama administration is a partial step in that direction). Also needed would be ratification of the Comprehensive Test Ban Treaty and negotiation of a global fissile material cut-off treaty. All of this would require the creation of ever more rigorous systems of verification and inspection, strengthening the capacity of the International Atomic Energy Agency and other monitoring bodies to provide protection against cheating or nuclear breakout.

Political Zero

Adopting these steps can lead progressively toward nuclear zero, but a parallel process will be needed to achieve what author Jonathan Schell referred to as "political zero." The development of amicable relationships among states is needed so they no longer feel the need to develop and threaten to use such weapons.[13] Disarmament depends on building trust and cooperative relations between nations. This means strengthening mechanisms for resolving conflicts that could lead to violence. All are part of a process of creating the conditions for a world without nuclear weapons.

Realizing these conditions will be a long-term process, one that seems distant in the current era of rising nativism and heightened tensions between Washington and Moscow. The present danger only increases the urgency of fostering dialogue. The process of negotiating for disarmament can help to increase understanding and improve political relations. The Reagan-Gorbachev summits created relationships of trust and cooperation and laid the foundation for historic levels of arms reduction that dramatically improved world security. The same could happen again in the future and could conceivably result on a regional level from US–North Korea dialogue for denuclearization of the Korean peninsula.

The utopians in the nuclear debate are not the advocates of disarmament but rather those who believe that we can continue to rely on the threat of nuclear terror without disaster striking. We should rely instead on the military realists who have warned against the nuclear danger and have offered practical steps for reducing and eliminating these weapons to create a safer and more secure future.

Notes

1. George P. Shultz, William J. Perry, Henry A. Kissinger, and Sam Nunn, "A World Free of Nuclear Weapons," *Wall Street Journal*, January 4, 2007.
2. In his classic 1957 volume *Nuclear Deterrence and Foreign Policy* (New York: Harper, 1957), Kissinger wrote that the effectiveness of nuclear deterrence requires the will to use such weapons and discussed options for limited and all-out war in US policy.
3. See the account of the Reykjavik summit, based on the official transcript of the talks, in Jonathan Schell, *The Seventh Decade: The New Shape of Nuclear Danger* (New York: Metropolitan Books, 2007), 193–97.
4. Paul Lettow, *Ronald Reagan and His Quest to Abolish Nuclear Weapons* (New York: Random House, 2005).
5. "Statements on a Nuclear Weapons Free World," Pugwash Conferences on Science and World Affairs, n.d., https://pugwash.org/history/resources/nwfw-statements/.
6. Australia, Department of Foreign Affairs and Trade, *Report of the Canberra Commission on the Elimination of Nuclear Weapons* (Canberra: DFAT, 1996), 9–12.
7. Robert S. McNamara, "Nobody Needs Nukes," *New York Times*, February 23, 1993.
8. William Burr and Robert Wampler, "'The Master of the Game': Paul Nitze and U.S. Cold War Strategy from Truman to Reagan," *National Security Archive Electronic Briefing Book* No. 139, October 27, 2004.
9. Paul Nitze, "A Threat Mostly to Ourselves," *New York Times*, October 28, 1999.
10. Lee Butler and Andrew J. Goodpaster, "Joint Statement on Reduction of Nuclear Weapons Arsenals: Declining Utility, Continuing Risks," Nuclearfiles.org, Project of the Nuclear Age Peace Foundation, December 4, 1996.

11. "Statement on Nuclear Weapons by International Generals and Admirals," *Arms Control Today* 26, no. 9 (November/December 1996): 15, 18.
12. Stansfield Turner, *Caging the Nuclear Genie: An American Challenge for Global Security* (Boulder, CO: Westview, 1997).
13. Jonathan Schell, *The Gift of Time: The Case for Abolishing Nuclear Weapons Now* (New York: Metropolitan Books, 1998), 218.

6

The Testimony of Witnesses

DANIEL HALL

The testimony of witnesses to the catastrophic humanitarian effects of nuclear weapon detonation, testing, and production has been a vital component of the international discourse on the humanitarian consequences of nuclear weapons. These often graphic testimonies disrupt the notion that discussions about nuclear weapons policy are only salient when confined to the sanitized realm of abstract military doctrines. On the contrary, the real stories of survivors have brought the lived experience of those who have personally suffered the effects of nuclear weapons into tension with ostensibly realist perspectives on nuclear weapons policy that typically ignore such experiences. As such, they offer a corrective to the discourse, asserting that the humanitarian consequences of nuclear weapons, with the fraught moral, ethical, and legal questions they carry, be properly placed not at the margins but instead at the center of all discussions and calculations about nuclear disarmament. For decades, witnesses such as *hibakusha* (those who survived the 1945 atomic bombings of Hiroshima and Nagasaki) as well as survivors of nuclear testing and production activities have been sharing their experiences around the world to advocate for a world free from nuclear weapons. Their decades of advocacy informed and shaped the Humanitarian Initiative, an international movement begun in 2010 to reframe the nuclear weapons discourse around humanitarian consequences that ultimately became the driving force for the adoption of the Treaty on the Prohibition of Nuclear Weapons (TPNW) in 2017.

Unspeakable Suffering

On August 6, 1945, at 8:15 a.m., an atomic bomb detonated above the city of Hiroshima, releasing heat exceeding temperatures on the surface of the sun, mechanical forces equal to fifteen thousand tons of TNT and lethal doses of radiation that would inflict multigenerational suffering and death. Ms. Setsuko Thurlow, a thirteen-year-old girl at the time, was 1.8 kilometers from ground zero. She remembers seeing a bright flash of light, feeling the strange sensation of floating in the air, and then losing consciousness. When she awoke she managed to crawl out from the debris of a collapsed building. "I looked around the outside world," she relates.

> Although it was morning, it was as dark as twilight because of the dust and smoke rising up in the air. I saw streams of ghostly figures, slowly shuffling from the centre of the city towards the nearby hills. I say "ghostly" because they did not look like human beings; their hair stood straight upward and they were naked and tattered, bleeding, burned, blackened and swollen. Parts of their bodies were missing, flesh and skin hanging from their bones, some with their eyeballs hanging in their hands, and some with their stomachs burst open, with intestines hanging out. We students joined the ghostly procession, carefully stepping over the dead and dying. There was a deathly silence broken only by the moans of the injured and their pleas for water. The foul stench of burned skin filled the air.[1]

On September 8 Dr. Marcel Junod traveled to Hiroshima, becoming the first foreign doctor to assess the effects of the atomic bombing and its victims. According to witnesses encountered by Junod, in a few seconds after the blast, "thousands of human beings in the streets and gardens in the town centre, struck by a wave of intense heat, died like flies. Others lay writhing like worms, atrociously burned. All private houses, warehouses, etc., disappeared as if swept away by a supernatural power. Trams were picked up and hurled yards away, as if they were weightless; trains were flung off the rails . . . . Every living thing was petrified in an attitude of acute pain."[2] For any who managed to survive, aftereffects would haunt them for the rest of their lives. Physical deformities, disabilities, and persistent social discrimination compounded the challenge of missed educational opportunities, limited prospects for marriage, and job opportunities denied.

Common to all *hibakusha* and especially acute for women as the birth of a child neared, was the lifelong fear and anxiety from radiological exposure and passing on radiation-related disabilities. Masao Tomonaga, director emeritus of the Japanese Red Cross Nagasaki Atomic Bomb Hospital, states that "the anxiety they still feel regarding potential aftereffects emerging in their own bodies or genetic effects in their offspring is quite beyond imagination. . . . An instantaneous exposure in August 1945 has kept survivors imprisoned by aftereffects for 70 years."[3]

Mission of Survivors

For nearly ten years after the bombing of Hiroshima and Nagasaki, US occupation forces strictly prohibited people from speaking or talking about the bombing and damage, including the miserable deaths of over three hundred thousand people. With the rise of the antinuclear movement in the country in 1954, however, many *hibakusha* found new hope and saw an opportunity to give meaning and purpose to their experiences through advocacy. Among the personal stories that *hibakusha* have shared, several common themes emerge, some of which I illustrate here.

For many *hibakusha*, their deep sense of mission was forged in the personal struggle to survive the aftermath of the atomic bombings itself. Ms. Setsuko Morita states:

> We crawled over Ozu Bridge. By that time, our burns were so painful that walking was difficult. In the river below, corpses floated by— adults, children, horses. Many got caught on bridge girders. Was this a bad dream? Was it hell? How could we believe that this was really happening? All we could think was: get back to school and find people to rescue our friends back at Toshogu Shrine. Supported only by a strong sense of mission and responsibility, we kept going.[4]

Driven to inform the public, especially young people, many *hibakusha* chose to revisit their unresolved traumas in spite of the heavy emotional and physical toll doing so took on their health. Ms. Kazuko Kawada, a bombing survivor, states, "When asked, 'What happened that day?'

some still tremble and remain silent. This profound anxiety seems peculiar to atomic bomb survivors. We still have never digested our experience thoroughly. We all carry intense feelings of grief, having so abruptly lost family members, friends, our entire communities and our normal daily lives."[5]

Also common to the testimonies of many *hibakusha* was a profound feeling of responsibility to speak for those who did not survive and a determination to remember them not as death statistics but instead as unique human beings. When asked to speak to Japanese students about her experience, Ms. Yoshie Oka accepted only under the condition that she speak to them in the actual communications bunker where her fellow classmates died. Ms. Oka states, "When the time came and I tried to speak in that room steeped in painful memories, recalling my dead friends left me at times speechless. Eventually, I was weeping. 'That girl used to sit here.... That one sat over there.' Their faces would rise up in front of me. The students who have to listen to me in those rooms probably feel uncomfortable. But when I speak there, I sense my dead classmates speaking to me."[6]

In a speech delivered at the May 2017 nuclear ban treaty negotiations, Ms. Setsuko Thurlow demonstrated this same sense of responsibility by bringing the moral weight of those who didn't survive to bear on the conscience of delegates attending the negotiations:

> For those of you delegates, who are genuinely serious about disarmament, I want you to feel the presence of not only the future generations who will benefit from your negotiations to ban nuclear weapons, but to feel a cloud of witnesses from Hiroshima and Nagasaki. The memories and images of those who perished have always supported and guided me. I think this is how many survivors have kept on living—to make sure that the deaths of their loved ones were not in vain. As you proceed through this week, I want you to also feel their support and presence. And do your job well! And know that we hibakusha have no doubt that this treaty can—and will—change the world.[7]

Some of the earliest precedents for such international advocacy were organized through civil society organizations such as the Japan Confederation of A- and H-Bomb Sufferers Organizations (Nihon Hidankyo), which was founded in August 1956. Nihon Hidankyo would go on to carry out a multifaceted movement under the banner of "No more *Hibakusha*." Its witness included advocacy inside and outside of Japan, at international conferences and on speaking tours, for the complete elimination of nuclear weapons.[8]

Decades of dedicated advocacy by *hibakusha* and other survivors of nuclear production and testing followed, laying the foundation for the Humanitarian Initiative. This international movement of governments, the international Red Cross and Red Crescent organizations, United Nations (UN) agencies, and nongovernmental organizations began in 2010 to reframe the nuclear weapons discourse around humanitarian consequences and ultimately became the driving force for the adoption of the TPNW in 2017.

Treaty on the Non-Proliferation of Nuclear Weapons

Beginning at the May 2010 Review Conference of the Parties to the Treaty on the Non-Proliferation of Nuclear Weapons (NPT), commonly known as the Nuclear Non-Proliferation Treaty, governments adopted by consensus a final document expressing their "deep concern at the catastrophic humanitarian consequences of any use of nuclear weapons" and reaffirmed "the need for all States at all times to comply with applicable international law, including international humanitarian law." At the May 2012 NPT Preparatory Conference, Switzerland delivered on behalf of 16 nations the first in a series of joint statements on the humanitarian impact of nuclear weapons. The statement drew a direct link to the 1945 atomic bombings: "When the horrific consequences of their use became apparent in Hiroshima and Nagasaki, the International Committee of the Red Cross (ICRC) took a clear position calling for the abolition of these weapons of 'extermination. . . . In addition to the immediate fatalities, survivors of the horrendous effects of a nuclear explosion would endure immeasurable suffering." The statement credited civil society with playing a crucial role "in raising the awareness about the dramatic humanitarian consequences as well as the critical implications of nuclear weapons" for international humanitarian law.[9] This was followed by 35 governments signing the NPT at the 2012 General Assembly First Committee session, 80 signing at the 2013 NPT Preparatory Committee, and then 125 signing at the 2013 General Assembly

First Committee session. At the April 2015 NPT session, 159 nations, four-fifths of all UN member states, signed the statement.

Concurrently, in November 2011 the International Red Cross and Red Crescent Movement, the largest humanitarian organization in existence, adopted a landmark resolution on the topic, finding "it difficult to envisage how any use of nuclear weapons could be compatible with the rules of international humanitarian law, in particular the rules of distinction, precaution and proportionality," and urged all states to negotiate a "legally binding international agreement" to prohibit and completely eliminate nuclear weapons. The resolution specifically cited "the testimony of atomic bomb survivors, the experience of the Japanese Red Cross Society and the ICRC in assisting the victims of the atomic bomb blasts in Hiroshima and Nagasaki and the knowledge gained through the ongoing treatment of survivors by the Japanese Red Cross Atomic Bomb Survivors Hospital."[10] The movement reaffirmed its commitment in November 2013 with the adoption of a four-year action plan toward the prohibition and elimination of nuclear weapons.

Humanitarian Impact of Nuclear Weapons Conferences

In March 2013, the International Campaign to Abolish Nuclear Weapons (ICAN), a coalition of nongovernmental organizations in one hundred countries, serving as the civil society partner, joined governments and international organizations for the first of three intergovernmental conferences to discuss for the first time together the catastrophic humanitarian impact of nuclear weapons. The first conference was held in Oslo, Norway, and was followed the next year with conferences in Nayarit, Mexico, and Vienna, Austria.

The Nayarit conference opened with testimony from five *hibakusha* who shared their experiences as survivors of Nagasaki and Hiroshima, describing also the long-term effects of a nuclear weapon detonation, the intergenerational effects from the perspective of a third-generation *hibakusha*, and the social and psychological impact of nuclear detonation. Ms. Setsuko Thurlow declared that "humanity and nuclear weapons cannot coexist." She scored "the inhumanity, illegality, immorality, and cruelty of the atomic bombings," the discrimination experienced by survivors known as "contaminated ones by nuclear poison," and the delayed effects of radiation that were still killing survivors sixty-nine years later. She also cited the psycho-social control of the Allied Forces Occupation Authority that "censored media coverage of survivors' suffering," confiscated diaries and letters and photographs, and silenced survivors into isolation that "deprived them of the normal grieving process."[11] She called for a nuclear weapons ban to break through the stagnation in the field of nuclear disarmament:

> Although we hibakusha have spent our life energy to warn people about the hell that is nuclear war, in nearly 70 years there has been little progress in the field of nuclear disarmament. We therefore urgently need a new path, one that recognizes the utterly unacceptable humanitarian consequences of nuclear weapons—weapons we have a moral obligation to prohibit. It is our hope that this new movement to ban nuclear weapons will finally lead us to a nuclear weapon free world.[12]

In his summary of the meeting, the chair of the conference called for the development of a legally binding instrument aiming toward the "70th anniversary of the Hiroshima and Nagasaki attacks" as the appropriate milestone for the goal and as such declared the Nayarit conference the "point of no return."[13]

At the 2014 Vienna conference, Ms. Thurlow expressed her support for this clear target. She voiced the frustration felt by *hibakusha* due to "lack of tangible progress toward nuclear disarmament" and directly confronted the traditionally dominant focus on military doctrine, asking how much longer "the Nuclear Weapon States [could be allowed] to continue threatening all life on Earth" and continue the "shifting of the world's attention to the doctrine of deterrence in the name of national and international security."[14] The conference also included testimony from survivors of nuclear weapons testing in Australia and the Marshall Islands. At the close of the conference, the Austrian government issued the Austrian Pledge (later renamed the Humanitarian Pledge) to "identify and pursue effective measures to fill the legal gap for the prohibition and elimination of nuclear weapons" that would go on to be endorsed by 107 states at the 2015 NPT review conference and hailed as the real outcome of a conference that failed to adopt a final document.[15]

The Nuclear Ban Treaty

The range of activities surrounding the Humanitarian Initiative involving governments, UN agencies, humanitarian organizations, and civil society organizations from 2010 to 2015 were followed by open-ended working group meetings throughout 2016 to propose concrete legal measures and norms necessary to achieve and maintain a world without nuclear weapons. At the May 4 meeting in Geneva, Ms. Setsuko Thurlow credited the Humanitarian Initiative for "reframing how we think and talk about nuclear weapons and [refocusing attention] from the military doctrine of deterrence to the real impact of nuclear weapons, on all living beings and our environment."[16] Governments voted overwhelmingly to adopt the open-ended working group report, and in December 2016 the UN General Assembly adopted a landmark resolution to convene a conference in 2017 to "negotiate a legally binding instrument to prohibit nuclear weapons, leading towards their total elimination."

During the ban treaty negotiations, Ms. Sue Coleman-Haseldine, an indigenous Australian nuclear test survivor, shared the experience of indigenous people in southern Australia who were exposed to the fallout from nuclear testing and experiments. She hailed the nuclear ban treaty as "an opportunity to assist countries to make amends to victims of nuclear weapons," to "acknowledge the permanent damage done to people, land and culture, across generations, and particularly for indigenous people worldwide," and to "require countries to address the needs of impacted people."[17] Ms. Karina Lester, a second-generation indigenous nuclear test survivor, also from southern Australia, voiced her strong support "to include a paragraph in the preamble that recognizes the disproportionate impact of nuclear testing on indigenous peoples around the world."[18] This ultimately was included in the treaty preamble. Ms. Masako Wada, assistant secretary-general of Nihon Hidankyo, expressed on behalf of the *hibakusha* that the draft convention of the treaty released on May 22 was a source of "tremendous hope" and that it showed "compassion on our suffering in the preamble" and "acknowledges the efforts of the *hibakusha* as part of the evidence for which the convention is to be adopted."[19] Ms. Yayoi Tsuchida, assistant general-secretary of the Japan Council Against Atomic and Hydrogen Bombs (Gensuikyo), urged that the appeal of the *hibakusha* that "humans cannot coexist with nuclear weapons" should find expression in the treaty, that they cannot wait any longer for "states possessing nuclear weapons to participate in the treaty," that all states regardless of their nuclear or nonnuclear status have an obligation to prohibit and eliminate nuclear weapons, and that the *hibakusha* will continue to "do [their] utmost." Ms. Setsuko Thurlow reminded delegates that their task was to "establish a clear, new, international standard . . . to declare, in no uncertain terms, that nuclear weapons are illegitimate, immoral and illegal."[20]

On July 7, 2017, 122 states voted for the adoption of the TPNW. Upon adoption, Ms. Izumi Nakamitsu, UN high representative for disarmament affairs, paid tribute to the "pioneering efforts and demand for progress" by members of civil society that made the treaty possible and "the heroic efforts" of *hibakusha* whose "unspeakable suffering and tireless endeavors [were] captured for the first time in a multilateral nuclear disarmament treaty."[21]

Nobel Peace Prize

On October 6, ICAN was awarded the Nobel Peace Prize for its "work to draw attention to the catastrophic humanitarian consequences of any use of nuclear weapons and for its ground-breaking efforts to achieve a treaty-based prohibition of such weapons."[22] The campaign issued a statement, calling the prize a tribute to the "tireless efforts of many millions of campaigners and concerned citizens worldwide" and "survivors of the atomic bombings of Hiroshima and Nagasaki—the *hibakusha*—and victims of nuclear test explosions around the world, whose searing testimonies and unstinting advocacy were instrumental in securing this landmark agreement."[23] On December 10, Ms. Setsuko Thurlow and ICAN executive director Beatrice Fihn jointly received the award on behalf of ICAN and delivered the Nobel Peace Prize lecture. In her speech, Ms. Thurlow shared that she stood in solidarity with those "people whose lands and seas were irradiated, whose bodies were experimented upon, whose cultures were forever disrupted" by the testing of nuclear weapons from "places with long-forgotten names, like Moruroa, Ekker, Semipalatinsk, Maralinga, Bikini."[24] She also offered a warning about the underlying thinking that tries to justify the existence of nuclear weapons. Thurlow criticized the "propaganda" that leads people to believe that the atomic bombs of Hiroshima and Nagasaki were "good bombs" that had ended a "just war," calling it a "myth that led to the disastrous nuclear arms race . . . that continues to this day." She rejected the notion that nuclear weapons are a "necessary evil," labeling them instead the "ultimate evil" that threatens to make the world "uninhabitable for future generations." Thurlow also called out the officials of nuclear–armed nations and their "accomplices" under the nuclear umbrella as each being an "integral part of a system of violence that is endangering humankind" and warned them to be "alert to the banality of evil."

Conclusion

The power of the witness of survivors to drive forward the Humanitarian Initiative and adoption of the TPNW has demonstrated that individuals have the agency to shift the direction of disarmament diplomacy. While the existing international legal landscape already included longstanding rules of distinction and proportionality in the use of force and a 1996 International Court of Justice advisory opinion that "the threat or use of nuclear weapons would generally be contrary to the rules of international law applicable in armed conflict,"[25] there was no law that prohibited nuclear weapons per se. The TPNW finally filled that legal gap in international humanitarian law, explicitly stigmatizing and prohibiting nuclear weapons, following the path of biological and chemical weapons. This legal shift is intrinsically tied to the moral journey and mission of the *hibakusha* and other survivors. Through their heart-wrenching testimonies, they conveyed the appalling humanitarian, health, and environmental consequences of nuclear weapons. In doing so, they disrupted the traditional consequentialist nature of disarmament diplomacy in which nuclear weapon states might consider reducing the role and value of nuclear weapons yet continue to justify possession and threats to use them because of the perceived military utility of deterrence. In contrast, *hibakusha* and other survivors entered the discourse from the deontological end of the ethical spectrum with a moral narrative that universally and completely rejected the legitimacy of nuclear violence because of the unacceptable harm and suffering resulting from use and, by extension, threat of use and indeed the very existence of nuclear weapons, based on the view that the only guarantee they will not be used again is through complete elimination. It seems entirely unlikely that the new legal framing of the TPNW would have been possible without this new moral framing embodied by the lived experience of *hibakusha* and other survivors. As legal expert Nobuo Hayashi shared during the Vienna Conference on the Humanitarian Impact of Nuclear Weapons, "Law stands on hollow ground where a solid moral conviction is absent."[26] The moral advocacy of *hibakusha* and other survivors grew into a movement and has come to reflect the moral perspectives of a broad range of civil society actors, including faith leaders and communities from East to West.[27] For example, in his 2009 nuclear abolition proposal issued in advance of the 2010 NPT review, Japanese Buddhist thinker Daisaku Ikeda reiterated his long-standing rejection of nuclear deterrence. "If we are to put the era of nuclear terror behind us, we must struggle against the real 'enemy.' That enemy is not nuclear weapons per se, nor is it the states that possess or develop them. The real enemy that we must confront is the ways of thinking that justify nuclear weapons; the readiness to annihilate others when they are seen as a threat or as a hindrance to the realization of our objectives."[28]

Similarly, at a conference held at the Vatican following the adoption of the TPNW on November 10, 2017, "Perspectives for a World Free from Nuclear Weapons and for Integral Disarmament," Pope Francis delivered a landmark address in which he rejected deterrence with nuclear weapons, condemning "the threat of use" and "their very possession." He went on to say that "They cannot constitute the basis for peaceful coexistence between members of the human family, which must rather be inspired by an ethics of solidarity. Essential in this regard is the witness given by the *Hibakusha*, the survivors of the bombing of Hiroshima and Nagasaki, together with other victims of nuclear arms testing. May their prophetic voice serve as a warning, above all for coming generations!"[29]

This growing conviction from *hibakusha* and other survivors, faith communities, academics, scientists, and others from the civil society realm will be vital for the success of the long-term project of convincing states that possess nuclear weapons that it is unacceptable. It offers a solid moral foundation to an ongoing process of delegitimizing nuclear weapons by undermining the legitimacy of valuing them regardless of their perceived military utility and in doing so provides a necessary corrective to a discourse that has been one-sided in its privileging of a step-by-step and building-block approach favored by nuclear-armed states. Together, they have the political capacity to continue tackling not only physical constraints such as stockpiles and testing but also normative and legal constraints. This is compatible with the December 2016 UN General Assembly resolution 71/258 that acknowledged that "a legally binding instrument prohibiting nuclear weapons would be an important contribution towards comprehensive nuclear disarmament . . . bearing in mind also that additional measures, both practical and legally binding, for the irreversible, verifiable and transparent destruction of nuclear weapons would be needed in order to achieve and maintain a world without nuclear weapons."[30] Should a multilateral agreement for the complete and verifiable elimination of nuclear weapons be achieved, it will be indebted to the moral courage of *hibakusha* and other survivors.

Notes

1. Setsuko Thurlow, "Testimony from a Hiroshima Atomic Bomb Survivor," statement delivered during the Testimony of Hibakusha session at the Second Conference on the Humanitarian Impact of Nuclear Weapons, Nayarit, Mexico, February 13, 2014.
2. Jakob Kellenberger, "Bringing the Era of Nuclear Weapons to an End," statement delivered to the Geneva Diplomatic Corps, Geneva, Switzerland, April 20, 2010.
3. Soka Gakkai International. "Human Beings Do Not Need Atomic Bombs," *Japan Times*, September 19, 2018. Soka Gakkai International (SGI) is a community-based Buddhist organization that has been collecting and publishing *hibakusha* testimonies since the 1970s. Some of the testimonies in this essay were drawn from its collection published as *Hiroshima and Nagasaki: That We Never Forget*, available for free download at https://sgi-peace.org/resources/hiroshima-and-nagasaki-that-we-never-forget.
4. Soka Gakkai Youth Division, *Hiroshima and Nagasaki: That We Never Forget* (Tokyo: Daisanbunmei-sha, 2017), 35.
5. Soka Gakkai Youth Division, 28.
6. Soka Gakkai Youth Division, 14–15.
7. Setsuko Thurlow, "Testimony from a Hiroshima Atomic Bomb Survivor on Behalf of the International Campaign to Abolish Nuclear Weapons," statement delivered at the UN Conference to Negotiate a Legally Binding Instrument to Prohibit Nuclear Weapons, Leading towards Their Total Elimination, New York, March 28, 2017.
8. Nihon Hidankyo, "About Hidankyo," http://www.ne.jp/asahi/hidankyo/nihon/english/index.html; http://www.ne.jp/asahi/hidankyo/nihon/english/about/about1-01.html.
9. Ambassador Benno Laggner, "Joint Statement on the Humanitarian Dimension of Nuclear Disarmament," statement delivered during the 2012

Preparatory Committee for the 2015 Nuclear Non-Proliferation Treaty Review Conference, Vienna, Austria, May 2, 2012.
10. Council of Delegates of the International Red Cross and Red Crescent Movement, "Council of Delegates 2011: Resolution 1, Working towards the Elimination of Nuclear Weapons," statement delivered at the Council of Delegates of the International Red Cross and Red Crescent Movement, Geneva, Switzerland, November 26, 2011.
11. Thurlow, "Testimony from a Hiroshima Atomic Bomb Survivor on Behalf of the International Campaign to Abolish Nuclear Weapons."
12. Thurlow, "Testimony from a Hiroshima Atomic Bomb Survivor on Behalf of the International Campaign to Abolish Nuclear Weapons."
13. Juan Manuel Gomez Robledo, "Chair's Summary of the Second Conference on the Humanitarian Impact of Nuclear Weapons," statement delivered at the Second Conference on the Humanitarian Impact of Nuclear Weapons, Nayarit, Mexico, February 13, 2014.
14. Setsuko Thurlow, "Hiroshima Peace Ambassador Shares Her Childhood Experience of Surviving the 1945 Atomic Bombing of Hiroshima," statement delivered at the Third Conference on the Humanitarian Impact of Nuclear Weapons, Vienna, Austria, December 8, 2014.
15. Michael Linhart, "Austrian Deputy Foreign Minister Presents the Austrian Pledge," statement delivered at the Vienna Conference on the Humanitarian Impact of Nuclear Weapons, Vienna, Austria, December 9, 2014.
16. Setsuko Thurlow, "Testimony from a Hiroshima Atomic Bomb Survivor," statement delivered at the Open-Ended Working Group on Taking Forward Multilateral Disarmament Negotiations, Geneva, Switzerland, May 4, 2016.
17. Sue Coleman-Haseldine, "Testimony from a Survivor of Nuclear Weapon Testing in South Australia," statement delivered at the UN Conference to Negotiate a Legally Binding Instrument to Prohibit Nuclear Weapons, Leading towards Their Total Elimination, New York, NY, March 28, 2017.
18. Karina Lester, "Testimony from Survivor of Nuclear Weapon Testing in South Australia Advocates for the Treaty Preamble to Include Language Acknowledging the Disproportionate Impact of Nuclear Testing on Indigenous Peoples around the World," statement delivered at the UN Conference to Negotiate a Legally Binding Instrument to Prohibit Nuclear Weapons, Leading towards Their Total Elimination, New York, NY, March 28, 2017.
19. Masako Wada, "Assistant Secretary General of Nihon Hidankyo Shares Her Perspective on the TPNW Draft Document on Behalf of Hibakusha," statement delivered at the UN Conference to Negotiate a Legally Binding Instrument to Prohibit Nuclear Weapons, Leading Towards their Total Elimination, New York, NY, June 19, 2017.
20. Setsuko Thurlow, "Testimony from a Hiroshima Atomic Bomb Survivor on Behalf of the International Campaign to Abolish Nuclear Weapons," statement delivered at the UN Conference to Negotiate a Legally Binding

Instrument to Prohibit Nuclear Weapons, Leading towards Their Total Elimination, New York, NY, March 28, 2017.
21. Izumi Nakamitsu, "Remarks from the High Representative for Disarmament Affairs on the Adoption of the TPNW," statement delivered at the UN Conference to Negotiate a Legally Binding Instrument to Prohibit Nuclear Weapons, Leading towards Their Total Elimination, New York, NY, March 28, 2017.
22. The Nobel Peace Prize for 2017.
23. Kevin Liffey, "Anti-Nuclear Campaign ICAN Says Nobel Peace Prize a 'great honor,'" *Reuters*, October 6, 2017.
24. Setsuko Thurlow, "2017 Nobel Peace Prize Acceptance Speech," speech delivered at the 2017 Nobel Peace Prize Award Ceremony, Oslo, Norway, December 10, 2017.
25. International Court of Justice, Advisory Opinion, 1996 I.C.J. 266.
26. Nobuo Hayashi, "International Norms and the Humanitarian Impact of Nuclear Weapons," statement delivered at the Third Conference on the Humanitarian Impact of Nuclear Weapons, Vienna, Austria, December 8, 2014.
27. RNS Press Release Service. "Faith communities issue interfaith statement calling for urgent action toward nuclear abolition at NPT PrepCom in Geneva." *Religion News*, April 26, 2018.
28. Daisaku Ikeda, "Building Solidarity toward Nuclear Abolition," 2009, https://www.daisakuikeda.org/assets/files/disarm_p2009.pdf.
29. Address of His Holiness Pope Francis to participants in the International Symposium "Prospects for a World Free of Nuclear Weapons and for Integral Disarmament," November 10, 2017.
30. General Assembly resolution 71/258, "Taking Forward Multilateral Nuclear Disarmament Negotiations," A/RES/71/258 (January 11, 2017).

7

Swords into Plowshares

CAROLE SARGENT

In July 2012, four years after the death of artist and peace activist Tom Lewis, three members of a group calling itself Transform Now Plowshares splashed his blood on the walls of a nuclear uranium storage facility. They chose Oak Ridge, Tennessee, the historic birthplace of the atomic bomb. As one of the oldest nuclear facilities, the Y-12 National Security Complex provided the enriched uranium for Little Boy, the bomb that killed well over one hundred thousand people in Hiroshima in 1945.

Y-12 protests have been customary throughout the history of Plowshares. Lewis himself joined a Plowshares convoy at Y-12 in 2005, blocking the road while Oak Ridge marked the sixtieth solemn anniversary of the Hiroshima bombing. When he knew he was dying, Lewis banked his blood to be used in future actions. Now here he was—posthumously—confronting Y-12 yet again.[1]

Plowshares is a pacifist movement organized to protest nuclear weapons. Its participants enact the prophecies of Isaiah 2:4 and Micah 4:3, whereby God's people beat swords into plowshares and spears into pruning hooks. Plowshare activists do this by entering nuclear facilities and military bases to beat on parts of weapons with household hammers to disarm them. In many actions, participants pour donated human blood carried in baby bottles on the weapons, then spray-paint slogans and string up police tape as their visual indictment of these weapons as criminal. During this witness they pray, read scripture, sometimes share home-baked bread, sing, and wait to be arrested rather than fleeing. Once the security guards arrive, the activists read a statement, often in the form of a prayer for the facility. After their arrest, although most hope for exoneration under the law, they do not try to evade judgment, as they consider both the trial and the subsequent prison sentences parts of the full action and its intended result.

Although the movement is multifaith, Plowshares culture skews Catholic. Many of its members are or used to be Catholic sisters and priests. Quite a few are military veterans, and most self-define as politically progressive. They are generally white, middle class, and college educated or beyond, and they can perform these actions at any age.[2] The majority are either single and childless or have grown children, because the few couples with young children have faced significant family issues when one or both parents are arrested. The activists' influences are Christ and the Bible, with many having been variously influenced by Dorothy Day, Martin Luther King Jr., Thomas Merton, Mahatma Gandhi, Alfred Delp, SJ, St. Joan of Arc, Pope John XXIII, and Óscar Romero, among abundant others.[3]

Plowshares has no defined structure, meetings, or bylaws, and it only exists when people come together to discern a new action.[4] Its impact has often been distorted by media depictions of it as occasional and offbeat activist theater. News stories tend to fixate on well-known popular culture figures such as brother priests Philip and Daniel Berrigan, both of whom were present at the first Plowshares action in 1980, later dramatized in a movie starring Martin Sheen. This imbalance of coverage toward iconic break-ins and mediagenic personalities can hide a much bigger story: the hundreds of successful actions that have taken place in six countries—the United States, the Netherlands, Germany, Australia, Sweden, Italy, and Great Britain—over more than forty years. The media tendencies to simplify and sensationalize can also emphasize the work of men. When news stories do include women, they often focus on the cuteness factor, such as in the case of then-octogenarian Megan Rice, a sister of the Society of the Holy Child Jesus (SHCJ) who with Michael Walli and Gregory Boertje-Obed entered Y-12. Rice was profiled on MSNBC, in the *New Yorker*, on the BBC, and worldwide but often more as a quirky elder than as a thoughtful activist with well-discerned principles.[5]

A Catholic Phenomenon with Protestant Predecessors

Plowshares is young as a movement, but its roots go back centuries. Scholars categorize it with post-Reformation Protestant pacifism claimed by the three historic peace churches: Mennonites, Church of the Brethren, and Quakers.[6] These all reject the just war theory that St. Augustine and St. Thomas Aquinas derived from Cicero, citing other parallel and older peace traditions that have too often been ignored in favor of an ahistorical fixation on just war.[7] Both Quakers and Mennonites encourage their members to be conscientious objectors in wartime, and although the military occasionally cooperates, other times this objection can lead to arrest and incarceration.

Plowshares also belongs to the post-1900 antiwar organizing traditions such as the 1914 International Fellowship of Reconciliation, the 1919 Women's International League for Peace and Freedom, the 1923 War Resisters League, and two 1957 responses to nuclear technology, the National Committee for a Sane Nuclear Policy and the Committee for Nonviolent Action. Plowshares is distinctive, however, because those were delineated and ongoing groups, whereas its structure is quite fluid.

All of the pre–nuclear era groups suffered US membership losses during World War II because of the general popularity of the nation's reasons for going to war. The atomic bombs the US dropped on Japan were long perceived as having ended the war, and even some future pacifists initially celebrated their promise.[8] Later during the Cold War, and especially throughout the Cuban Missile Crisis, the American public again broadly accepted a nuclear arms race as necessary to stop Russia and defend against communism. Because of this swing toward popular embrace of weapons-based peacekeeping, several groups arose to counter the scramble for ever-updated nuclear technology.

The first known action that resembled what Plowshares would become happened in 1958, when former US Navy commander Albert Bigelow sailed into the Eniwetak Pacific testing zone, forcing a halt to nuclear tests. Many others followed. For example, in 1977 the Clamshell Alliance, formed to protest the building of nuclear power plants, mobilized 1,400 people to occupy the Seabrook facility in New Hampshire. Groups such as these inspired more efforts, such as Mobilization for Survival and Three Mile Island Alert in the 1970s.

Most directly, however, Plowshares developed from three key influences: the Catholic Worker movement of the early and mid-twentieth century; anti–Vietnam War actions inspired by the Baltimore Four, the Catonsville Nine, the DC Nine, and the Milwaukee Fourteen and their ilk beginning in the late 1960s; and the Jonah House community and the related Atlantic Life Community of the 1970s. It was against the backdrop of these and many more that the first Plowshares group of eight organized in 1980. Plowshares also inspired other groups, such as the Lenten Desert Experience at the Nevada Test Site in 1982, motivated by nuclear test protests that had taken place in the desert since the 1950s, and the subsequent and ongoing Nevada Desert Experience, attracting many who also participate in Plowshares.

Some Plowshares activists grew up in households with subscriptions to Dorothy Day and Peter Maurin's newspaper, *The Catholic Worker*. Catholic Workers became some of the earliest antinuclear protesters, having organized against New York's fallout shelter drills since the mid-1950s, so the movement had a natural influence on that post–World War II generation coming of age in the 1960s. To this day some of the most common Catholic Worker practices influence Plowshares. For example, Clarification of Thought meetings that are standard features of Catholic Worker houses inspired the Plowshares group discernment model. Many houses such as the Dorothy Day Catholic Worker in Washington, DC, facilitated by Art Laffin and Kathy Boylan, share participants with Plowshares. However, acceptance of Plowshares' unique radicalism is not universal among Catholic Workers, and there have been some controversies. Plowshares tends to reflect the Catholic Worker's Christian anarchist history, because even though it derives its membership and inspiration from the Catholic Church, it acts in ways that are not authorized by the Church and in fact sometimes contravene the Church's official recommendations.

The Structure of Plowshares Actions

Plowshares is not a formal organization. It exists only through its actions, discerned after a long period of prayer and study. A person may be invited to join a Plowshares prayer circle. Most of these small groups coalesce over the course of at least a year, forming a plan to enter a chosen nuclear site. An individual's steps toward Plowshares involve long and careful consideration on both sides. Candidates typically have participated in other activities first, such as protesting at the Pentagon or the White House. Fr. Steve Kelly, SJ, who is a veteran of several Plowshares actions and has served over seven years in prison, including stretches in solitary confinement, explains that "you don't just roll out of bed one day and decide to do Plowshares."⁹ As volunteers become well known in like-minded communities and express interest, they may be invited to a series of prayer meetings. The group then works together as a body of between one and nine people, choosing a uniquely named action (e.g., Trident Nein Plowshares, Pershing Plowshares, Gods of Metal Plowshares, Silo Pruning Hooks Plowshares, Weapons of Mass Destruction Here Plowshares, Nuclear Navy Plowshares, etc.). The group disperses and the unique name is retired after all sentences are served.

No religious congregation formally endorses Plowshares, but some, notably the Jesuits, the SHCJ, the Society of the Sacred Heart of Jesus (RSCJ), and the Dominican Sisters of Grand Rapids (OP), acknowledge and even accept its unique call to the conscience of individual members. Catholic teaching frames and respects moral conscience as a necessary judgment of human reason, and individuals with well-formed consciences may sometimes discern alone with God. Since most religious congregations would never force any member to disregard a sincere call of conscience, most tend to tolerate a Plowshares activist or two in their midst. For their part, Plowshares activists try to protect their superiors and sisters and brothers by not giving specific reasons for absences, thus shielding the congregation from the legal consequences of a conspiracy charge. This isn't mere "don't ask, don't tell," however, for it goes to something deeper: genuine room within the perceived strictures of religious life to honor calls of individual conscience as a movement of the Holy Spirit. Sometimes superiors will endorse officially, although it is rare. As one Jesuit provincial, Fr. Patrick Lee, wrote to Fr. William Bichsel in what he acknowledged was one of the hardest letters he had ever written, "I see your role in our province as a prophet." He missioned Fr. Bichsel to "hear and respond to what is in that deepest part of your heart" by going to the Trident Submarine Base in Bangor, Washington, for a Plowshares protest.¹⁰ Support at that level is rare, however, and some congregations such as the SHCJ were more conventionally resistant at first but gradually came to accept the work, with varying amounts of agreement or disagreement depending on whom one asks.

Before each court trial a Festival of Hope takes place in anticipation, with veteran activists and supporters traveling in from all over to encourage the current team; videos from some festivals are posted on YouTube. The trials themselves sometimes take on a convivial atmosphere as supporters pack the courtrooms to follow the proceedings. There have been peace parades, marches, singing in the streets, and various creative, theatrical forms of public prayer. While encouraging, though, the mood is not frivolous, for all defendants face serious charges. Court cases are considered the heart of any action. The goal is not prison but rather acquittal on the merits, a morally ideal outcome that has not yet been achieved in the United States. However, a few judges have been more sympathetic. A rare acknowledgment in court that activists could be right happened in the early 1980s after Plowshares activists entered a Sperry plant. After the guilty verdict, US district judge Miles Lord suspended their sentence with this declaration: "What is so sacred about a bomb, so romantic about a missile? Why do we condemn and hang individual killers while extolling the virtues of warmongers? What is that fatal fascination which attracts us to the thought of mass destruction of our brethren in another country?"[11] A few others have allowed defendants to go on probation and do community service instead of reporting to prison. Art Laffin notes that some groups were not prosecuted at all. He documents thirteen cases in the United States, England, Scotland, Ireland, New Zealand, and Australia with better outcomes. In six cases people were found not guilty, but never in the United States. In five cases the activists were never charged or the charges were dropped. Two cases resulted in hung juries, although both were eventually retried and convicted. The vast majority of Plowshares trials, however, do end with both conviction and incarceration.

Defense strategies evolve as the law adapts to antinuclear activism. For example, some defense teams refuse to select members of the jury. Instead, they publicly insist that a random group should be able to come to a fair conclusion. This refusal to stack the jury can signal integrity to jurors who might not otherwise have any way to know who these activists are. Lawyers have often been present, especially Anabel Dwyer of the Lawyers' Committee on Nuclear Policy; Francis Boyle of the University of Illinois College of Law; Bill Quigley, director of the Law Clinic and the Gillis Long Poverty Law Center at Loyola University New Orleans; and the law firm of Orrick, Herrington & Sutcliffe with the legal team of Karen Johnson-McKewan, Judy Kwan, and James Hsiao.

Plowshares members also sometimes represent themselves, with their lawyers only advising from the sidelines. This strategy of pro se allows each activist to speak testimony into the record that a judge might otherwise block. Self-representation can also give a defendant the opportunity to flip the trial and try to indict the builders of nuclear weapons. Tensions can rise as judges generally try to restrict the case to written law (did they enter or didn't they?) and defendants attempt to argue the illegality of the weapons themselves. "Our goal," said Martha Hennessy, granddaughter of Dorothy Day, referring to her participation in the Kings Bay Plowshares action of 2018 and echoing similar words by Catholic sister Anne Montgomery, RSCJ, "is to put nuclear weapons on trial."[12] Specifically, "we would like the federal courts to allow expert testimony to examine the legality of the US nuclear arsenal."[13]

Some arguments used by Plowshares activists, with or without counsel, have worked well in multiple court cases. First, some invoke the Nuremberg trials as authorizing citizens to intervene any time the US government commits crimes against humanity as defined by international law. The use of nuclear weapons falls under this type of crime, they contend, because weapons by definition target civilians, a clear human rights violation. The Dominican sister Ardeth Platte, OP (who was the original for the nun in the book that inspired the Netflix series *Orange is the New Black*), Carol Gilbert, OP, Jackie Hudson, OP, and Anne Montgomery, RSCJ clarified that their acts were not civil disobedience but rather civil resistance mandated under Nuremberg and international laws.[14] Platte and Gilbert said they were holding the US government accountable for adhering to its own laws. Judges have not accepted this defense, however, and routinely instruct the jury to ignore it.[15]

Second, some seek jury nullification, persuading a jury to deliver a not-guilty verdict according to its conscience rather than following either written law or the judge's instructions (thus nullifying the judge's orders).[16] Defense lawyer William Kuntsler first attempted jury nullification in these contexts with the Catonsville Nine in 1968. Historian Howard Zinn encouraged it successfully when he testified for the Camden 28 in 1973, resulting in full exoneration (albeit pre-Plowshares), and it remains a standard tactic whenever practical.

Third, activists point out that nuclear weapons are, in fact and by definition, illegal and have been for decades. Former US attorney general Ramsey Clark, who consistently defended antiwar and antinuclear activists from the 1970s until shortly before his death in 2021 and who testified at many Plowshares trials, maintained that Y-12 and facilities like it are illegal under the Nuclear Non-Proliferation Treaty, which he personally signed on behalf of the United States in 1968.

Fourth, Clark was also a proponent of the necessity defense, claiming that the action of breaking a law was only done to avoid greater harm. Although it has not succeeded for Plowshares, some climate activists have used this argument successfully, including the Climate Defense Project in 2017.

Fifth, "some property has no right to exist" is an argument from the Catonsville Nine Statement of 1968 that has carried over into Plowshares. It says in part that "Hitler's gas ovens, Stalin's concentration camps, atomic-biological-chemical weaponry, files of conscription, and slum properties are examples."[17] In other words, it is not a crime to attempt to dismantle something that never should have existed in the first place. Others cite the immorality of profiting from killing people. Or they argue that federal and state money spent on nuclear weapons steals from the poor by overallocating tax trillions for an unwinnable arms race.

Many judges successfully bar defendants from saying anything about nonviolence or the larger issues that might identify themselves as peace activists to the jury. In most Plowshares cases prosecutors enter what is known as a "motion in limine," in other words a pretrial motion to prohibit Plowshares defendants from using any affirmative defenses by agreeing at the very start of the trial that certain evidence—in their case humanitarian motivations and the core illegality of nuclear weapons—cannot be admitted as evidence or discussed. This can lead to considerable sorrow on the part of jurors who only learn after the trial who it was they just found guilty. Remorseful jurors have even been known to seek out Plowshares defendants before sentencing to apologize.[18]

Sentences range from fines to imprisonment to both, and incarceration becomes part of the overall witness and a rich opportunity for ministry. Many activists develop pastoral friendships with prisoners, holding Bible studies and treating the prison experience as a spiritual sojourn. Some become powerful advocates for incarceration reform, lobbying against unfair sentencing and inequities they witness on the inside. Prison becomes a way to be closest to the poor and to understand how powerless they are when routinely strip-searched, deprived of basic necessities, and otherwise humiliated. The firsthand experience of incarceration gives activists a unique perspective and authority about, for example, the national trend toward for-profit prisons.

Plowshares activists can receive concessions because of class, white privilege, religious status, and their nonviolent reputation. The full-time religious refuse to pay their fines as a matter of conscience, for they maintain that they did nothing wrong, but the courts also categorize them as indigent because they do not own property even though they may be supported by a congregation. Other activists live communally and under the poverty line to avoid paying taxes that support the war machine, so they also fall under the threshold for repayment of fines.

However, activists also share in the inequities of prison life, such as being remanded to solitary confinement "for their protection" even though solitary is generally classified as cruel and even as torture, being strip-searched for no reason, or being sent from facility to facility as punishment for organizing. Some do make the best of it. Fr. Steve Kelly describes prisons as "monasteries of the 20th and 21st century" and uses solitary as a place for the practice of prayer.[19] Greg Boertje-Obed notes that it can be oddly noisy in solitary, so you can sometimes communicate with other prisoners through walls and pipes, leading to a kind of fellowship. Nevertheless, solitary confinement constitutes hard time and leaves permanent psychological wounds.

Conclusion: A Legacy of Controversy

Servant of God Dorothy Day was a consistent supporter of those who burned draft cards and selective service records, and she believed in filling prisons as a form of nonviolent protest. However, it is impossible to speculate what she would say today. She expressed concern about certain rougher methods carried over from the Catonsville era, such as blocking employees who tried to interrupt the actions and destroying property by hammering on it.[20] But as Tom Lewis insisted, no one was harmed even slightly, and "there's a fundamental difference between violence to property and violence to people, and the two can't be associated as one."[21]

Some Plowshares actions have also led to unforeseen consequences. For example, the Y-12 leadership fired a security guard shortly before his eligibility for retirement because he did not shoot at activists who were in the kill zone. He said he knew they were harmless, whereas his backup colleague (who kept his job) cuffed them roughly, placing them facedown on the ground.

Churches also are not at all in agreement. More conservative Catholics who identify with law-and-order patriotism tend to accept national nuclear strength, considering it an essential form of peacekeeping. Some are scandalized that Catholic priests and sisters would even consider breaking any written law, even to heed the deepest call of conscience. Phil Berrigan recalled a Catholic Federal Bureau of Investigation agent exasperated in 1968 at arresting two priests for the Catonsville Nine action after having earlier done so for the Baltimore Four. All the agents were "irritated by our insouciance and anxious to make us pay for breaking the law." The Catholic agent "blushed with anger. 'Him again!' he shouted, pointing one large fist at my head, 'Good God, I'm changing my religion.'"[22]

The consistent whiteness of Plowshares activists also raises questions. However, supporters generally contend that true racial diversity within Plowshares is not possible, as browner activists would risk being shot or killed in nuclear facility free-fire zones, and they could be targets in prison. Consequently, many see Plowshares as a responsible use of white privilege in the service of social justice against crimes of the rich and powerful.

Members of some peace communities, including some Catholic Workers, have even accused Plowshares of harming the overall peace movement. They prefer more moderate and diplomatic efforts such as the International Campaign to Abolish Nuclear Weapons, winner of the 2017 Nobel Peace Prize and of which Sister Ardeth Platte was a part.

It is probably Tom Lewis himself, as a founding participant in both Catonsville and Plowshares actions, who framed it best, contending the movement grew up over time.[23] He felt the intensive discernment process of Plowshares showed spiritual growth in the post-Catonsville era, eventually creating true community. The center and the edge have long coexisted. I conclude from this study that they need one another more than either may acknowledge fully.

Notes

1. I document this action in detail in Carole Sargent, *Transform Now Plowshares: Megan Rice, Gregory Boertje-Obed, and Michael Walli* (Collegeville, MN: Liturgical Press, 2022). For the authoritative origins of Plowshares by two of its founding activists, see Arthur Laffin and Anne Montgomery, RSCJ, *Swords into Plowshares: Nonviolent Direct Action for Disarmament* (New York: Harper & Row, 1987). Thanks to Sr. Megan Rice, SHCJ, Sr. Ardeth Platte, OP, Sr. Carol Gilbert, OP, and Art Laffin of the Dorothy Day

Catholic Worker in Washington, DC; Martha Hennessy, granddaughter of Dorothy Day; and Paki Wieland of CODEPINK. For a fuller history of Plowshares, see Sharon Erickson Nepstad, *Religion and War Resistance in the Plowshares Movement* (New York: Cambridge University Press, 2009); and Dan Zak, *Almighty: Courage, Resistance, and Existential Peril in the Nuclear Age* (New York: Blue Rider Press/Penguin, 2016).

2. Members take seriously how white privilege affects their impact, a point discussed later in this essay.
3. For demographics, see the first chapter of Nepstad, *Religion and War Resistance in the Plowshares Movement*. See also Philip Berrigan, *Fighting the Lamb's War: Skirmishes with the American Empire* (Monroe, ME: Common Courage, 1996), 96.
4. George Mische, "Inattention to Accuracy about 'Catonsville Nine' Distorts History," *National Catholic Reporter*, May 17, 2013. Technically the second Plowshares action was solo, when Peter DeMott found keys in a van at the General Dynamics Electric Boat shipyard in Groton, Connecticut, and rammed the van into the body of a Trident submarine, but it was a spontaneous decision by an individual, not a planned action.
5. For more details about the global media, see Sargent, "Introduction," in *Transform Now Plowshares*.
6. Nepstad, *Religion and War Resistance in the Plowshares Movement*, 34. For a longer history of the movement, see Dan McKanan, "Introduction," in *Doing Time for Peace: Resistance, Family, and Community*, ed. Rosalie Riegle, xiii–xvi (Nashville, TN: Vanderbilt University Press, 2012).
7. Drew Christiansen, SJ, "Nuclear Abolition and the Catholic Peace Tradition," Berkley Center for Religions, Peace & World Affairs, March 4, 2014, https://www.youtube.com/watch?v=XcgDdKutAF4, at 8:29.
8. Tsuyoshi Hasegawa counters the contention that the bombs ended World War II. Tsuyoshi Hasegawa, *Racing the Enemy: Stalin, Truman, and the Surrender of Japan* (Cambridge, MA: Harvard University Press, 2005).
9. Fr. Steve Kelly, SJ, interview with the author, July 2017.
10. Patrick J. Lee, SJ, Missioning letter to Fr. William J. Bichsel, SJ, October 23, 2009, Disarm Now Plowshares, https://disarmnowplowshares.wordpress.com/2009/12/13/missioning/.
11. John LaForge, "The Judge Who Assailed Worship of the Bomb," *Beyond Nuclear International*, December 1, 2019, https://beyondnuclearinternational.org/2019/12/01/the-judge-who-assailed-worship-of-the-bomb.
12. Martha Hennessy, interview with Maria Benevento for *National Catholic Reporter*, July 30, 2018.
13. Martha Hennessy, correspondence with the author, January 18, 2019.
14. Some such as Megan Rice, SHCJ, and her Plowshares mentor, Anne Montgomery, RSCJ, defined it as "divine obedience." See Montgomery's chapter "Divine Obedience," in Laffin and Montgomery, *Swords into Plowshares*, 25.
15. Nepstad, *Religion and War Resistance in the Plowshares Movement*, 80.

16. Andrew D. Leipold, "Rethinking Jury Nullification," *Virginia Law Review* 82, no. 2 (March 1996): 253–54.
17. Catonsville Defense Committee, "The Catonsville Statement," May 17, 1968, Dean Pappas Collection, Enoch Pratt Free Library, Baltimore, Maryland.
18. See, for example, Disarm Now Plowshares, "Hearts Open, Come Together," December 23, 2010, https://youtu.be/Rdvj9Mid718.
19. Fr. Steve Kelly, SJ, correspondence with the author, December 3, 2018, from the Glynn County Detention Center, where he was incarcerated for the Kings Bay Plowshares 7 action.
20. Thomas Merton, "Nonviolence Does Not—Cannot—Mean Passivity," *Ave Maria*, Vol. 108, Congregation of the Holy Cross, 1968.
21. Riegle, *Doing Time for Peace*, 26.
22. Berrigan, *Fighting the Lamb's War*, 106.
23. Riegle, *Doing Time for Peace*, 26.

PART III

Toward a World without Nuclear Weapons

8

National Attitudes toward Nuclear Deterrence

JAMES E. GOODBY

On November 10, 2017, at a Vatican conference, Pope Francis delivered a speech that offered a guide to the self-preservation of the human race. He said in essence that reliance on nuclear weapons as a means of managing international security affairs must be phased out because too much is at stake to go on believing that nuclear weapons bring security.[1] What was new and crucially important about his statement was his judgment that time is running out on the gamble that nuclear deterrence can continue forever as the bedrock of international security without a catastrophic event caused by an accident, a miscalculation, or a deliberate decision to use nuclear weapons.

Are the nations listening? Are those people who make policy acting in a way that suggests they have heard and understood what Pope Francis was saying on that day in 2017? Tragically, it appears that neither policymakers nor ordinary people are heeding his prophetic words.

Who Has Nuclear Weapons?

Currently, nine nations possess nuclear weapons. Five nuclear weapon states are acknowledged as such in the Nuclear Non-Proliferation Treaty (NPT): Great Britain, China, France, Russia, and the United States. These nations are also permanent members of the United Nations Security Council.

Four other nuclear-armed nations refused to become signatories of the NPT, although one of them, North Korea, was a non–nuclear-armed member of the NPT before its government began conducting missile test flights and nuclear test explosions.

Israel has never acknowledged that it has nuclear weapons but is widely believed to have around eighty warheads/bombs. Pakistan and India have nuclear weapons, and each denounced the NPT as discriminatory because the NPT members decline to accept these nations as nuclear weapon states.

Extended Deterrence: "The Nuclear Umbrella"

Several other nations allied with the United States have relied on US nuclear weapons to defend them if they are attacked: the European member nations of the North Atlantic Treaty Organization and Australia, Japan, and South Korea in the Asia-Pacific region. Several of these nations could readily construct nuclear weapons and the means of delivering them if they decided to do so.

New Complexities of Nuclear Deterrence

Neither these five recognized nuclear weapon states under the NPT nor the four other nuclear-armed states that reject the NPT have made any serious move to drop nuclear deterrence as a key element in their defense posture. None of the nations under the US nuclear umbrella have shown any willingness to renounce nuclear deterrence as a key component of their defensive arrangements.

The bipolar nuclear deterrence system of the Cold War has been succeeded by a more complex one. Three nuclear weapon states act essentially at the global level: the United States, China, and Russia. Four other countries possessing nuclear weapons operate at the regional level: Israel, India, Pakistan, and North Korea. Two others have serious global interests, but their nuclear deterrent forces operate primarily at a regional level: France and the United Kingdom.

What this complex system suggests is that nuclear war could break out because of a regional conflict and that nuclear weapon states that operate at the global level could become involved. During the Cold War, this kind of nuclear war was known as "catalytic" because a third party might trigger a conflict between the two superpowers, the United States and the Soviet Union. Today, a potential catalytic war is close to being the norm. For example, if India and Pakistan engaged in an exchange of nuclear fire against each other, this would almost certainly require China and the United States to go on high alert and probably move their nuclear forces in a way that might look threatening in Washington and Beijing. If North Korea proceeds to develop its nuclear capabilities, the movements of US forces in response to some action on the part of North Korea could lead to movements by China or Russia of their nuclear forces, and this might be perceived as threatening by Washington and New Delhi.

Nuclear deterrence has become a more complicated and dangerous way to manage interstate relations. If cyberwarfare and unmanned drones and space systems are added to the mix, the stability that is seen in retrospect as the product of nuclear deterrence during the Cold War can no longer be taken for granted. Quite the contrary. Nuclear weapons inject a major uncertainty into interstate relations under conditions complicated by the interaction of more nations that possess nuclear weapons and more weapons systems that can confuse decision makers' understanding of what is happening.

Who Declares the Right to Initiate Nuclear War?

The United States and Russia each have made clear that they entertain the possibility of first use of their nuclear weapons; that is, their official statements of policy regarding use of nuclear weapons declare their willingness to use nuclear weapons even if nuclear weapons have not been used by other states possessing nuclear weapons. Both the United States and Russia are devoting considerable amounts of money to making their nuclear forces more effective and usable in the circumstances they imagine might exist in the future. China has joined them in this policy, and a multination nuclear arms race has become increasingly likely during the last few years.

The 2018 Nuclear Posture Review, issued during the Trump administration, stated that nuclear weapons will be used only in "extreme circumstances." It has many similarities with President Barack Obama's Nuclear Posture Review, but officials explained that major cyberattacks on the United States and nonnuclear attacks against US nuclear command and control systems are possible reasons for first use. The Nuclear Posture Review also proposed a low-yield nuclear warhead option for the

Trident II submarine-launched ballistic missile and a new sea-launched cruise missile.[2]

Russia's nuclear use doctrine permits first use of nuclear weapons if chemical or biological weapons are used against Russia or its allies or if the very existence of the Russian state is jeopardized by a massive attack with nonnuclear weapons. Russia is also modernizing its nuclear arsenal.

NATO countries, including Britain and France, have declared that nuclear weapons are part of the alliance's defense posture. Use policy, as described in NATO's public statements, says that nuclear weapons will only be used as a "last resort." This means that US, British, and French nuclear weapons could be used first, if necessary, to defend against an overwhelming attack with nonnuclear weapons.

In the Middle East, Israel evidently has a policy of not permitting any other state in the region to acquire nuclear weapons. This has required Israel to destroy nuclear facilities in Iraq in 1981 and in Syria in 2007.[3] Iran also has been the target of surreptitious attacks against its nuclear programs. Since Israel has never said that it possesses nuclear weapons, it has not had to state the conditions under which they would be used.

In South Asia, many experts consider the initiation of nuclear war a high risk. Territorial disputes generate tensions between India and Pakistan and between India and China. India and Pakistan have an argument between them over Jammu and Kashmir dating back to their independence in 1947. Armed conflict has broken out between India and its two neighbors over these disputed areas, including recently as this chapter was being written. There is in South Asia an ever-present opportunity for miscalculation and high levels of tension.

Pakistan and India developed the infrastructure for nuclear weapons capabilities through civil nuclear power plants. India showed that it had the capability to build a nuclear weapon by testing a device it said was for peaceful uses in 1974. In 1998, India broke out of its "recessed deterrence" mode with a series of five nuclear test explosions. Pakistan immediately followed suit with its own series of six test explosions. Since then, each country has refrained from nuclear test explosions but has devoted wealth, industrial capacity, and technological expertise to building nuclear warheads and the means of delivering them, including missiles, bombers, and submarines. Analysts consider that the military postures the two neighbors have developed are fraught with dangers of nuclear weapons use if combat should break out between them.

Pakistan has built short-range so-called tactical nuclear weapons systems and has mated nuclear warheads with these delivery systems so they can be ready for use at any time. India is considering doing the same but does not seem to have done so as of this writing. Instead India, the dominant military power in South Asia, has adopted a strategy of being prepared to launch a conventional attack on Pakistan without mobilizing to do so. Pakistan has found this Indian posture quite unsettling, and analysts consider that Pakistan might use its tactical nuclear weapons against a standing-start Indian invasion, anticipating that nuclear use on its own territory would not prompt an Indian nuclear response. India has a policy of not using nuclear weapons first in any conflict, while Pakistan reserves the right to use nuclear weapons first if it is attacked.

The takeover of Afghanistan by the Taliban has prompted new concerns in New Delhi and elsewhere about the rise of radical influences in Pakistan. These concerns will add to uncertainties in South Asia.

The delicate relationship between these two nuclear-armed powers is complicated by the fact that China and India also are nuclear rivals and that India calculates its nuclear requirements not just against Pakistan but also vis-à-vis China.

China's Nuclear Challenge

Until recently China had slowly built a capability for producing nuclear warheads and delivery systems, and the pace of new deployments of nuclear weapons had been in keeping with China's policy of avoiding excessive provocation while building up its economic strength. Under President Xi Jinping, China is exploiting its position as a rising great power to exert pressure on its neighbors in the South China Sea and to challenge American naval power in the region. This is threatening Taiwan. President Xi seems determined to present the world with the specter of a new and aggressive nuclear weapon state.

As of 2018, the Nuclear Notebook of the *Bulletin of the Atomic Scientists* could report that "there is no sign that the Chinese government has officially diverted from its traditional nuclear policy—a pledge not to use nuclear weapons first, not to use nuclear weapons against nonnuclear countries or in nuclear weapon–free zones, and to maintain only a minimum deterrent designed to ensure a survivable second-strike capability."[4]

At that time, the Nuclear Notebook estimated that "China has a stockpile of approximately 280 nuclear warheads for delivery by 120 to 130 land-based ballistic missiles, 48 sea-based ballistic missiles, and bombers." The Nuclear Notebook also pointed out that most missiles carried only 1 warhead each and that China is thought to store most of its warheads in its central storage facility.[5]

China clearly has decided to invest heavily in its defense capabilities, including its nuclear forces. No longer is China content with a modest nuclear deterrent force capable of a retaliatory strike if it is attacked. New silos for ballistic missiles are being built. New ships for its navy are being constructed.

Most ominously, China tested a new weapons system in August 2021 that married a vehicle capable of orbiting Earth with a hypersonic maneuverable missile that could strike any point on the planet with little hope of being intercepted. This type of weapons system encourages preemption through either a boost-phase attack or antisatellite weapons, either of which could trigger a nuclear war. This is a strong argument for negotiation between the United States and China aimed at changing the hostile relations between them.

North Korea: A Question Mark

North Korea's determined pursuit of nuclear weapons dates back to the 1950s and the policies of Kim Il-sung, the founder of the state. Kim Jong-un, the present leader, mounted a vigorous campaign in 2017 to develop a thermonuclear warhead and a ballistic missile with a range sufficient to reach mainland US territory. He appears to have achieved that capability and has threatened to use nuclear weapons against the United States but has not yet moved to build a fleet of intercontinental ballistic missiles.

The Singapore summit between President Donald Trump and Chairman Kim in 2018 yielded a document the two men approved, and it could have provided the basis for a step-by-step reduction in North Korea's nuclear weapons program. The Trump administration's record of US–North Korea discussions includes numerous letters between Trump and Kim, but neither these private exchanges nor face-to-face meetings between them yielded a settlement. Kim has resumed testing of missiles, although he is still showing restraint in developing long-range missiles. As of this writing, he has not resumed nuclear test explosions.

Pope Francis has challenged us to think seriously about two fundamental issues:

> What could quickly change these national attitudes?
> Could nuclear war be avoided through a gradual process of evolutionary change?

First, as to quickly changing national attitudes, three developments would have a powerful effect on national policies around the world:

> A nuclear explosion in a major city;
> Strong leadership by the United States and Russia, who possess the world's largest nuclear arsenals; and
> A detente between the United States and China that heads off a nuclear arms race.

How might a nuclear explosion in a major city occur? Several possibilities need to be considered:

> Terrorists or a rogue state smuggle a nuclear bomb into a major city and either detonate it or threaten to detonate it.
> A nation loses control of one of its ready-to-launch nuclear weapons systems, perhaps through cyberattack, and its preprogrammed target is struck as a result.
> An error in a warning system leads a nuclear release authority to conclude that its nation is under attack, and nuclear-armed missiles are launched to retaliate and to limit damage from remaining missiles in the supposed attacker's inventory.

Admittedly, even this type of catastrophe might not be enough to wean surviving leaders away from reliance on nuclear weapons. The sense that such a powerful weapon must bring safety to its possessor is deeply ingrained. Still, the death and destruction from even limited nuclear war would be so incomprehensibly large that a lasting moral impact might be imprinted on human societies. This is the optimal outcome. An escalation of nuclear war to global levels is also possible, and this is likely why Pope Francis urges humanity to abandon nuclear deterrence.

How about gradually reducing reliance on nuclear deterrence through diplomacy? In theory, this could result from the leadership of the two most powerful nuclear weapon states, the United States and Russia, joined by other nations in a joint enterprise. Nations such as China and India may not be impressed by gradual reductions in the arsenals of the United States and Russia, but if a group of states—some nuclear-armed, some not—banded together to join Russia and the United States in actions that convincingly showed a serious intent to move toward minimal levels of nuclear weapons, the impact could be quite significant.

It is conceivable that a gradual shift in attitudes toward nuclear weapons might happen as a result of wise leadership in major nations. For example, leaders might come to power in Moscow, Washington, Beijing, and elsewhere who perceive that nuclear war would end life as we know it. Accountability of leaders for such vastly destructive actions will come about when the enormity of their responsibility "reach[es] men's very souls," as Pope John XXIII put it.[6] This is the essence of the idea of integral disarmament, which he discussed in 1963. Pope Francis spoke of this idea, using those specific words, in his November 2017 speech. Reducing the centrality of nuclear weapons in the thinking of national leaders can come about as a result of fundamental changes in thinking about relationships between adversary nations. This is a secular way of describing what Pope John XXIII and Pope Francis meant by integral disarmament.

President Obama, speaking at Hiroshima on May 27, 2016, voiced a similar idea: "The scientific revolution that led to the splitting of an atom requires a moral revolution as well."[7] He added that "we must recognize our connection to one another as members of one human race." The same idea was expressed by Pope Francis, who said that nuclear weapons "cannot constitute the basis for peaceful coexistence between members of the human family, which must rather be inspired by an ethics of solidarity."[8]

A gradual shift in attitudes toward nuclear weapons is inherent in the idea of "integral disarmament," whether that idea is expressed in spiritual or secular terms. But how do we encourage gradual changes in human relations? First, it must be said that formal treaties and agreements on nuclear weapons have generally not been very successful in achieving integral disarmament. The US-Russia relationship is a case in point. The most enduring obstacles to reaching agreements with the Soviet Union/Russia in nuclear negotiations, as these have materialized during the last several decades of experience with these negotiations, stem from deeply embedded political attitudes. These control much of what the leaderships in Moscow and in Washington say and do regardless of who is in charge. There was a brief change in the pattern during the period when Ronald Reagan and Mikhail Gorbachev were in charge of their nations. Important and far-reaching political changes took place then.

Russia typically has been determined to be seen as an equal partner of the United States on the world stage. In nuclear negotiations, this is manifested in some cases as a demand for parity in US and Russian nuclear forces. Putin's rejection of Obama's Berlin appeal for negotiations for deeper strategic reductions probably was motivated in part by a perception that Obama was not treating him and Russia as equals in global affairs.

It is hard for the leaders of a nation that sees itself as exceptional, such as the United States, to accept the notion of cooperation between peers on the world stage. But history suggests that when Washington, Moscow, and other nations work as equals in a shared enterprise, the outcome is often quite positive. "Positions of strength" policies have to take account of the need for cooperation at some point.

The brief period of stunning changes in US-Russia relations during the Reagan-Gorbachev era, aided and abetted by the US secretary of state, George P. Shultz, showed that obstacles to US-Russia cooperation can be overcome. But they are deep-rooted obstacles stemming from significantly different calculations about the security needs of each country. Sustained and determined leadership in both countries can overcome entrenched opinions about security needs and guide their nations toward new solutions. But differing histories and geopolitical environments inform Russian and American assumptions about the world around them. These cannot be changed, but they can be recognized, and "work-arounds" can be devised. It is possible that Russia and the United States could rekindle the flame of hope that burned so brightly during the Reagan-Gorbachev years.

Can advancing technology reduce the fixation on nuclear weapons as essential for safety? One obstacle that blocked progress toward international nuclear agreements for decades has become easier to manage. This is the issue of monitoring and verifying compliance with agreements. Russia has accepted the need for on-site inspections and accountability and is more comfortable with intrusive inspections systems than it was in the past. The verification provisions for the New START treaty are being implemented faithfully by both sides despite tensions between the two countries.

But technology has also encouraged the spread of missile capabilities around the world, and this no doubt affected Moscow's view of the utility of the Intermediate-Range Nuclear Forces Treaty and led it to violate the terms of that treaty. Russia also appears to value its short-range nuclear forces more highly than ever.

Reductions in nuclear force leads to concerns about the vulnerability of remaining nuclear forces and their ability to successfully execute a second strike. Missile defense is particularly troublesome in this regard, as defenses aimed at one country (e.g., North Korea) can be perceived as threatening the deterrent capability of other countries (e.g., Russia and China), stimulating them to increase and modernize rather than reduce nuclear weapons. Advanced conventional weapons can also be perceived as threatening deterrence, stimulating increases and modernization rather than reductions.

Each holder of nuclear weapons sees its security problem as not just the nuclear weapons of the others but also as a host of additional technical issues. Technologies on the horizon for precision conventional systems, autonomous systems, counterspace weapons, and cyber could complicate maintenance of stable deterrent forces and frustrate arms control negotiations by stimulating increases in nuclear forces.

Can Limits on Nuclear Weapons Use Lead to Gradual Loss of Interest in Nuclear Weapons?

The argument against initiation of the use of nuclear weapons is strong on both moral and realpolitik grounds. The possession of nuclear weapons by nine countries, the growing potential for regional conflict involving some of those nuclear-armed countries, the advancing technologies that undermine nuclear deterrence, and the growing risk of nuclear use by accident, miscalculation, or cyberattack could lead to a conclusion that the risks of continued indefinite reliance on deterrence are greater than the risks of reductions and eventual elimination. This point evidently underlies the thinking of Pope Francis. One fundamental fact to recognize is this: a nuclear war has never been fought. Technical analyses can quantify the physical scale of the destruction that might be caused by nuclear war, but only through the lens of morality and ethics can the historical consequences of that destruction be understood and accountability be judged.

An example of how gradual change could come about incrementally, without formal agreements, is the nonuse of nuclear weapons in combat ever since August 1945. The reasons for this are unclear, although the obvious consequences of engaging in a nuclear war in terms of unparalleled death and destruction must have been understood by most decision makers. The various names given to the condition of nonuse are "self-deterrence" (John Lewis Gaddis), "tradition of non-use" (Thomas Schelling), and "taboo" (by several, most notably Nina Tannenwald).[9]

But is it also possible that national leaders have shrunk from using nuclear weapons from a sense of ethics and morality? Did the images of what happened at Hiroshima and Nagasaki bring home to generations of politicians and military leaders the evil inherent in destroying whole populations?

A sense of morality did permeate the discussions among American policymakers at the time of the Cuban Missile Crisis in October 1962, but what was on their minds was not Hiroshima and Nagasaki but rather the Japanese surprise attack on Pearl Harbor and the sense that America did not do such things.[10] This is an important point because it suggests that how nations choose to behave does not rest solely on the fear of nuclear weapons but also rests on a widely shared belief in how the nation's leaders should act when considering the use of force. This consideration makes it entirely possible to believe that integral disarmament can come about through a sense of moral revulsion among the nations, a revulsion caused by their reliance on the destruction of lives and civilization to maintain peace when there are other alternatives.

Can that same feeling of what is right and wrong in national behavior be extended to possession of nuclear weapons and the threat to use them? In short, can moral revulsion against the very idea of relying on nuclear weapons for security lead nations to renounce nuclear weapons and nuclear deterrence? This is what Pope Francis is asking of us in the name of humanity's survival. Could moral revulsion at least lead nations to renounce the first use of nuclear weapons and to take steps to affect the operations of their nuclear forces while seriously negotiating for their elimination?

These questions cannot be answered with any degree of certainty, but it is reasonably certain that the statements of religious leaders will add to the weight of the argument against relying indefinitely into the future on nuclear deterrence for safety. But political leaders will have to carry the ball themselves. As John Kennedy said, "on earth God's work must truly be our own."[11]

Humanitarian concerns have been raised about the use of nuclear weapons that have evidently had a powerful impact on the negotiation of the so-called Ban Treaty, a document designed to prohibit the possession of nuclear weapons. It lacks any provisions that would prescribe how this could be done in practice, and all of the states possessing nuclear weapons have refused to join it.

The most difficult political and technical questions about eliminating nuclear weapons arise in regard to the last five hundred nuclear weapons of a US-Russia reduction program. This is where the focus of study should be on any effort to carry out the mandate to eliminate this existential threat to humanity. Nuclear and non–nuclear weapon states could join in such a study.

For this reason, another agreement that has the support of the nuclear weapon states and contains agreed provisions for deep reductions in nuclear weaponry will be necessary. Presently, there are no negotiations underway among the nuclear-armed nations. Without filling that negotiations gap, there can be little hope for moving toward the world that Pope Francis and other leaders have advocated.[12]

Other steps to resolve disputes must be taken on a regional basis in the Middle East, South Asia, and Northeast Asia. Regional disputes have been the drivers of nuclear ambitions in each of these regions. The presence of nuclear weapons in these regions has made it more difficult to resolve the underlying disputes.[13] All the major nations have a fundamental interest in seeing these conflicts end and nuclear weapons eliminated or at least made more difficult to use. Peace in the Middle East and South Asia is especially indispensable to integral disarmament and should be a moral imperative for the United Nations Security Council.

Perhaps most serious of all the obstacles to changing attitudes toward nuclear deterrence is the reemergence of a nuclear arms race between the United States and Russia and now potentially a new nuclear arms race between China and the United States. Aside from jeopardizing prospects for deeper reductions in strategic nuclear forces, this will make a cooperative security relationship among the United States, Russia, and China more difficult to achieve across the board, which will affect nations around the world.

Need for a Public Dialogue

Underlying all of the actions that states could take to measure up to the moral stance outlined by Pope Francis are the attitudes and opinions of ordinary people around the world. Unless citizens are well informed of the hazards of nuclear weapons and understand the moral reasoning for ceasing to include nuclear weapons in their nations' deterrent and war-fighting policies, support for moving away from policies of the past will not exist. This situation can be corrected, but it will require a determined and sustained campaign by religious and private organizations of all kinds united under the banner of creating the conditions that will resist the threat of nuclear war.

Notes

1. Pope Francis, "Address of His Holiness Pope Francis to Participants in the International Symposium 'Prospects for a World Free of Nuclear Weapons and for Integral Disarmament,'" November 10, 2017.
2. Adam Mount and Abigail Stowe-Thurston, "What Is U.S. Nuclear Policy, Exactly?," *Bulletin of the Atomic Scientists*, April 18, 2018.
3. Isabel Kershner, "Ending Secrecy, Israel Says It Bombed Syrian Reactor in 2007," *New York Times*, March 21, 2018.
4. Hans M. Kristensen and Robert S. Norris, "Chinese Nuclear Forces, 2018," *Bulletin of the Atomic Scientists*, 74, no. 4 (2018): 289–95. Both authors are affiliated with the Federation of American Scientists.
5. Kristensen and Norris.
6. Pope John XXIII, *Pacem in terris*, 113.
7. The Obama White House, "President Obama's Remarks at Hiroshima Peace Memorial," May 27, 2016, Medium, https://medium.com/@Obama WhiteHouse/president-obamas-remarks-at-hiroshima-peace-memorial -6a27716f82d9.
8. Pope Francis, "Address."
9. Nina Tannenwald, *The Nuclear Taboo: The United States and the Non-Use of Nuclear Weapons Since 1945* (Cambridge: Cambridge University Press, 2007).

10. Mark White, "Robert Kennedy and the Cuban Missile Crisis: A Reinterpretation," *American Diplomacy*, September 2007.
11. John F. Kennedy, Inaugural Address, January 20, 1961, John F. Kennedy Presidential Library and Museum.
12. See George Shultz and James Goodby, eds., *The War That Must Never Be Fought: Dilemmas of Nuclear Deterrence* (Stanford, CA: Hoover Institution Press, 2015). Shultz and Goodby provide a discussion of opportunities and obstacles facing those who favor less reliance on nuclear deterrence.
13. See James Goodby, *Approaching the Nuclear Tipping Point: Cooperative Security in an Era of Global Change* (Lanham, MD: Rowman & Littlefield, 2017).

9

6 + 6 = 9

Law and Nuclear Weapons

DAVID A. KOPLOW

This chapter addresses law, not mathematics, but it relies on a simple, albeit crudely mistaken, arithmetic formula to make a point about international and domestic law, nuclear disarmament, proliferation, and frustrated aspirations. The first "6" in the title refers to Article VI of the 1968 Nuclear Non-Proliferation Treaty (NPT),[1] the cornerstone instrument in the global effort to impede the further dissemination of nuclear weapons and the capability to develop them. Article VI contains the fundamental disarmament commitment: the promise by the countries that continue to possess nuclear weapons to pursue negotiations in good faith to limit and abolish them.

The second "6" in the title refers to Article VI of the US Constitution, known as the supremacy clause.[2] This provision establishes treaties as "the supreme Law of the Land" in the United States, equivalent to federal statutes, subordinate only to the Constitution itself as a rule of law binding upon US courts and other organs of government.

Finally, the "9," unfortunately, represents the number of states around the world that are widely understood to possess nuclear weapons today. The fact that the number remains so high, fifty years after the conclusion of the NPT, is a sad commentary on the combined failures of the two primary legal authorities cited above to accomplish the objectives that their authors so earnestly sought and that the world still so desperately needs.

The following pages trace how the failure to honor the rule of law embodied in the NPT and the Constitution has contributed to the longevity and the dispersal of the world's stockpiles of nuclear weapons, perhaps the most devastating threat that the human species has ever faced. The essay addresses both the macro level (i.e., the legal obligations imposed on the United States as a whole) and the micro level (i.e., the plight of an individual member of the military services or a civilian located in the chain of command who might be confronted with an illegal order to employ nuclear weapons).

The Nuclear Non-Proliferation Treaty

The NPT constitutes a precarious balancing act, attempting to reconcile the somewhat conflicting interests of differently situated groups of states. Virtually all other major arms control treaties have always been fully symmetric, in establishing exactly equal rights and responsibilities for all parties, without reserving special perquisites for those countries that happened to be the first to develop a particular category of weapons or that possessed the arms in the greatest numbers. Uniquely, the NPT formally creates two nonintersecting categories of parties: the nuclear weapon states, which had already tested nuclear weapons before the treaty was concluded and who were allowed to continue to hold them, and the non–nuclear weapon states, which have pledged never to cross the nuclear weapons threshold. Under the treaty, only 5 countries qualify as nuclear weapon states (China, France, Russia, the United Kingdom, and the United States, not just coincidentally the same 5 that are permanent members of the United Nations Security Council). All the other 186 parties are forever locked into non–nuclear weapon state status. Importantly, 4 crucial nonparties (India, Israel, North Korea, and Pakistan) have stayed away from the treaty, at least in part because of this "discriminatory" structure.[3]

The NPT is often said to rest on three pillars: nonproliferation (the non–nuclear weapon states' commitment not to acquire the portentous weapons), disarmament (Article VI, elaborated next), and peaceful uses (the agreement to share the benefits of nuclear energy for electricity generation, nuclear medicine, and other civil applications). While each pillar has engendered its own controversies, as reflected in the rancorous review conferences held every five years to assess the ongoing track record of NPT implementation, the focus here is on the most problematic aspect, Article VI.

Article VI is hardly a paragon of drafting clarity and precision. Its single sentence provides that "Each of the Parties to the Treaty undertakes to pursue negotiations in good faith on effective measures relating to cessation of the nuclear arms race at an early date and to nuclear disarmament, and on a treaty on general and complete disarmament under strict and effective international control." The commitment to "pursue negotiations in good faith" is surely vague, but it is not hopelessly vague. No timetable for completing the negotiations is specified, and no specific sequence of intermediate steps is indicated, but those gaps do not deprive the text of all content. The concept of "good faith" does have legal meaning; in multiple other contexts, international and domestic US legal authorities have fleshed out this key phrase. Good faith requires all participants to strive sincerely toward reaching agreement, not simply "going through the motions" while inflexibly insisting on their own starting positions; they must engage in a genuine give-and-take. Certainly, parties cannot legitimately disavow the goals specified in Article VI, adopt policies that deliberately make their accomplishment more difficult, or interpose ceaseless delay and insurmountable preconditions.[4] As the International Court of Justice expressed the point in its celebrated and unsatisfying 1996 advisory opinion "Legality of the Threat or Use of Nuclear Weapons," "the legal import of that obligation goes beyond that of a mere obligation of conduct; the obligation involved here is an obligation to achieve a precise result—nuclear disarmament in all its aspects—by adopting a particular course of conduct, namely, the pursuit of negotiations on the matter in good faith."[5]

An objective observer must now conclude that by any calculus, more than fifty years of perpetuating the divide between nuclear weapon and non–nuclear weapon states—what some call "nuclear apartheid"—is exorbitant. Yes, the nuclear inventories of the United States and Russia have been dramatically drawn down from their Cold War heights; by some measures, the world's collective stockpile of deployed nuclear weapons has been reduced by 90 percent. But getting to zero is nowhere in sight. Instead, we see furious recapitalization of the nuclear arsenals and associated infrastructures in most nuclear weapon states, clearly indicating the intention to retain these Armageddon devices for indefinite decades into the future. Most tellingly, for purposes of Article VI, there have been no nuclear negotiations between nuclear weapon states (good faith or otherwise) since the conclusion of the US-Russia New START treaty in 2010,[6] and all the nuclear weapon states boycotted the global process for developing the 2017 Treaty on the Prohibition of

Nuclear Weapons.[7] Notably, Article VI is an obligation for "each of the parties," but as a practical matter, a special emphasis falls on the nuclear weapon states and particularly the two that possess the lion's share of the inventories—the United States and Russia. But how can anyone contend that Article VI is being fulfilled today when nobody is talking?

The Supremacy Clause

Article VI of the US Constitution also reflects a cumbersome drafting deficit. Its clause 2 states, in eighteenth-century style, "This Constitution, and the Laws of the United States which shall be made in Pursuance thereof; and all Treaties made, or which shall be made, under the Authority of the United States, shall be the supreme Law of the Land; and the Judges in every State shall be bound thereby, any Thing in the Constitution or Laws of any State to the Contrary notwithstanding."

At first blush, this passage seems to define the Constitution, the federal laws, and treaties as all being supreme, but subsequent interpretation has established that some authorities are more supreme than others. Federal laws (i.e., statutes) are supreme only when they are "in Pursuance" of the Constitution, so a statute that exceeds or conflicts with the Constitution is denied supremacy and is invalidated as "unconstitutional." Treaties are handled somewhat differently here: they are supreme if they are "under the Authority of the United States," which might suggest that a treaty need not be "pursuant to" the Constitution. Indeed, that is not a frivolous postulate. In some other countries, treaties (especially treaties respecting fundamental human rights) can depart from the domestic constitution and effectively supersede or amend it. In the United States, however, a different position prevails, and subsequent case law has established that the language of Article VI was asymmetric only to preserve as supreme the treaties that were concluded *prior to* the adoption of the US Constitution (notably, the peace treaty with Great Britain that ended the American Revolutionary War). In sum, a treaty, just as a statute, is legally binding, weighty, and inferior only to the Constitution.[8]

For purposes of this essay, the fundamental effect of the supremacy clause is to ensure that a treaty is law, meaning it can be enforced by US courts; can displace prior inconsistent federal and state legislation; and has the same teeth as other domestic legal authority. Under a famous 1900 US Supreme Court case, denominated after a ship called the *Paquete Habana*, "International law is part of our law, and must be ascertained and administered by the courts."[9] Moreover, under Article II, section 3, of the Constitution, the president has a duty to "take Care that the Laws be faithfully executed."[10] That is, even if the president disagrees with the general purpose or the specific thrust of a law, including a treaty that may have been made by his or her long-ago predecessors, he or she is obliged to carry it out. It is not merely a political choice for the United States to implement the provisions of the NPT; it is a genuine legal requirement.[11]

Of course, legal procedures offer several escape hatches from a treaty obligation that is regarded as burdensome, obsolete, or dysfunctional. Treaties can be amended or replaced; the United States, like all other parties, also has the legal right to withdraw from the NPT, on three months' notice, if extraordinary events jeopardize its supreme interests.[12] But until those momentous steps are taken (following the terrible example of North Korea, the only party ever to exercise the NPT withdrawal option), the treaty—including the Article VI obligation—is fully in force for the United States.

The mathematic equation in the title of this essay illustrates one of the adverse consequences of the failure to cleave to these legal obligations. The number of nuclear-equipped states has crept inexorably up to the current nine and shows no signs of abating. If the United States and the other nuclear weapon states disregard or downplay their NPT obligations to advance "in good faith" and "at an early date" toward nuclear abolition, how can they expect the basic bargain of that treaty to endure? How can their leaders and diplomats maintain, with any kind of straight face, that other countries should continue to eschew nuclear weapons when the planet's most powerful actors have found it impossible to escape their own nuclear addiction? If we want international law to be honored, we have to model that behavior ourselves, as our reciprocal legal obligations so clearly specify.

Superior Orders

We turn now from big-picture questions about national obligations to small-picture questions about personal responsibilities and commitments. That is, what is a US person to do when confronted by illegal government action? For example, what if a US government official in the Department of State is instructed by a more senior leader to disregard the NPT's commitment to negotiate in good faith toward nuclear disarmament, with the guidance that we are just going to put that effort onto the back burner for another few years or decades? In the worst case, what if a US military officer who is part of the operational chain of command is issued an illegal order to use a nuclear weapon in a circumstance when such a launch would be in violation of the international law of armed conflict?[13] Many other people of good faith may also find their hands dirty in the nuclear weapons enterprise: they research, build, and maintain the explosive devices and the associated delivery systems; they write and promulgate the doctrines and strategies for the use of the arms; and they vote appropriations of tax funds for those apocalyptic purposes.[14]

This essay does not have to contend that all possible uses of nuclear weapons would be illegal—even the International Court of Justice's advisory opinion declined to go that far. But surely at least some potential applications of the ultimate weapon would be violative of fundamental, universal codes.

The irreconcilable yin-yang of military law in this area consists of two somewhat conflicting propositions. On the one hand, military service members are obligated to carry out all lawful orders promptly, thoroughly, and without question. Good military order and discipline often require rote adherence to orders from superiors during peacetime and war, even when they impose considerable costs to self and others. The military structure is not a democracy, and deployment of nuclear weapons could entail the apex case of a requirement for unblinking obedience and speed.

On the other hand, a service member is also obligated—by international law and by the domestic US Uniform Code of Military Justice—to disobey a manifestly illegal order. Since the Nuremberg tribunals for Nazi war criminals, it has been universally accepted that "I was just following orders" is not an admissible defense, and a measure of reflective judgment is required. Soldiers are not steeped in constitutional law, but they are accountable. It is not civil disobedience or conscientious objection to refuse a patently illegal order; it is actually loyal adherence to a supervening legal responsibility.[15]

How is a service member to reconcile these competing imperatives? There can be no generic answer to that excruciating choice; it must be a case-by-case response to an impossible situation. As Gen. John Hyten, then leading the US Strategic Command, put it, military leaders must perpetually contemplate these awful responsibilities, but the bottom line is clear: an officer must resist an illegal order to employ nuclear weapons, because "if you execute an unlawful order, you will go to jail."[16]

A similar burden can fall upon civilians, especially those in senior governmental positions, whose oath of office ("to defend the Constitution") should compel them not to be complicit in a manifestly illegal order to employ nuclear weapons in violation of clear international or domestic law. Of course, any such true conflict would be exceedingly rare. A presidential instruction to use a nuclear weapon would ordinarily be entitled to a presumption of regularity; after all, the president may be uniquely aware of factual circumstances that would make reliance on the ultimate weapon legitimate. A lawful order, including one that was "merely" unwise or offensive to the recipient's personal moral code, must be obeyed. Still, an inescapable burden reposes with all subordinate officials: they shall not carry out a manifestly illegal order.[17]

Conclusion

This short essay can only raise, not resolve, these legal puzzles, and we can hope that they remain merely hypothetical. But the commitment to the rule of law, both domestic and international, means that these riddles do not lie wholly within the realm of policy, strategy, or ethics. The faulty arithmetic of law is relevant, too.

Notes

The author is Scott K. Ginsberg Professor of Law at the Georgetown University Law Center. The views expressed in this manuscript are those of the author and do not necessarily reflect the official policy or position of the Department of Defense or the US government.

1. Treaty on the Non-Proliferation of Nuclear Weapons, opened for signature July 1, 1968, 21 U.S.T. 483, 729 U.N.T.S. 161.
2. US Constitution, article VI, clause 2.
3. India, North Korea, and Pakistan have each overtly conducted explosive tests of nuclear weapons and proclaimed their status as possessors of nuclear weapons, while Israel is generally acknowledged as owning nuclear weapons but has maintained a posture of neither confirming nor denying

possession of them, and it is the policy of the United States to support that ambiguity. See Arms Control Association, "Nuclear Weapons: Who Has What at a Glance," June 2018; and David S. Jonas, "Variations on Non-Nuclear: May the 'Final Four' Join the Nuclear Nonproliferation Treaty as Non-Nuclear Weapon States While Retaining Their Nuclear Weapons?," *Michigan State Law Review* (2005): 417.
4. Elizabeth J. Shafer, "Good Faith Negotiation, the Nuclear Disarmament Obligation of Article VI of the NPT, and Return to the International Court of Justice," presented at the international seminar "Abolition of Nuclear Weapons, War and Armed Forces," sponsored by the University of Costa Rica Faculty of Law and the International Association of Lawyers Against Nuclear Arms, January 26, 2008, San Jose, Costa Rica; Steven Reinhold, "Good Faith in International Law," *UCL Journal of Law and Jurisprudence* (2013): 40; and Martin A. Rogoff, "The Obligation to Negotiate in International Law: Rules and Realities," *Michigan Journal of International Law* (1994): 141.
5. International Court of Justice, "Legality of the Threat or Use of Nuclear Weapons," Advisory Opinion, I.C.J. Reports 1996, 226, 263, para. 99.
6. Treaty between the United States of America and the Russian Federation on the Measures for Further Reduction and Limitation of Strategic Offensive Arms, signed April 8, 2010.
7. Treaty on the Prohibition of Nuclear Weapons, opened for signature 2017, entered in force 2021.
8. *Marbury v. Madison*, 5 US 137 (1803); *Missouri v. Holland*, 252 US 416 (1920); and *Reid v. Covert*, 354 US 1 (1957).
9. *The Paquete Habana; The Lola*, 175 US 677, 700 (1900).
10. US Constitution, Article II, section 3. See Edward T. Swaine, "Taking Care of Treaties," 108 *Columbia Law Review*, no. 2 (2008): 331.
11. If a treaty is non–self-executing, then it does not by itself provide an immediately actionable rule of decision for a US court but is nonetheless binding as international and domestic law. See Duncan B. Hollis and Carlos M. Vazquez, "Treaty Self-Execution as 'Foreign' Foreign Relations Law," in *Oxford Handbook of Comparative Foreign Relations Law*, ed. Curtis A. Bradley, 467–84 (New York: Oxford University Press, 2019); and Stephen P. Mulligan, "International Law and Agreements: Their Effect upon U.S. Law," Congressional Research Service, Report 7-5700, RL32528, September 19, 2018, 15-17.
12. Treaty on the Non-Proliferation of Nuclear Weapons, Articles VIII and X.1.
13. Charlie Dunlap, "Have Presidents Ever Given the Military Illegal Orders?," *Lawfire* (Duke University blog post), March 10, 2016; and James E. Baker, "Obedience to Orders, Lawful Orders and the Military's Constitutional Compact," Just Security Good Governance Paper No. 21, November 2, 2020.

14. Burkhard Bleul, "The Nuclear Question: Pious Hopes and Real Opportunities," *Ethics and Armed Forces: Controversies in Military Ethics and Security Policy*, no. 1 (2020): 85–89.
15. Gary D. Solis, *The Law of Armed Conflict: International Humanitarian Law in War*, 2nd ed. (Cambridge: Cambridge University Press, 2016), 373–416; *Manual for Courts-Martial United States*, Part IV ¶14 b(2)(a)(i) (2012 ed.).
16. Reuters, "U.S. Nuclear General Says Would Resist 'Illegal' Trump Strike Order," November 18, 2017.
17. Anthony J. Colangelo, "The Duty to Disobey Illegal Nuclear Strike Orders," *Harvard National Security Journal* 9 (2018): 84–120; Mary B. DeRosa and Ashley Nicolas, "The President and Nuclear Weapons: Authorities, Limits, and Process," Nuclear Threat Initiative Paper, December 2019; Taylor Griffin, "Are There Legal Grounds to Disobey a Presidential Order to Launch a Nuclear Weapon?," Roughly Explained, August 9, 2017; Pauline Shanks Kaurin, "Professional Disobedience: Loyalty and the Military," The Strategy Bridge, August 8, 2017; Peter Feaver, "Will the Military Obey President Trump's Orders?," *Foreign Policy*, February 29, 2016; Rebeccah Heinrichs, "Trump, National Command Authority, and Lawful Orders," RealClearDefense, November 27, 2017; Hitomi Takemura, "Disobeying Manifestly Illegal Orders," *Peace Review* 18, no. 4 (2006): 533; and Christopher Fonzone, "What the Military Law of Obedience Does (and Doesn't) Do," American Constitution Society Issue Brief, March 2018.

10

Abolition in the Context of General Disarmament

PIERCE S. CORDEN

The nuclear weapon introduced into the world a new way to cause destruction. It used the energy released by the fission of atoms, notably the 235 isotope of uranium and the 239 isotope of plutonium, and the fusion of atoms, notably the 2 and 3 isotopes of hydrogen, deuterium, and tritium. The energy releases by weapons utilizing the fission and fusion of atoms are, in practice, some thousands to millions of times greater than those from the explosion of weapons utilizing chemical reactions. The explosion of a nuclear weapon also releases radioactivity, which can be dispersed far beyond the point of detonation. Thus, nuclear weapons are justifiably considered a weapon of mass destruction, defined as such by the United Nations (UN) in 1948 along with biological, chemical, and radiological weapons.[1]

Since nuclear weapons were twice used in war in 1945 at the conclusion of World War II, there have been many test explosions of such weapons, and currently they have been incorporated into the arsenals of up to nine states. The total warhead number reached a peak in the mid-1980s of some seventy thousand. The total number is now thought to be around fifteen thousand.[2] In some cases, the weapons are held in bilateral or trilateral conflicting situations: Pakistan, China, and India; North Korea and the United States; and the Russian Federation, the United States, and China. In a conflict between the North Atlantic Treaty Organization (NATO) and Russia, the nuclear weapons of the United Kingdom and France would be relevant. Israel, which maintains an ambiguous stance, acts in ways to deny nuclear weapons to other states in the region.

The NATO situation perhaps best illustrates the linkage between nuclear weapons and conventional weapons. At the outset, NATO considered its situation vis-à-vis the Soviet Union and the Warsaw Pact one of conventional inferiority and believed that Western nuclear weapons served as a counter. Today, the Russian Federation appears to consider that it is at a disadvantage in the conventional balance with the West. And the conventional weapon agreements developed in the 1980s, when the situation was still bloc to bloc, have not been modified to address the current situation whereby NATO has expanded to the east, Byelorussia seems oriented toward Moscow, and Ukraine, Moldova, and Georgia are caught in the middle.[3]

Accordingly, the interlinking of nuclear weapons, embodied in the doctrinal notion of "extended deterrence," and of conventional weapons is an important factor in pursuing the elimination of nuclear weapons. This linkage has been recognized for decades, with efforts at the end of the 1950s and early 1960s dedicated to dealing with not just the global security threats posed by the new category of nuclear weapons but also conventional weapons within the context of general and complete disarmament. These efforts extended as far as the publication by the United States of documents, including provisions to be agreed on, that would codify general and complete disarmament.[4]

The international conflicts of that time overtook all such efforts at general and complete disarmament, and conventional arms control did not figure prominently in disarmament efforts for more than a decade and then principally in the framework of the East-West conflict. NATO and Warsaw Pact states initiated the mutual and balanced force reduction negotiations in 1973 that, although they did not result in an agreement, paved the way for the more successful negotiation of the Treaty on Conventional Armed Forces in Europe, signed at the Paris conference in 1991. During that same period parallel efforts were devoted to the development of confidence- and security-building measures, culminating in the Vienna Document embodying a range of such measures, adopted at that same Paris conference.[5]

Early efforts to cap and reverse the nuclear arms competition, primarily between the Soviet Union and the United States, resulted in a number of agreements directed mostly at nuclear weapons, including the 1959 Antarctic Treaty (which also prohibits conventional weapons on that continent); the 1963 Limited (or Partial) Test Ban Treaty prohibiting nuclear tests in the atmosphere, underwater, or in outer space; and the 1967 Outer Space Treaty prohibiting the installation of nuclear weapons in outer space and providing that the moon and other celestial bodies shall be used exclusively for peaceful purposes. The 1967 treaty has not been interpreted to preclude military use of outer space for communications, navigation, and intelligence purposes. The Seabed Treaty of 1972 prohibits nuclear weapons in that environment.

The signing of the Nuclear Non-Proliferation Treaty (NPT) in 1968 was the culmination of these initial efforts for nuclear arms control. It defines the nuclear weapon states as the five that had then tested nuclear weapons—the United States, the Soviet Union, the United Kingdom, France, and China—and provides that all other parties to the NPT, of which there are now 186, are non–nuclear weapon states. The NPT provides for substantial verification of the non–nuclear weapon states to ensure that they do not acquire nuclear weapons. These states accept safeguards on their peaceful nuclear programs implemented by the International Atomic Energy Agency. There are no provisions in the treaty requiring verification of the military programs or actions of the nuclear weapon states, although at least the United States has voluntarily placed some of its peaceful nuclear facilities under safeguards similar to those accepted by the non–nuclear weapon states. On the other hand, fissile materials that can be used in the production of nuclear weapons can be taken out of safeguards by both nuclear weapon states and non–nuclear weapon states to be put to nonweapon nuclear use as fuel for naval nuclear reactors powering ships: aircraft carriers, submarines, icebreakers, and other categories. This is a specific illustration of the overlap between military capabilities not considered to constitute nuclear weapons but heavily involved with the constituent material of nuclear weapons that will need to have careful consideration in agreeing to arrangements abolishing nuclear weapons.

The NPT famously contains Article VI, which makes explicit the linkage between the process of eliminating nuclear weapons and the larger process of reducing if not eliminating the military capabilities of states within the international system constituting the UN: "Each of the Parties to the Treaty undertakes to pursue negotiations in good faith on effective measures relating to cessation of the nuclear arms race at an early date and to nuclear disarmament, and on a treaty on general and complete disarmament under strict and effective international control."[6]

While not often cited, the preamble to the NPT also makes reference to general and complete disarmament and does so in a way that places the objective within the larger framework of the UN. The concluding paragraphs of the preamble read as follows:

> Desiring to further the easing of international tension and the strengthening of trust between States in order to facilitate the cessation of the manufacture of nuclear weapons, the liquidation of all their existing stockpiles, and the elimination from national arsenals of nuclear weapons and the means of their delivery pursuant to a Treaty on general and complete disarmament under strict and effective international control.
>
> Recalling that, in accordance with the Charter of the United Nations, States must refrain in their international relations from the threat or use of force against the territorial integrity or political independence of any State, or in any other manner inconsistent with the Purposes of the United Nations, and that the establishment and maintenance of international peace and security are to be promoted with the least diversion for armaments of the world's human and economic resources.[7]

It is noteworthy that the first of these paragraphs explicitly addresses the means of delivering a nuclear weapon to a target. The subsequent efforts to reduce the role of nuclear weapons has focused in great measure on limiting and reducing delivery systems, ballistic missiles and aircraft being the most relevant of these.

However, four states that have tested nuclear weapons or are widely considered to possess such weapons are not party to the NPT: India, Pakistan, Israel, and North Korea. It seems clear that all of these states will need to become involved not just in the elimination of nuclear arsenals; they will also need to address security concerns posed by conventional weapons as well as by other types of weapons of mass destruction. The ongoing conflicts between India and Pakistan, the chemical and possible biological weapons of North Korea, and the tensions in the Middle East posed by the several conflicts there, including the sad events involving the use of chemical weapons in Syria and the Israeli–Iranian and wider Israeli–Middle Eastern impasses, provide ample evidence of this necessity.

The subsequent Treaty on the Prohibition of Nuclear Weapons was opened for signature in 2017 following a rapid negotiation process earlier that year. In its preamble, the treaty establishes links to the objectives of broader disarmament and the preeminent role of the UN in seeking nonmilitary solutions to conflict in two preambular paragraphs. The first links the treaty to the "full" implementation of the NPT, thus to include the obligations in its Article VI to nuclear and general and complete disarmament:

> *Reaffirming also* that the full and effective implementation of the Treaty on the Non-Proliferation of Nuclear Weapons, which serves as the cornerstone of the nuclear disarmament and non-proliferation regime, has a vital role to play in promoting international peace and security.[8]
>
> *Recalling* that, in accordance with the Charter of the United Nations, States must refrain in their international relations from the threat or use of force against the territorial integrity or political independence of any State, or in any other manner inconsistent with the Purposes of the United Nations, and that the establishment and maintenance of international peace and security are to be promoted with the list diversion for armaments of the world's human and economic resources.[9]

The Holy See has recognized the broader context of disarmament that must be addressed in the process of eliminating nuclear weapons. In October 2016 the UN Office of Disarmament Affairs released a report, "Rethinking General and Complete Disarmament in the 21st Century," and the Holy See's UN Permanent Observer Mission released a commentary on the report, "Remarks at Side Event: Rethinking General and Complete Disarmament in the 21st Century, New York, 27 October 2016."[10]

The Permanent Observer Mission's paper cited the encyclical of Pope John XXIII, *Pacem in terris*, issued shortly after the Cuban Missile Crisis. The encyclical puts the elimination of nuclear weapons in the broader context of disarmament: "the stockpiles which exist in various quantities should be reduced equally and simultaneously by the parties concerned; that nuclear weapons should be banned, and finally that all come to an agreement on a fitting program of disarmament, employing mutual and effective controls." Pope John had in mind an even broader framework than that envisioned by the UN Charter: "the fundamental principle on which our present peace depends must be replaced by another, which declares that the true and solid peace of nations consists not in quantity of arms but in mutual trust alone."[11] Regardless of the aspirations embodied in mutual trust alone, the more immediate tasks provide a context for nuclear and general and complete disarmament strikingly similar to that of Article VI of the NPT.[12]

Pope Francis has continued to stress the importance of addressing both nuclear disarmament and the larger context of the threats to international peace and security arising from conventional weapons, to include the trade—licit and illicit—in conventional weapons feeding contemporary conflicts. The Permanent Observer Mission's paper cited Pope Francis's address to the US Congress in September 2015 as well as his address to the UN General Assembly later that month. In Washington the pope said,

> Being at the service of dialogue and peace also means being truly determined to minimize and, in the long term, to end the many armed conflicts throughout our world. Here we have to ask ourselves: Why are deadly weapons being sold to those who plan to inflict untold suffering on individuals and society? Sadly, the answer, as we all know, is simply for money: money that is drenched in blood, often innocent blood. In the face of this shameful and culpable silence, it is our duty to confront the problems and to stop the arms trade.[13]

In view of the reemergence of rivalries among the great powers, most if not all nuclear armed and some of which rely on other states for their weapons, stopping the arms trade is one important component of proceeding to and achieving general and complete disarmament.

In his remarks to the UN General Assembly, Pope Francis cited the role of the UN Charter, arguing that "war is the negation of all rights and a dramatic assault on the environment. If we want true integral human development for all, we must work tirelessly to avoid war between nations and peoples."[14] These thoughts sum up war in the twenty-first-century world at the interstate level or between national groups as the antithesis of human well-being, including the need to situate our lives in a nurtured environment.

The Permanent Observer Mission's statement cites explicitly the linkage between the elimination of nuclear weapons and steps leading to general and complete disarmament of chemical, biological, radiological, and conventional weapons. Added to this broad appraisal should be technologies that are emerging as types of weapons that threaten large-scale disruption to societies, such as the malicious interruption of electronic communications, the control of vital systems such as electricity generation and distribution, and the command and control of nuclear weapons themselves. The control of not only nuclear weapons but also nonnuclear weapons and technologies will require internationally agreed measures to ensure that agreements are being respected. Bodies such as the Organization for the Prohibition of Chemical Weapons, the International Atomic Energy Agency, and the Provisional Technical Secretariat of the Comprehensive Nuclear-Test-Ban Treaty illustrate how monitoring and verification can be implemented.

To conclude, the elimination of nuclear weapons will necessarily require substantial changes in the global array of nonnuclear weaponry and technologies. In a nuclear weapon–free world, doctrines for the use of nuclear weapons that include responses to the use of other mass destruction weapons against the nuclear weapon state or its allies and doctrines that envision a role for nuclear weapons if the very existence of a state is threatened will of necessity need to be replaced with a global security architecture in which nonnuclear forces do not pose such threats to other states. Similar issues will need to be resolved not only in the East-West context but also in South Asia, Northeast Asia, and the Middle East.

The new architecture will also of necessity embody greatly reduced numbers of weapons and greatly modified roles for armed forces possessed by states. Whether this architecture is feasible within the present international structure of the UN, the Security Council in particular, will be a challenge. Perhaps the steps that have been taken since the end of World War II, a number of which have been cited above and also include the Convention on Conventional Weapons, the Arms Trade Treaty, and the Ottawa Convention prohibiting antipersonnel land mines, can provide some optimism that more general disarmament is not unrealistic.

Notes

1. UN Commission for Conventional Armaments, resolution adopted at its thirteenth meeting, August 12, 1948, S/c.3/32/Rev. 1, 2.

2. Federation of American Scientists, "Status of World Nuclear Forces," September 2020, https://fas.org/issues/nuclear-weapons/status-world-nuclear-forces/.
3. Richard Sokolsky, "The New NATO-Russia Military Balance: Implications for European Security," Carnegie Endowment, 2017, https://carnegieendowment.org/files/3-8-17_Richard_Sokolsky_Russia_Military_Balance.pdf.
4. Program for general and complete disarmament under effective international control submitted by the delegation of the United States of America to the Ten Nation Committee on Disarmament, June 27, 1960, TCND/7. See also the United States Program for General and Complete Disarmament in a Peaceful World, Department of State publication 7277, Disarmament Series 5, released September 1961.
5. See revised Vienna Document 2011—Confidence- and Security-Building Measures, https://2009-2017.state.gov/t/avc/cca/c43837.htm.
6. United Nations, Office for Disarmament Affairs, "Treaty on the Non-Proliferation of Nuclear Weapons," opened for signature 1968, entered into force 1970.
7. United Nations.
8. United Nations, Office for Disarmament Affairs, "Treaty on the Prohibition of Nuclear Weapons," opened for signature 2017, entered into force 2021.
9. United Nations.
10. United Nations, Office for Disarmament Affairs, UNODA Occasional Papers No. 28, October 2016; and Permanent Observer Mission of the Holy See to the United Nations, "Week in Review," November 4, 2016. The Nuncio followed up with a statement in the First Committee on general and complete disarmament, October 16, 2017.
11. Pope John XXIII, *Pacem in terris*.
12. See also Pope John XXIII, *Gaudium et spes*, nos. 77–83.
13. Pope Francis, address to the US Congress, September 24, 2015.
14. Pope Francis, address to the UN General Assembly, September 25, 2015. The pope has continued to address the inability of war, including the role of nuclear deterrence, to enable a lasting future for humanity. See Pope Francis, *Fratelli tutti*, nos. 255–62.

11

New Models

Building Capacities for Nuclear Cooperation

RICHARD A. LOVE

Work on arms control, disarmament, and nonproliferation has stalled. The United States has pulled out of the Intermediate-Range Nuclear Forces Treaty, and both the United States and Russia have terminated the Open Skies Treaty. They have, however, agreed to extend the New START treaty, and at their June 16, 2021, meeting in Geneva, Presidents Joe Biden and Vladimir Putin agreed to explore wide-ranging talks on strategic stability, which will address cybersecurity as well as nuclear disarmament. Yet bilateral, formal treaties between the United States and Russia are not the only means to advance arms control and nonproliferation. Another option involves multilateral nonproliferation, arms control, and disarmament activities. The Proliferation Security Initiative (PSI) offers one model for forward movement.[1]

The Proliferation Security Initiative: An Alternative to Traditional Arms-Control Models

The PSI is a different model for approaching arms control and nonproliferation. It is not a traditional arms control treaty. The PSI is a growing coalition of like-minded countries that plan, exercise, and execute interdiction operations aimed at disrupting the traffic in materials and technologies involving missiles and weapons of mass destruction and missiles (WMD).

When George W. Bush became president in 2001, his administration, in action and declaratory policy, clearly favored more unilateral efforts internationally over what the president and adviser John Bolton viewed as slow, least–common denominator international compacts pursued through traditional treaties and agreements through, for example, the United Nations (UN) or other binding international forums. The PSI was initiated by a US president who was suspicious of traditional arms control, disarmament, and nonproliferation treaties and was not a fan of multilateral conventions or the UN. So, why did a president so critical of multilateralism initiate a multilateral approach to countering WMD?

The concept for the PSI was largely developed in response to concern over the growing threat of nuclear proliferation as highlighted by the *So San* interdiction incident in 2002. In December 2002, US intelligence assets tracked an unflagged vessel, the *So San*, as it departed North Korea toward an unknown destination; it was assumed to be bound for the Middle East. Acting on a request from the United States, Spanish special operations forces, staged from the Spanish frigate *Navarro*, intercepted and boarded the *So San*. While searchers found a great deal of cement, the declared cargo, they also discovered nonmanifested Scud-B missiles, warheads, and fuel oxidizer. The Bush administration, facing protests from North Korea and Yemen, conceded that the weapons and their components were the legally acquired property of the Yemeni government. Indeed, during this time the administration complimented Yemen for being a staunch ally in the global war on terror. Subsequently, Spanish forces released the *So San* to deliver its cargo to Yemen, convincing the Bush administration that more work was needed in the interest of nonproliferation. As Bush reportedly said to his national security team at the National Security Council, "Tell me again, why exactly was this a good idea?"

The National Security Council staff subsequently put together a "tiger team," a small group of national security experts on WMD proliferation, to investigate the *So San* case.[2] The team delivered a number of key findings, asserting that views on the legality of maritime interdiction on the high seas were inconsistent not only across states and with other international actors such as the UN but even within the United States. These inconsistencies were also between departments (as when the US State Department disagreed with the Department of Defense) and even within departments (e.g., within the Department of Defense, the legal interpretations of the Joint Chiefs of Staff differed from those of the Office of the Secretary of Defense). The team also concluded, perhaps even more strikingly, that few states had criminalized activities such as WMD transiting their domestic waters. For a vast majority of states, trafficking in WMD on, through, or over their sovereign territory was not a criminal offense. They concluded that the status quo was insufficient to meet the current WMD proliferation threat. A new initiative was needed, a new concept in proliferation prevention in which taking action operationally was encouraged, and cooperation and information sharing would be promoted. States would demonstrate resolve by openly testing interdiction concepts at sea, on land, and even in the air domain through exercises. Equally important, the new initiative included experts from the legal and operational communities, who would address interdiction concepts and develop a clearer and common understanding of interdiction, interception, and the legal framework for operational proliferation prevention.

Applying lessons learned from the embarrassing *So San* incident, the Bush administration worked with a cadre of other countries to develop and implement the PSI as a multilateral effort, based on countries accepting a statement of interdiction principles. At a meeting in Krakow, Poland, in May 2003, eleven states—Australia, France, Germany, Italy, Japan, the Netherlands, Poland, Portugal, Spain, the United Kingdom, and the United States—politically committed at the head-of-state level to take more action for proliferation prevention and to work together to develop practical measures to interdict WMD shipments and their delivery systems at sea, in the air, and on land.

In subsequent meetings the Bush administration developed a set of general principles. These principles, created within the framework of existing international and state-based agreements and laws, enable partner states to disrupt and interdict the illegal proliferation of WMD. The principles themselves are not overly long and serve as common ground for interdiction.[3] They emphasize that the PSI is an activity, not an organization; that political commitment to the principles is required to join the PSI; and that there would not be negotiated memberships because the PSI's purpose is for states to act and be proactive. Countries that commit themselves to the PSI are "endorsers" not members, as there is not a treaty to formally ratify or regime to which the PSI countries belong. The "Statement of Interdiction Principles" emphasizes self-policing by states endorsing the PSI, especially over ships that are flagged in their states, and encourages the practice of flag states to grant permission to other states to conduct searches and to expand participation in the

PSI in order to cut the number of available proliferation avenues, thus imposing additional costs and risks to proliferators:

> PSI participants are committed to the following interdiction principles to establish a more coordinated and effective basis through which to impede and stop shipments of WMDs, delivery systems, and related materials flowing to and from states and non-state actors of proliferation concern, consistent with national legal authorities and relevant international law and frameworks, including the UN Security Council. They call on all states concerned with this threat to international peace and security to join in similarly committing to:
>
> 1. Undertake effective measures, either alone or in concert with other states, for interdicting the transfer or transport of WMD, their delivery systems, and related materials to and from states and non-state actors of proliferation concern....
> 2. Adopt streamlined procedures for rapid exchange of relevant information concerning suspected proliferation activity, protecting the confidential character of classified information provided by other states as part of this initiative, dedicate appropriate resources and efforts to interdiction operations and capabilities, and maximize coordination among participants in interdiction efforts.
> 3. Review and work to strengthen their relevant national legal authorities where necessary to accomplish these objectives, and work to strengthen when necessary relevant international laws and frameworks in appropriate ways to support these commitments.
> 4. Take specific actions in support of interdiction efforts regarding cargoes of WMD, their delivery systems, or related materials, to the extent their national legal authorities permit and consistent with their obligations under international law and frameworks, to include:
>   a. Not to transport or assist in the transport of any such cargoes to or from states or non-state actors of proliferation concern, and not to allow any persons subject to their jurisdiction to do so.
>   b. At their own initiative, or at the request and good cause shown by another state, to take action to board and search any vessel

flying their flag in their internal waters or territorial seas, or areas beyond the territorial seas of any other state, that is reasonably suspected of transporting such cargoes to or from states or non-state actors of proliferation concerns, and to seize such cargoes that are identified.

c. To seriously consider providing consent under the appropriate circumstances to the boarding and searching of its own flag vessels by other states, and to the seizure of such WMD-related cargoes in such vessels that may be identified by such states.

d. To take appropriate actions to (1) stop and/or search in their internal waters, territorial seas, or contiguous zones (when declared) vessels that are reasonably suspected of carrying such cargoes to or from states or non-state actors of proliferation concern and to seize such cargoes that are identified; and (2) enforce conditions on vessels entering or leaving their ports, internal waters, or territorial seas that are reasonably suspected of carrying such cargoes, such as requiring that such vessels be subject to boarding, search, and seizure of such cargoes prior to entry.

e. At their own initiative or upon the request and good cause shown by another state, to (a) require aircraft that are reasonably suspected of carrying such cargoes to or from states or non-state actors of proliferation concern and that are transiting their airspace to land for inspection and seize any such cargoes that are identified; and/or (b) deny aircraft reasonably suspected of carrying such cargoes transit rights through their airspace in advance of such flights.

f. If their ports, airfields, or other facilities are used as transshipment points for shipment of such cargoes to or from states or non-state actors of proliferation concern, to inspect vessels, aircraft, or other modes of transport reasonably suspected of carrying such cargoes, and to seize such cargoes that are identified.[4]

There has been demand for the types of training and capacity building exercises undertaken by PSI endorsing states. The original 11 PSI partners have grown to a group of 107 participating and supporting states.[5]

Challenges of the PSI

There are, however, some concerns regarding the PSI approach to countering WMD. The PSI is a novel departure from traditional approaches to proliferation prevention in many aspects. It was designed not to seek universal membership but instead to remain a loosely organized "activity," not organized under the UN framework or other international governing authority. The PSI does not have a centralized governing body or a secretariat to implement political decisions, nor does it have a dedicated cadre of experts who can leverage "institutional knowledge" for future events. The PSI is intentionally represented as a "political" commitment rather than a legal one, and as such it does not require any compellence actions under international law. This allows each state to take action only when deemed politically justified according to each endorsing state's interpretations of its own domestic and international laws and to take action independently or in small associations. Thus, there are no "whole of PSI" proliferation prevention tactical or operationally focused actions generally, nor are there specific WMD PSI-mandated interdictions.

Because there is no PSI organization per se, no headquarters, and no PSI staff located in Geneva or The Hague to process requests for information or verify compliance, the PSI lacks institutional memory.[6] Instead, it works due to the high-level political commitment of its member states, coupled with having the operational capacity to interdict when and where necessary. But commitment may wane with changes in administration and leadership without an international organization to continue momentum. Each interdiction opportunity is administered on a case-by-case basis predicated on the unique characteristics of the specific events as they unfold. Not all member states are involved in each operation, but it is assumed that those that can assist will. The purpose here is to foster a bias for action whereby states are predisposed to work together to stop the illegal transfer of WMD technology, materials, components, and knowledge.

The downside of such a decentralized approach is that no one is in charge, and interdiction is left to the discretion of endorsing states. This has undermined efforts to reach out to private industry and engage the shipping industry in public-private partnerships to combat WMD proliferation.[7] PSI industry outreach has yielded less than what was hoped for. Since there is no single PSI—no standing group, organization, body, or even board for industry to engage with—industry can quite rightfully ask who speaks for it, who can make commitments, who adjudicates differences, and what force or authority a political commitment to a statement of principles actually has.

Also, without a PSI body, there is no single unit keeping score, cataloging information on PSI interdictions, successes, failures, and lessons learned. While endorsing countries may do this for their own activities, no one gathers the information for all, and no country has access to the information of others. Since PSI participation is voluntary and nonbinding, its sustainability is a concern.

Benefits of the PSI

The PSI breaks with proliferation prevention efforts of the past and creates a flexible and dynamic framework that can quickly respond to a fast-moving WMD proliferation crisis.[8] Since the PSI is an activity rather than an organization, the result is a group of like-minded states that agree to be bound by certain principles.[9] They include a commitment to interdict transfers to and from states and nonstate actors of proliferation to the extent of their capabilities. They also include legal authorities to develop internal and cooperative procedures to facilitate the exchange of proliferation-related information with other countries. Additionally, states commit to strengthening their national legal authorities to facilitate interdiction and to take specific action in support of interdiction efforts.

By design, the PSI does not seek universality. It is not governed by a secretariat and does not have a large, fixed staff and is not guided by the decisions of an executive board. The PSI brings the best of what an endorsing state can offer and requires no more. The barriers to entry are low. A participant makes a political commitment to do more under the PSI concept and then it endorses a set of interdiction principles.[10] While all states were invited to both join the PSI and agree to a statement of principles, the PSI acknowledges that not all states will agree to do so. That suited the eleven founding endorsees just fine, since active involvement was viewed as more important than merely signing up as many as possible.

The PSI is operationally focused. Its countries regularly engage in international interdiction training exercises, and its partners clearly improved their capabilities to interdict suspect shipments. Some of these improvements, operational in nature, depended on security forces and law enforcement officials improving their ability to better identify, inspect, and stop materials that could be used in dangerous weapons development programs. This learning process was facilitated by regular interactions among PSI partners in the military, legal, law enforcement, information, and diplomatic communities who gathered to refine operational concepts to conduct interdictions. The robust exercise program that formed one of the foundational cornerstones of the PSI also improved operational activities. Indeed, the PSI exercise program was and is one of the only global, interagency, and multinational exercise programs that allow countries to practice applying the range of interdiction tools, often in coordination with partner countries where nonendorsing states can participate as observers.[11]

The PSI has been successful in persuading signatories to work domestically to strengthen laws and cooperatively to stop the trafficking of WMD-related material and technology to and from states and organizations that present a proliferation risk. PSI partner states commit to interdiction efforts using shared intelligence, timely communication, and multilateral action.

This process was evident in, for example, the interception of the ship BBC *China*. The United States shared with Germany and Italy intelligence developed from its operations targeting the A. Q. Khan network. This intelligence identified the likelihood that a Malaysian company was shipping nuclear technology to Libya via Dubai aboard a German-registered vessel. Acting on that intelligence and with operational assistance from the US Navy, German and Italian officials coordinated the diversion of the ship to Italy. This operation represents the type of multilateral interdiction effort laid out in the PSI. PSI advocates point to the fact that Muammar Qadhafi did not make any substantial public moves to initiate WMD rollback until after the interception of BBC *China* and its cargo of centrifuge components.

As the PSI continues to expand its membership and its activities, it not only complicates the efforts of proliferators but also strengthens nonproliferation norms, providing a concrete means of security cooperation with allies and friends and demonstrating that coordinated actions among like-minded states can be achieved without having to create new organizations or more formalized bureaucracies.

Progress along several fronts has established the PSI global network of partnerships. Countries have committed to a statement of interdiction principles. Guidelines and processes are in place for the collection, analysis, and sharing of intelligence. New ship-boarding agreements are extending available legal authorities. Operational experts from participating states meet regularly to develop improved intelligence, military, and law enforcement capabilities to support interdiction activities. These capabilities are being refined in a robust exercise program.

The PSI as a Model for Today

Today when traditional arms control, disarmament, and nonproliferation negotiations are not advancing, the multilateral, cooperative activities of the PSI present an alternative model.

The Trump administration was not committed to arms control, disarmament, and nonproliferation efforts. It pulled out of landmark treaties, such as the Intermediate-Range Nuclear Forces Treaty. And the administration was building new nuclear weapons. Traditional models of arms control, disarmament, and nonproliferation are not working today.

But another lane is open. The Trump administration was committed to building upon the success of the PSI framework and developing ways to strengthen and continue the activity. The strong statement in January 2018 committing the PSI states of the Operational Experts Group to support UN Security Council Resolutions 2375 and 2397 demonstrate this commitment.[12] The goal is to extend both the functional reach of the PSI framework and the breadth of international participation. In tandem with other elements of the global nonproliferation agenda, the solid diplomatic and operational foundation of the PSI provides a basis for making progress in strengthening proliferation prevention efforts.

Notes

1. This chapter is drawn from a larger book manuscript, Dr. Richard Love, *The Proliferation Security Initiative: A New and Effective Model for Proliferation Prevention.*

2. Susan J. Koch, "Proliferation Security Initiative: Origins and Evolution," Occasional Paper 9 (Washington, DC: National Defense University Press, 2012), 6–7.
3. Proliferation Security Initiative, Chairman's Statement at the Third Meeting, Foreign Ministry of France, Third Meeting of the PSI, September 3–4, 2003.
4. The White House, "Statement of Interdiction Principles," a declaration issued by the Proliferation Security Initiative, Paris, September 4, 2003, https://2009-2017.state.gov/t/isn/c27726.htm.
5. "Endorsing States List," Proliferation Security Initiative, February 4, 2019, https://www.psi-online.info/psi-info-en/botschaft/-/2205942.
6. Ian Williams, "Proliferation Security Initiative: Ten Years On," Arms Control Now, May 28, 2013.
7. US Department of State, Office of the Spokesman, "London PSI Meeting Advances Public-Private Partnership to Combat WMD Proliferation," September 26, 2006. The London meeting was the third industry outreach meeting. The first, in August 2004, focused on the container line industry in Copenhagen, Denmark. The second, in September 2005, was concerned with the air cargo industry in Los Angeles, California.
8. Erin Harbaugh, "The Proliferation Security Initiative: Counterproliferation at the Crossroads," *Strategic Insights* 3, no. 7 (July 2004): 2.
9. Foreign Ministry of Poland, "Chairman's Statement at the 1st Anniversary PSI Meeting," Krakow, Poland, May 31–June 1, 2004, US Department of State Archive.
10. See US Department of State, "Remarks of John R. Bolton, Under Secretary for Arms Control and International Security Affairs," Proliferation Security Initiative Meeting, Paris, France, September 4, 2003, where he laid out the statement of interdiction principles.
11. For one perspective on the Australian experience with PSI exercises, see Australian Government, Department of Defence, "Australian Contributions to Foreign Hosted PSI Exercises," http://www.defence.gov.au/psi/other.asp.
12. "Joint Statement from Proliferation Security Initiative (PSI) Partners in Support of United Nations Security Council Resolutions 2375 and 2397 Enforcement," Media Note, US Department of State, January 12, 2018.

12

Nuclear Abolition and Global Human Needs

LAWRENCE J. KORB

The era of significant arms control agreements between the major nuclear powers—the United States and Russia, which between them currently possess 13,300 of the world's 14,465 nuclear weapons—that have reduced the number and cost of nuclear weapons and led some to believe that nuclear weapons, such as chemical and biological weapons, would be abolished is in danger of ending. From the 1963 Limited Test Ban Treaty, which banned nuclear testing in the atmosphere, to the 2011 New START Agreement, between Presidents Barack Obama and Vladimir Putin, which limited the two countries to no more than 1,550 deployed nuclear weapons on no more than 700 deployed delivery vehicles, the major nuclear powers have concluded dozens of bilateral agreements and supported several multilateral arms agreements.

As a result of these agreements, the total number of nuclear weapons on both sides has dropped from about sixty thousand in 1972 to about thirteen thousand today. Moreover, the agreements have provided extremely intrusive inspections to ensure that both parties are living up to the terms of the agreements. These US-Russian arms control treaties have been concluded by both Democratic and Republican presidents as well as Soviet Communist party leaders and Russian presidents. In addition to the arms control agreements, the two major nuclear powers have also made a number of executive agreements designed to avoid provocative actions or mistakes that could lead to a nuclear exchange. These included establishing a hotline in 1963 and signing the Incidents at Sea Agreement in 1972.

In addition to the bilateral agreements, the United Nations has brokered a number of treaties with the majority of the global community to limit the spread and testing of nuclear weapons. These agreements have included the Nuclear Non-Proliferation Treaty of 1968, the Comprehensive Test Ban Treaty of 1996, and the Treaty on the Prohibition of Nuclear Weapons of 2017. Unfortunately, these global treaties have not been ratified by all of the world's leading powers. For example, the US Senate failed to ratify the Comprehensive Test Ban Treaty, and none of the nine nations that currently possess nuclear weapons ratified the 2017 treaty. They did, however, set a global norm that nuclear weapons should never be used again and that nonnuclear states should not develop nuclear weapons. For example, the international community has put significant sanctions in place against countries such as Iran and North Korea for violating the Nuclear Non-Proliferation Treaty.

These bilateral and multilateral treaties have improved global security in a number of important ways. First, they have reduced the number of nuclear weapons possessed by the United States and Russia. Second, the treaties have motivated many countries not to develop their own nuclear weapons in the first place and several nations, such as South Africa and Iran, to actually give up or stop producing these weapons. Third, the treaties have significantly reduced the funding that nations have and continue to spend on these weapons of mass destruction.

An Unraveling Web of Treaties

There are at least four reasons why the era of arms control may be ending. First, US president Joseph Biden and Russian president Vladimir Putin renewed the New START treaty in February 2020 and agreed to begin discussions on strategic stability. The renewal assures both sides of up to eighteen inspections a year of the other's nuclear sites to ensure compliance. Any new agreements will be far more difficult to achieve, however, because of new evasive delivery systems and cyberwarfare technologies. In addition, both sides are interested in bringing other members of the nuclear club, especially China, under any new agreements.

Second, in order to get enough support from Republican members for a two-thirds vote in the Senate necessary to ratify the New START treaty in 2011, President Obama had to agree to undertake a significant modernization program for all three legs of the US nuclear arsenal. This program will not only dramatically increase the targeting and kill capability of US strategic nuclear weapons but will also commit the United States to maintaining New START treaty limits for the foreseeable future. Moreover, it will cost the United States close to $2 trillion over the next thirty years. President Donald Trump compounded the problem by endorsing the nuclear modernization program and also proposing, in his 2017 nuclear posture review, the addition of funds to develop two new tactical nuclear weapons. This will not only add billions of dollars to the cost of the modernization program but also could actually lower the threshold for using nuclear weapons.

Third, in 2002 President George W. Bush unilaterally withdrew the United States from the Anti-Ballistic Missile (ABM) Treaty that was negotiated by President Richard Nixon and General Secretary Leonid Brezhnev in 1972 and limited each side to deploying no more than a single ABM system. President Bush claimed that this step was necessary for the United States to deal with the nuclear threat from the "axis of evil" countries, Iran, Iraq, and North Korea. Moreover, he argued that the Soviet Union, with whom this treaty was negotiated, no longer existed. Both of these reasons were incorrect. Not only did none of the three members have nuclear weapons at that time, but defense against intercontinental ballistic missiles is technologically impossible. By this time the Russians had not only abided by all of the treaties signed by Brezhnev but also assumed the treaty responsibilities of the Soviet Union as a predecessor state. The Russians also believed that ABM technology could be used to undermine their own nuclear deterrence against an attack by NATO's superior conventional forces. Claiming that ABM deployments were necessary to protect Europe from Iranian nuclear attacks, President Bush had compounded the problem by proposing to deploy ballistic missile defenses in Poland and the Czech Republic. While the Obama administration modified the Bush plan somewhat by placing Aegis Ashore missile defense systems in Poland and Romania, it did not placate the Russians.

The Trump administration compounded the problem by unilaterally withdrawing from the Iran Nuclear Accord. Not only were the Iranians actually abiding by the terms of the agreement, but the Russians were also a signatory.

Fourth, after mutual recriminations, in 2019 both the United States and the Russian Federation withdrew from the Intermediate-Range Nuclear Forces Treaty, an agreement that marked the end of the Cold War by reducing tensions between the two powers in Europe.

The Human Costs of Nuclear Modernization

This new era of strategic competition now underway is not only dangerous but also expensive, and it will divert funds from other global needs. Imagine what the approximately $2 trillion that the United States plans to spend modernizing its nuclear arsenal could do to deal with hunger and disease in this country or around the world. As the Second Vatican Council declared, "the arms race is an utterly treacherous trap for humanity, and one which ensnares the poor to an intolerable degree."[1]

Currently, the nine nuclear powers spend over $100 billion a year on nuclear weapons. Since the United States and Russia account for about 75 percent of these expenditures, this number will rise significantly as the two nations undertake their massive nuclear modernization programs. As the International Campaign to Abolish Nuclear Weapons points out, there is no doubt that the production, maintenance and modernization of nuclear forces diverts vast public resources away from such areas as health care, education, climate change, migration, disaster relief, and development assistance. Diverting about half the money spent in nuclear weapons would help the global community meet the UN's 2030 Sustainable Development Goals. Nuclear weapons spending is more than twice the development assistance provided to Africa and equal to the gross domestic product of Bangladesh, a country of about 160 million people.

To reverse this dangerous trend and divert funds to global needs, the United States should immediately begin working on a treaty that will reduce the number of deployed nuclear weapons to no more than one thousand. This is something that was done when previous arms reduction agreements were nearing their expiration dates. In addition, the United States should allow the Russians to inspect the proposed missile defense sites in Poland and Romania to demonstrate that they are not offensive weapons. In return, the United States should ask that we be able to inspect the Russian 9M729 missile, which violates the Intermediate-Range Nuclear Forces Treaty. Finally, the United States should formally adopt a "no first use" policy for these weapons—something it refused to do in the Cold War when the Soviets had superior conventional forces, a situation that no longer exists—and commit itself to eventually joining the 2017 treaty prohibiting the possession of nuclear weapons.

These negotiations should be occasions for the Holy See, other diplomats, and international civil society to make the global fund for development proposed by Pope Francis an integral part of an arms control regime designed for the abolition of nuclear weapons. As he wrote in his 2021 World Day of Peace Message, "What a courageous decision it would be to establish a 'Global Fund' with the money spent on weapons and other military expenditures, in order to permanently eliminate hunger and contribute to the development of the poorest countries."[2] Even as we work to end the danger of nuclear war, we should also take deliberate steps to build a peace that will provide a dignified life for all humanity and sustain conditions for the integrity of creation generations into the future.

Notes

1. Second Vatican Council (1965), *Gaudium et spes: Pastoral Constitution on the Church in the Modern World*, no. 81.
2. Pope Francis, "A Culture of Care as a Path to Peace," 54th World Day of Peace Message, January 1, 2021.

PART IV

Evolution of Just War

13

Nuclear Disarmament

Ethical Challenges at or Near Zero

GERARD F. POWERS

After decades of "utopian" appeals in official Catholic Church statements, nuclear disarmament has gone mainstream. Since the end of the Cold War and especially since 9/11, a chorus of prominent political and military figures has embraced nuclear disarmament as a policy goal. That goal was given added momentum with the 2017 Treaty on the Prohibition of Nuclear Weapons (TPNW), which entered into force in 2021. The TPNW enjoyed strong support from the Holy See and occasioned the most explicit papal condemnation of nuclear deterrence to date.[1]

Pope Francis has given new prominence and clarity to the Holy See's long-standing efforts to delegitimize the nuclear status quo and place the moral imperative of disarmament at the center of the nuclear agenda. Since the end of the Cold War, the Holy See has been increasingly concerned that the nuclear powers have not fully realized the potential nuclear peace dividend. Instead, they have reversed course and embarked on the largest nuclear modernization programs since the early 1980s while dismantling much of the existing arms control regime. In its increasingly urgent calls to abandon deterrence and embrace disarmament, the Holy See provides a critically important moral vision of a possibility that can scarcely be imagined now. But more is needed.

The credibility of that vision will depend on addressing two ethics gaps. The first—the pastoral implications of the pope's prudential judgment that nuclear deterrence is no longer morally acceptable—is covered by other chapters in this volume. I address the second gap: the need to develop an ethic of nuclear disarmament that is as sophisticated as the ethic of nuclear use and deterrence developed during the Cold War.[2]

Two sets of policy issues deserve more attention by Catholic ethicists. The first involves the extent to which current approaches should be adapted to address issues of defense and deterrence at or near zero: disarmament intervention, missile defense, and existential or virtual deterrence. The second considers the extent to which nuclear disarmament requires a paradigm shift toward a system of cooperative security in which nuclear and conventional disarmament proceeds apace and the rights and responsibilities of sovereign states and international institutions are significantly reshaped. The process of nuclear disarmament can and should move with new urgency now, but its ultimate success requires further moral reflection on these and other issues.

Defense and Deterrence in a Time of Disarmament

Many Church statements call for a move beyond nuclear deterrence.[3] But if the world eliminated nuclear weapons, that would not change the need for new forms of deterrence with their fresh moral challenges. As arsenals are reduced to low numbers, states might rely on immoral countervalue (targeting of cities) rather than counterforce (targeting of military assets) strategies to deter the use of nuclear weapons.[4] Moving to zero could make nuclear weapons even more valuable, more usable, and more destabilizing, since keeping a few or being able to reconstitute an arsenal quickly could offer a tremendous strategic advantage.[5] Moreover, the risk of nuclear terrorism by nonstate actors or proliferation by rogue states would be reduced but not eliminated with a global ban.

One answer is to adapt and extend existing approaches to arms control, nonproliferation, and counterproliferation. The first two have been far more effective in limiting the number of states with nuclear weapons than many predicted. The International Atomic Energy Agency and national governments have considerable expertise in cooperative threat reduction, tracking and controlling fissile materials, and verifying compliance with nuclear disarmament agreements. Technological developments should make these and other efforts even more effective. Whether these measures would be able to ensure compliance with global zero involves technical, security, and political questions to which ethics has little to add.

Disarmament Intervention

A counterproliferation strategy that raises challenging moral questions is whether the use of force would be justified to enforce global zero. The 2003 US invasion of Iraq should have been the death of the misbegotten doctrine of preventive war.[6] But some form of the doctrine is likely to gain even greater salience to counter nuclear holdouts or breakouts as the world moves toward zero.[7] Calls for an ethic of "disarmament intervention" could emerge. Unilateral disarmament intervention is not new. It is considered to be illegitimate because it involves the preventive use of force against a potential danger, not defense against actual aggression. Moreover, in cases such as Israel's 1981 attack on Iraq's Osirak nuclear reactor and the 2003 US intervention in Iraq, it involved a double standard, since those using force to prevent nuclear proliferation were nuclear weapon states. If, however, military intervention was in support of wider international efforts to achieve or maintain global nuclear disarmament, the moral calculus would be different at least to the extent that there would no longer be a double standard.[8] Even then, however, disarmament intervention would raise a host of moral concerns.

George Weigel's argument for preventive force exemplifies the problem. He argues for expanding the definition of "defense against aggression" to acknowledge that "in the hands of certain kinds of states, the mere possession of weapons of mass destruction constitutes an aggression—or, at the very least, an aggression-waiting-to-happen."[9] Such a redefinition would be problematic. It would entail a sharp and dangerous departure from existing constraints on just cause, which limit force to defense against actual, not potential, aggression. Moreover, if possession of weapons of mass destruction constituted aggression, what about intent to possess?[10] A doctrine of unilateral disarmament intervention, however well intentioned, would justify force based on highly subjective and speculative judgments about the potential threat posed by the nature and presumed intentions of a government that has or seeks nuclear weapons capabilities. Such an approach would lack the moral certitude necessary to justify force. It would easily lead to what John Courtney Murray called the "dangerous fallacy involved in [the] casting up of desperate alternatives" (i.e., between preventive war and catastrophic nuclear breakout).[11] A doctrine of disarmament intervention would also set a dangerous precedent, undermining international peace and stability. The doctrine might dissuade some countries from pursuing nuclear weapons but might just as likely encourage others to do so.

The more difficult moral question is whether disarmament intervention could be justified if authorized by a reformed (e.g., more representative and without the veto power of the five permanent members, China, France, Russia, the United Kingdom, and the United States) United Nations (UN) Security Council acting under its authority to maintain international peace and security or under an expanded understanding of the responsibility to protect (R2P). Since the TPNW is justified as a response to the "catastrophic humanitarian consequences that would result from any use of nuclear weapons" and the need to respect international humanitarian law, enforcing a ban would be consistent with at least two of the grounds for invoking R2P: preventing war crimes and crimes against humanity.[12] Adapting R2P to serve the humanitarian goal of nuclear disarmament would reinforce the idea that the international community should assist states in meeting their obligations under the TPNW and a follow-on nuclear disarmament treaty. This would prioritize nonmilitary responses when a state is unwilling or unable to disarm. It would also impose highly restrictive procedural and substantive constraints on coercive forms of disarmament intervention. The precautionary principles of proportionality and probability of success, for example, would be calibrated to match a range of potential means of intervention from targeted sanctions to cyber weapons to major military strikes.

Even under such constraints, however, disarmament intervention would not escape many of the problems associated with unilateral preventive force. Even with restrictive constraints, it could threaten the very human rights and international peace and stability that the UN Security Council, R2P, and disarmament are meant to protect. Moreover, as with unilateral intervention, it would privilege relatively few states with sophisticated conventional militaries that could take action, with UN Security Council authorization, against less powerful states; it would not be a tool for dealing with major powers. Finally, it would be fraught with all the moral challenges associated with military intervention. If force were strictly limited to eliminating nuclear weapons capabilities, it might not work or might only temporarily stop a nuclear program. If force were used to change a recalcitrant regime, it would entail all the challenges of occupation and state building that have been evident in Iraq, Libya, Afghanistan, and elsewhere. In short, perhaps a case could be made for disarmament intervention, under UN auspices, in extraordinary cases, but it would not be the morally preferred mode of enforcing global zero.

Missile Defense

Another potentially more constructive strategy to counter nuclear holdouts or cheaters could be shared missile defense, an idea, Jonathan Schell insists, that "is almost certain to be resurrected if and when the idea of abolition is next seriously raised."[13] In launching the Strategic Defense Initiative in 1983, the Reagan administration claimed that it was morally superior to the nuclear status quo because it promised to transcend a deterrence based on mutual assured destruction and, if shared, would make nuclear abolition possible. In a lengthy 1988 report, the United States Catholic Conference opposed the deployment of missile defenses.[14] The bishops concluded that, while the ethic of intention that sought to justify missile defense as a way to transcend deterrence was legitimate, the morality of SDI also depended on an ethic of consequences. They were especially concerned about the negative impact on arms control agreements, in particular the Anti-Ballistic Missile Treaty; that SDI could contribute to a new offensive-defensive arms race; that it could undermine the stability of deterrence; and that its cost could be morally disproportionate. While much has changed since the bishops' report, the validity of most of its concerns has been borne out.

But would a different assessment of missile defense be warranted if the world approached or achieved zero? In current US policy, missile defense is intended to defend only against limited nuclear threats.[15] With no or only a few nuclear weapons and continued technological developments, would such limited missile defenses become more feasible, effective, stabilizing, and affordable? The challenges would remain daunting. Unless all dual-capable delivery systems were banned, for example, it would be very difficult for missile defenses to discriminate between missiles carrying nuclear and conventional weapons. Moreover, missile defenses would be useless against weapons delivered by ship or truck, and they have already led to a new arms race to develop weapons to elude, overwhelm, or attack them.[16] Missile defenses would also entail space-based interceptors that would militarize space and cyber weapons that could be used for both defensive and offensive purposes. If missile defenses were shared or were under international supervision, that would help address the bishops' concern that it would be destabilizing and would impede disarmament.[17] But the challenges in coordinating a variety of complex and different missile defense systems could be even more daunting than collaborating on a disarmament treaty.[18] The cost of missile defense against a few nuclear weapons would likely be more manageable and justifiable but would remain exorbitant, especially in light of other pressing human needs and its limited efficacy. At best, then, missile defense could supplant some, though not all, forms of deterrence at or near global zero.[19]

Virtual Deterrence

If disarmament intervention and missile defense are problematic strategies for enforcing global zero, what about existential or virtual deterrence?[20] "Existential deterrence," a term coined by McGeorge Bundy, assumes that a nation would be deterred from launching a first strike because it feared an adversary's capacity to retaliate, regardless of that adversary's force structure, targeting policies, or intent.[21] According to Bryan Hehir, existential deterrence was the implicit theory of deterrence in the bishops' 1983 peace pastoral.[22] Bundy and the bishops wrote in a Cold War context. Could the concept apply at or near zero, where the fear of nuclear retaliation is significantly reduced or nonexistent? Schell argues that it could because, "even in a world without nuclear weapons, deterrence would, precisely because the bomb in the mind would still be present, remain in effect." The fact that one cannot disinvent nuclear weapons, he argues, would be "as much a source of reassurance as it would be a danger."[23] Sidney Drell and James Goodby contend that a form of virtual or latent deterrence could work, since the capacity to reconstitute a nuclear arsenal would deter other countries from doing so. But it would have to be just one part of "sustained proactive cooperation" among nations, based on their shared interests in maintaining nuclear zero. Such cooperation would include defining parameters for permitted latent nuclear capabilities, verifying compliance with strict controls on nuclear activities and counterproliferation programs, and deploying early-warning systems and defenses against nuclear attack.[24]

On its face, virtual deterrence would seem impermissible given Pope Francis's condemnation of even the possession of nuclear weapons (which presumably includes retaining the capacity to possess). A proper reading of the pope's position, however, suggests that a virtual deterrent could, in fact, be morally permissible. In 1982, Pope John Paul II enunciated an "interim ethic" on nuclear deterrence: "In current conditions," he said, "'deterrence' based on balance, certainly not as an end in itself but as a step on the way toward a progressive disarmament, may still be judged morally acceptable."[25]

This interim ethic on deterrence was always a function of context, not time. In 2017, Pope Francis, following similar statements by Pope Benedict and numerous senior Vatican officials over the past two decades, made a prudential moral judgment that the strict conditions for the moral acceptability of deterrence were not being met based on his reading of signs of the nuclear times very different from those Pope John Paul II faced in 1982. Despite deep cuts in US-Russian nuclear stockpiles, the Holy See has argued that the nuclear powers did not cash in on the "peace dividend" that was supposed to come with the end of the Cold War but instead largely abandoned arms control initiatives and pursued major nuclear modernization programs that were dangerous and an unjust use of resources.[26] Pope Francis did not abandon his predecessor's formula but made a prudential judgment that nuclear deterrence was not being used as a step toward disarmament and had become an end in itself, a principal impediment to disarmament.[27] In the entirely different scenario of a world at or near nuclear zero, Pope Francis's prudential judgment would arguably not apply because deterrence would now be used in the way envisioned by Pope John Paul II's formula: as a step toward or to maintain disarmament. At or near global zero, a deterrence ethic based on virtual deterrence would be tightly linked to a nonnuclear ethic that combined nonproliferation with abolition.

Even if the Holy See's moral assessment of deterrence provides room for a deterrent based on the possession of a small nuclear arsenal near zero or the ability to rebuild one quickly at zero, other problems would have to be addressed. Would such "easy" forms of deterrence fail, as critics claim?[28] Would they invariably devolve into a morally problematic conditional intent to use indiscriminate or disproportionate force? Would maintaining and especially reconstituting a nuclear capacity contribute to instability in a crisis? Moreover, a world in which a few powers dominate because of their capacity to reconstitute their nuclear arsenal—or retain superiority in conventional or cyber weapons—would not reduce the incentive for nations to retain or obtain a nuclear capacity and could spark a conventional arms race. Such disparities would constitute an unacceptable de facto double standard that would differ in quality but not in kind from that enshrined in the Nuclear Non-Proliferation Treaty, which, in practice, prohibits most states from obtaining nuclear weapons while permitting a few to retain theirs.

Disarmament intervention, missile defense, and virtual deterrence are three current defense strategies that could be adapted to help make a world free of nuclear weapons more feasible. Each would be easier to justify at or near zero than under current circumstances, especially if they were just one part of a package of policy responses prioritizing nonmilitary measures. But they would not be free of moral and strategic problems. Therefore, it is necessary to consider the extent to which nuclear disarmament requires not just adapting existing approaches but also a major paradigm shift toward a system of cooperative security.

Nuclear Disarmament and Cooperative Security

Since Hiroshima, the Catholic Church's calls for progress toward nuclear disarmament have been made in the context of a rather idealistic vision of a just and peaceful political order. A case in point is Pope John XXIII's encyclical, *Pacem in terris*. It was a response to the Cuban Missile Crisis, yet instead of providing a detailed moral evaluation of nuclear weapons, it offered a framework for a positive or just peace (*tranquilitas ordinis*): that of a rightly ordered political community with people living in truth, charity, freedom, and justice directed toward the common good.[29]

A New International Order

Linking nuclear disarmament to a vision of a new international order, as the Church has done, is not uncontroversial. It raises long-debated questions about the theory of change associated with arms control and nuclear disarmament. Does nuclear zero depend on a major transformation to a system of cooperative security, as the Church insists, or does such a linkage impose an unrealistic and unnecessary precondition for nuclear disarmament? In other words, how much of a transformation of the international system is needed for nuclear zero to become a reality? Is it relatively modest reform of the current order that builds on cooperative systems of arms control, such as those already in place for existing nuclear and chemical weapons treaties? Is it a paradigm change as unimaginable as the end of the Cold War? Or is it of an even more radical nature, since, as transformative as the end of the Cold War was, it did not deliver the full peace dividend and new world order that the Holy See and others called for?

The US bishops' 1983 peace pastoral called for nuclear disarmament within the context of a positive vision of peace, but its main focus was the ethics of nuclear use and deterrence in the context of the Cold War's negative "peace of a sort."[30] The bishops' 1993 document on the post–Cold War order framed the nuclear issue more directly in terms of positive peace:

> In 1983, a dominant concern was the ethics of nuclear weapons. Today, this concern, while still critically important, must be considered in the context of a more fundamental question of the ethical foundations of political order: How do we achieve *Pacem in Terris'* vision of a just and stable political order, so that nations will no longer rely on nuclear weapons for their security?[31]

Most other Church documents on nuclear weapons since the end of the Cold War have also framed the nuclear question in these broader terms of the need for a positive peace based in human and cooperative security. They call for abandoning a realist approach that considers nuclear weapons central to national security and international stability, a system based on what Pope Francis calls the "mentality of fear" and the "false security" of weapons of mass destruction.[32] Just as Schell argues that nuclear abolition could be the starting point for dealing with even more challenging global threats such as climate change, Pope Francis sees nuclear disarmament as removing an impediment to the kind of cooperative security needed to build a positive political peace.[33] In other words, the Church propounds a dialectical theory of change by which political peace and nuclear disarmament are mutually reinforcing: political peace makes nuclear disarmament possible and vice versa. Nuclear disarmament is both a means and an end. Furthermore, this theory of change presumes that, as with efforts to eradicate slavery and disease, eliminating nuclear weapons and establishing political peace will not be a static, once-and-for-all achievement. Rather, it will be a product of constantly changing, innovative, and necessarily contingent efforts to achieve communities of right relations in many different places and at many different levels of society.[34]

Interestingly, many realists would agree with the Church's basic premise that nuclear disarmament goes hand in hand with major changes in international affairs, while they might disagree on whether such changes are feasible.[35] Some prominent proponents of nuclear disarmament do not accept this theory of change. Robert McNamara, for one, supported the US bishops' 1993 call to pursue nuclear disarmament as a policy goal but criticized their linking disarmament to what he considered a politically unrealistic and unnecessary precondition of creating new systems of cooperative security.[36] Many supporters of the TPNW make a similar argument. The calls by Henry Kissinger, George Shultz, William Perry, and Sam Nunn for a world free of nuclear weapons are premised on a changed international security framework that incorporates an idealist dimension, but they do not presume the need for the kind of radical change in international affairs envisioned by Church statements on nuclear weapons.[37]

Building on their work, James Goodby and Steven Pifer outline a "joint enterprise" for a world without nuclear weapons that many realists could embrace. It would include not only a properly structured, verifiable, and enforceable global treaty but also a complex set of treaties dealing with related issues (e.g., cybersecurity, fissile materials, civil nuclear power, and nuclear terrorism), as well as regional treaties (e.g., nuclear-free zones and conventional arms control). It would also require success in addressing political conflicts and instability in the Mideast, the Korean Peninsula, South Asia, and elsewhere.[38] Clearly, one need not embrace the Church's cosmopolitan ethic and its idealist calls for a transformed international order to make a case for nuclear disarmament. In fact, arguments for disarmament that do not presume such paradigmatic change might be more persuasive, especially given realism's predominance in the nuclear debate.

If that is the case, what of the Church's claim that nuclear disarmament should be part of a larger project of developing new systems of human and cooperative security? Maryann Cusimano Love provides an answer in this volume: that the Church's theological and moral vision of a positive peace, which includes concepts such as reconciliation that are not normally part of the nuclear lexicon, help explain why more progress hasn't been made on nuclear disarmament since the end of the Cold War. A broader perspective is also needed to deal with the failed and failing states and the authoritarian and aggressive regimes that will impede achieving and maintaining nuclear zero. As Drew Christiansen explains, just war thinkers have to engage the just peace tradition to better understand alternatives to force and what counts as a just peace.[39] The challenge for Catholic scholars is to connect with the work done by specialists in diplomacy, international law and institutions, national security, science and technology, peace studies, and other disciplines to put much-needed policy and institutional flesh on the principled bones of the Church's call for disarmament and new systems of human and cooperative security.

Conventional Disarmament

One issue requiring further ethical reflection is the relationship between nuclear and conventional disarmament. "Integral disarmament," a term from *Pacem in terris*, was the organizing theme of the November 2017 Vatican symposium at which Pope Francis condemned the possessing of nuclear weapons.[40] In his essay in this book, Pierce Corden traces how the Church has linked the long-term goal of abolishing nuclear weapons to the need for general disarmament.

That nuclear and conventional disarmament should go hand in hand is contested by both nuclear disarmament skeptics and optimists. Nuclear disarmament skeptics contend that nuclear weapons have deterred major conventional wars between the great powers and that nuclear zero would lead to new great power conflicts.[41] Moreover, nuclear zero could catalyze new conventional arms races among former nuclear states and their allies who had relied on extended deterrence. Those on the losing end of those arms races as well as rogue states would have strong incentives for nuclear breakout.

Some nuclear disarmament optimists propose a different scenario. They contend that conventional forces could replace and, in some respects, improve upon nuclear deterrence because their flexibility, usability, and effectiveness make them a more credible deterrent.[42] Andrew Futter and Benjamin Zala acknowledge that advanced conventional weaponry—a combination of missile defense, precision antisatellite and antisubmarine technologies, and artificial intelligence—could be highly destabilizing and impede nuclear disarmament. But if there were rough parity in advanced conventional weaponry capabilities, it could also be an incentive for nuclear disarmament as nuclear weapons became more vulnerable and risky and less useful politically and militarily. This, they argue, would be a nuclear disarmament that is "technologically driven rather than based on politics, ethics or morals."[43]

The Church's integral disarmament approach is skeptical about both nuclear or conventional deterrence as long-term solutions. In response to nuclear disarmament skeptics, a 2014 Vatican study document dismissed as "specious" the claim that nuclear weapons reduce the risk of conventional war. According to the document, nuclear weapons have not deterred wars between nuclear powers or between nonnuclear and nuclear nations, nor have they deterred major terrorist attacks on nuclear states. Moreover, nuclear weapons themselves have been a casus belli in cases such as the Cuban Missile Crisis and the 2003 Iraq intervention.[44] The document concluded:

> The "peace of a sort" provided by nuclear deterrence is a misnomer and tends to cloud our collective vision. . . . [T]he misleading assumption that nuclear deterrence prevents war should no longer inspire reluctance to accepting international abolition of nuclear arsenals. If it ever was true, today it has become a dodge from meeting responsibilities to this generation and the next.[45]

Even if the skeptics are correct that nuclear weapons have deterred major great power wars, the Church has rejected the use of nuclear weapons to deter conventional war because of the moral problems with nuclear use and deterrence. Therefore, given the risk that nuclear zero could, in fact, make the world safer for conventional war, it makes good sense to work for both nuclear and conventional disarmament. The close connection between the Intermediate-Range Nuclear Forces Treaty and the Treaty on Conventional Armed Forces in Europe is perhaps the best example of the importance of linking the two.[46]

In some ways, the optimists who are betting on technologically driven nuclear disarmament exemplify the technocratic paradigm that Pope Francis has so forcefully argued against in *Laudato si'*. No doubt new technologies will continue to reshape the nuclear-conventional dynamic and could impede or contribute to nuclear disarmament.[47] But, as the pope insists, technological developments have to be accompanied by "a development in human responsibility, values and conscience."[48] Technology alone is no substitute for developing morally appropriate political solutions.

Corden points out that a nuclear-free world will require the development of a new global security architecture that embodies greatly reduced numbers of weapons of all kinds and greatly modified roles for armed forces. As the Church advocates for that new security architecture, it will have to ensure that linking nuclear and conventional disarmament does not become an excuse for the international community to do nothing on either. The Church and Catholic scholars will also have to clarify how much conventional disarmament is needed and how that relates to a nation's right to self-defense. Does integral disarmament ultimately entail a rejection of the just war tradition in favor of an effort to ban war itself, as recent popes have envisioned? These are some of the highly contested issues that will need further scrutiny.

Limits to Sovereignty

Another issue related to the Church's vision of cooperative security is the extent to which nuclear abolition will require a major rethinking of the rights and responsibilities of sovereignty. What McGeorge Bundy said in reviewing the US bishops' peace pastoral remains true today: "If anything could have led people to abandon their nation-centered ways, it should have been the bomb.... [Those] preoccupied by nuclear danger have fixed on national sovereignty as the basic obstacle to the exorcism of the specter."[49]

If a global ban is to be effective, both nuclear and nonnuclear nations will have to give up some of their rights of sovereignty to regional and international institutions, which in turn will have to be given much more capacity and authority than they now have.[50] The significant expansion of nuclear power in the next twenty years will fuel proliferation unless the International Atomic Energy Agency is significantly strengthened and nations agree to much more intrusive inspections, stronger safeguards, and tougher sanctions. Article 4.6 of the TPNW envisions "a competent international authority or authorities" that would have "to negotiate and verify the irreversible elimination of nuclear weapons programs." That would involve highly intrusive measures to identify nuclear materials and verify, enforce, and ensure compliance. As mentioned, missile defenses would also have to be shared or put under some common authority. For these and other reasons, the rights of sovereignty and the limits on UN authority (and that of other multilateral bodies) will have to be rethought to make a global ban on nuclear weapons a reality. All nations will have to be willing to embrace an ethic of restraint in accepting limits on their sovereignty and forgoing nuclear weapons as a source of national security in the name of the global good. Because of the risks their weapons pose to the world, the nuclear states will bear an especially heavy moral burden to forgo pretensions of military, political, and economic dominance and instead accept limits on their sovereign prerogatives as they lead in building a system of cooperative security that will make a global ban more likely and sustainable.

Conclusion

"Ought" implies "can." Nuclear disarmament will never be accepted as a moral imperative much less a legitimate policy objective unless we can escape what Schell calls the "profound fatalism" that is based on "an anxiety or conviction that the bomb, though a human creation, is somehow immune to human control."[51] Can the world escape this denial of responsibility, which borders on the sin of despair? Schell believes that it can because the firmest foundation for a nuclear-weapons-free world already exists and would only be strengthened once the world gets to zero: that is, "the nuclear moral taboo, a deep revulsion against nuclear destruction."[52] Former US defense secretary William Perry made a similar point in endorsing the TPNW. Citing Max Kampelman on the "power of the ought," Perry contends that while the treaty itself will not eliminate nuclear weapons, "it establishes key ideals necessary to push us further up the [nuclear-free] mountain" and "offers inspiration to combat the sense of hopelessness that many feel when confronting this daunting problem."[53]

Reinforcing the nuclear taboo on use, questioning the morality of nuclear deterrence, and upholding the vision and moral imperative of nuclear disarmament remain the Church's most significant contributions to the process of nuclear disarmament. But more is needed. Catholic scholars must join policy specialists in making the case that nuclear disarmament is not a utopian dream but rather an achievable goal in which the cure of disarmament is not worse than the disease of deterrence. This essay highlights a few of the issues that deserve further ethical reflection as this process moves forward: disarmament intervention, the role of missile defense, virtual deterrence, and the extent to which nuclear disarmament requires major paradigm shifts in international relations in which nuclear and general conventional disarmament would proceed apace and the rights and responsibilities of sovereign states and international institutions would be radically reshaped. Clearly, the nuclear status quo is morally untenable. The process of nuclear disarmament can and must proceed apart from addressing these and other end-state issues. But a more sophisticated moral case for disarmament that can address these issues is essential if momentum toward nuclear zero can be sustained for the decades needed for it to become a reality.

Notes

1. Address of His Holiness Pope Francis to Participants in the International Symposium "Prospects for a World Free of Nuclear Weapons and for Integral Disarmament," November 10, 2017, 3–5; Address of The Holy Father, Peace Memorial (Hiroshima), November 24, 2019.
2. This essay updates and significantly expands my previous article, "The Nuclear Ethics Gap," *America*, May 17, 2010, 11.
3. Pope Francis, *Fratelli tutti*, no. 262; Message of Pope Francis: UN Conference to Negotiate Legally Binding Instrument to Prohibit Nuclear Weapons, March 23, 2017.
4. Cf. Brad Roberts, "On Adapting Nuclear Deterrence to Reduce Nuclear Risk," *Daedalus* 149, no. 2 (Spring 2020): 72–73.
5. For an argument that technological developments have made disarmament destabilizing, see Keir A. Lieber and Daryl G. Press, "Why Nuclear Disarmament and Strategic Stability Are Incompatible," in *Nuclear Disarmament: A Critical Assessment*, ed. Bård Nikolas Vik Steen and Olav Njølstad (Abingdon, UK: Routledge, 2019), 45.
6. Gerard Powers, "Would an Invasion of Iraq Be a 'Just War'?," United States Institute of Peace Special Report #98, January 2003.
7. For an argument that the threat or use of preemptive or preventive force could be justified to stop nuclear proliferation in some rare cases, such as Iraq, North Korea, and Iran, see Sidney D. Drell and James E. Goodby, *The Gravest Danger: Nuclear Weapons* (Stanford, CA: Hoover Institution Press, 2003), 34–44.
8. Cf. Charles L. Glaser, "Was Nuclear Disarmament Ever Alive?," in *Nuclear Disarmament*, 25, 38.
9. George Weigel, "The Just War Tradition and the World after September 11," *Catholic University Law Review* 51, no. 3 (2002): 707.
10. J. Bryan Hehir, "The Moral Measurement of War: A Tradition of Change and Continuity," a paper for the conference "The Sacred and the Sovereign," University of Chicago Divinity School, October 20, 2000.
11. John Courtney Murray, *We Hold These Truths: Catholic Reflections on the American Proposition* (New York: Sheed and Ward, 1960), 266–67.

12. Preamble, Treaty on the Prohibition of Nuclear Weapons, July 7, 2017.
13. Jonathan Schell, *The Seventh Decade: The New Shape of Nuclear Danger* (New York: Metropolitan Books, 2007), 198.
14. United States Catholic Conference, *A Report on the Challenge of Peace and Policy Developments, 1983–1988* (Washington, DC: United States Catholic Conference, 1988).
15. Keith B. Payne, "The Great Divide in U.S. Deterrence Thought," *Strategic Studies Quarterly* 14, no. 2 (2020): 16–48.
16. Philip E. Coyle, "Radical Departures from the Status Quo and Their Impacts on Nuclear Non-Proliferation and Disarmament," in *Nuclear Disarmament*, 265, 269–270. For an argument that missile defense could work near zero but not at zero, see Marvin Schaffer, "Moral Nuclear Deterrence: The Ascendancy of Missile Defense," *Foresight: The Journal of Futures Studies, Strategic Thinking and Policy* 14, no. 3 (2012): 260–71.
17. David Cortright and Raimo Väyrynen, *Towards Nuclear Zero* (London: International Institute for Strategic Studies, 2010), 150–54.
18. Charles L. Glaser, "Was Nuclear Disarmament Ever Alive?," in *Nuclear Disarmament*, 25, 29.
19. Tom Sauer argues for no (best) or limited theater (second best) ballistic missile defense at zero. See Tom Sauer, "Nuclear Elimination with or without Missile Defence?," *Cambridge Review of International Affairs* 25, no. 3 (2012): 433–450.
20. These terms are used in a variety of different ways. Some authors, for example, distinguish among minimal deterrence, existential deterrence, and post-existential deterrence. See Tom Sauer, "A Second Nuclear Revolution: From Nuclear Primacy to Post-Existential Deterrence," *Journal of Strategic Studies* 32, no. 5 (2009): 745–67.
21. McGeorge Bundy, "The Bishops and the Bomb," *New York Review of Books*, June 16, 1983.
22. See, e.g., J. Bryan Hehir, "There's No Deterring the Catholic Bishops," *Ethics and International Affairs* 3, no. 1 (March 1989): 277, 288.
23. Schell, *The Seventh Decade*, 220–21.
24. Sidney D. Drell and James E. Goodby, *A World without Nuclear Weapons: End-State Issues* (Stanford, CA: Hoover Institution Press, 2009), 12–31.
25. Pope John Paul II, "Message to the UN General Assembly," June 7, 1982, no. 8.
26. Study Document, "Nuclear Disarmament: Time for Abolition," Permanent Mission of the Holy See to the United Nations and Other International Organizations in Geneva, December 8, 2014.
27. Gerard Powers, "Papal Condemnation of Nuclear Deterrence and What Is Next," *Arms Control Today* 48, no. 4 (May 2018): 6–11.
28. For a critique of idealist proposals to eliminate nuclear weapons or realist approaches to existential and other variants of "safe" deterrence theories, see Keith B. Payne, *Shadows on the Wall: Deterrence and Disarmament*

(Fairfax, VA: National Institute Press, 2020). For a critique of Cold War–era theories of existential deterrence, see Lawrence Freedman, "I Exist; Therefore I Deter," *International Security* 13, no. 1 (1988): 177–95.
29. Pope John XXIII, *Pacem in terris* (1963). For a helpful summary of Catholic teaching on peace, see Kenneth Himes, "Peacebuilding and Catholic Social Teaching," in *Peacebuilding: Catholic Theology, Ethics and Praxis*, ed. Robert J. Schreiter, R. Scott Appleby, and Gerard F. Powers (Maryknoll, NY: Orbis, 2010), 268–69.
30. National Conference of Catholic Bishops (NCCB), *The Challenge of Peace: God's Promise and Our Response* (Washington, DC: United States Catholic Conference, 1983).
31. *The Harvest of Justice Is Sown in Peace*, 1993, 31.
32. Address of His Holiness Pope Francis to Participants in the International Symposium "Prospects for a World Free of Nuclear Weapons and for Integral Disarmament," 3.
33. Schell, *The Seventh Decade*, 216–17; Pope Francis, Address to the 75th Session of the UN General Assembly, September 25, 2020; and Pope Francis, Letter to President, UN Conference to Negotiate Legally Binding Instrument to Prohibit Nuclear Weapons. For Catholic perspectives on political peace, see Drew Christiansen, "Catholic Peacemaking, 1991–2005: The Legacy of Pope John Paul II," *Review of Faith and International Affairs* 4, no. 2 (2006): 22; and Heinz-Gerhard Justenhoven, "The Peace Ethics of Pope John Paul II," *University of St. Thomas Law Journal* 3, no. 1 (2005): 110–38.
34. Himes, "Peacebuilding and Catholic Social Teaching," 269.
35. See, e.g., Brad Roberts, "Nuclear Ethics and the Ban Treaty," in *Nuclear Disarmament*, 112.
36. Author's conversation with Robert McNamara at United States Conference of Catholic Bishops headquarters, Washington, DC, February 22, 1999.
37. George P. Shultz, William J. Perry, Henry A. Kissinger, and Sam Nunn, "A World Free of Nuclear Weapons," *Wall Street Journal*, January 4, 2007. For a detailed analysis of the approach taken by the four, see David Cortright's essay in this volume and Philip Taubman, *The Partnership: Five Cold Warriors and Their Quest to Ban the Bomb* (New York: Harper Collins, 2012). Max M. Kampelman's argument about the "power of ought" had some influence on the four. See Max M. Kampelman, "Bombs Away," *New York Times*, April 24, 2006, A-19.
38. James E. Goodby and Steven Pifer, "Creating the Conditions for a World without Nuclear Weapons," in *The War That Must Never Be Fought: Dilemmas of Nuclear Deterrence*, ed. George Shultz and James Goodby (Stanford, CA: Hoover Institution Press, 2015), 473.
39. Drew Christiansen, "The Social and Moral Responsibilities of Knowledge Workers," in *A World Free from Nuclear Weapons: The Vatican Conference on Disarmament*, ed. Drew Christiansen, SJ, and Carole Sargent (Washington, DC: Georgetown University Press, 2020), 120, 124–25.

40. For the proceedings of the conference, see Christiansen and Sargent, eds., *A World Free from Nuclear Weapons*.
41. See, e.g., Michael Desch, "No More Nukes? An Exchange," *Commonweal*, February 23, 2018, https://www.commonwealmagazine.org/no-more-nukes; Kenneth Waltz, "More May Be Better," in *The Spread of Nuclear Weapons: A Debate*, ed. Scott Sagan and Kenneth Waltz, 1–45 (New York: Norton, 1995); and Kenneth Waltz, "The Great Debate," *The National Interest*, September–October 2010, 92.
42. For a rebuttal of the "nuclear peace" argument and an argument that strengthened conventional forces could replace nuclear deterrence, see Benoit Pelopidas, "A Bet Portrayed as a Certainty: Reassessing the Added Deterrent Value of Nuclear Weapons," and Steven Pifer, "A Realist's Rationale for a World Without Nuclear Weapons," in *The War That Must Never Be Fought*, 5–55, 81–107.
43. Andrew Futter and Benjamin Zala, "Emerging Non-Nuclear Technology and the Future of the Global Nuclear Order," in *Nuclear Disarmament*, 207, 220.
44. Holy See, "Nuclear Disarmament." A casus belli is "an act or situation provoking or justifying war" (Oxford English Dictionary).
45. Holy See, "Nuclear Disarmament." For a detailed critique of arguments that nuclear zero would increase the risk of nuclear proliferation and conventional war, see Benoit Pelopidas, "A Bet Portrayed as a Certainty: Reassessing the Added Deterrent Value of Nuclear Weapons," in *The War That Must Never Be Fought*, 5–55.
46. Cortright and Väyrynen, *Towards Nuclear Zero*, 77–80.
47. See, for example, Robert H. Latiff, *Future Peace: Technology, Aggression, and the Rush to War* (Notre Dame, IN: University of Notre Dame Press, 2022); Nobumasa Akiyama, "The Impact of AI on Nuclear Deterrence and Military Strategy, including the Ethical Implications," in *Proceedings of the Workshop "Robotics, AI and Humanity: Science, Ethics and Policy"* (May 16–17, 2019), ed. Joachim von Braun, Stefano Zamagni, and Marcelo Sánchez Sorondo (Vatican City: Scripta Varia 144, 2019, E-Pub); Gregory M. Reichberg et al., "Warring with Machines: Military Applications of Artificial Intelligence and the Relevance of Virtue Ethics," Oslo Peace Research Institute Project, January 2020–December 2023; and Maryann Cusimano Love, *Global Issues beyond Sovereignty*, 5th ed. (Lanham, MD: Rowman & Littlefield, 2020), 345–84.
48. Pope Francis, *Laudato si'*, no. 105.
49. McGeorge Bundy, "The Bishops and the Bomb," *New York Review of Books*, June 16, 1983.
50. The need for a global public authority to safeguard security, justice, development, human rights, and other aspects of the global common good is a consistent theme in Catholic social teaching. See Pope John XXIII, *Pacem in*

terris (1963), nos. 136–38; and Second Vatican Council (1965), *Gaudium et spes*, no. 81.
51. Schell, *The Seventh Decade*, 18.
52. Schell, 220.
53. William J. Perry, "Why the United States Should Support the Treaty on the Prohibition of Nuclear Weapons," *Bulletin of Atomic Scientists*, January 22, 2021. For an argument that the TPNW will not contribute to nuclear disarmament as much as the widely accepted norms against battlefield use and testing of nuclear weapons, see Michael Krepon, "Bombs, Bans, and Norms," Arms Control Wonk (blog network), November 6, 2016.

14

Just Peace and Nuclear Disarmament

MARYANN CUSIMANO LOVE

Nuclear weapons do not build peace; rather, they "create nothing but a false sense of security," Pope Francis tells us. "They cannot constitute the basis for peaceful coexistence between members of the human family, which must rather be inspired by an ethics of solidarity."[1]

Pope Francis and world leaders call for a world free of nuclear weapons. We need a new nuclear ethics to move toward this policy of deep nuclear disarmament. I propose an ethics of just peace to guide us toward a world free of nuclear weapons. During the Cold War, conflict between the United States and the Soviet Union froze and was institutionalized in nuclear deterrence: a mobilization of deadly weapons, not a peace plan. It is time to move from the negative peace of the Cold War to a positive peace based on right relationships.

Nuclear deterrence was based on the presumption that nuclear Armageddon or the threat of nuclear genocide were the only relationships possible among the nuclear powers. Globalization changed this, making more and deeper and more varied relationships possible, even among adversaries.[2] With better relationships possible, we have a moral obligation to pursue them. Just peace principles and practices have worked in war zones around the world helping to prevent war, manage conflict, and build sustainable peace. We must now apply just peace principles and practices to nuclear disarmament.[3]

Just peace is the mutually constitutive and interactive commitment to and pursuit of social cohesion and equity in both orientation/aim and action. I offer the following just peace criteria, drawn from studies and interviews of grassroots Christian institutions and peacebuilders:[4]

- Just cause (protecting, defending, and restoring the fundamental dignity of human life and the common good);
- Right intention (aiming to create a positive peace);
- Participation (respecting human dignity means including societal stakeholders, state and nonstate actors, women, and previous parties to the conflict);
- Restoration (repair of the human as well as the physical infrastructure);
- Right relationship (creating or restoring just social relationships both vertically and horizontally);
- Reconciliation (healing the communal and individual wounds of war);[5] and
- Sustainability (developing structures that can help peace endure over time).[6]

Like strands in a rope, just peace principles build upon one another and are most successfully put into practice when applied together.

Just cause and right intention. These first two norms are the motivations that drive building a just peace. The rest of the just peace principles detail how to build a positive peace, and each principle is associated with practices to implement the norms. Just peace principles and practices are supported by religious rationales, international law, cognitive psychology, and pragmatic professional standards. Like the legs of a chair, these supports strengthen just peace principles and appeal to both faith-based and secular peacebuilders.

To move toward deeper disarmament, we need to build deeper relationships. Wars, even cold wars, damage relationships between countries and peoples. Wars end, but they do not always end with positive peace based on right relationships. The Cold War ended with a cold peace, not with disarmament, demobilization, reintegration, restoration, truth telling, and the other tools of just peace that have been so helpful in ending other wars.[7]

Participation. Engagement with the other is necessary to acknowledge the human dignity of parties to a conflict. This participation can take many practical forms, such as dialogue, deep respectful listening, common action on projects of mutual concern, and formal structures for ensuring multistakeholder input and interaction with peace processes.[8] Participation helps build right relationship by acknowledging and respecting the dignity of all including previously oppressed or marginalized peoples, not just elites. Cold War disarmament processes were undertaken by elite government arms negotiators (primarily white men) in the United States and the Soviet Union, excluding other countries and peoples impacted by nuclear arms. The Nunn-Lugar Cooperative Threat Reduction (CTR) Program expanded participation beyond political elites in Moscow and Washington to people harmed by the Cold War nuclear weapons complexes in Kazakhstan, Belarus, and Ukraine. Support for the CTR program expanded to European countries through the G8 Global Partnership against the Spread of Weapons and Materials of Mass Destruction and included scientists and researchers, not just political and military leaders. Senators Sam Nunn and Richard Lugar wanted to further expand the CTR program to include the participation of other countries, especially India and Pakistan, but there wasn't political will in Congress for expanded participation. Countries and people impacted by nuclear weapons have exerted their agency by establishing nuclear weapons–free zones and by enacting the Treaty on the Prohibition of Nuclear Weapons (entered into force 2021). Following the model of the 1999 Anti-Personnel Mine Ban Treaty (also known as the Ottawa Convention), the humanitarian impact of nuclear weapons conferences, and the treaty process culminating in the Treaty to Prohibit Nuclear Weapons, victims of the use and testing of nuclear weapons were invited to participate in the treaty negotiations because they had been excluded from the previous decades of nuclear disarmament discussions. Participation must be widened beyond government officials and scientists in order to both honor human dignity and build constituents in favor of deeper disarmament.

Expanding participation beyond bilateral approaches is necessary for principled as well as practical reasons, particularly at a time when bilateral relations are strained. Nonstate venues must be pursued, as should multilateral cooperation and multilateral processes. The Nuclear Security Summits, the Proliferation Security Initiative/Partnerships to Prevent Proliferation, and the Global Threat Reduction Initiative that removed plutonium and highly enriched uranium from eighteen countries, more than enough for one hundred bombs, are important models that ought to be revived and continued. Multilateral and nongovernmental organization cooperation in all-hazard foreign consequence management agreements and exercises also deepen relationships among a wider variety of stakeholders.

Increasing the outreach and participation of countries such as South Africa and Argentina that gave up their nuclear weapons programs would ground multilateral conversations in the connections between nuclear reduction and greater resources available for development. These countries have already walked this path of demilitarizing in the nuclear arena in order to focus on development and have much to offer the global conversations.

Participation is important for both principled and practical reasons. In international relations we talk about "boomerang" politics and forum shopping. When politics is blocked in one venue, you pursue alternate forums. Foreign consequence management, capacity sharing, and joint training and exercises helpful in disaster relief would also help if radiological dispersal devices (dirty bombs) or nuclear weapons are detonated, whether by accident or by terrorists. Unfortunately, this is a real concern. When ISIS seized the Nineveh plains, it stole over eighty pounds of (non–weapons grade) uranium from Mosul University in Iraq in June 2014. While this material has reportedly since been recovered, nuclear materials are still decentralized in many insecure locations. We cannot wait until bilateral relations improve to further the nuclear safety and security, disarmament, Nuclear Non-Proliferation Treaty, and non-nuclear use agendas. Widening the net of participation and relationship building and the issues that we use to encourage cooperation can keep momentum moving while bilateral relations and disarmament talks are stalled.

Right relationship. This can be operationalized in practices of acknowledgment, respect, and efforts to correct unjust patterns of exploitation. Expanding meaningful participation in decision making is another means of building just relationships. To stop countries and statesmen from seeking respect through nuclear weapons, we must creatively seek other avenues to demonstrate respectful relations, as South Korea did through its skillful Olympic diplomacy. Right relationships of trust can be strengthened through disarmament's regular interactions of inspections, information sharing, transparency, and accountability of nuclear weapons and materials. Negotiating a new agreement to follow the New START treaty when it expires in 2026 will extend the regular relationships between US and Russian arms inspectors. It will also extend the forum for resolving disagreements; a respectful, fair, and regularized process for asking questions; receiving information; and addressing each other's concerns with treaty compliance and understanding of new weapons systems or weapons research. Deeper disarmament by the United States and Russia, which together possess more than 90 percent of the world's nuclear weapons, is required by the Nuclear Non-Proliferation Treaty. Making good on their commitments in that treaty will build right relationships with the nonnuclear states that are parties to the Treaty to Prohibit Nuclear Weapons.

Restoration. Usually one of the first and easier tools of just peace is restoration, but that has not been the case with nuclear weapons. A standard tool of restoration is disarmament, demobilization, and reintegration, which includes compensation to war victims and economic development opportunities to spur defense conversion to civilian economic activities. The Megatons to Megawatts Program was an example of defense conversion; the fissile material from decommissioned nuclear bombs was turned into electricity. At the height of the program, 10 percent of electricity in the United States came from decommissioned nuclear bombs. As part of the CTR program, some restoration and reintegration was offered to former Soviet nuclear weapons scientists, who were offered other scientific jobs and relocation in order to prevent nuclear proliferation.

But restoration did not move beyond scientists and has not been offered to victims of nuclear weapons. The Radiation Exposure Compensation Act of 1990 and the Nuclear Claims Tribunal were slow and inadequate in compensating those harmed by the nuclear weapons complex, and the compensation fund ran out for Pacific Island victims of nuclear testing. While some uranium miners and veterans received compensation, many more died or were denied restoration, including Native Americans, Pacific Islanders, women, children, and members of the wider community exposed to nuclear testing and the hazardous waste of nuclear weapons production. Some disarmament occurred, but without demobilization thousands of weapons remain on hair-trigger alert with a widely spread risk over air, land, and sea due to the triad force structure. Restoration of the safety of people and the planet requires not only decreased arms but also removing them from hair-trigger status, reducing the spread and increasing the safety of the weapons during drawdown, cleaning up the nuclear weapons sacrifice zones, and reintegrating workers from the nuclear complex into new jobs and industries. Disarmament of the mind and heart have also not occurred. Restoration can use many practices including, for example, economic development, environmental remediation, trauma healing, healing of memories, soul repair, medical interventions, and rebuilding physical infrastructures such as for water supply. The radiological contamination and environmental damage of the nuclear age have been long lasting, as has the cultural damage to impacted communities, particularly indigenous peoples forced from their homes.

Reconciliation. Truth telling, public apologies, acknowledgment, reparations, punishment, building just institutional structures, forgiveness, and so on are all part of reconciliation, which usually comes later, not first. Participation, right relationship, and restoration are usually addressed first in order to move individuals and societies closer to the goal of reconciliation. A just peace approach to nuclear weapons must include truth telling and public education about the full and continuing costs of the nuclear age as well as truth telling about the many nuclear accidents, nuclear near misses, thefts and losses of nuclear materials, and the fact that atomic weapons alone caused the end of neither World War II nor the Cold War peace.[9]

After the Cold War there was no reconciliation between the United States and Russia or between Russia and the newly independent states. There was no truth and reconciliation commission, and there were no transparency and public apologies for crimes or acknowledgment of harms done during the war and no systems to reintegrate former foes with symbolic politics that built a wider and deeper public support for peace with Russia. Sports and cultural diplomacy are ways to restore cultural connections.

Sustainability. Sustainability is key to making just peace take root over time and space, including our common home and future generations. Usually there is a sequence to just peace norms, with participation and restoration in order to rebuild right relationships moving first and efforts at reconciliation following later. Sustainability holds these norms together. Whereas restoration and reconciliation must work through the harms of the past, sustainability moves just peace to the future tense. Sustainability protects the lives and rights of future generations of people and the planet, ensuring that communities are building a durable peace that will last. The Nuclear Security Summits, the CTR program, and the G8 Global Partnership were efforts to create more long-term multilateral structures, but these were not sustained in the Trump administration.

Expanding disarmament beyond the extended New START treaty is an important way to sustain the nuclear arms reductions that already have occurred as the United States and Russia define future and deeper disarmament processes.

Honoring treaties is a way to make peace sustainable, lasting beyond any particular president or administration. The US withdrawal from the Intermediate-Range Nuclear Forces Treaty in 2019 and the Open Skies Treaty in 2020 undermined trust and sustainability. The 2019 treaty outlawed a very destabilizing class of weapons, ground-launched missiles with ranges from 500 to 5,500 kilometers, which escalate conflict, offer little time for decision makers to respond, and increase the risk of accidental nuclear war. The Intermediate-Range Nuclear Forces Treaty created a safer world, causing the destruction of nearly 2,700 destabilizing nuclear and conventional missiles in the United States, Russia, and the Soviet successor states. A dangerous arms race has already begun. The United States and Russia are testing and developing new weapons systems. Sustainability also requires continued environmental cleanup of polluted nuclear weapons sites such as Hanford, Washington, and Oak Ridge, Tennessee. Attempts to curtail environmental laws, including changing the Magna Carta of environmental legislation, the National Environmental Protection Act, undermine sustainability, participation, and truth telling.

It is never too late to do the right thing. Just peace principles and practices have worked in war zones around the world and can advance nuclear disarmament as well. Globalization makes better relationships possible; just peace principles and practices work to make those relationships equitable. Cooperating in other arenas yields benefits in its own right and also helps build a more just peace, building relationships of trust that may have spillover effects in the nuclear arena. All wars end. Whether they end well or badly depends on us, on what we do to build a more just and lasting peace.

Notes

1. Pope Francis, 2017 Vatican disarmament conference.
2. Maryann Cusimano Love, *Global Issues* (Lanham, MD: Rowman & Littlefield, 2019); and Maryann Cusimano Love, *Beyond Sovereignty* (New York: Cengage, 2011).
3. My research is based on two decades of participant-observer research, document review, and interviews with peacebuilders around the world, examining how Church institutions are working to build a more just peace and how peace practitioners use religious ideas and imagination to guide their actions.
4. A longer discussion of this research is available in Maryann Cusimano Love, "Just Peace," manuscript; and Maryann Cusimano Love, "What Kind of Peace Do We Seek? Just Peace Institutionalized," in *Peacebuilding: Catholic Theology, Ethics, and Praxis*, ed. R. Scott Appleby, Robert Schreiter, and Gerard F. Powers, 56–91 (Maryknoll, NY: Orbis: 2008).
5. Daniel Philpott, "Reconciliation," in *Peacebuilding: Catholic Theology, Ethics, and Praxis*, ed. R. Scott Appleby, Robert Schreiter, and Gerard F. Powers, 92–124 (Maryknoll, NY: Orbis: 2008); and Daniel Philpott, *Just and Unjust Peace: An Ethic of Political Reconciliation* (New York: Oxford University Press, 2012).
6. Caritas Internationalis, *Peacebuilding: A Caritas Training Manual*, 2nd ed. (Vatican City: Caritas Internationalis, 2006), especially "Peacebuilding Principles and Framework"; and Tom Bamat, Mark Rogers, and Julie Ideh, *Pursuing Just Peace* (Baltimore: Catholic Relief Services, 2008), especially the overview by David Steele and the chapter "Synthesis: Gleanings on Process-Structures."
7. Maryann Cusimano Love, "Building a Better Peace: A Future Worthy of Our Faith," *America*, July 21, 2015.
8. Pope Francis, *Fratelli tutti*.
9. Eric Schlosser, *Command and Control: Nuclear Weapons, the Damascus Accident, and the Illusion of Safety* (New York: Penguin, 2013); and Ward Wilson, "The Myth of Nuclear Deterrence," *The Nonproliferation Review* 15, no. 3 (2008): 421–39.

15

Peacebuilding and Nuclear Deterrence

DANIEL PHILPOTT

In recent decades the ethics of war and peace has expanded from traditional questions about the justice of war to the dilemmas of building peace. Thought has followed praxis as a wave of countries around the world have confronted pasts of colossal violence and injustice associated with war and dictatorship. Characteristic practices include trials, the building of the rule of law, disarmament, reparations, truth telling, the social reintegration of combatants, apologies, forgiveness, and amnesties.

The emergent question is not what is a just war but rather what is a just peace. Catholic and other Christian ethicists are among those who have entered this discussion and have contributed at least two major ideas from the Christian tradition: first, the notion, found in the Bible and echoed throughout the tradition, that peace consists not merely in the absence of violence but also in the presence of justice, and second, the concept of reconciliation, meaning the restoration of right relationship in the aftermath of widespread violence and injustice.[1] What insights might peacebuilding carry for dilemmas surrounding nuclear weapons?

This question begs another: If nuclear weapons occasion the building of a just peace, exactly what sort of violence or injustice do they involve? In contrast to most of the settings around the globe that have given rise to the ethic of peacebuilding, where deaths and other human rights violations are denominated in commas and zeroes, nuclear weapons have elicited deaths on this scale—and in fact have only been used in combat at all—on one occasion seventy-four years ago. The US bombings of Hiroshima and Nagasaki continue to demand certain peacebuilding measures—namely truth telling, acknowledgment, and forgiveness—but the problem that nuclear weapons have posed for peace since remains to be settled.² More than a few analysts, after all, have made the case that nuclear weapons are responsible for the "long peace" that persisted through the Cold War—keeping it from being a hot war—and has endured to the present day.³ A peace in which "safety will be the sturdy child of terror, and survival the twin brother of annihilation," as Winston Churchill phrased it memorably, may fall far short of a just peace but is far superior to the violence among great powers that characterized the first half of the twentieth century, these analysts contend.

That nuclear weapons are a condition of violence that calls for peacebuilding, then, must be argued, not merely assumed. Offering just such an argument, to great fanfare, has been none other than Pope Francis, who in 2017 joined 121 other countries in signing the Treaty on the Prohibition of Nuclear Weapons on behalf of the Holy See and delivered two major addresses decrying nuclear weapons, in the second of which he condemned "the threat of their use, as well as their very possession," a censure whose scope seemed to exceed that of previous popes.⁴ Aiming to motivate his Catholic followers and other activists to rid the world of nuclear weapons—the second address was delivered to a symposium attended by eleven Nobel laureates and some three hundred diplomats and civil society representatives—Pope Francis cited the risk of a nuclear accident, the ineffectiveness of nuclear deterrence, the catastrophic effect of the use of nuclear weapons, the perpetuation of a mentality of fear, and the diversion of resources that could be used for fighting poverty and promoting human development.⁵

It is hard to dispute that these features of nuclear weapons detract from a just peace and call for peacebuilding. The world's states, fourteen of which possess nuclear weapons, including the United States and Russia, which possess 93 percent of them, cannot be said to be reconciled or living in right relationship when many of them, again including the United States and Russia, brandish a standing threat to wipe out a large portion of one another's populations, even should they regard this threat as a means to peace and stability and hope never to carry it out. The long peace surely falls far short of a just peace.

In two respects, though, Pope Francis's statements raise questions. First, it is unclear whether his condemnation of the possession of nuclear weapons truly is a development of papal teaching and if so what it entails. Previous popes, dating back to the pleas of Pope Benedict XV in World War I, have called consistently for international mutual disarmament. Once the nuclear age began, they extended this call to nuclear disarmament. Both Pope St. John Paul II and the US Catholic bishops in their letter of 1983 "The Challenge of Peace" made nuclear disarmament the strict condition for their reluctant permission of nuclear deterrence, which John Paul II termed an "interim ethic."[6] Pope Francis's language, however, sounded as if he was taking a further step and condemning even the possession of nuclear weapons. Was he?

On a strong reading, Pope Francis was declaring the mere possession of nuclear weapons intrinsically immoral. The Church has taught from its earliest days that some actions are always and everywhere sinful—adultery, theft, murder—and since the Second Vatican Council has stressed ever more emphatically that certain practices in the social and political realms are intrinsically immoral, for instance, exploitative labor, torture, slavery, abortion, and indiscriminate warfare.[7] Did Pope Francis purport to add nuclear deterrence to this list?

Probably not. He inserted his strong words "their very possession . . . is to be firmly condemned" between a preceding clause, "if we take into account the risk of an accidental detonation," and a succeeding clause lamenting a "mentality of fear" that extends to the "entire human race." What is suggested here is that the pope is directing attention to certain grave drawbacks of nuclear weapons in an effort to accentuate the "interim" and "strictly conditional" nature of deterrence and to increase the urgency of disarmament. What is lacking here is the "always and everywhere" language of the intrinsically immoral. Critically lacking too are calls for the kinds of measures that would attend such a categorical condemnation, ones analogous to the counsel that a pastor would give to an adulterer: cease and desist at once; gradual disentanglement is not an option. Pope Francis did not call upon states to destroy their weapons and renounce their doctrines of deterrence immediately and unilaterally, advise military and governmental officials involved in maintaining the deterrent to walk away without hesitation, or inform Catholics of the implications of this new teaching for the sacraments of reconciliation, Eucharist, and last rites. He took none of the pastoral measures that would follow from a teaching that the mere possession of nuclear weapons is intrinsically immoral.

The second question arising from Pope Francis's remarks concerns his reasons for disarmament, which depend on political, strategic, and even technical judgments that do not follow automatically from the moral teachings of the Church. If Pope Francis is arguing not that the possession of nuclear weapons is intrinsically evil but rather that the world would be more just and peaceful in the absence of these weapons, then he is burdened to defend his views that deterrence is ineffective and that the risk of accident is unacceptably high against the argument that nuclear weapons secure the long peace, a peace that could be defended plausibly as a lesser evil than the alternatives. And he must explain how it is that nuclear disarmament yields dividends for human development, which is not obvious. "More bang for the buck" was a major rationale that led US policymakers to adopt a strategy of massive retaliation in the early 1950s, which they were convinced was a far cheaper strategy than a conventional defense of US interests against the Soviet Union and China.[8] Although today's strategic environment is quite different, the economics of foregoing deterrence and the benefits for reducing poverty are far from certain. These questions do not imply that Pope Francis's arguments cannot be defended but instead underline that such arguments belong to the empirical and social scientific domain and do not admit of settled answers.[9] So too, a peacebuilding strategy based on these arguments will always remain tentative.

A clearer, more radical condemnation of deterrence—and approach to peacebuilding—would emerge from the stronger absolutist interpretation of Pope Francis's remarks (which I have argued was not what he meant). Something quite like this position is defended in what may well stand as the most forceful, rigorous, and clear argument in the large literature on nuclear deterrence, John Finnis, Joseph M. Boyle Jr., and Germain Grisez's 1987 book *Nuclear Deterrence, Morality and Realism*.[10] The authors belong to an influential school of Catholic moral theology pioneered by Grisez, one of whose key achievements is a defense of absolute moral norms against consequentialist or "proportionalist" views, a position that would prove central to their assessment of nuclear weapons.

What Finnis et al. condemn is somewhat different than the mere possession of nuclear weapons; it is rather the intention to kill civilians that deterrence involves. This intention is conditional, to be sure, but is nevertheless exercised through the elaborate policies, procedures, and weapons systems involved in constructing and securing the deterrent. The authors stand squarely in the Catholic tradition, which has always condemned the intentional killing of innocents. The US bishops affirmed in their 1983 letter that a deterrent that targets civilian populations also would violate the principle of discrimination, a cornerstone of a Christian ethic of war.[11] They refrained from condemning the US policy of deterrence outright, though, because they were convinced that it did not explicitly target civilians.

This is where Finnis et al. demur. The critical moral problem with the US deterrent, they argue, is not precisely its targeting policies, which may well aim at military assets, but rather the intention to kill civilians, which US policymakers never have refrained from articulating. Finnis et al. demonstrate meticulously that even in the era of flexible response and war-fighting strategies that began in the 1960s and continued through the writing of their book, policymakers consistently incorporated open threats of "city swapping," "final retaliation," "massive retaliation," and "unacceptable damage" into US deterrence policy.[12] Policymakers did not articulate these threats accidentally or incidentally but instead viewed them as essential for effective deterrence against an enemy that possesses a parallel capacity for massive destruction.

Finnis et al. judge it highly unlikely that deterrence strategy could be revised so as to avoid this murderous intention. They consider and reject as unrealistic a purely counterforce deterrent, one aimed only at military targets. The only morally sound course of action, they conclude, is unilateral disarmament on the part of nuclear states and immediate cessation of complicity with deterrence on the part of government and military officials. They do not reach this judgment blithely or optimistically but rather with the expectation that it would result in the Soviet conquest of Western societies that are far more just in character. They insist, though, as the Church has always insisted, that murder is always wrong as an end or a means, as an executed action or as a simple intention. They quote Cardinal John Henry Newman's view that "non-moral evil and suffering can never be equivalent to even a venial sin one commits" and conclude with a poignant reflection on the Kingdom of Heaven as the realm where faithfulness in respecting human life is eternally rewarded.[13] Their argument is reminiscent of that of one of the twentieth century's greatest Catholic philosophers, Elizabeth Anscombe, who closed her 1961 essay "War and Murder" with this retort to the argument that nuclear weapons were necessary to defend the Church in the West:

> It is not a vague faith in the triumph of the spirit over force (there is little enough warrant for that), but a definite faith in the divine promises, that makes us believe that the Church cannot fail. Those, therefore, who think they must be prepared to wage a war with Russia involving the deliberate massacre of cities, must be prepared to say to God: "We had to break your law, lest your Church fail. We could not obey your commandments, for we did not believe your promises."[14]

Like Finnis et al., Anscombe was not driven to her position by a "third way" stance in the Cold War but rather by her insistence that a murderous intention is always and everywhere forbidden.

Not long after Finnis et al. published their book, the Cold War ended. Western powers' threat of massive civilian death did not end, however, and remains US policy today. Perhaps a renunciation of deterrence would have less dire consequences than Finnis et al. believed it would have had in the 1980s. Some analysts argue that the United States now has so great a superiority in conventional weapons that it could deter a nuclear attack from Russia, China, or North Korea through counterforce threats alone.[15] If one believes with Pope Francis that nuclear deterrence is ineffective, then unilateral disarmament would likely have little consequence for—and may even improve the state of—peace and stability. These, again, are strategic debates whose outcome is uncertain. What is clear in light of traditional Christian teaching is that one cannot intend the death of an innocent person without separating oneself from God. When an entire society intends the death of another society's civilians, then this society, much like the Israelites of the Old Testament, has turned away from God collectively and is manifestly not at peace.

How Then to Build Peace?

What strategy for peacebuilding arises from this analysis? I opened this essay by observing the emergence of a peacebuilding ethic comprising the kinds of practices that have come to be common in addressing the past wounds of armed conflict and dictatorship. Yet, I noted that nuclear deterrence is different. Nuclear weapons have been used only once, and their subsequent role in global politics has not resulted in direct casualties or the widespread violations of human rights that are characteristic of war and dictatorship. An even bigger difference is the lack of a social consensus on the justice of nuclear weapons. Many peacebuilding practices—truth commissions, reparations schemes, etc.—in recent years are based on standards such as human rights that enjoy a strong popular consensus even if there is less agreement about who violated whose rights and why. Little social consensus exists in nuclear armed states, by contrast, on whether nuclear weapons (or deterrence, use, or possession, depending on how the question is put) are just. There is no broad consensus, for instance, that nuclear deterrence ought to be an interim ethic, that time is running out on the acceptability of this ethic, and that multilateral disarmament is morally imperative, as Pope Francis and contributors to this volume argue. Still less is there consensus on the view of nuclear deterrence that I have endorsed, namely that it involves an immoral intention that ought to be renounced at once by states and by individuals who are complicit in cooperating with this intention.

Given this lack of consensus, it is unsurprising that few peacebuilding measures have taken place with respect to nuclear weapons. An important but partial exception is arms control, for instance, the Strategic Arms Reduction Treaty process, which was advanced most recently through the agreement of 2010 between the United States and the Russian Federation. Progress is halting, though. Only in the past few years, the United States and Russia mutually withdrew from the Intermediate-Range Nuclear Forces Treaty, which they signed in 1987. Beyond arms control, few of the practices that have come to be associated with peacebuilding have taken place. In an insightful set of remarks at a conference on nuclear weapons in May 2016, political scientist Maryann Cusimano Love pointed out that in the aftermath of the Cold War, the United States and Russia for the most part did not undertake the sort of peacebuilding practices that have come to be standard in recent years, some of which took place between former enemies after World War II: contrition, forgiveness, the airing of truth, and the building of common institutions for the purpose of advancing peace.[16] Nor has the United States apologized for history's only use of nuclear weapons.

It is unlikely that a popular consensus on the injustice of nuclear weapons and nuclear deterrence or, still more, any peacebuilding practices regarding nuclear weapons will emerge any time soon. Even arms control looks unpromising at the moment, though this is the most likely practice to regain momentum. Among the other practices, perhaps the most urgent, given this state of affairs, is the telling of truth. This will not take the form of a truth commission—not any time soon, at any rate—but instead involves those who are convinced of the injustice of nuclear deterrence seeking, with renewed vigor, to persuade their fellow citizens of this injustice: an evangelization of justice. This effort might begin with Catholic populations, whose Church teaches the absolute, exceptionless character of the norm that forbids intentionally killing the innocent and might then be extended to other citizens on the basis that this norm is one of natural law.[17] Urgent too is educating these same citizens that current nuclear deterrence doctrines involve the threats of retaliation against civilians, a reality that many have forgotten since the end of the Cold War.

A strategy in this evangelization might be based on the concept of moral ecology that William Barbieri discusses in his essay in this volume and that he illustrates through Pope Francis's encyclical on the natural environment, *Laudato si'*. My own interpretation of our moral ecology would stress the interdependence of the wide popular acceptance of nuclear deterrence and the wide acceptance of other intrinsic moral evils. In delivering a talk to high school students on the jettisoning of sexual mores in the 1960s, Archbishop Fulton Sheen located the origins of the problem at "8:15 in the morning, the 6th of August, 1945." More recently, contemporary Catholic evangelists Chris Stefanick wrote that "it has been said that 'the fruit of abortion is nuclear war.' The logic is that abortion creates a society where human life isn't valued above all else, where the end justifies the means, and where moral absolutes can be obliterated by good intentions. All of that was engrained in our nation's psyche 30 years before *Roe v. Wade*. I think it would be more accurate to say, 'The fruit of nuclear war was abortion.'"[18]

Hiroshima and Nagasaki plowed the soil, in terms of moral norms, for the adoption of massive retaliation by US policymakers in the early 1950s. Once wide swaths of societies had accepted nuclear deterrence based on retaliation against civilians as a fundamental part of their defense postures—thus normalizing murder into the fabric of their common life—it was unsurprising that they would make similar judgments about the practice of abortion, which has now taken over sixty million lives in the United States and is practiced at high rates in other nuclear states such as the United Kingdom, France, Russia, China, and India. Hiroshima and Nagasaki were preceded in turn by the practice of indiscriminate bombing of cities in Germany and Japan on the part of the United States and the United Kingdom during World War II. Here too the norm against murder was violated, as Jesuit moral theologian John Ford, SJ, explained in his 1944 article in *Theological Studies*, which he courageously wrote during the war.[19] It was in reaction to these practices that *Gaudium et spes*, the pastoral constitution of which was devoted to social and political questions, declared emphatically that "Any act of war aimed indiscriminately at the destruction of entire cities of extensive areas along with their population is a crime against God and man himself. It merits unequivocal and unhesitating condemnation."[20]

Significantly, Fr. Ford was one of the architects of the encyclical *Humanae vitae* in 1968, which upheld the Church's prohibition on contraceptive acts, another teaching about intrinsic evil that would be widely flouted in Western societies including by Catholics. Similarly, the writings of Anscombe contain arguments against nuclear deterrence as well as contraception.[21] Both Ford's and Anscombe's thought underscore the plausibility that wide social rejection of moral norms in one realm of life fosters a similar rejection in another, the idea of moral ecology.

If a widespread consensus on the immorality of deterrence were ever to emerge—which, again, I do not expect any time soon—we can hope that nuclear-armed states will renounce their deterrent postures and their attendant threats. Then, other measures of peacebuilding might take place, for instance, political apologies and acts of contrition performed by a head of state on behalf of an entire country. Since the 1990s, political apologies have become common in global politics. In most cases, heads of state apologize for crimes committed by previous heads of state in their own country. German presidents and chancellors, for instance, have expressed contrition for the crimes of the Nazi past beginning with Chancellor Willy Brandt's *Kniefall* before the monument to the victims of the Warsaw uprising in 1970 and continuing through numerous statements and gestures up through the present day. Other examples include US president George H. W. Bush's apology to Japanese Americans interned in World War II, US president Bill Clinton's apology for his failure to intervene in the Rwanda genocide and for US complicity in human rights violations in Guatemala during the Cold War, and scores of other instances from around the world.[22]

What gives heads of state authority to apologize for crimes committed by other heads of state? Injustices committed by heads of state, people in uniform, or anyone acting in the name of the state have two dimensions: personal and collective. The personal dimension relates to the act of the individual perpetrator alone, for which only he or she is guilty and only he or she can atone for, a possibility that ends with the individual's death. The collective dimension is the sense in which the entire society—in whose name the leader or the person in uniform acts—is implicated in the injustice. It is this dimension for which a subsequent head of state—speaking in the name of the entire society—could apologize. Through apology, a head of state names an injustice as an injustice, accepts responsibility for it (at least for the collective dimension), renounces it as a source of national pride, invites the members of the society to remember the deed as an unjust one, and asks for forgiveness from the victims of the injustice or their representatives.[23]

In principle, a United States president or the head of another nuclear state could apologize rightfully for the deterrence policy that has threatened (and thus intended) the deaths of innocents or, in the US case, for the bombings of Hiroshima and Nagasaki. In the US case, the president's apology would be directed toward citizens of the former Soviet Union (including representatives of those now deceased) and living survivors of the Hiroshima and Nagasaki bombings and representatives of those who have died.

If a US president or other head of a nuclear state were to apologize, what sort of effect might it have? In addition to the primary or intrinsic reasons for apology, there is this question of what sort of consequences one would have for peace and reconciliation. Would it unify a society in condemnation of past injustices?[24] Or would it produce a bitter backlash that would serve only to lead a society away from contrition? In 2016, President Barack Obama became the first sitting US president to visit Hiroshima and did so to advance peace and reconciliation. He insisted, though, that he was not apologizing for the US bombing, no doubt in part to stave off criticisms that he was embarking on an "apology tour." Had he apologized he surely would have faced a popular backlash in the United States, where a 2015 Pew Research Center survey showed that 70 percent of Americans over age sixty-five considered the atomic bombs justified, while 47 percent of those eighteen to twenty-nine years old thought the same.[25] Such a backlash would have mimicked that in Japan, the very country that he was visiting. There, prime ministers began to apologize robustly for war crimes that the Japanese army had committed in World War II, yet they elicited strong and wide criticisms from nationalist factions resulting in a divisive public dispute that did little for the cause of contrition.[26] One wonders whether if Obama had apologized he would have created a dynamic that would have made contrition more acceptable in Japan, even while he risked unpopularity in the United States.

Apologies—at least implicitly—request forgiveness, still another practice of peacebuilding that deals with past injustice. Whereas apologies have burgeoned in global politics, forgiveness is comparatively rare on the part of heads of states, speaking for collectivities. True, it has become more common among victims in the past generation and has taken place in societies facing past injustices such as South Africa, Uganda, Northern Ireland, and El Salvador. It is almost unheard of, though, on the part of heads of state. I have argued elsewhere that on the same grounds that leaders may apologize in the name of collectivities, they also, in principle, could forgive in the name of collectivities.[27] It is a practice that could go far to build peace and reconciliation between states but one that stands in need of pioneers.

To speak of peacebuilding with regard to nuclear deterrence requires faith. It is to explore possibilities that are distant. Nuclear issues, though, are inherently apocalyptic. The prospect of nuclear war is the prospect of destruction of biblical proportions. The risk of this destruction is one from which even the most cool-headed, realist advocate of deterrence cannot distance oneself. If such an individual can broach the apocalypse, though, then why cannot the peacebuilder do the same? The Christian peacebuilder also appeals to end times and biblical proportions but stresses the truly final outcome: reconciliation of all things, a new Heaven and new Earth. To place oneself on the side of the moral law is to side with the commandments that will be vindicated at that time. To engage in practices of reconciliation and peacebuilding is to prepare for this time and the ultimate, definitive, repair that it will bring.[28]

Notes

1. For explorations of these questions, see Robert J. Schreiter, R. Scott Appleby, and Gerard F. Powers, *Peacebuilding: Catholic Theology, Ethics, and Praxis* (Maryknoll, NY: Orbis Books, 2010); Daniel Philpott and Gerard F. Powers, *Strategies of Peace: Transforming Conflict in a Violent World* (Oxford: Oxford University Press, 2010); Daniel Philpott, *Just and Unjust Peace: An Ethic of Political Reconciliation* (Oxford: Oxford University Press, 2012); and John Paul Lederach, *Building Peace: Sustainable Reconciliation in Divided Societies* (Washington, DC: United States Institute of Peace, 1997).
2. See Daniel Philpott, "Why Obama Should Apologize for Hiroshima," *New York Daily News*, May 26, 2016.
3. See, for instance, John Lewis Gaddis, "The Long Peace: Elements of Stability in the Postwar International System," *International Security* 10, no. 4 (Spring 1986): 99–142; and Michael C. Desch, "No More Nukes? An Exchange," *Commonweal*, February 9, 2018. For an argument that the spread of nuclear weapons would actually contribute to global peace, see Kenneth Waltz, "The Spread of Nuclear Weapons: More May Be Better," *Adelphi Papers*, No. 171 (London: International Institute for Strategic Studies, 1981).
4. Quoted from an excerpt in Gerard Powers, "Papal Condemnation of Nuclear Deterrence and What Is Next," *Arms Control Today*, May 2018.
5. On the threat of a nuclear accident, see the important work of Eric Schlosser, *Command and Control: Nuclear Deterrence, the Damascus Accident and the Illusion of Safety* (New York: Penguin Books, 2013).
6. National Conference of Catholic Bishops of the United States, *The Challenge of Peace: God's Promise and Our Response* (Washington, DC: United States Catholic Conference), February 1, 1984; and John Paul II, "Message of His Holiness John Paul II to the General Assembly of the United Nations," June 7, 1982.
7. Second Vatican Council (1965), *Gaudium et spes: Pastoral Constitution on the Church in the Modern World*, nos. 181–82; and John Paul II, *Veritatis splendor*, August 6, 1993, no. 80.
8. See John Lewis Gaddis, *Strategies of Containment* (Oxford: Oxford University Press, 1982), 132–34.
9. To be sure, respected scholars and policymakers have joined in the case for total global mutual disarmament. See George P. Schultz, William J. Perry, Henry A. Kissinger, and Sam Nunn, "A World Free of Nuclear Weapons," *Wall Street Journal*, January 4, 2007.
10. John Finnis, Joseph Boyle, and Germain Grisez, *Nuclear Deterrence, Morality and Realism* (Oxford: Oxford University Press, 1987).
11. *The Challenge of Peace*, 532.
12. See, for instance, *Nuclear Posture Review Report*, US Department of Defense, April 2010, 30.

13. Finnis et al., *Nuclear Deterrence, Morality and Realism*, 382. They quote Newman at greater length in their notes on page 389 as saying "the Catholic Church holds it better for . . . all the many millions on [the earth] to die of starvation in extremest agony, as far as temporal affliction goes, than that one soul . . . should commit one venial sin, should tell one willful untruth, or . . ."
14. G.E.M. Anscombe, "War and Murder," in *Nuclear Weapons: A Catholic Response*, ed. Walter Stein, 43–62 (London: Sheed and Ward, 1961).
15. Keir Lieber and Daryl Press, "The Rise of U.S. Nuclear Primacy," *Foreign Affairs*, March/April 2006. It is not the task of Lieber and Press in this piece to advocate a renunciation of threats to civilians or a pure counterforce strategy. Their argument points to the technological possibility of these courses of action.
16. Cusimano Love delivered her remarks at the conference "Nuclear Proliferation, Deterrence, and Disarmament: Evolving Catholic Approaches," convened by the Nuclear Threat Initiative in London on May 24, 2016.
17. John Paul II, *Veritatis splendor*, nos. 79–83.
18. R. Jared Staudt, "The Anniversary of Hiroshima: John Paul II and Fulton Sheen on the Bomb and Conversion," *Catholic World Report*, August 6, 2014.
19. John C. Ford, "The Morality of Obliteration Bombing," *Theological Studies* 5, no. 3 (September 1944): 261–309.
20. Second Vatican Council (1965), *Gaudium et spes: Pastoral Constitution on the Church in the Modern World*, nos. 80, 221–22.
21. G.E.M. Anscombe, *Faith in a Hard Ground: Essays on Religion, Philosophy, and Ethics*, ed. Mary Geach and Luke Gormally (Exeter, UK: Imprint Academic, 2008), 170–98.
22. Philpott, *Just and Unjust Peace*, 198–200.
23. Philpott, 200–206.
24. Much of what I have learned about the determinants of effective apologies is from Ji Eun Kim, "Good and Bad Apologies: Determinants of Successful State Apologies," PhD diss., University of Notre Dame, 2017.
25. President Obama's visit is discussed and this statistic is cited in Philpott, "Why Obama Should Apologize for Hiroshima."
26. Jennifer Lind, *Sorry States* (Ithaca, NY: Cornell University Press, 2008), 26–101.
27. Philpott, *Just and Unjust Peace*, 279–84.
28. Finnis et al.'s final chapter of *Nuclear Deterrence, Morality and Realism* is a powerful account of the connection between acting justly in this life and the Kingdom of Heaven.

16

Prophetic Indictment or Deliberative Discussion?

BERNARD G. PRUSAK

A little more than halfway through their 1983 pastoral letter "The Challenge of Peace," the US bishops acknowledge voices "call[ing] us to raise a prophetic challenge to the community of faith—a challenge which goes beyond nuclear deterrence."[1] Those prophetic voices rejected the position, embraced at that time by the majority of the US bishops and Pope John Paul II, that nuclear deterrence was an acceptable "interim ethic" so long as disarmament was the ultimate goal.[2] One of those voices, Thomas Merton, claimed that "there is simply no 'good end' that renders [the] risk [of nuclear war] permissible" and questioned whether rationalizations for "wielding the threat of nuclear destruction" do not constitute cooperation in evil.[3]

As other contributions to this volume document, leading voices in the Roman Catholic Church, not least Pope Francis, have begun to sound more like Merton than like the US bishops in the 1980s. Prophetic indictment of not only the use but also the very possession of nuclear weapons is no longer limited to the likes of Merton, the Berrigans, and activist groups such as Plowshares. Thus, in a 2017 address Pope Francis commended the "prophetic voice" of the *hibakusha*, the survivors of the bombings of Hiroshima and Nagasaki, and condemned the "very possession" of nuclear weapons.[4] In his visit to Hiroshima in late November 2019, Francis reiterated that condemnation.[5] Cardinal Robert McElroy of San Diego has claimed that "the possession itself of [nuclear] weapons is now condemned, regardless of the intention."[6] And Drew Christiansen, the editor of this volume, wrote in *La Civiltà Cattolica*, a journal with close ties to the Vatican, that "we should cease to imagine nuclear weapons as tools for us to manage, but rather as a curse we must banish,"⁷ language that "The Challenge of Peace" reserved for the arms race but that prophetic voices in the preceding half century applied to the weapons themselves.⁸

Pope Francis's November 2019 visit to Japan, which included stops in both Nagasaki and Hiroshima, brought attention to the Vatican's renewed diplomacy on nuclear weapons, which this volume also aims to serve. To that end, one could argue that more attention now needs to be given to the question of how people who fervently wish for a world rid of nuclear weapons should go about arguing for it. More precisely, what is the rhetorical strategy that is best geared to the goal of ridding the world of nuclear weapons? As the moral theologian Cathleen Kaveny explains in her book *Prophecy without Contempt: Religious Discourse in the Public Square*, prophets demand unambiguous compliance with unconditional moral imperatives.⁹ By contrast, what she calls "deliberators" allow that moral rules need to take into account complex circumstances, human weakness, ignorance, and sin.¹⁰

Kaveny gives three examples of pressing moral issues that, in her judgment, currently are not ripe for the rhetoric of prophetic indictment: animal rights, gun control, and climate change.¹¹ Her reasons for this judgment differ for each of the issues, but key questions include, first, whether would-be prophets can draw on at least some of the fundamental commitments of our present political community or only on the commitments of a utopian community they imagine and hope for,¹² and second, whether what is at issue is indeed moral failure rather than good faith disagreement about the relevant underlying facts.¹³ With respect to the first question, would-be prophets who cannot draw on commonly recognized moral commitments are not likely to get a hearing. Instead, they are likely to alienate people and thereby set back their cause. To put the point differently, even "norm entrepreneurs" who aim to jar people out of moral passivity and acquiescence need leverage from deeply rooted norms. With respect to the second question, if what is really at issue is good faith disagreement about the relevant underlying facts, railing about moral failure would indict, ironically, precisely the would-be prophets for failing to come to terms appropriately with the question at hand.

How do things stand, then, with the pressing moral issue of nuclear weapons in the twenty-first century? Is it currently ripe for prophetic indictment, or does that rhetorical strategy risk backfiring under present conditions?[14]

To begin with, the would-be prophet surely can draw on widely shared and deeply held commitments to denounce any use of nuclear weapons that directly targets civilian populations or that "unintentionally" though foreseeably kills and maims massive numbers of civilians.[15] The prophet can also draw on common moral commitments in denouncing any systems, strategies, or policies that would either increase the likelihood of nuclear warfare among the current nuclear powers or stimulate nuclear proliferation, thereby both imperiling peace in unstable regions such as Northeast Asia and making it more likely that terrorist organizations will acquire a nuclear device.[16] In this regard, the signs of the times have been ominous over the last several years. If as Pope John Paul II claimed, "the condemnation of evils and injustices . . . is an aspect of the Church's prophetic role,"[17] prophets have a lot of material to work with, from North Korea's expansion of its ballistic missiles program to Russia's violation of the Intermediate-Range Nuclear Forces Treaty to the Trump administration's withdrawal from the Joint Comprehensive Plan of Action with Iran and abrogation of the treaty in response to Russia's violations. The agreement between the Biden administration and Vladimir Putin's Russia to extend the New START treaty, which limits the countries' nuclear arsenals, is a rare piece of good news.

The would-be prophet seems to be on shakier ground in denouncing nuclear deterrence as such, as opposed, for example, to strategies of nuclear deterrence that court a destabilizing arms race. Documents such as the Vatican's 2014 white paper "Nuclear Disarmament: A Time for Abolition" make it difficult to pin down the Church's official position. Gerard Powers has proposed that the Vatican's call for abolition is "not based on a moral rejection of the concept of deterrence itself, but a prudential judgment . . . about the morality of the particular structure of deterrence as it exists today."[18] That interpretation is supported by passages in the white paper,[19] but the reader also finds statements such as "it must be admitted that the very possession of nuclear weapons, even for purposes of deterrence, is morally problematic."[20]

Whatever the Vatican's current position on deterrence as such, it is indeed horrible that nations would have "a policy which makes it a mark of the good serviceman to be willing, in the appropriate circumstances, to commit murder on a gigantic scale."[21] Moreover, it is chilling to hear a serviceperson reflect that "you have to know you would follow through."[22] Yet for all that, it is not obvious that the US bishops' question in "The Challenge of Peace," "May a nation threaten what it may never do?" must have the answer "no."[23] (Here this essay differs from Gregory Reichberg's.)[24]

The argument that the answer to this question must always be "no" typically turns on the claim that it is morally impermissible to do evil that good may come of it.[25] According to this argument, it is evil for a nation to intend the massacre of civilians for its own preservation. Yet that has been US policy since the Cold War. It is not only Catholic ethicists who find this policy evil. In his 2017 book *The Doomsday Machine*, Daniel Ellsberg, of Pentagon Papers fame, laments that "what is missing . . . in the typical discussion and analysis of historical or current nuclear policies is the recognition that what is being discussed is dizzyingly insane and immoral."[26] An anticonsequentialist thinker such as Elizabeth Anscombe might take the argument a step further: because the use of nuclear weapons would be evil and because there is no point in stockpiling weapons that a nation must never use, nations with nuclear weapons should simply get rid of them without calculating the possible consequences.

There are, however, several objections to this line of argument. First, is the choice of nuclear deterrence for fear of nuclear blackmail by a hostile power—and presumably either annihilation or subjugation—rightly depicted as a choice to do evil that good may come of it? Or should it be depicted instead as a choice between two evils, full stop (which is how the French bishops, for example, saw it in their 1993 statement *Gagner la paix*).[27] In that analysis, nuclear deterrence might be defended as less evil than annihilation or subjugation. This brings us to the second objection: Is a threat to do evil, made in the hopes that it will never have to be carried out, as wrong morally as actually doing the evil? Surely not: not all evils are equally wrong.[28] In that case, why would a lesser evil (nuclear deterrence) not be permitted if it has the consequence of preventing a greater evil (annihilation or subjugation)? Finally, if we are considering how to counter a threat of aggression, arguably the question to ask is not what we would be permitted to do after the act of aggression that we hope to prevent but rather what we are permitted to do in the course of trying to prevent it.[29]

Imagine, with apologies in advance for the thought experiment, that someone threatens your child's life. Is it morally permissible for you to threaten in turn the life of that person's child in order to save your own child? Clearly it would be morally impermissible for you to kill the other person's child, but according to this objection, that is the wrong consideration in the circumstances. Focusing, as you surely would, on how to counter the threat against your own child, it is much less clear that it is wrong for you to make the threat against the other person's child not only as a bluff but instead as a threat that you are seriously prepared to carry out.

The point of articulating these objections is not to defend current US policy or that of any of the current nuclear powers. Ellsberg is right: "what is being discussed is dizzyingly insane and immoral."[30] And Anscombe is right, I believe, to reject consequentialism as a moral theory. Instead, the point is to indicate that the morality of nuclear deterrence is deeply contested.[31] Deep-rooted commitments can be invoked to defend it, such as the conviction that it is "a fundamental duty of political leadership . . . to protect the citizenry from harm," just as it is a fundamental duty of parents to protect their children, which is the analogy at the heart of the preceding paragraph's gruesome thought experiment.[32] The upshot is that nuclear deterrence as such does not appear ripe for prophetic indictment, which Reichberg likewise appears to acknowledge with his concession that unilateral disarmament "would be to invite nuclear blackmail, a position into which no state, mindful of its obligations, could place itself."[33]

If that is correct, then deliberative discussion about how to reduce the present dangers of nuclear catastrophe is the order of the day. Ellsberg may present a helpful model here to Catholic leaders. His rhetoric against the "modernization" of the US nuclear arsenal to improve first-strike capability is prophetic, but he allows the legitimacy of maintaining, for now, a minimal nuclear deterrent.[34] His example demonstrates that even prophets should not restrict themselves to prophetic denunciation. Just saying "no" will not do.[35]

In this regard, it is worth noting that the thought experiment above hardly suggests that deterrence is a stable equilibrium, especially in our multipolar world where the actions of third parties—say, North Korea or China or an American president on mind-altering steroids—can introduce new, destabilizing calculations. Nearly fifty years ago, the moral theologian Paul Ramsey presented a similar thought experiment involving the feud between the Hatfields and the McCoys.[36] In the heat of the moment when the eldest Hatfield has in his sights the youngest McCoy and the eldest McCoy aims for the youngest Hatfield, the focus is on the vulnerable children. After a while, though, attention is likely to turn to the weapons themselves, on the grounds that protecting the weapons is protecting the children. Yet if one side, say the McCoys, protects its weapons so well that they become indestructible, then that side endangers its children anew because the equilibrium the McCoys had with the Hatfields is destabilized: the Hatfields' weapons are vulnerable in a way that the McCoys' are not, which gives the Hatfields reason to use their weapons before they can be destroyed. Thus, technological breakthroughs improving the speed of delivery systems and the destructive power of the weapons also threaten to destabilize the cease-fire between the families. The upshot is that what had appeared to be a stable, if mad, plan of peace is exposed as a high-risk game of chicken. For all that, until the families can reach a peace based on trust and mutual disarmament, deterrence is their only choice.

Whether the policy of deterrence makes trust harder to establish is a good question, but it is not one that can be answered in the abstract without attention to the actual prospects for diplomatic breakthroughs. Here a claim made by Gerard Powers in this volume and elsewhere is to the point: if nuclear disarmament is the policy goal, we need a new ethics of nuclear defense and deterrence that recognizes and takes seriously the new threats that getting rid of nuclear weapons would likely conjure in a world where neither the evil of the human heart nor the knowledge of how to make nuclear weapons can be wished away.

To recall, the second question that Kaveny asks us to consider is whether there is good faith disagreement about the relevant underlying facts. In that case, prophetic indictment would again be ill-conceived. By way of example, Pope Francis has made a number of empirical claims about nuclear weapons. One is that they threaten "catastrophic humanitarian and environmental effects,"[37] which is indisputable. A second is that they divert attention and funding from "the real priorities facing our human family, such as the fight against poverty, the promotion of peace, the undertaking of educational, ecological and healthcare projects, and the development of human rights."[38] Given that the cost of US nuclear forces is estimated to run as high as $2 trillion over the next thirty years, the pope's point appears well taken. At the same time, the far greater share of military spending is on conventional warfare, with the upshot that it can plausibly be claimed, in good faith, that "it is hard to see clear connections between the nuclear programs of nine countries . . . and the grave political, economic, and social problems plaguing the developing world."[39]

Once more, the point of articulating objections to prophetic discourse about nuclear deterrence is not to defend current US policy or the policies of any other nuclear power. To the contrary, this essay has been intended as an invitation to Catholic leaders to reflect on the rhetorical strategy that is most likely to advance the goal of nuclear disarmament. Jesus instructed his disciples, whom he sent out like sheep into the midst of wolves, to be both wise as serpents and innocent as doves (Matthew 10:16). If sheep can also be serpents and doves, perhaps the Church's leaders can find a way to mix the thunder of the prophet on some issues of nuclear policy with the prudence and humility of the deliberator on others. Nothing less is likely to succeed in moving us a step closer to multilateral nuclear disarmament.

Notes

1. National Conference of Catholic Bishops, *The Challenge of Peace: God's Promise and Our Response* (Washington, DC: United States Catholic Conference, 1983), no. 198.
2. For insightful analysis of the bishops' "interim ethics," see Gerard Powers, "From Nuclear Deterrence to Disarmament: Evolving Catholic Perspectives," *Arms Control Today*, May 2015. That "evolution" is evident in the reevaluation of "The Challenge of Peace" published in 1998 by seventy-five US Catholic bishops associated with Pax Christi, available from Canadian Coalition for Nuclear Responsibility, http://ccnr.org/pax_christi.html. See also the US bishops' earlier "pastoral reflection on the moral life," *To Live in Christ Jesus* (Washington, DC: United States Catholic Conference, 1976), 10. "As possessors of a vast nuclear arsenal, we must also be aware that not only is it wrong to attack civilian populations but it is also wrong to threaten to attack them as part of a strategy of deterrence."
3. Thomas Merton, "Nuclear War and Christian Responsibility," *Commonweal*, February 6, 1962.
4. Pope Francis, "Address to Participants in the International Symposium 'Prospects for a World Free of Nuclear Weapons and for Integral Disarmament,'" November 10, 2017.
5. Pope Francis, "Address of the Holy Father," Peace Memorial, Hiroshima, November 24, 2019. "The use of atomic energy for purposes of war is immoral, just as the possessing of nuclear weapons is immoral, as I already said two years ago."

6. See Gerard O'Connell, "Nuclear Disarmament Now a 'Moral Imperative' as Pope Rejects Deterrence," *America*, November 13, 2017.
7. Drew Christiansen, "The Church Says 'No' to Nuclear Weapons: Pastoral and Moral Implications," *La Civiltà Cattolica*, May 14, 2018, 8.
8. See, for example, Phil Berrigan, shortly before his death in 2002, as quoted in Jim Forest, *At Play in the Lions' Den: A Biography and a Memoir of Daniel Berrigan* (Maryknoll, NY: Orbis, 2017), 278. "I die with the conviction, held since 1968 and Catonsville, that nuclear weapons are the scourge of the earth; to mine for them, manufacture them, deploy them, use them, is a curse against God, the human family, and the earth itself."
9. Cathleen Kaveny, *Prophecy without Contempt: Religious Discourse in the Public Square* (Cambridge, MA: Harvard University Press, 2016), 261.
10. Kaveny.
11. Kaveny, 324.
12. Kaveny, 323.
13. Kaveny, 325.
14. Cf. Judith Valente, "Paths to Peace," *U.S. Catholic*, September 2018, 28–33, quoting figures such as Tom Cornell, Jim Forest, and Martha Hennessy.
15. One of the weaker moments of "The Challenge of Peace" appears in its statement that a strike against "industrial or militarily significant economic targets within heavily populated areas . . . would be . . . morally disproportionate, even though not intentionally indiscriminate" (no. 182). See Robert W. Tucker, "Morality and Deterrence," *Ethics* 95 (1985): 461–78, who notes that "one might almost suspect the bishops of a fine irony here" unless they really do subscribe to "the notion of the 'intentless' destruction of entire societies" (472).
16. See Sidney D. Drell and James E. Goodby, *The Gravest Danger: Nuclear Weapons* (Stanford, CA: Hoover Institution Press, 2003), 24 and 109, for a dire reckoning of the consequences of a nuclear-armed North Korea. If the Bush administration's response to the terrorist attacks of September 11, 2001, is any indication, a terrorist attack on a US city with a nuclear device likely would lead to severe restrictions on civil liberties and far-flung military adventurism.
17. Pope John Paul II, *Sollicitudo rei socialis* (December 30, 1987), no. 41.
18. See Powers, "From Nuclear Deterrence to Disarmament."
19. See Holy See, "Nuclear Disarmament: Time for Abolition," in *Nuclear Deterrence: An Ethical Perspective*, ed. Mathias Nebel and Gregory M. Reichberg, 87–97 (Chambésy, Switzerland: Caritas in Veritate Foundation, 2015). "In the absence of further progress toward complete disarmament, and without concrete steps toward a more secure and a more genuine peace, the nuclear weapon establishment has lost much of its legitimacy" (89).
20. Holy See.
21. Anthony Kenny, *The Logic of Deterrence* (Chicago: University of Chicago Press, 1985), 54.

22. See Paul Sonne, "How an ICBM Commander Learned to Stop Worrying and Love the Bomb," *Washington Post*, September 1, 2018.
23. *The Challenge of Peace*, no. 137.
24. See also Reichberg's longer paper "The Morality of Nuclear Deterrence: A Reassessment," in *Nuclear Deterrence: An Ethical Perspective*, 9–31. Reichberg's crucial claim is that "to place oneself in a position where failure [of a deterrent threat] would in all likelihood entail [immoral action, namely, massive nuclear retaliation] is itself morally objectionable" (22). In my judgment, that claim needs further argumentation than Reichberg provides.
25. See John Finnis, Joseph Boyle, and Germain Grisez, *Nuclear Deterrence, Morality and Realism* (Oxford: Oxford University Press, 1987), 327.
26. Daniel Ellsberg, *The Doomsday Machine: Confessions of a Nuclear War Planner* (New York: Bloomsbury, 2017), 348.
27. See *Gagner la paix* (November 8, 1983), no. 39, Doctrine sociale de l'Église catholique, https://www.doctrine-sociale-catholique.fr/textes-des-conferences-episcopales-francophones/254-gagner-la-paix#Gagner%20la%20paix. "Affronté à un choix entre deux maux quasiment imparables, la capitulation ou la contre-menace, on choisit le moindre sans prétendre en faire un bien!"
28. Cf. Jeff McMahan, "Deterrence and Deontology," *Ethics* 95 (1985): 517–36, esp. 527–29.
29. See Gerald Dworkin, "Nuclear Intentions," *Ethics* 95 (1985): 445–60, esp. 459.
30. Ellsberg, *The Doomsday Machine*, 348.
31. For what may be the most philosophically fascinating and complex discussion in the literature, see Gregory Kavka, "Some Paradoxes of Deterrence," *Journal of Philosophy* 75 (1978): 285–302.
32. Reichberg, "The Morality of Nuclear Deterrence," 19.
33. Reichberg, 26.
34. See Ellsberg, *The Doomsday Machine*, 345.
35. See further Peter Steinfels' insightful review of Ellsberg's book in *America*, December 27, 2017.
36. Paul Ramsey, "The Hatfields and the Coys," in *The Just War: Force and Political Responsibility*, 168–77 (Lanham, MD: University Press of America, 1983 [1968]).
37. Pope Francis, "Address to Participants in the International Symposium."
38. Pope Francis.
39. Michael C. Desch, "No More Nukes? An Exchange" (with Gerard Powers), *Commonweal*, February 9, 2018.

PART V

Conscience Formation

17

Formation of Conscience Regarding the Development, Possession, and Use of Nuclear Weapons

MARGARET R. PFEIL

Pope Francis's position carries many implications, and one emerges clearly for consideration: What work is needed, ethically and theologically, to help form the consciences of US citizens regarding the possession and use of nuclear weapons? The United States possesses the most nuclear warheads of any nation in the world (about 6,800) after Russia (about 7,000) and remains the only nation to have used nuclear weapons in warfare. Yet there is shockingly little public awareness of corresponding responsibilities, particularly the foundational obligation of forming conscience rightly.

Conscience

Conscience, Richard Gula has remarked, "is another word like 'sin'—often used but little understood."[1] It involves the capacity to discern and choose the morally right course of action in a particular situation. In doing so, a person brings to bear a lifelong process of formation of conscience. Each person has the obligation to form his or her conscience as fully as possible and to follow it.

Because the human person is social, conscience and the process of its formation are also socially situated. Adequate formation of conscience on a given issue will entail several steps, including seeking full and accurate information, consultation of trusted persons with expertise relevant to the situation, consideration of the Church's teaching found in Scripture and tradition, drawing upon the wisdom of personal and communal experience, and, most importantly, prayerful discernment of the movement of the Holy Spirit as one seeks to apply guiding moral values in a particular case. As I anticipate making a certain choice, I am invited to ask who I am becoming as a person in relationship to God. Will this choice express the full freedom and authenticity of the person God created me to be, as one made in God's image?

Applying this general framework of formation of conscience to the nuclear context involves unpacking several categories of information for discernment. First, systemic considerations are especially relevant for the formation of personal and social conscience in the case of nuclear weapons due to the particular circumstances governing their development and production. Second, the highly toxic nature of fissile material requires awareness of the real risks of nuclear waste and contamination, particularly in relation to the most vulnerable members of the biotic community. Third, nuclear weapons pose a limit situation for humans' relationship with the rest of creation, drawing attention to the link between genocide and ecocide. Holding these three aspects of nuclear weapons together, it is possible to approach the formation of personal and social conscience through specific questions for personal and communal discernment with the support of the ecclesial community.

The Systemic Aspect of Nuclear Weapons

In her seminal work on secrecy, Sissela Bok notes that those working on the Manhattan Project, some of the world's greatest scientists of the time were not informed about the

> scope and aim of their research, though they often guessed. They were asked to disguise the nature of their work in letters to friends and relatives, or to talk in empty terms. . . . When looking for a site for the project, . . . townspeople were falsely told that the project had to do with the manufacture of electric missiles.
> Without feedback and debate concerning their undertaking, and without day-to-day contact with the rest of the world, the scientists were an easy prey to complete absorption in their task, and to denying or rationalizing away any doubts about their own role.[2]

Driven at least in part by the excitement and sense of power born of secrecy, they continued working on the project even after Germany's surrender in spring 1945.

Jean-Michel Oughourlian, a longtime collaborator of René Girard, writes that "desire cannot exercise its energy except in the presence of a resistance, and that energy increases in direct proportion to the strength of the resistance."[3] The secret and elite nature of the scientists' work added an extra layer of resistance to the already potent, scientifically driven desire to develop atomic bombs. By early 1944, what had proved to be a highly motivating object of desire for many scientists—that is, developing nuclear capability before Nazi Germany and keeping that technology out of Germany's control—had lost its power. Germany no longer posed a threat in that regard. For others, the real political aim of the race to build the atomic bomb was to attain leverage over the Soviets. In March 1945 Gen. Leslie Groves, director of the Manhattan Project, acknowledged as much in casual dinner conversation among colleagues at Los Alamos.[4]

For Joseph Rotblat, a young Polish-born physicist present at the dining table, Groves's aside proved decisive in shaping his own opposition to the project. At a time when Germany could still have prevailed, Stephanie Cooke recounts, "Russian soldiers were dying by the thousands in order to defeat the Germans, and Groves was speaking of them as if they were the enemy, more than the Germans."[5] Thereafter, Rotblat resigned from the Manhattan Project on moral grounds. Later in 1955, he would coauthor a letter with Einstein and others to the general public opposing the nuclear arms race.

But Rotblat's colleagues continued working on the bomb, he told Cooke, mainly out of "'pure and simple scientific curiosity—the strong urge to find out whether the theoretical calculations and predictions would come true.'"[6] Robert Oppenheimer confirmed this view in a November 1945 speech at Los Alamos. "If you are a scientist you cannot stop such a thing. If you are a scientist you believe that it is good to find out how the world works; that it is good to find out what the realities are; that it is good to turn over to mankind at large the greatest possible power to control the world and to deal with it according to its lights and values."[7]

Following Jacques Ellul, Darrell Fasching writes of Oppenheimer's assessment that "we can call this the 'technical imperative': If it can be done it must be done. When one of the [Manhattan] project scientists, Leo Szilard, tried to get a letter of protest from the scientists in Chicago to President Truman, it was effectively subverted 'for security reasons.' Technical experts were not supposed to raise ethical questions about mass death: they were supposed to follow orders with unquestioning obedience."[8]

For his part, Rotblat did not find Oppenheimer's account persuasive, holding that the scientists did indeed bear moral responsibility for their participation in the project. "The majority [of scientists]," he recalled, "were not bothered by moral scruples; they were quite content to leave it to others to decide how their work would be used."[9]

Fasching explores the possible roots of this sort of abdication of moral responsibility, pointing to a process of "doubling" that occurs in a technical bureaucracy such as the one that governed the Manhattan Project scientists. In this process, an individual is simply one small part of a hierarchical order of decision making and performs a discrete task directed toward a larger purpose that may remain obscure to him or her:

> Such bureaucracies neutralize our capacity to be ethical by separating ends and means. Unlike my personal life, where I choose both what I shall do (ends) and how I shall accomplish it (means), in a bureaucracy those in authority higher up are believed to be in the best position to see the big picture and choose the ends. Those technical experts lower down in the hierarchy are simply expected to use their knowledge and skill to provide the means for carrying out ends chosen by others higher up, with unquestioning obedience. Not having chosen the ends, one does not have to feel responsible for one's actions.[10]

Ervin László, a prominent systems philosopher, observes that when viewed systemically, groups take on a sort of personality of their own. Baseball teams and business corporations might replace all of their personnel at once, and still their organizations would continue forward. These groups constitute "wholes" in which the constituent parts maintain certain qualities of relationship among themselves. For a corporation, László writes, the particular identity of its employees matters less than whether "there are a sufficient number of persons with sufficient qualifications in the proper relationships to each other and to their tools and instruments. Hence such entities exhibit a certain uniqueness of characteristics as wholes. They cannot simply be reduced to the properties of their individual parts."[11]

The proper functioning of a system depends on open channels of communication among the interactive parts, allowing the group or entity to make necessary adjustments in response to feedback. In social systems, theorist Joanna Macy emphasizes, individual members must make decisions for themselves as part of the integrity of the whole. In the case of the Manhattan Project, Rotblat along with Szilard demonstrated that they as individuals stood in moral opposition to the direction of the group's efforts, and they acted accordingly, following their consciences.

But, the dominant cultural milieu of the project greased the skids for those who did not want to take personal responsibility for their part in the whole effort. Rotblat's own crystallization of conscience depended on receiving, almost by accident, key data about the real moral object of the work in which he participated. Measured by the narrow end of building atomic bombs, the means of secrecy served the Manhattan Project well. Measured by the moral health of the social system and its members, however, the withholding of such relevant information as the true object of their common work complicated the ethical task for each person involved.

The example of the Manhattan Project scientists highlights a formidable challenge in forming consciences with a view toward nuclear disarmament. In addition to the formation of personal conscience, members of society will need to attend to social conscience: How might communities and institutions support proper formation of conscience for not only individuals but also the whole social group? For members of the military, scientific, and manufacturing communities responsible for the production, maintenance, and potential use of nuclear weapons, what ecclesial support might be necessary to help them resist the systemic pressures of the "technical imperative" and undertake the difficult task of forming their consciences as fully as possible?

For those more indirectly involved in the nuclear weapons industry but no less responsible for formation of conscience, how might the Church encourage greater personal and communal awareness? In his 1961 farewell address, President Dwight Eisenhower, according to Stephanie Cooke, "warned against not only 'unwarranted influence' by the military-industrial complex but the 'danger that public policy could itself become the captive of a scientific-technological elite.'"[12] However, Cooke cautions, "that warning has largely been ignored, allowing a huge, secretive, self-rationalizing system to take on a life of its own, backed by history, money, power, and a default conviction in its own inevitability."[13]

I think of taxpayers and investors who, perhaps unwittingly, continue to finance the research, development, and assembly of nuclear weapons at tremendous socioeconomic and environmental cost. Analysis of US government budget data provided by Kingston Reif, director of disarmament and threat reduction policy at the Arms Control Association, projects the total cost of US nuclear forces over the next thirty years to be between $1.25 trillion and $1.46 trillion. These prices are in "then-year dollars," meaning they are adjusted for future inflation.[14] Through the expansive reach of transnational corporations, the nuclear weapons industry is spread throughout the United States and across the globe by design. Every taxpayer and likely most workers with 401(k) investments are complicit in some way, but few of us have ever been invited to form our consciences sufficiently to realize the fact of our involvement and its moral implications.

The military-industrial complex about which Eisenhower raised alarm has only become more enmeshed with the everyday lives of Americans. It has numbed consciences, personal and social, and fostered a false consciousness in which "national security" is used as a sort of hypnotic suggestive trigger to advance an "anything goes" approach to generating profit by way of war making and preparations for war. At the 2017 Vatican nuclear disarmament conference, Nobel laureate Jody Williams, who led a worldwide movement to ban land mines, contested the term "national security." Whenever someone uses that phrase, she challenges the person to define its meaning. In so doing, she supports formation of conscience both personal and social.

Nuclear Waste and Contamination

Another facet of formation of conscience regarding the nuclear weapons industry is its production of highly toxic waste. For all the scientific and technological expertise required to develop nuclear weaponry, the waste disposal issue, once receiving attention, has proved to be an even more difficult challenge. Arjun Makhijani, Stephen Schwartz, and William Weida say that it involves prediction "of the behavior of long-lived fission products and fissile materials for tens of thousands of years, a span of time longer than all of recorded history."[15]

As established by the Atomic Energy Act of 1946, Makhijani, Schwartz, and Weida write that the Atomic Energy Commission (AEC) as a governmental institution wielded formidable "financial, legal, and de facto juridical and regulatory power." It was not until 1947, however, that the commission began attending to the effects of toxic materials used in nuclear production. The committee asked to investigate this issue "reported that the disposal of contaminated waste, 'if continued for decades, presents the gravest of problems. This is one of the areas of research that cannot be indefinitely postponed.'" Forty years elapsed, they write, "before the government began to address seriously the consequences of placing bomb production ahead of environmental concerns."[16] The culture within the AEC did not support examination of waste and contamination issues. They cite Carroll L. Wilson, the first general manager of the AEC: "Chemists and chemical engineers were not interested in dealing with waste. It was not glamorous; there were no careers; it was messy; nobody got brownie points for caring about nuclear waste. The Atomic Energy Commission neglected the problem."[17]

The fact that the AEC supervised but did not actually operate the nuclear weapons complex added another layer of complication to the decision-making process in addressing nuclear waste. Makhijani, Schwartz, and Weida outline the systemic challenge:

> The production of nuclear weapons was considered so difficult that only corporations were presumed to have the expertise to carry it out. This government-owned, contractor-operated system was inherited from the Manhattan Project, when the immense engineering capabilities of large corporations (such as DuPont and General Electric) and universities (such as the University of California) were used to design the weapons and to build and operate the factories that processed the materials used for the first atomic bombs.... Before corporations agreed to do the job, however, they insisted that they be completely free of liability for their actions, even when these actions were negligent.[18]

In the post–Cold War era, the United States has found itself poorly equipped to deal with nuclear waste. Helen Caldicott cites the National Academy of Sciences as having determined that "two-thirds of the government sites involved in nuclear weapons production will never be decontaminated. Long-term stewardship will be required for 100 of the 144 sites, and many will remain dangerously radioactive for tens or even hundreds of thousands of years."[19] At Rocky Flats, where plutonium bomb cores were made, "workers have dubbed more than two dozen areas 'infinity rooms' because radiation monitors go off the scale inside them. These rooms ... have been sealed and are off-limits."[20] Certain areas deemed beyond decontamination now carry the designation "national sacrifice zones," such as the Oak Ridge complex in Tennessee and the Hanford Reservation in Washington.[21]

The metaphorical language of infinity rooms and national sacrifice zones belies the actual consequences of the headlong pursuit of nuclear power with very little thought given to the long-term ramifications for material creation. In Girard's theory of mimetic violence, even bitter rivals can unite against a common enemy, a scapegoat sacrificed for the advantage of the unified parties. The apocalyptic scenes described by Pedro Arrupe, SJ, and other survivors of Hiroshima and Nagasaki portended further sacrificial scapegoating.[22] If it was possible to obliterate whole cities in the name of geopolitical strategy—not just Hiroshima and Nagasaki but also Tokyo, Dresden, and other populated areas before them—it was not a large leap to rationalize the sacrifice of the rest of material creation. Earth itself and all its inhabitants and ecosystems became a scapegoat for the pursuit of what was thought to be the ultimate power, now ostensibly under human control.

The persistent problem of nuclear waste reveals that human technical expertise in splitting the atom did not signify total mastery of nuclear energy. To date, the United States does not have a permanent disposal facility or proven technical means to process and store the detritus of the nuclear military-industrial complex.

The default option seems to be further exploitation of Indigenous communities, Indigenous environmental activist Winona LaDuke notes. "Much of the world's nuclear industry has been sited on or near Native lands. Some 70 percent of the world's uranium originates from Native communities, whether Namibia's Rossing Mine, Australia's Jabulikka Mine, Cluff Lake, or Rabbit Lake Mine in Diné (Navajo) territory."[23] Navajo land is home to over one thousand abandoned uranium mines. Absent any federal standards or organized plan for reclamation of uranium mines, some Indigenous communities such as the Navajo and Laguna Pueblo have undertaken their own reclamation work.[24]

In addition to the challenge of environmental remediation, Indigenous communities also face significantly elevated rates of disease and death as a result of unsafe mining policies. In spite of reliable European studies in the 1940s showing the health hazards posed by uranium mining, including increased risk of lung cancer for miners working in settings with poor or no ventilation, the AEC did not ventilate the mines and chose not to warn the miners at risk.

> More than 4,100 miners—including more than 1,500 Navajos—became the subject of what was essentially an experiment to determine the health effects of exposure to high levels of radon in such mines. These workers received a formal apology from the government in 1990 and are eligible for compensation up to $100,000 under the Radiation Exposure Compensation Act (signed by President George Bush on October 15, 1990). . . . There have been problems in actually obtaining compensation, however, especially among Native Americans, who often do not have the written documentation, such as marriage licenses, required by the Department of Justice to establish their claims.[25]

If existing US nuclear reactors operate to the end of their licensing terms, they will have generated an estimated seventy-five thousand to eighty thousand metric tons of nuclear waste.[26] LaDuke points out that Native communities are vulnerable to nuclear dumping due to their sovereign status, relative lack of infrastructure, and a growing environmental justice movement that offers better protection to off-reservation communities.[27] Plagued by intergenerational poverty, some Native communities have been readily persuaded by seemingly lucrative financial offers. As the federal government increased pressure on Indigenous communities to accept nuclear waste, "over 31% of Native Americans living on reservations had incomes below the federal poverty line."[28] The government's nuclear waste negotiator, David Leroy, went so far as to argue that "Native responsibility to hold nuclear waste emanates from the 'superior Native understanding of the natural world' and the fact that we are 'our brother's keeper.'"[29]

Indigenous communities have long borne the brunt of nuclear carelessness. Los Alamos Laboratory sits atop sacred burial grounds of the Pueblo community, and the Trinity test occurred just upwind from the Mescalero Apache Indian Reservation.[30] In 1951, the AEC established the Nevada Test Site on Western Shoshone territory, where 1,054 nuclear devices were exploded above and below ground until 1992.[31] Virginia Sanchez, a Western Shoshone who grew up nearby, began the Nuclear Risk Management for Native Communities Program in 1993. She recalls that "the Atomic Energy Commission and then the Department of Energy would deliberately wait for the clouds to blow north and east before conducting above-ground tests, so that the fallout would avoid any heavily populated areas such as Las Vegas and Los Angeles."[32] Makhijani and Schwartz report that "as a result of fallout from US atmospheric testing between 1945 and 1963, an estimated 70,000 to 800,000 people in the United States and around the world have died or will die prematurely from a fatal cancer attributable to the testing (a comparable number would be attributable to the Soviet testing program)."[33]

The AEC circulated a pamphlet in Nevada and southern Utah in the mid-1950s assuring residents that their radiation exposure from nuclear testing fallout would be minimal.[34] Meanwhile, following complaints and a threat of litigation from the Eastman Kodak Company located near Lake Ontario in New York that measurable levels of highly radioactive fallout around their facilities following atomic detonations at the Nevada Test Site posed serious risks to their film products, the AEC granted security clearance to executives at Kodak and several other photographic companies to access daily updates about testing and predicted areas of heavy fallout so they could adjust their production schedules accordingly.[35]

The privileging of corporate interests over those of the general public and of Indigenous communities in particular reflected the systemic moral disorder of the Manhattan Project. With no opportunity for public debate and with misinformation from the federal government about the actual risks of radioactive fallout, individual members of the social system, particularly those on the margins, were not in a position to offer feedback directed toward structural transformation.

As a condition of the United States signing the Comprehensive Test Ban Treaty in 1996, the Department of Energy demanded funding for expansion of nuclear weapons programs, including the design of new warheads, at their labs. The Stockpile Stewardship and Management Program receives $5 billion annually. "Thus," Helen Caldicott summarizes, "violation of both [the Comprehensive Test Ban and Nuclear Non-Proliferation] international treaties designed to control the spread of nuclear weapons was built into acceptance of the CTBT," which the US Senate has yet to ratify.[36]

Linking Genocide and Ecocide

Viewed historically, as Jonathan Schell observes, "the peril of human extinction in a nuclear holocaust is the middle term that links genocide and ecocide."[37] The development of nuclear weapons took root in a trend toward the increasing destructive capacity of conventional weaponry and concomitant disregard for noncombatant life as well as ideological rationalizations for extermination of whole peoples and cultures. It is no wonder, Schell says, that generally people are not eager to ponder the prospect of nuclear annihilation.

Turning a blind eye has also extended to the exponentially growing destructive effects of human activity on the natural environment. Nuclear weapons development prepared the way for a sort of inertial acceptance of mass extermination of not just the human species but also the whole ecosphere. "In other words," Schell emphasizes, "nuclear weapons and nuclear strategy, which actually trade on genocide for political purposes, called mutual assured destruction, threaten not just individual people, in however large numbers, but the order of creation, natural and human, and this is something new."[38]

As László's theory suggests, at stake here are not only the individual members of a wide variety of systems—familial, social, political, economic, cultural, ecological—but also the very relational structures that bind them together and provide the context for their existence. Schell puts it succinctly: "It is the integrity and perdurance of these life-forms, which are truly the books of life, that endow each 'kind'—whether this is one of the peoples that make up the human species, the human species itself, other species, or ecosystems—with an immortality that is unshared by their individual members."[39]

The magnitude of the prospect of ecocide means that formation of conscience regarding the possession and use of nuclear weapons must involve communal and ecclesial structures of support that encourage dialogical exploration of these manifold strands of interconnection woven into the very fabric of God's creation, reflecting Trinitarian interrelationship as Pope Francis emphasized in the encyclical *Laudato si'* (On Care of Our Common Home).[40]

What follows is a potential guide for ongoing formation of conscience at the personal and social levels. These categories of questions could be used in the context of small group discernment in which the participants could encourage one another to seek relevant and necessary information and hold each other accountable in the process of forming conscience and taking appropriate action.

An Examen for Ongoing Formation of Conscience

Personal Responsibility

Am I actively seeking out information needed to discern the morality of possession and use of nuclear weapons?

What are my sources of information?

Have I supported efforts in my parish and local community to gather the necessary information and to discuss it publicly?

Have I invited others to engage in communal discernment and prayer together regarding nuclear weapons?

Personal and Communal Complicity

Cooperation with evil. What is the nature of my involvement with nuclear weapons? What are the social, economic, cultural, political, and ecological dimensions of my involvement? And of my local community? And of my ecclesial community?

Material. Am I directly involved in the design, production, manufacture, maintenance, or military preparedness to deploy and use nuclear weapons?

Remote. Do I indirectly support the design, production, manufacture, maintenance, or military preparedness to deploy and use nuclear weapons (e.g., through my voting record, my tax dollars, my financial investments, my silence on nuclear policy issues, or my lack of solidarity with those directly and negatively affected by nuclear weapons production, including Indigenous peoples, workers, communities, and ecosystems exposed to nuclear waste)? Have I asked this question in the contexts of my local community and my ecclesial community as well?

Imagining Alternatives

If US society moves toward disarmament, what possibilities for peace might emerge? Eliminating deterrence as a framework may free the imagination to conceive of alternative approaches.

Are there ways to live into the just and stable peace of right relationship with God, neighbor, and all of creation and to receive the gift of Christ's peace?

Following Conscience

Am I taking steps to act in ways aligned with my moral discernment regarding nuclear weapons? And am I active in encouraging my local and ecclesial communities to take such steps?

If I have become aware of kinds and levels of complicity, what am I doing to address that moral disorder? For example:
- Have I considered a change of employment?
- Have I offered support to others who deem it necessary to change employment as a result of their discernment process?
- Have I considered personal and communal financial divestment?
- Have I engaged in disarmament advocacy efforts?
- Have I encouraged my local community and parish to do so?

Notes

1. Richard Gula, *Reason Informed by Faith: Foundations of Catholic Morality* (Mahwah: Paulist Press, 1989), 123.
2. Sissela Bok, *Secrets: On the Ethics of Concealment and Revelation* (New York: Pantheon Books, 1982), 199.
3. Jean-Michel Oughourlian, *The Genesis of Desire (Studies in Violence, Mimesis & Culture)*, trans. Eugene Webb (East Lansing: Michigan State University Press, 2010), 29.
4. Stephanie Cooke, *In Mortal Hands: A Cautionary History of the Nuclear Age* (New York: Bloomsbury, 2009), 25–26.
5. Cooke, 26.
6. Cooke, 31, from the author's interviews with Joseph Rotblat in London, June 25, 2004, and January 25, 2005. All quotations of Rotblat will be taken from this source unless otherwise noted.
7. Robert Oppenheimer, "Speech to the Association of Los Alamos Scientists" (Los Alamos, November 2, 1945), in *Robert Oppenheimer: Letters and Recollections*, ed. Alice Kimball Smith and Charles Weiner (Cambridge, MA: Harvard University Press, 1980), 317.
8. Darrell J. Fasching, "Ethics after Auschwitz and Hiroshima," *Bridges* 5 (March 1998): 8.
9. Cooke, *In Mortal Hands*, 32.
10. Fasching, "Ethics after Auschwitz and Hiroshima," 14.

11. Ervin László, *The Systems View of the World: A Holistic Vision for Our Time* (New York: George Braziller, 1972), 5.
12. Cooke, *In Mortal Hands*, 407. See also Dwight D. Eisenhower, "Farewell Address to the American People, January 17th, 1961," Dwight D. Eisenhower Presidential Library, https://www.eisenhowerlibrary.gov/sites/default/files/file/farewell_address.pdf.
13. Cooke, *In Mortal Hands*, 407.
14. Kingston Reif for the Arms Control Association, "U.S. Nuclear Modernization Programs," August 2018.
15. Arjun Makhijani, Stephen I. Schwartz, and William J. Weida, "Nuclear Waste Management and Environmental Remediation," in Stephen I. Schwartz, ed., *Atomic Audit: The Costs and Consequences of U.S. Nuclear Weapons since 1940* (Washington, DC: Brookings, 1998), 370.
16. Makhijani, Schwartz, and Weida, 356–57.
17. Makhijani, Schwartz, and Weida, 357.
18. Makhijani, Schwartz, and Weida.
19. Helen Caldicott, *The New Nuclear Danger: George W. Bush's Military-Industrial Complex* (New York: New Press, 2002), 64.
20. Makhijani, Schwartz, and Weida, "Nuclear Waste Management and Environmental Remediation," 373n60.
21. Cooke, *In Mortal Hands*, 341. See also Caldicott, *The New Nuclear Danger*, 63–64.
22. Kevin Burke, ed., *Pedro Arrupe: Essential Writings* (Maryknoll, NY: Orbis Books, 2004), 39–51.
23. Winona LaDuke, *All Our Relations: Native Struggles for Land and Life* (Chicago: Haymarket Books, 2015), 97.
24. Peter H. Eichstaedt, *If You Poison Us: Uranium and Native Americans* (Santa Fe, NM: Red Crane Books, 1994), 172–74.
25. Arjun Makhijani and Stephen I. Schwartz, "Victims of the Bomb," in *Atomic Audit*, 402.
26. LaDuke, *All Our Relations*, 97.
27. LaDuke, 100.
28. Public Citizen, "Radioactive Racism: The History of Targeting Native American Communities with High-Level Atomic Waste Dumps," Nuclear Information and Resource Services, n.d., http://www.nirs.org/wp-content/uploads/radwaste/scullvalley/historynativecommunitiesnuclearwaste06142005.pdf, citing the 1990 US Census.
29. LaDuke, *All Our Relations*, 101, citing an interview with Nilak Butler, a former Indigenous Environmental Network council member.
30. Public Citizen, "Radioactive Racism," note 4.
31. LaDuke, *All Our Relations*, 98.
32. LaDuke, 99, citing an interview with Virginia Sanchez, September 16, 1997.
33. Makhijani and Schwartz, "Victims of the Bomb," 395.

34. Makhijani and Schwartz, 423, citing the Atomic Energy Commission, "Atomic Tests in Nevada."
35. Makhijani and Schwartz, 422–23.
36. Caldicott, *The New Nuclear Danger*, 44.
37. Jonathan Schell, "Genesis in Reverse," *Bulletin of the Atomic Scientists* 63 (January/February 2007), 27. See also Fasching, "Ethics after Auschwitz and Hiroshima," 10.
38. Schell, "Genesis in Reverse," 27.
39. Schell, 29.
40. Pope Francis, *Laudato si',* nos. 111, 138, 171, and 240.

18

Catholic Conscience and Nuclear Weapons

JOSEPH J. FAHEY

The earliest Christians embraced pacifism in response to the Sermon on the Mount. Christians rejected bloodshed, whether it be capital punishment, gladiatorial contests, or military service. They were called to the higher ministry of reconciliation, and the *lex talionis* (retaliation in kind) of old was replaced by the call to love even our enemies. This grand law of love characterized Christian life in the early centuries when Christians were persecuted by Roman authorities for their fidelity to the Gospel of Jesus. When Roman soldiers converted to Christianity, they rejected bloodshed and hatred of enemies, embracing instead active love for all. St. Martin of Tours (316–397 CE) was representative when he stated, "Hitherto I have served you as a soldier, let me now serve Christ.... I am a soldier of Christ and it is not lawful for me to fight."

The conscientious witness of the early Christians to renounce bloodshed and service in military forces has continued down to our own time. This was true even when, beginning in the fifth century, some in the Church embraced the just war theory, even in the savage bloodshed of the Crusaders (twelfth to thirteenth centuries) and later the conquistadors (sixteenth to eighteenth centuries). While pacifism retreated to monastic and clerical life after the fifth century, there were nevertheless many examples of individuals and small groups that maintained the peacemaking witness of the early Christians. We also do well to remember that the embrace of just war was done reluctantly, and as late as 1000 CE various penitentials and *The Peace of God* and *The Truce of God* severely restricted weapons in war, the number of those who could be killed in war, and the time of year when fighting to could take place. Even during the brutal Crusades there were peace movements that opposed bloodshed. The Third Order of St. Francis, which exempted laypeople from military service, is but one example of medieval peace movements. Hence, while the term "conscientious objection" is of recent origin, the obligation to conscientiously observe severe restrictions on war and to opt instead for nonviolent alternatives is quite old in Christian history.

While members of the historic peace churches—Mennonites, Brethren, and Quakers—have traditionally been exempt from military service, the idea that Roman Catholics could refuse military service with the approval of ecclesiastical authorities occurred only after World War II. During World War I, for example, Ben Salmon, an American Catholic war resister, opposed the war on the Church's teaching on just war and was imprisoned and sentenced to death for his stand. He sought support from clergy but received none. The few Catholics who resisted World War I simply did so without clerical or hierarchical support.

During World War II, Catholics in many warring countries were urged on by the hierarchy in their native land to serve in the military. There were Catholic conscientious objectors, but few received any official support as in the case of Blessed Franz Jägerstätter in Austria, whose priest and bishop refused to support him in his refusal to serve in the Nazi army. I interviewed some World War II Catholic conscientious objectors, and almost all told me that no priest would support them.

Catholic Teaching on Peace and War

A dramatic change on Church teaching on conscientious objection to war took place after World War II. These quotations, among many, represent that change:

St. John XXIII:

Therefore, in this age of ours which prides itself on its atomic power, it is irrational to believe that war is still an apt means of vindicating violated rights. (1963, *Pacem in terris*, no. 127)

Vatican Council II:

We cannot fail to praise those who renounce the use of violence in the vindication of their rights and who resort to methods of defense which are otherwise available to weaker parties, provided that this can be done without injury to the rights and duties of others or to the community itself. (*Gaudium et spes*, no. 78)

Every act of war directed to the indiscriminate destruction of whole cities or vast areas with their inhabitants is a crime against God and man which merits firm and unequivocal condemnation. (*Gaudium et spes*, no. 80)

Therefore it must be said again: the arms race is an utterly treacherous trap for humanity and one which injures the poor to an intolerable degree. It is much to be feared that if this race persists, it will eventually spawn all the lethal ruin whose path it is now making ready. (*Gaudium et spes*, no. 81)

Compendium of the Social Doctrine of the Church:

Every member of the armed forces is morally obliged to resist orders that call for perpetrating crimes against the law of nations and the universal principles of this law. Military personnel remain fully responsible for the acts that they commit in violation of the rights of individuals and peoples, or of the norms of international humanitarian law. Such acts cannot be justified by claiming obedience to the orders of superiors. (no. 503)

Conscientious objectors who, out of principle, refuse military service in those cases where it is obligatory because their conscience rejects any kind of recourse to the use of force or because they are opposed to participation in a particular conflict, must be open to accepting alternative forms of military service. "It seems just that laws should make humane provisions for the case of conscientious objectors who refuse to carry arms, provided they accept some other form of community service." (no. 503)

Pope Francis, in his address to the participants in the international symposium "Prospects for a World Free of Nuclear Weapons and for Integral Disarmament":

Nor can we fail to be genuinely concerned by the catastrophic humanitarian and environmental effects of any employment of nuclear devices. If we also take into account the risk of an accidental detonation as a result of error of any kind, the threat of their use as well as their very possession is to be firmly condemned. For they exist in the service of a mentality of fear that affects not only the parties in conflict but the entire human race. International relations cannot be held captive to military force, mutual intimidation, and the parading of stockpiles of arms. Weapons of mass destruction, particularly nuclear weapons, create nothing but a false sense of security. They cannot constitute the basis for peaceful coexistence between members of the human family, which must rather be inspired by an ethics of solidarity. (November 10, 2017)

Perhaps the most hotly debated item in the 1983 US bishops' pastoral letter "The Challenge of Peace" was the question of whether nuclear deterrence would be condemned as intrinsically evil. If so, the pastoral implications—especially for scientists and technicians who design and make nuclear weapons and military personnel who serve in any capacity in nuclear warfare—were enormous. The US bishops, however, did not condemn deterrence and the possession of nuclear weapons, adopting instead the position of Pope John Paul II in a 1982 letter to the United Nations that "deterrence based on balance, certainly not as an end in itself but as a step on the way toward a progressive disarmament, may still be judged morally acceptable." As chief of US chaplains, US Navy admiral Msgr. John O'Connor told me in 1976 that "if nuclear deterrence is condemned, no superior officer involved in nuclear weapons warfare would be able to trust a Catholic under his command."

Pope Francis's 2017 statement that "the threat of their use [nuclear weapons], as well their very possession is to be condemned" leaves no room for doubt or distinction: Nuclear weapons are intrinsically evil. Hence, nuclear weapons may not be developed and may not be used as a deterrent, and they may not be used in warfare. In fact, the very act of making nuclear weapons is itself intrinsically evil, since the manufacture of nuclear weapons steals funds that should be used to promote the universal common good. Catholic teaching is unambiguous on this subject.

Therefore, those nations that manufacture and possess nuclear weapons are engaged in an intrinsically evil act. This evil act directly involves those scientists who design these weapons, the manufacturers who make the weapons, the politicians who approve the funds to create the weapons, and the members of the military who are assigned to bombers, missile silos, and naval vessels that will fire these weapons when ordered to do so.

Catholic Teaching on Cooperation with Evil

Catholic teaching holds that cooperation with evil takes two forms: formal and material. People formally cooperate when they concur with the intent or act that is evil and perform the evil act itself. In this case, a person is guilty of evil when he or she directly designs, funds, manufactures, uses nuclear weapons. Material cooperation with evil means that one does not approve of the intent or the act that creates nuclear weapons but nevertheless contributes in some way to the existence of nuclear weapons. Material cooperation may be immediate if a person does not support the intent to do evil but nevertheless contributes in some way without which the evil act cannot be done. Material cooperation may be mediate when a person participates in evil in an indirect and nonsupportive way.

When we apply these principles to the possession of nuclear weapons and their use for deterrence purposes, the conscience of those involved is challenged by these facts:

1. People are formally guilty of cooperation with evil when their intention and actions are to directly design, fund, or manufacture nuclear weapons. This group includes scientists, political leaders, corporations that manufacture nuclear weapons, and military personnel who are deployed to maintain and use nuclear weapons. Formal cooperation with evil is always gravely morally wrong. A moral action that is gravely wrong in Catholic teaching is a mortal sin.

2. People are materially guilty of cooperation with evil when they are not directly involved in the design, funding, manufacture, or deployment of nuclear weapons but nevertheless commit actions without which nuclear weapons cannot be produced. People are guilty of immediate cooperation with evil when they provide the material (capital) that is essential for the immoral act to occur. Citizens who pay taxes that in part fund nuclear weapons are guilty of immediate material cooperation with evil, since these taxes result in nuclear weapons research, development, and deployment. People may engage in mediate cooperation with evil if they provide material that is not necessary for the commission of

the immoral act. Hence, military personnel such as cooks, medics, and office personnel may not be guilty of cooperation with evil (although as citizens that portion of their federal taxes directed to weapons of mass destruction may result in immediate cooperation with evil for which they are morally culpable).

Hence, Church teaching on cooperation with evil poses a most serious challenge to the consciences of very large segments of society in nuclear weapons–producing countries (together the United States and Russia produce 95 percent of nuclear weapons, with the United States by far in the lead in overall military spending and arms exports). When Church teaching was that nuclear weapons possession was acceptable as long as disarmament was being pursued, scientists, politicians, defense corporations, soldiers, and citizens could continue to participate in nuclear weapons planning and production although with a most uneasy conscience.

But at last, the fiction of nations producing weapons while at the same time seeking disarmament has been exposed. The nuclear arms manufacturers and their governmental cronies have lied to us long enough.

The fact is that the nuclear weapons–producing powers—mainly the United States—never intended to do anything but produce more plentiful and more powerful nuclear weapons if for no other reason than these weapon systems are highly profitable. And it is a fact that the United States always intended to use these weapons in warfare and continued to do so under former president Donald Trump.

A Universal Responsibility

Pope Francis has exposed the obscenity of the nuclear arms race that only races for profit at the expense of people. He has issued a clarion call to peace that the world simply cannot ignore. And we do well to remember that the Catholic Church has issued many, many statements condemning the arms race even of conventional weapons since the pontificate of Benedict XV before World War I. Was not the conventional bombing of Hamburg and Dresden and Tokyo not more horrific than Hiroshima and Nagasaki?

The large number of Catholic citizens who are involved directly or indirectly with the production of nuclear weapons are going to need a good deal of assistance as they examine their consciences on the question of whether they can keep their jobs or continue to pay taxes. Catholics in the military have a special burden of conscience that will demand a special wisdom to discern whether they are guilty of formal cooperation with evil. Courage will be demanded of all as they find that there is no longer any safe place to stand or any time to wait for nations to begin nuclear disarmament. Citizens—including those in the military—simply cannot wait for their governments to act. Tragically, the burden is on each of us. We must be prepared to stand alone if necessary in the face of nuclear catastrophe. But we are not alone. Catholic teaching tells us that the God of love is with us and that Jesus has shown us in the Sermon on the Mount how to make peace. Catholic teaching on world governance is the blueprint for a world of peace for all!

The following proposals are designed to assist in the formation of conscience for faithful Catholics—and all people of goodwill—who wish to form a correct conscience on the matter of nuclear weapons.[1]

Policy Planners

A faithful Catholic who is tasked with planning, developing, and providing funds for weapons of war can no longer assist in any way with the preparation of nuclear weapons (or conventional weapons of mass destruction). This will undoubtedly cause a crisis in conscience for those who had heretofore formed policy on the earlier teaching on the acceptance of deterrence. These policy planners, from corporate executives to elected and appointed political officials, must be instructed that nuclear planning is now a condemned activity by the Catholic Church and that they should seek employment in fields other than that of nuclear planning. (Given the Church's strong teaching, however, on aversion to any kind of arms preparation and spending, these officials will do well to consider alternative forms of defense such as nonviolent national defense, diplomacy, and the pursuit of a governed world where war itself will be banned.)

Military Service

A faithful Catholic on active military duty who is involved with planning or supervising the deployment of nuclear weapons and those who serve in aircraft and on surface naval ships and submarines can no longer in good conscience serve in any capacity that involves the very possession and possible use of nuclear weapons. Provision must be made in civil and military law for those who conscientiously object to any military service that even remotely deals with nuclear weapons. Catholics who are refused assistance by military officials to join conventional military forces or to seek an honorable discharge for reasons of conscience should be supported by Church officials and lay Catholics with legal and moral assistance. Selective conscientious objection is a Catholic teaching that should be enshrined in civil law.

Civil Society

Faithful Catholics who are citizens of those nations that possess nuclear weapons have a moral duty to vote for officials who will support their nation signing the Treaty on the Prohibition of Nuclear Weapons. If they are given an opportunity to vote directly for budget items that involve nuclear weapons, they should vote in the negative. Catholic dioceses and parishes should make information available to Catholics about Church teaching on the condemnation of deterrence and nuclear weapons along with materials on peacemaking, nonviolence, and the necessity of banning war through international law and governance.

Educators

Those in the teaching profession—from grade school through university—can assist mightily in helping Catholics to become informed about the condemnation of deterrence and nuclear weapons. Catholic schools and parishes should provide instruction for those of draft age who must decide if they will register for military service. Catholic colleges and universities should be distinguished by offering programs in peace and justice studies that offer all students the opportunity to examine matters of conscience and war.

Global Governance

Disarmament of any kind is simply not going to happen while we continue the system of sovereign nation-states. People want security and protection, which can only be truly found in a system of world governance in which international law replaces the international anarchy of today. Law can replace war and sinful military spending if we make the United Nations a system of democratic global governance. In the words of St. John XXIII in *Pacem in terris*, "Today the universal common good presents us with problems which are world-wide in their dimensions; problems, therefore, which cannot be solved except by a public authority with power, organization and means co-extensive with these problems, and with a world-wide sphere of activity. Consequently the moral order itself demands the establishment of some such general form of public authority" (no. 137).

The Vatican and local conferences of bishops should prepare a pastoral plan on the urgency of disarmament and the necessity for a freely chosen democratic Global Union of states that will not only outlaw war but also ensure the safety of our fragile planet for all generations to come.

Note

1. See also the essays in part VII, "Responsible Actors," in this volume.

19

The Conundrum of Deterrence

A Practical Christian Response

LISA SOWLE CAHILL

Two decades into the twenty-first century there are about seventeen thousand nuclear weapons in the world, a situation that Catholic social teaching—especially papal teaching—deplores and condemns. Yet most voters and politicians in the United States are disengaged from if not opposed to nuclear disarmament as an urgent public mandate.[1] Many who find the situation worrisome or downright terrifying do not know where to begin to change institutionalized policies of nuclear possession and deterrence that followed the first and only (so far) use of nuclear bombs—by the United States against two Japanese cities in 1945. Work by activists, Church leaders, and international government representatives and policymakers to abolish nuclear weapons has made progress in recent decades.[2] But the advances have had limited impact on the behavior of nuclear and would-be nuclear states and are hardly a priority of voters in the United States and other nations experiencing a resurgence of nationalist, protectionist right-wing politics.[3]

A first thesis of this essay is that while both possession and serious threat to use nuclear weapons are immoral, nuclear deterrence still presents a moral conundrum because decision makers must enter a de facto ongoing situation in which these immoral policies are a point of departure and set conditions for and parameters of available paths to deterrence. Those negotiating for disarmament (in contrast to prophetically denouncing nuclear weapons) must employ nuclear policy as a medium. This is why ecclesial representatives such as Pope John Paul II and the US Catholic bishops conceded that deterrence is provisionally tolerable or even acceptable, even though such a policy presumably entails a determination to do, should deterrence fail, that which is flatly and egregiously immoral. Those who work for change within nuclear-dependent political systems shoulder the burden of nuclear injustice to some extent.

A second thesis of this essay is that while Christian ethics can provide no moral analysis that clearly resolves this problem, it offers a way forward in the form of practical ecclesial and political action. The key to reducing and ultimately removing the conundrum of nuclear deterrence is broad-based political mobilization, undertaken with a morally idealistic yet pragmatic sensibility. Tangled human situations in which good and evil are mixed call for context-specific discernment and the hope that human solidarity and the inherent appeal of justice can overcome tribalistic fear and what Augustine called the *libido dominandi* (lust for domination). A resource for this second thesis is the encyclical *Laudato si'* on lack of political will and social change.

The Conundrum of Deterrence

As other chapters in this volume have argued, the use of nuclear weapons has never been approved in Catholic social teaching, although John Courtney Murray claimed that Pius XII did not rule it out.[4] Certainly popes since Vatican II have spoken out strongly against the nuclear arms race not only because nuclear weapons (even so-called limited or tactical nuclear weapons) kill indiscriminately and leave long-lasting lethal effects but also because the disproportionate expenditures they require is already an injustice to the poor. Nevertheless, John Paul II and the US Catholic bishops stated that deterrence policies could provide an acceptable moral framework within which to work for disarmament as long as progress toward that goal was steady and significant.[5] Not only has that criterion not been met, but heightened focus on successful deterrence has meant that refinement of nuclear systems and capacities has overtaken the idea that the ultimate aim is elimination.[6]

Despite conditional acceptance, nuclear deterrence has never been justifiable in reasoned ethical terms, a point well argued by another contributor to this book, Gregory Reichberg.[7] The most fundamental problem is that if a threat to use nuclear weapons in response to a first attack by an adversary is to be credible, it must be backed by a serious, public, and demonstrable determination to follow through should an attack occur. That virtually requires a command and launch system that responds automatically to an incoming attack, eliminating any *in via* reconsideration of the consequences or morality of retaliation by those who are attacked first. It has been argued that just such a system is in place in the United States.[8] Yet assurances in 2017 by the head of the Strategic Air Command, Gen. John Hyten, that he would not execute an "illegal" command from the president to launch a nuclear weapon open up a margin of ambiguity and of morality in what would otherwise be a policy failing several just war criteria, most blatantly noncombatant immunity and right intention.[9] Surely popes and bishops have approved deterrence only on the tacit premise that nuclear weapons would not in fact be used. But this does not remove the moral ambiguity of the policy itself as explicitly rejecting that premise.

Advocates of Catholic social teaching as well as officials such as General Hyten are in a morally anomalous situation insofar as to effect change, they must cooperate with or even participate in the institutions from which they dissent. "We are all involved in webs of relationships that enable people to achieve their good or bad ends, whether by good or bad means."[10] Our entanglement in the web raises the prospect of morally wrong complicity with the bad ends and means. One tool of Catholic moral theology that is often invoked to alleviate such tensions is the principle of cooperation.[11] As moral theologian Gerard Magill notes, "the purpose of the principle is to clarify how good moral decisions can be made, even when there is complicity in wrongdoing."[12] One is culpable for the evil aspects or outcomes of the actions or policies with which one cooperates if one's contribution is formal in the sense that one approves the evil result. If one does not desire or approve the outcome, then one's action is considered material and not necessarily culpable. Whether material cooperation is culpable depends on how necessary it is to the execution of the evil effect. The principle of cooperation provides further distinctions to evaluate its connection to the evil caused by the principal actor.

Degrees of material cooperation can be distinguished on the basis of whether the action is part of or overlaps with that of the principal agent or is distinct from and secondary to it (immediate and mediate cooperation). The latter sort of cooperation (mediate) can be further analyzed in terms of how close it is to the principal action in space or time or chain of causality (proximate or remote).[13] If one's cooperation is material, mediate, and even remote (the evil aspect is not desired and is a remote and indirect consequence in time and space of the agent's own action, one that would be accomplished even without the agent's participation), then one is not morally guilty of the resulting evil. These distinctions do not amount to a clear formula for defining immoral complicity, but beyond ruling out deliberate participation in evil, they also post strong warning signals around close connections to it. The more close or direct the agent's cooperation, the weightier the justification must be. "In sum, the principle of cooperation provides a moral compass to distinguish immoral complicity from an honorable commitment to diminish evil by combining hope and realism in a world of compromised values and sinful actions."[14]

While the principle of cooperation is helpful in distinguishing degrees of culpability, moral theologians of the past have been too quick to see it as resolving moral quandaries and absolving the agents caught up in them. First, even agents who cannot on the whole be regarded as blameworthy still bear some responsibility for evil aspects of a morally justifiable action that was entangled in webs of good and evil. Second, remedial and compensatory action is required.[15] These two provisions are recognized when nuclear deterrence is accepted only within a strong and overarching condemnation of violence as an acceptable path to peace and when remediating conditions are set, such as negotiations toward disarmament. Even so, and as Catholic social teaching instructs, any cooperation with policies enabling the continued possession and threatened use of nuclear weapons are morally fraught courses of action that properly result in uneasy consciences. Nuclear deterrence is a moral conundrum because it is both theoretically unjustified and practically necessary as a condition for negotiating arms reduction and nuclear abolition.

A Practical Christian Response

Probably the two most common and visible Christian ethical responses to nuclear weapons and nuclear deterrence are to insist and demonstrate that they are incompatible with Bible, theology, and authoritative teaching and to urge international agreements and United Nations (UN) control over nuclear proliferation and use as well as over the current unstable possession of nuclear arms by at least eight nation-states. In addition, a smaller number of theorists and policy advisers are working on concrete paths to better international relations and more successful nuclear arms control. Such responses are necessary but inadequate.

First, while it is certainly true that the very existence of nuclear arms contradicts the gospel, derivative theologies, and right reason, it is necessary to come to terms with the fact that no move can be made from these sources to policy changes without going through diverse political and military intermediaries (including voters) who have access to policy formation. Here we enter the realm of moral negotiation, compromise, and ambivalence where even finding an adequate language of engagement can be difficult.

Second, international treaties and law are important and influential, a recent example being the 2017 UN Treaty on the Prohibition of Nuclear Weapons, which the Holy See was one of the first states to sign and ratify. But the problem here is twofold: treaties are toothless unless they are ratified and implemented (ratification by fifty states would make the treaty law, and more than that number have signed it, but a much smaller number have ratified it, and none of the signers are states actually possessing nuclear weapons). In any event, though the UN has considerable moral authority, an asset of the treaty,[16] it lacks enforcement mechanisms. The same is true of agreements between states and of national policy domestically. Bilateral agreements will not be observed and domestic policy will not be conformed to arms reduction if practical incentives and citizen buy-in are lacking. In the networked new world order, global governance must be handled in a way that is more fragmented yet alliance building, more bottom-up and midlevel-out than top-down. Domestic policy depends similarly on the consent of those domestic stakeholders whose support the government needs (whether voters or local elites), accomplished through alliance building.[17]

The Christian Catholic response must go beyond naming the injustices of nuclear weapons, calling for their abolition, protesting defense policy,[18] or demanding (as papal Catholic social teaching is wont to do)[19] that the UN step in and correct the errors of nation-states. All of these moves will be effective only if and because they manage to reshape the broader and deeper cultural imagination that is supportive of or resigned to the potential use of nuclear weapons. Apparently, few Americans buy the "nuclear taboo" and indeed prioritize protecting American troops and interests even if it means killing millions of foreign noncombatants.[20] The biggest and most important challenge is to rally the worldwide institutional presence of Catholicism and the civil society and professional roles of its members to instigate cultural and worldview changes in the social environments that are maintaining the present dangerous and immoral nuclear scenario.

We find a model in *Laudato si'*, where Pope Francis identifies the tendency of UN summits to produce an "ineffectual outcome document" (e.g., on climate change) due to the opposition of "countries which place their national interests above the global common good."[21] Pope Francis neither expects the UN to take control, anticipates that a top-down Vatican document will command the attention of Catholics everywhere, nor limits his sights to Catholics and Catholic practice. Instead, he cites seventeen or more local bishops' conferences, urges Catholics and non-Catholic partners to build momentum through public education, and draws on vision-expanding resources such as poetry, prayer, and a YouTube video.[22]

Pope Francis has called nonviolence "a style of politics for peace."[23] This style involves symbolic strategies of conversion, such as the prayer vigil he held for peace in St. Peter's Square in 2013 and the photo of a small boy at Nagasaki that he shared with journalists because "it is more moving than 1000 words."[24] A politics for peace requires pragmatic creativity that can find workable solutions to looming dangers and intractable conflicts, including (as General Hyten himself proposes) international diplomacy in an atmosphere of respect, with prioritization of mutual benefits over threats and demands.

Speaking to the UN in 2017 on negotiations to abolish nuclear weapons, Pope Francis recognized that globalization and interdependence mean that responses to the nuclear weapons threat must be "collective and concerted," involving not only nation-states but the military, private business, religious communities, civil societies, and international organizations.[25] Later that same year, he explicitly condemned simple possession of nuclear weapons and praised the "healthy realism" motivating the "alliance between civil society, states, international organizations, churches, academics and groups of experts" that had come together to make and back the 2017 UN treaty prohibiting nuclear weapons.[26]

It is the strength of this alliance and its ability to infiltrate the cultures and politics of nuclear-possessing states that will define the practical impact of the treaty and the world's (non?)nuclear future. Catholics in partnership with like-minded Christian denominations, religious traditions, humanitarian organizations, governmental representatives at multiple levels, and political movements can and must do more to make what Pope Francis terms "effective and inclusive" progress toward a world without nuclear weapons.[27] Networking at every level of society, they must prioritize nonviolent means of conflict transformation, counter xenophobic politics with a politics of solidarity, and make national and international leaders more accountable to constituencies that are newly energized against the dangerous reality of nuclear proliferation.

Notes

1. This was confirmed by a Stanford University study in 2017. See Clifton B. Parker, "Public Opinion Unlikely to Curb a US President's Use of Nuclear Weapons in War, Stanford Scholar Finds," *Stanford News*, August 8, 2017. See similar results in "U.S.-Japan Opinion Survey, 2017," University of Maryland Critical Issues Poll, January 8, 2018, https://criticalissues.umd.edu/sites/criticalissues.umd.edu/files/us-japan_opinion_survey.pdf, presented at the Brookings Institution, January 8, 2018, https://www.brookings.edu/wp-content/uploads/2018/01/fp_20180108_north_korea_transcript.pdf.
2. In July 2017, a majority of the world's nations adopted an agreement to ban nuclear weapons. See International Campaign to Abolish Nuclear Weapons, "Signature/Ratification Status of the Treaty on the Prohibition of Nuclear Weapons," http://www.icanw.org/the-treaty/.
3. See Ariel Edwards-Levy, "Voters Say Health Care Is a Top Issue in the 2018 Election—A Good Sign for Democrats," *Huffington Post*, April 6, 2018. Edwards-Levy also names and ranks other voter priorities such as immigration and the economy.
4. John Courtney Murray, *We Hold These Truths: Catholic Reflections on the American Proposition* (New York: Doubleday, 1964), 243–53.
5. See John Paul II, "Message to the UN Second Special Session on Disarmament," June 7, 1982; and National Conference of Catholic Bishops, "The Challenge of Peace: God's Promise and Our Response," Washington, USCC, 1983.
6. Gerard Powers, "From Nuclear Deterrence to Disarmament: Evolving Catholic Perspectives," Arms Control Association, May 2015.
7. Gregory M. Reichberg, "The Morality of Nuclear Deterrence: A Reassessment," in *Nuclear Deterrence: An Ethical Perspective*, ed. Mathias Nebel and Gregory M. Reichberg, 9–31 (Chambésy, Switzerland: Caritas in Veritate Foundation, 2015). See also Reichberg's chapter "Philosophical Debate on Nuclear Deterrence" in the present volume.
8. Bruce Blair, "What Exactly Would It Mean to Have Trump's Finger on the Nuclear Button?," *Politico*, June 11, 2016.

9. Deutsche Welle, "US General John Hyten Would Resist 'Illegal' Trump Nuclear Launch Order," November 19, 2017. See also Reuters staff, "U.S. Nuclear General Says Would Resist 'Illegal' Trump Strike Order," November 18, 2017.
10. Anthony Fisher, *Catholic Bioethics for a New Millennium* (Cambridge: Cambridge University Press, 2012), 71.
11. See M. Cathleen Kaveny, "Complicity with Evil," *Criterion* (2003), esp. 24–25. For further discussion, see Helen Watt, ed., *Cooperation, Complicity and Conscience* (London: Linacre Centre, 2005).
12. Gerard Magill, "A Moral Compass for Cooperation with Wrongdoing," in *Voting and Holiness: Catholic Perspectives on Political Participation*, ed. Nicholas P. Cafardi (Mahwah, NJ: Paulist Press, 2012), 139.
13. See Anthony Fisher, "Cooperation in Evil: Understanding the Issues," in Watt, *Cooperation*, 29–32.
14. Watt, *Cooperation*, 150.
15. Michael Walzer makes a similar point regarding the ethics of war and the principle of double effect. Michael Walzer, *Just and Unjust Wars: A Moral Argument with Historical Illustrations*, 5th ed. (New York: Basic Books, 2015), 153–59.
16. Ray Acheson, "How Prohibiting Nuclear Weapons Changed the World," *The Nation*, July 6, 2018.
17. See Anne-Marie Slaughter, *A New World Order* (Princeton, NJ: Princeton University Press, 2004); Maryann Cusimano Love, *Beyond Sovereignty: Issues for a Global Agenda*, 4th ed. (Boston: Wadsworth, 2011); and Stewart Patrick, "The Unruled World: The Case for Good Enough Global Governance," *Foreign Affairs* 93, no. 1 (2014): 58–73.
18. The website of the United States Conference of Catholic Bishops includes eloquent position papers and letters calling for action against nuclear weapons by the US government and its highly placed officials. However, as John Paul II said in 1982, "To the extent that the efforts at arms reduction and then of total disarmament are not matched by parallel ethical renewal, they are doomed in advance to failure" ("Message to the UN Second Special Session on Disarmament," no. 12). There must be a "necessary struggle at the level of the consciences of peoples to take their responsibility" if genuine progress is to take place (no. 13).
19. See, for example, Benedict XVI, *Caritas in veritate*, no. 67.
20. Parker, "Public Opinion," 2.
21. Pope Francis, *Laudato si'*, no. 169; see also no. 54.
22. *Laudato si'*.
23. Pope Francis, "Nonviolence: A Style of Politics for Peace," World Day of Peace Message, 2017.
24. Catholic News Agency, "On flight to Chile, Pope Gives Journalists Photo Showing 'Fruits of War,'" January 15, 2018.

25. Pope Francis, "Message to the United Nations Conference to Negotiate a Legally Binding Instrument to Prohibit Nuclear Weapons Leading to Their Total Elimination," March 28, 2017.
26. Pope Francis, "Address to Participants in the International Symposium 'Prospects for a World Free of Nuclear Weapons and for Integral Disarmament,'" November 10, 2017.
27. On this same point, see Maryann Cusimano Love, "Resurrection Politics and Banning the Bomb," *Peace Policy*, November 6, 2017. See also Maryann Cusimano Love, "Building a Better Peace: A Future Worthy of Our Faith," *America*, July 21, 2015; and Marie Dennis, "Clear Guidance toward Nuclear Abolition," Berkley Forum for Religion, Peace and World Affairs, November 16, 2016.

20

Pastoral Accompaniment

Pope Francis's Approach to the Human Vocation

DREW CHRISTIANSEN, SJ

The first principle of the natural law, Thomas Aquinas taught, is "Do good and avoid evil."[1] In the twentieth century when it came to systemic evil, Mohandas Gandhi, Martin Luther King Jr., and their followers taught us that we must do more: resist evil. If resistance to evil intensifies the Thomistic injunction to avoid evil, Pope Francis's moral teaching strengthens the injunction to do good. It attempts to make men and women alert to the promptings of the Spirit within them to grow morally and spiritually. In the dominant traditional approaches to ordinary pastoral care, the goals were to assist penitents in knowing their sins, perhaps assessing their complicity in evil, and repenting of the evil they had done.[2] Francis's approach, while not neglecting the acknowledgment of sin and the need for repentance, is concerned above all with nourishing the desire for good and the aspiration for holiness.

Pope Francis's model of pastoral accompaniment has resonances with Gregory the Great's manual on the care of souls,[3] but its immediate sources are found more in the Spiritual Exercises of Saint Ignatius Loyola and the writings of Saint Peter Faber, one of Ignatius's first companions noted for his gentleness and expert spiritual direction.[4] Pope Francis is distinguished by his insistence that even in the sinner there is a desire to advance in goodness, what Ignatius described as "the progress of souls," defined as love of God and neighbor and growth in the virtues.[5] Francis's approach to pastoral care retrieves the integration of confessional practice and spiritual direction that preceded the modern period. It is likewise a corrective to a post-Kantian secular ethics focused on universal minimal norms and a revisionist natural law theory built around the absolute claims of primary goods, where moral ideals were given scant attention.[6]

Conscience and Discernment

Pope Francis is known for his preaching of God's mercy and disparagement of moral legalism. A less noticed but no less important teaching is his insistence that even in most sinners there is a latent aspiration for goodness. He appeals to the conviction that the Holy Spirit is at work in everyone, believer and unbeliever alike, inspiring them to be better and do more, what Jesuits call the *magis*, the greater good. It is as if he turned Luther's *simul iustus et peccator* (at once justified and a sinner) into *simul peccator et sanctus* (at once a sinner and a saint) but with an accent on the potentiality, in God's mercy, for every person's growth in goodness and sanctity.

In his inaugural interview with Antonio Spadaro, SJ, for *America*, "With a Big Heart Open to God," Francis appealed for understanding for a troubled woman who nonetheless "wants to move forward in her Christian life."[7] For Francis we are all sinners, but backward-looking moral legalism locks people into their identity as sinners, at best repentant sinners, and in so doing represses the aspiration to do better, to grow morally. By contrast, Francis tells us, "Confession . . . is the place in which the Lord's mercy inspires us *to do better.*"[8] Following the Jesuit axiom of "the progress of souls,"[9] Francis holds that conscientious living consists of far more than avoiding and repenting sin; it is rather "to move forward in the Christian life," responding to what morally "fascinates and attracts more, what makes the heart burn."[10] Francis not only makes room for serious consideration of ideals but also makes them essential to personal moral and spiritual development.

The role of pastoral care, as Francis conceives of it, is to assist men and women to respond to the greater good in their lives. Attending to the full ambit of the moral life, pastoral ethics assigns greater weight to moral ideals, "Gospel values" as Paul VI called them, than to minimal universal moral norms.[11] For the person growing in moral awareness, what to others may seem an optional moral ideal is existentially a goal incumbent on that person to fulfill.

In terms of our own discussion on nuclear deterrence and abolition, a pastoral moral theology means liberating those with responsibility for defense and security to grasp their own vocations to do the better thing by taking steps to advance the elimination of nuclear weapons. Total elimination of nuclear weapons is not a quixotic quest but instead is the better and greater good of a positive, nonnuclear peace that releases resources for the development especially of the world's poor, a world without nuclear weapons and with integral development for all. The good that attracts the aspiring person is a world without nuclear weapons enjoying the positive gifts of peace. One consequence of that moral advance is to redefine and modify the moral theology that allowed conditional permission for nuclear deterrence, as Pope Francis did in his condemnation of deterrence in his November 10, 2017, address.[12] The greater good in this case will also entail resisting the evil of strategies of deterrence and their justification.

The Limits of Just War Casuistry

Humanity's moral progress has depended on those who have sought to do more and better. At its best, earlier Catholic teaching on nuclear ethics has been a provisional, interim ethic that understood its need to give way, with the advance of disarmament, to a world without nuclear weapons. Clinging to a provisional ethic of deterrence to the neglect of abolition, however, has led to a situation whereby nuclear strategy has gone far along the path to ignoring any moral restraints so that for several years nuclear strategists have identified multiple nonnuclear confrontations in which to employ nuclear weapons and design more flexible weapons that increase the risk of nuclear war.[13]

The need for a new way of thinking derives, then, not just from the need for personal accompaniment of officials through the moral dilemmas they face but also especially because just war thinking and the casuistic method to which it belongs reach the limits of their usefulness when it comes to nuclear weapons.[14] Nuclear war-fighting is not like armed combat in any other field. Even late twentieth-century nuclear strategists tried to maintain a "fire break" between nuclear and conventional weapons. Morally speaking, the Samson Option—destroying all creation or even some part of it for the sake of a limited good, even preservation of a sovereign state—is no option at all.[15] The Second Vatican Council made clear that the old maxim *Fiat iustitia, ruat caelum*—"Let there be justice though the heavens fall"—is not an option for Catholics or anyone.

It solemnly declared that "any act of war aimed indiscriminately at the destruction of entire cities or of extensive areas along with their populations is a crime against God and [humanity]. It deserves unequivocal and unhesitating condemnation."[16]

Nuclear weapons are never a legitimate means of defense. Of course, there are those who have insisted on "thinking the unthinkable."[17] But that formula is more than a verbal paradox; it is an abuse of human reason in its fullest sense. It attempts to extend technical rationality divorced from the deeper sources of human understanding beyond its rightful limits.

Aquinas called this technical rationality *ratio*, that is, deductive (logical) reasoning, and the deeper (intuitive) form of knowing *intellectus*, that is, real or personal knowledge arising from full engagement with the realities at stake.[18] The US bishops in their 1983 pastoral letter "The Challenge of Peace" understood that distinction when they gave only conditional warrant to deterrence narrowly defined but condemned nuclear warfare outright.[19] President John F. Kennedy appealed to that deeper form of rationality when, in his 1963 American University address, he said that disarmament "is the rational end of rational men."[20] To think rightly about nuclear ethics, we need to tap into those deeper existential sources of moral wisdom. It is on just this point that Pope Francis's holistic approach to moral judgment can be of help to us in applying his condemnation of nuclear deterrence to real-life circumstances and to the responsibilities of those working in the national security establishment.

Pastoral Accompaniment

According to Pope Francis, pastoral care involves building relationships "where the most profound questions and daily concerns are shared, where deeper discernment about our experiences and life itself is undertaken in the light of the Gospel, for the purpose of directing individual and social decisions towards the good."[21] Evangelical discernment, he writes, "strives to recognize—by the light of the Spirit—a call which God causes to resound in the historical situation itself. In this situation, and through it,"[22] he affirms, "God calls the believer."[23] Since God's Spirit is active in everyone, the same can be said of all men and women of goodwill.[24]

So, discernment does not look primarily to what everyone is called to do through observance of basic and universal moral standards but rather to what I am called to do—to the greater good I am called to effect. It is a personal call. Eventually the world may come to agree that the abolition of nuclear deterrence is morally required, as it did in regard to the abolition of slavery and in the establishment of universal human rights, but first we are responsible to heed the personal call of conscience for us to effect change today.

The legendary psychologist Erik Erikson would call this testing of one's call "a life crisis," a period of moral growth and decision in which a person's identity is reshaped in responding to a grave problem facing humanity.[25] Nuclear abolition is the crisis of our age.[26] To an attentive, morally responsible person, Pope Francis's condemnation of nuclear deterrence signals that morally aware people should be about finding ways to contribute to the abolition of nuclear weapons, beginning with the rejection of the strategy of deterrence. In this context responsible moral agents should examine the courses of action open to them: Shall I promote negotiated disarmament more vigorously? Shall I resign or transfer to another branch of service? Shall I openly protest? Shall I resist from within? Shall I disobey? Shall I shift the direction of my research? Should I study alternative means of defense? The role of pastoral workers—bishops, pastors, teachers, and counselors—is to accompany people in discerning their paths of action as they take up this call.

Pope Francis offers a general rule for pastoral accompaniment that may serve as a point of reference for us. The pope writes that Jesus "looked on the men and women whom he met with love and tenderness, accompanying their steps in truth, patience and mercy as he proclaimed the Gospel of the Kingdom."[27] He concludes that "the Lord is also with us today as we seek to practice and pass on the Gospel."[28] We may adapt the last sentence for our purposes, saying that the Lord is also with us today as we seek to practice and pass on the Gospel of peace.[29]

The specific tasks of pastoral moral accompaniment may include the following forms of care:

- Education on the Church's teaching on peace and war and more broadly on the movement to abolish nuclear weapons;
- Serving as a sounding board for questions, doubts, and probings;
- Airing the costs of discipleship and sharing the stories of heroic peacemakers;

- Assisting counselees to attain spiritual freedom in their decisions;
- Resisting movements of evil in oneself and in the world around us;
- Praying together for the gift of discernment;
- Exploring various courses of action, assessing the options, and settling on one from among them on which to act;[30] and finally,
- Confirming that a decision has validation in prayer and life.

All these measures presuppose that pastor and discerner are seeking together "a more excellent way" where "God's kingdom reigns not only in our hearts but in society" so that "universal fraternity, justice, peace and dignity" have a greater place in our common life."[31] Commitment to this kind of world, Francis promises, "always generates history."[32]

For Pope Francis, like Pope Paul VI before him, there can be "a legitimate variety of possible options" to achieve the same goal. As Paul wrote in "A Call to Action," "The same Christian faith can lead to different commitments."[33] The responses of nuclear scientists, ranging from those at the Lawrence Livermore National Laboratory to the dialogues sponsored by Oakland's Bishop John Cummins during the 1980s with theologians and ethicists from the Graduate Theological Union in Berkeley, demonstrated just such a variety of ways to respond to the moral problematic raised by the US bishops' 1983 peace pastoral "The Challenge of Peace." Some chose to change their careers, returning to academia; others switched to less compromising lab work such as verification and monitoring technology, and still others shifted their studies within the labs to the development of renewable technologies. A similar variety of paths is open to today's weapon scientists, military personnel, and policymakers when they consider Pope Francis's condemnation of deterrence. The role of pastoral accompaniment is to assist such conscientious men and women to find their own path in response to the nuclear question.

The Second Vatican Council understood discernment of the signs of the times as participation in humanity's taking responsibility for its own history. Humanity, the council wrote, "is becoming aware that it is responsible to guide aright the forces [it] has unleashed."[34] Like Pope Francis, moreover, the council insisted that human beings realize their humanity when they pursue goals "in a spontaneous choice of what is good, and [procure for themselves], through effective and skillful action, apt means for that end."[35] The human vocation before God is precisely to exercise responsible freedom in the face of the challenges of the day, among which the foremost is the abolition of nuclear weapons. In purely secular terms, abolition may seem a utopian ideal. But by the light of faith, it is one of those solutions that are "fully human" in keeping with humanity's deepest vocation.[36] In their accompaniment of members of the nuclear establishment, pastors, spiritual directors and others will be assisting their fellow disciples to integrate their role responsibilities with their fundamental vocations as human beings to realize, with God, a still greater good in the form of a world free of nuclear weapons where all peoples will be better able to enjoy the fruits of peace.[37]

Notes

1. Thomas Aquinas, *Summa Theologiae*, IIa IIae, 1.94.a.2. I use the customary formula "Do good and avoid evil." The standard Blackfriars translation, however, uses the more active "Pursue (or love) good" and "flee evil," dynamic translations that are more consistent with living a life of virtue rather than the simple avoidance of sin. This active rendering is quite congruent with the vision of the moral life Pope Francis gives us in his pastoral writings. Both contrast with the kind of confessional practice and moral casuistry that focuses on sin and its avoidance. They emphasize the dynamic nature of the moral life, the attraction of the good, and the natural aversion to evil.
2. See Albert R. Jonsen and Stephen Toulmin, *The Abuse of Casuistry: A History of Moral Reasoning* (Berkeley: University of California Press, 1988); and John Mahoney, *The Making of Moral Theology: A Study of the Roman Catholic Tradition* (Oxford, UK: Clarendon, 1987). See also James M. Gustafson, *Protestant and Roman Catholic Ethics: Prospects for Rapprochement* (Chicago: University of Chicago Press, 1978).
3. On Gregory's *Liber Pastoralis* and its applications today, see Thomas C. Oden, *Care of Souls in the Classic Tradition* (Minneapolis: Fortress, 1984).
4. Antonio Spadaro, "With a Big Heart Open to God: An Interview with Pope Francis," *America*, September 30, 2013. For Pope Francis's sources, see George E. Ganss, ed., *Ignatius Loyola: Spiritual Exercises and Selected Works* (Mahwah, NJ: Paulist Press, 1991), "Spiritual Exercises," nos. 328–26 (205–7); and Pierre Favre, *The Spiritual Writings of Pierre Favre: The Memoriale and Selected Letters and Instructions* (Brighton, MA: Institute of Jesuit Sources, 1996).

5. The phrase "progress of souls" is particularly characteristic of Ignatius's advice to working Jesuits. Typically it referred to increase in the love of God and neighbor and growth in the virtues. See Joseph N. Tylenda, ed., *Counsels for Jesuits: Selected Letters and Instructions of Saint Ignatius Loyola* (Chicago: Loyola University Press, 1985).
6. For a standard rendering of contemporary philosophical ethics as (minimal) universal norms, see William K. Frankena, *Ethics*, 2nd ed. (New York: Pearson, 1988). For the revisionist natural law view that primary goods involve absolute norms that may never be violated, see John Finnis, *Natural Law and Natural Rights*, 2nd ed. (Oxford, UK: Clarendon, 2011). For a philosophical defense of ideals in the moral life, see Nicholas Rescher, *Ethical Idealism: An Inquiry into the Nature and Function of Ideals* (Berkeley: University of California Press, 1987).
7. Spadaro, "With a Big Heart Open to God."
8. Spadaro (my emphasis).
9. Spadaro.
10. Spadaro.
11. Cardinal Maurice Roy, "Reflections by Cardinal Maurice Roy on the Occasion of the Tenth Anniversary of the Encyclical 'Pacem in Terris' of Pope John XXIII (April 11, 1973)," in *The Gospel of Peace and Justice: Catholic Social Teaching Since Pope John*, ed. Joseph Gremillion (Maryknoll, NY: Orbis, 1976), 531–67.
12. Pope Francis, "Address of His Holiness Pope Francis to Participants in the International Symposium 'Prospects toward a World Free of Nuclear Weapons and for Integral Disarmament,'" November 10, 2017.
13. On strategies that call for nuclear responses to nonnuclear challenges, see James Goodby, "National Attitudes toward Nuclear Deterrence," in this volume.
14. See Gregory Reichberg, "Philosophical Debate on Nuclear Deterrence," in this volume.
15. "Samson Option" was the code name of the Israeli nuclear weapons program, taking its name from the ancient Israelite hero and judge Samson who died in his destruction of the Philistine temple at Gaza (Judges 16:4–30). Seymour Hersh recounts the development of modern Israel's nuclear capacity in *The Samson Option: Israel's Nuclear Arsenal and American Foreign Policy* (New York: Random House, 1991). The Israeli policy contemplated launching a massive retaliatory nuclear strategy if Israel was threatened with being overrun by its enemies.
16. Second Vatican Council (1965), *Gaudium et spes: Pastoral Constitution on the Church in the Modern World*, no. 80.
17. Herman Kahn, *Thinking about the Unthinkable* (New York: Horizon, 1962); and Herman Kahn, *Thinking about the Unthinkable in the 1980s* (New York: Simon and Schuster, 1984).

18. The premier study of this point in the epistemology of Aquinas is Pierre Rousselot, *The Intellectualism of Saint Thomas* (New York: Sheed and Ward, 1935). For a modern alternative rooted in the same insight, see Michael Polanyi, *Personal Knowledge: Towards a Post-Critical Philosophy* (Chicago: University of Chicago Press, 1958).
19. National Conference of Catholic Bishops of the United States, *The Challenge of Peace: God's Promise and Our Response* (Washington, DC: United States Catholic Conference), February 1, 1984, 604–88.
20. For a study of Kennedy's American University speech, see Jeffrey Sachs, *To Move the World: JFK's Quest for Peace* (New York: Random House, 2013).
21. Pope Francis, *Evangelii gaudium*, no. 77.
22. *Evangelii gaudium*, no. 154.
23. *Evangelii gaudium*.
24. *Evangelii gaudium*, no. 142.
25. On the role of unfolding history in personal identity, see Erik Erikson, *Identity: Youth and Crisis* (New York: Norton, 1968). On the historical crisis in the mature religious personality, see Erik Erikson, *Gandhi's Truth: On the Origins of Militant Nonviolence* (New York: Norton, 1969), esp. "Homo Religiosus," 395–409.
26. I adapt the notion of nuclear abolition as the generational challenge of our time from the suggestion of the late psychologist Rollo May, who argued that just as sex was the problem of the Victorians, so too violence was the challenge of our generation. See his *Power and Innocence: A Search for the Sources of Violence* (New York: Norton, 1972).
27. Pope Francis, *Amoris laetitia*, no. 60.
28. *Amoris laetitia* addresses the questions of marital love. It gives special attention to accompaniment of engaged couples, of those in troubled marriages, and especially of those with histories of troubled marriages desirous of returning to the Eucharist.
29. The phrase "the Gospel of peace" can be found in Ephesians 6:15, but it is a strong theme in the Gospel of Luke (1:79; 2:14, 29; 19:41–43; 24:37, and passim) in Jesus's dismissal of those he has healed.
30. Another pattern for communal discernment of the signs of the times can be found in Pope Paul VI, "A Call to Action" (*Octogesima adveniens*), in *Catholic Social Thought*, 280–303, no. 4. There Christian communities are called upon "to draw principles of reflection, norms of judgment and directives for action from the social teaching of the Church ... to discern the options and commitments which are called for to bring about ... changes seen to be urgently necessary." While the condemnation of nuclear deterrence is an exceptionally strong "directive," for responsible parties the goal, I believe, is the same: "to discern the options and commitments" necessary to bring about change in the form of "a world free of nuclear weapons."
31. Pope Francis, *Evangelii gaudium*, no. 180.
32. *Evangelii gaudium*, no. 181.

33. *Octogesima adveniens*, no. 50.
34. *Gaudium et spes*, no. 9.
35. *Gaudium et spes*, no. 17.
36. *Gaudium et spes*, no. 11.
37. James Goodby has asked how we know that "the greater good," "the magis," is not a deception and a warrant for imposing one's will on others. It is hard to answer that question without an appreciation for the process of spiritual direction. A simple answer, however, is first that the burdens of the call fall on the discerners. They must bear the costs of their call humbly, or at least, gently, without imposing on others. Their methods are those of persuasion and nonviolence. They will also find themselves personally transformed, ready to listen, be patient, reach out to the other, etc.

Finally, I describe the ultimate goal as "a world free of nuclear weapons where all peoples will be better able to enjoy the fruits of peace." To be integral disarmament, a world without nuclear weapons must be one of positive peace that includes development, human rights, ecological integrity, and the other components of peace recognized by Catholic social teaching and secular theories of global justice. (A positive peace contrasts with a negative peace, which is simply the absence of war.)

PART VI

Moral Education

21

Reviving Disarmament Education

KELSEY DAVENPORT

Achieving the goal of a world free of nuclear weapons faces numerous challenges. Among them, a decline in engagement by the general public is of special concern. Precipitated by the perception that the nuclear threat has decreased since the end of the Cold War, public disinterest has fostered a mindset that eliminating nuclear weapons is a desirable but unachievable goal.

While serving as United Nations (UN) secretary-general, Kofi Annan (1997–2006) highlighted how public apathy and disengagement on nuclear weapons issues has emerged as an obstacle to disarmament efforts:

> It is striking for someone of my generation to think that an entire new generation of human beings is coming to maturity without an ever-present terror of nuclear catastrophe. Yet it is so, and that is for the better. The downside, however, is ignorance of the real dangers that do exist, especially the legacy of nuclear weapons inherited from the last century. Moreover, the companion of ignorance is complacency: what we know little about, we care little to do anything about.[1]

Annan went on to argue that enhancing and strengthening disarmament education efforts can play a critical role in rectifying the growing apathy toward the nuclear threat and empowering the public to support steps toward a nuclear weapons–free world. Realizing Annan's vision requires tailoring disarmament education resources to demonstrate that the nuclear threat is still proximate and pairing information with impactful steps that individuals can take to advance the goal of eliminating nuclear weapons.

The Declining Saliency of the Nuclear Threat

Since the end of the Cold War, perceptions of the threat posed by nuclear weapons declined dramatically. Cold War generations lived under an omnipresent threat of nuclear war. Governments sought to foster ideological consensus supporting nuclear deterrence as a security imperative and drew attention to nuclear risk. The prevalence of fallout shelters, government-supported educational videos emphasizing the nuclear threat and how to survive a strike, and robust media coverage of events such as the Cuban Missile Crisis also highlighted the proximity and immediacy of the nuclear threat.[2]

While state-centered efforts to highlight nuclear superiority and garner support for nuclear deterrence were antithetical to disarmament efforts, it did ensure a high level of saliency and increased knowledge about nuclear issues throughout the Cold War. Emphasis of the proximity and relevance of the nuclear threat actually helped spur grassroots antinuclear campaigns and civic actions in support of disarmament.

For post–Cold War generations, however, nuclear weapons are viewed as archaic, historic, and a far less immediate threat when compared to other international security challenges. A 2018 study from the RAND Corporation demonstrates that Generation X and millennials are far less concerned about the proliferation of nuclear weapons and nuclear threats than baby boomers.[3] The report notes, for instance, that 83 percent of baby boomers expressed concern about the risk posed by North Korea's nuclear weapons, compared to 67 percent of Generation X, and 63 percent of millennials who expressed worry. These post–Cold War generations view terrorism, climate change, and cybersecurity as far more pressing security threats.

This shift is unsurprising. The threats that millennials and Generation X view as more urgent security challenges are the lived experiences of their generations. Terrorism and climate change are visible, relevant threats consistently in the news. Nuclear weapons are more commonly a history lesson than a current event, and while certain crises, such as North Korean nuclear and long-range missile tests, may propel nuclear weapons issues back into the public eye, these are fleeting exposure when compared to the persistent visibility of these other challenges.

Additionally, the public generally believes that nuclear disarmament is a desirable but unachievable goal. According to a world public opinion poll in 2000, respondents in twenty-two countries (a mix of nuclear weapon states and non–nuclear weapon states) overwhelmingly supported nuclear disarmament. Seventy-six percent favored or strongly favored a verifiable international agreement eliminating all nuclear weapons on a specific timetable. However, failure to realize the goal of nuclear abolition instills the impression that nuclear disarmament is impossible to achieve. In a 2008 poll of US citizens, 69 percent of respondents agreed that the world would be safer if nuclear weapons were eliminated. However, 84 percent of those favoring elimination agreed that it was not possible because knowledge of nuclear weapons is too widespread and there is no way to prevent other states from acquiring them.[4]

This disbelief in the possibility of eliminating nuclear weapons decreases agency by creating the impression that disarmament is not feasible and therefore not urgent. The public is less inclined to invest in addressing "impossible" solutions to intangible threats. The disbelief also gives states and political leaders the space to rhetorically support a world free of nuclear weapons while claiming that the conditions are not yet right for negotiating a treaty on disarmament and justifying the maintenance of nuclear arsenals as "necessary" for security.

The perception that the nuclear threat will be omnipresent along with the enormity of the disarmament challenges may also translate into avoidance of the issue. Three experts from the Stevens Institute of Technology, Kristyn Karl (professor of political science), Ashley Lytle (professor of psychology), and Alex Wellerstein (director of the science and technology studies program) reported in the *Washington Post* that 53 percent of Americans "deliberately avoided reading news about nuclear threats" and 76 percent are "indifferent to or preferring to ignore the idea that nuclear attacks could occur."[5]

Tailoring Disarmament Education Efforts to Empower the Public

A wide variety of disarmament education resources already exist at the international, national, and local levels. Disarmament education is promoted by the UN, individual state governments, academics, and numerous nongovernmental organizations (NGOs).[6] As a result of these disparate contributions, there is a plethora of educational resources highlighting the threat posed by nuclear weapons, refuting the arguments that nuclear weapons are necessary for security, and laying out the path toward their elimination. Moving forward, strengthening disarmament education will require tailoring new and existing resources to make the nuclear threat more relevant and proximate to the public. It also requires laying out discrete steps with demonstrable impact toward nuclear abolition that empowers the public to invest in pursuing disarmament.

Making Nuclear Weapons More Visible and Relatable

To increase salience, disarmament education efforts must focus on making nuclear weapons more visible and more relatable. Individuals are more inclined to take action and invest emotionally in an issue if it impacts them or people they care about or when it ignites passion or outrage. Highlighting basic facts about nuclear weapons helps give tangible context to the nuclear threat, but increasing knowledge about a topic does not necessarily equate to increasing saliency. Relying solely or heavily on facts can actually be counterproductive because it can overwhelm the intended audience and fail to build an emotional connection that recognizes the urgency of the threat and empowers them to be part of the solution.

Disarmament education efforts should increasingly look to alternative modes of communicating, including utilizing narrative and storytelling, to impart information in a way that makes the nuclear threat more personal and relatable. This was less necessary during the Cold War when the threat of nuclear strike was ever present and highly visible. The public was already convinced that nuclear weapons posed an urgent threat and impacted them personally.

Creative methods for communicating on nuclear issues can deliver facts while fostering a more personal connection by demonstrating how nuclear weapons continue to impact communities, even if the weapons themselves cannot be seen. This makes the threat posed by nuclear weapons more visible. Examples of powerful storytelling efforts that are increasingly utilized in disarmament education efforts include highlighting the environmental consequences of producing and maintaining nuclear weapons and the continued toxic legacy of nuclear testing. Tailoring education efforts to highlight direct impacts on communities helps foster that emotional connection by making the nuclear threat personal.

A number of groups engaged in disarmament education are working to develop resources that utilize new validators and creative methods of communication. The Outrider Foundation, for instance, is an organization that balances imparting information about the devastation of a nuclear strike with empowerment of grassroots supporters of disarmament. Its website is designed to make the nuclear threat more visible and relatable.[7] The site uses storytelling and interactive graphics to demonstrate the impact of nuclear weapons. For example, a series of pieces demonstrate the human cost of building and maintaining nuclear weapons by illustrating how communities around the world have suffered from uranium mining and nuclear testing. Imparting fact through narrative in this fashion helps forge personal connections with the nuclear threat that foster engagement.

N Square is another group using creative methods to communicate the nuclear threat.[8] N Square emphasizes cross-sector collaboration to highlight the nuclear risk and accelerate progress toward disarmament. The group has engaged with screenwriters and game designers, for instance, to embed nuclear narratives in different forms of media to make the risk more proximate. N Square also reaches people through mediums they engage with on a regular basis, such as TV and video games.

Making the nuclear threat more relevant and visible also requires making the topic more accessible. In the United States as in most other nuclear-armed countries, a small group of decision makers determine nuclear policy and communicate it using terms such as "deterrence," "strategic stability," and "escalation dynamics." This use of exclusionary language discourages public engagement and solidifies elite-level control over nuclear issues. Some disarmament education resources fall into the trap of discussing nuclear policy using these terms that, while commonplace in the field, are less accessible to the general public. Instead, disarmament education should act as an equalizer by discussing nuclear weapons without relying on technical jargon and breaking down concepts used by policymakers in a way that empowers the public to challenge the status quo. The UN Office for Disarmament Affairs has curated a collection of resources aimed at different educational levels designed to address this challenge, including books, games, and lesson plans.⁹

Similarly, it is important to consider who is delivering the message. Champions of the nuclear disarmament movement are less well known to post–Cold War generations. Fostering leadership that younger generations can identify with makes the threat of nuclear weapons more proximate and can incentivize engagement. A new grassroots group, Beyond the Bomb, is seeking to create a new nuclear disarmament movement led by young people.¹⁰ The group characterizes the nuclear threat as a form of violence and oppression, themes that resonate with post–Cold War generations, and engage in actions that appeal to that demographic.

Another tactic that can be powerful in demonstrating the continued relevancy of the nuclear threat but should be used carefully is highlighting the devastating consequence of a nuclear strike or the accidental detonation of a nuclear weapon. A nuclear war or a nuclear strike are concepts that are abstract and difficult to imagine, yet disarmament education efforts sometimes take for granted that people "know" what will happen in the event of a nuclear detonation. But post–Cold War generations have not taken part in a duck and cover drill and are unlikely to have studied in any depth the impact of dropping nuclear weapons on Hiroshima and Nagasaki. Talking in specifics about circumstances that could lead to a strike and the devastating impacts of a nuclear detonation makes the threat more imaginable and personal. Another way to highlight nuclear risk to make the threat more urgent and personal is to incorporate nuclear accidents, or so-called Broken Arrow incidents, into educational materials. (The military uses the code name Broken Arrow to refer to events involving the unexpected loss, theft, or inadvertent detonation of nuclear weapons.) Broken Arrow episodes demonstrate the danger of even possessing these weapons and point to how even if the public trusts its leaders to avoid nuclear war, eventually the world will run out of luck.

Few people realize, for instance, that at least six nuclear weapons have been lost since 1950 and never recovered or that a plane malfunction resulted in two three-megaton nuclear warheads (two hundred times more powerful than the bomb dropped on Hiroshima) falling near Goldsboro, North Carolina, in 1961. Five of six safety mechanisms failed on one of the warheads, causing US secretary of defense Robert McNamara to later note that "by the slightest margin of chance, literally the failure of two wires to cross, a nuclear explosion was averted."[11] Had the bomb detonated, it would have produced a fireball with a radius of about two kilometers and caused third-degree burns to anyone within eighteen kilometers of the explosion.

Demonstrating the number of casualties and the environmental devastation that would result from an attack on a particular city or explaining the impact of a nuclear exchange on global food supplies can grab people's attention. Appealing to fear is an important resource for disarmament education efforts to draw upon. Nonetheless, playing solely to the public's fear can be paralyzing rather than motivating. As the UN noted in its definition of disarmament education, the goal is empowerment and prompting communities to take action. Accordingly, it is critical that disarmament education pairs information with action steps that create outlets for individuals and groups to act on their concerns.

A section on the Outrider Foundation website allows individuals to see the impact of a nuclear strike on their city, and immediately below is the link "Learn What You Can Do about Nukes" that provides an immediate channel for those motivated to take action. Since the website was launched in early 2018, the interactive graphic simulating nuclear strikes has attracted more than two million visitors.

Intersectionality

The threat of nuclear weapons does not exist in a vacuum. Disarmament education efforts, however, often silo off the nuclear threat because of the uniqueness of the risk and because the primary justification for nuclear weapons is to deter nuclear war. But global threats are becoming increasingly intertwined. Placing the nuclear threat in a broader context demonstrates the relationship between nuclear weapons and other areas of concern that already enjoy high saliency in the general public. One way to do this is to highlight the relationship between nuclear disarmament and more proximate and visible issues that are spurring people to take action. Climate change is increasingly identified by the public as the biggest threat facing the planet, and nuclear weapons have a toxic environmental legacy, to say nothing of the environmental impact of a potential nuclear exchange. Highlighting the environmental consequences of nuclear testing, a nuclear strike, maintenance of arsenals, and the difficulties of disposal of nuclear waste demonstrates that there is a relationship between the nuclear threat and the environmental degradation. If disarmament education embraces the climate change cause and explains how these issues are related, the environmental community may be willing to reciprocate. Beyond the Bomb has taken some steps in this direction. The organization worked with several environmental groups to include nuclear policy into discussions around the Green New Deal, a popular environmental policy in the United States with considerable support from young people. This type of authentic intersectionality in disarmament education will not only make the nuclear threat more relevant but can also invite new audiences into the conversation on eliminating nuclear weapons.

Similarly, connections can be made between nuclear weapons and security concerns such as terrorism, which post–Cold War generations identified as more pressing for them. Nuclear weapons are largely associated with states, but few know that al-Qaeda had a nuclear weapons program and was conducting experiments relevant to building a nuclear bomb in Afghanistan. Illustrating how terrorists could use nuclear or radiological materials to build a dirty bomb makes the threat less abstract. Forging connections between issues that the broader public is already concerned about makes nuclear weapons more tangible, visible, and comprehensible.

Another tactic that illustrates the reality of nuclear weapons is to highlight the cost of maintaining and upgrading the nuclear arsenals. People care about what they are paying for and the opportunity costs of maintaining systems that they would prefer to eliminate. While the global costs of maintaining and upgrading nuclear arsenals are difficult to calculate because of opaque defense budgets, the United States alone will spend an estimated $634 billion in updating and maintaining its nuclear arsenal from 2021 through 2030.[12] Pointing out the cost of maintaining an arsenal that does not address the primary twenty-first-century security threats facing the United States and propagating the news that the majority of individuals support abolishing nuclear weapons makes for a powerful data set that resonates with the public.

The emphasis of the opportunity cost to maintaining nuclear weapons is an element that UN secretary-general António Guterres emphasized in his 2018 global agenda on disarmament. While the focus of this effort includes other conventional and unconventional weapons, the secretary-general highlights that educational efforts should also focus on "the positive effects that disarmament has on socioeconomic development."

Combining Aspirational Goals with Concrete Steps

Overcoming public apathy and increasing engagement on nuclear disarmament also require demonstrating that the goal of nuclear abolition is possible. The goal of nuclear disarmament was clearly established in the first UN General Assembly resolution in 1946 and later solidified in the 1970 Nuclear Non-Proliferation Treaty, but there are no established timelines or universally agreed upon actions to advance toward the elimination of nuclear weapons.[13] The failure to achieve a goal set more than seventy years ago contributes to public apathy and the perception that disarmament is improbable.

While the slow progress toward disarmament invites public apathy, the goal of eliminating nuclear weapons is also difficult for the public to grapple with. What does a nuclear-free world look like? Is it possible to verify the elimination of nuclear weapons? What does it mean to support nuclear disarmament? Articulating answers to these questions so that the public understands what it means to be "for" disarmament is a critical component of disarmament education. Members of the current generation in particular prefer to donate their time, rather than money, to causes they care about, and they prefer collaborative actions with demonstrable impact.

Disarmament education faces the difficult challenge of setting aspiration goals that excite the public's imagination and match the urgency of the threat. At the same time, advocates must lay out measurable steps that allow engaged individuals to see that they are having an immediate impact. The opportunities for impact differ widely from community to community, so unity around a shared goal is also necessary. Disarmament education programs therefore have to tailor the steps toward that goal more locally. A number of grassroots groups that work toward disarmament, such as Physicians for Social Responsibility, are navigating this balance by pursuing and supporting city council and state legislature resolutions supporting nuclear disarmament along with national legislation restricting the US president's sole authority to launch nuclear weapons.[14] Other resolutions are now supporting the larger national campaign on no first use of nuclear weapons with legislation introduced in the US Congress. These incremental steps at the local level increase public engagement and empowerment by demonstrating that the improbable is possible. They also show that individuals and communities can play a role in advancing the goal of elimination.

Conclusion

Recent events have led to a resurgence of public and media interest in the threat posed by nuclear weapons. Disarmament education efforts must seize this moment of increased awareness of the nuclear threat to capture the public's imagination. This is a critical opportunity to take advantage of the existing wealth of disarmament resources and tailor them to the public in a way that demonstrates that the nuclear threat is an urgent yet solvable challenge.

Selected Resources and Campaigns

"Disarmament Education: Resources for Learning." UN Office for Disarmament Affairs, https://www.un.org/disarmament/education/index.html.

"The Facts." International Campaign to Abolish Nuclear Weapons, http://www.icanw.org/the-facts.

"Fact Sheets." Arms Control Association, https://www.armscontrol.org/factsheets.

"K=1 Project." Columbia Center for Nuclear Studies, https://k1project.columbia.edu.

"Learn about Nuclear Weapons." Swedish Physicians against Nuclear Weapons, http://laromkarnvapen.se/en.

"No Nukes," PAX, https://nonukes.nl.

"NTI Education Center." Nuclear Threat Initiative, https://www.nti.org/learn/education-center.

"Nuclear Notebook." *Bulletin of the Atomic Scientists*, https://thebulletin.org/nuclear-risk/nuclear-weapons/nuclear-notebook.

"Nuclear South Asia: A Guide to India, Pakistan, and the Bomb." Stimson Center Nuclear Learning, https://www.nuclearlearning.org/courses/nuclear-south-asia.

"Nuclear Weapons." Nuclear Age Peace Foundation, https://www.wagingpeace.org/issues/nuclear-weapons/nuclear-deterrence.

"Nuclear Weapons." The Outrider Foundation, https://outrider.org/nuclear-weapons.

"Reaching Zero." Global Zero, https://www.globalzero.org/reaching-zero.

"Resources." Beyond the Bomb, https://beyondthebomb.org/get-involved/resources.

"Resources Guide on Nuclear Disarmament for Religious Leaders and Communities." Religions for Peace. https://www.rfp.org/wp-content/uloads/2020/10/Nuclear-Disarmament-Resource-Guide-English.pdf.

"UNFOLD ZERO." A Project of PragueVision, PNND, Basel Peace Office, Mayors for Peace, 2020 Vision Campaign, Aotearoa Lawyers for Peace, and Global Security Institute.

Notes

1. UN General Assembly, "United Nations Study on Disarmament and Nonproliferation Education: Report of the Secretary General," 57th Session, August 30, 2002.
2. One of these more well-known efforts was the 1951 *Duck and Cover* film, which led to schoolchildren across the country practicing for a nuclear attack by hiding under their desks. That film was produced in part by the US Federal Civil Defense Administration, which was created in 1950 to highlight the threat posed by communism. The National Education Association was consulted on the duck and cover film project, and a committee of teachers recommended it in 1952 for screening to first, second, and third graders. This is one of several government-supported projects designed to garner support for US nuclear policies. For more information, see Claire Hope, "Cold War Educational Propaganda and Instructional Films, 1945–1965 (MA thesis, Virginia Commonwealth University, 2011).
3. Marek N. Posard, Jennifer Kavanagh, Kathryn A. Edwards, and Sonni Efron, *Millennial Perceptions of Security: Results from a National Survey of Americans* (Santa Monica, CA: Rand, 2018).
4. Nigel Hey, "Survey Shows Public Concerned Over National Security, Still Supports Nuclear Arsenal," Nuclear Age Peace Foundation, August 25, 2000.
5. Kristyn Karl, Ashley Lytle, and Alex Wellerstein, "A Nuclear Bomb Might Not Kill You. But Not Knowing How to Respond Might," *Washington Post*, January 14, 2019.
6. The UN in particular has played a prominent role in recognizing the importance of strengthening disarmament education. Disarmament education, as defined by the UN, is focused not solely on the provision of information but also on empowering individuals and communities to take steps to advance the goal of eliminating nuclear weapons. The UN maintains a website (https://www.un.org/disarmament/education/index.html) on disarmament education that includes access to resources and reporting on state disarmament efforts. The website also includes a nonexhaustive list of NGOs involved with nuclear disarmament education resources. These NGOs in particular play a critical role, serving as independent sources of information and assessment for civil society, policymakers, and the media.
7. "Nuclear Weapons," The Outrider Foundation, https://outrider.org/nuclear-weapons.
8. N Square, http://www.nsquare.org.
9. Peace and Disarmament Resources for Teachers and Students, UN Office for Disarmament Affairs, https://education.unoda.org/teachers-students.html.
10. Beyond the Bomb, https://beyondthebomb.org/why-we-fight.

11. "Broken Arrow Incidents," Atomic Heritage Foundation, https://www.atomicheritage.org/history/broken-arrow-accidents.
12. Projected Costs of US Nuclear Forces, 2021–30, Congressional Budget Office, May 2021.
13. The first UN General Assembly resolution in 1946 called for the creation of a commission to ensure "the elimination from national armaments of atomic weapons and all other major weapons adaptable to mass destruction." When the text of the Nuclear Non-Proliferation Treaty was finalized in 1967, Article VI of the treaty called negotiations in good faith on "a treaty on general and complete disarmament under strict and effective international control." States that possess nuclear weapons outside of the treaty—India, Israel, and Pakistan—have also expressed support for global nuclear disarmament.
14. "To Abolish Nuclear Weapons, PSR Chapters 'Think Globally, Act Locally,'" Physicians for Social Responsibility, April 20, 2018.

22

The Nuclear History Boot Camp

DAVID HOLLOWAY

In November 2017, Pope Francis noted in an address to a Vatican symposium on disarmament that nuclear weapons "create nothing but a false sense of security."[1] "They cannot," he pointed out, "constitute the basis for peaceful coexistence between members of the human family, which must rather be inspired by an ethics of solidarity." It was wrong to rely on nuclear weapons as the basis of international security. What was needed was "integral disarmament," embracing not only the dismantlement of nuclear arsenals but also humanity's social, economic, and spiritual development. He urged the symposium's participants to pursue that goal "with patience and constancy, in the trust that the Lord is ever at our side."

Pope Francis's address was a call to action. It was also a reflection on the history of nuclear weapons. December 2018 marked eighty years since the discovery of nuclear fission made such weapons a realistic prospect. Since the bombing of Hiroshima and Nagasaki in August 1945, nuclear weapons have not been detonated in war. The history of nuclear weapons has nevertheless been long and eventful. There is much to reflect on. How might that reflection contribute to Pope Francis's goal of integral disarmament?

Over the last eight years I have had the good fortune to take part in the Nuclear History Boot Camp. This is part of a wider project, the Nuclear Proliferation International History Project, which is based at the Woodrow Wilson International Center for Scholars in Washington, DC, and has been funded by the Carnegie Corporation of New York. The principal investigators on the project are Christian Osterman, director of the History and Public Policy Program at the Wilson Center, and Leopoldo Nuti, a professor of international history at the Roma Tre University. The Nuclear History Boot Camp is one of the main activities organized by the project. Every year for the last eight years it has brought together fifteen or sixteen graduate students from around the world for ten days in the small town of Allumiere in the hills north of Rome. The boot camp is housed in a former NATO communications base, which was taken over by Roma Tre after the Cold War. Our Italian hosts have created an outstanding communal experience. Breakfast and lunch are taken at the base, but we all have dinner together at 8:00 p.m. in one of the restaurants in the town. This contributes to the collegiality (and conviviality) of the boot camp and makes it not only an intellectually stimulating experience but a very enjoyable one as well.

I have been one of four faculty members who stay for the whole ten days. The others are Pulitzer Prize–winning nuclear historian Martin Sherwin, arms control expert Joseph Pilat, and Leopoldo Nuti, who directs the boot camp. Other faculty members come in for a day or several days, making presentations and having discussions with the fellows. Faculty give talks about different aspects of the history of nuclear weapons, while the fellows make presentations about their own work. Some of them are completing their PhD dissertations; others are still formulating their research topics. The boot camp is essentially a ten-day running seminar, with everyone taking part in all the sessions.

The agenda for the boot camp depends to some degree on the research topics the fellows are pursuing, but there is a list of topics that we try to include almost every year. Among these are the decision to use the atomic bombs on Hiroshima and Nagasaki; the failure of early efforts to bring atomic energy under international control; the development of the hydrogen bomb; the US-Soviet nuclear arms race and arms control; the major nuclear crises including, of course, the Cuban Missile Crisis; the Nuclear Non-Proliferation Treaty and efforts to stop the spread of nuclear weapons; nuclear weapons and the end of the Cold War; the role of antinuclear movements; the rivalry between India and Pakistan; and efforts to construct a global nuclear order. Among the other topics we have looked at are the medical consequences of Hiroshima and Nagasaki, the health effects of radioactive fallout from nuclear tests, and the environmental consequences of nuclear activities. The history of nuclear weapons is the history of not only suffering and threats but also efforts to prevent nuclear war and ultimately to abolish nuclear weapons.

Most of the fellows we select are historians, although a number have been political scientists with historical interests. Anthropologists and science and technology studies students have taken part as well. We have enough applicants to the boot camp to be able to make sure that each cohort is truly international. The fellows have come from a range of countries including Argentina, Brazil, China, France, Germany, India, Ireland, Israel, Italy, Japan, the Netherlands, Pakistan, Poland, Russia, Serbia, South Africa, South Korea, Turkey, Ukraine, the United States and the United Kingdom. Every year we have a good mix of disciplines and national backgrounds. That diversity contributes greatly to the intellectual vitality of the boot camp. The Nuclear History Boot Camp has also taken steps to create and sustain links among the approximately 120 graduates of the boot camp. There is a Facebook page, there are regular emails about new documents and new research, and panels of boot campers have been organized at conferences. These measures have had considerable success in building a community of young scholars working on nuclear history.

The fellows bring their own perspectives with them. We have sessions on doing archival work in different countries, writing international history, and the ethical issues that sometimes arise in doing research. We do not try to impose particular interpretations of historical events; there is plenty of lively debate and discussion. Presenters, both faculty and fellows, do advance their own views. We encourage discussion of the various presentations including questions that are probing in nature but try to do that in a supportive way, because a major goal of the boot camp is to encourage research on the history of nuclear weapons.

Doing nuclear history is a way of reflecting on our nuclear present and our nuclear future. There is much to think about apart from the terrible destructiveness of nuclear weapons. Let me point to three examples. The first is the dangers that nuclear weapons create. We have come close to nuclear war through accidents and miscalculation. The Cuban Missile Crisis of 1962 was the most dangerous time, but there were other crises too. The dangers should not be forgotten. A second lesson is the importance of restraint. The Cuban Missile Crisis can serve as an example again. If President John F. Kennedy had not resisted the advice of Gen. Maxwell Taylor and Robert McNamara to respond to the shooting down of the U-2 plane over Cuba on Saturday, October 27, by attacking all the Cuban air defenses, we could have had a nuclear war. It was Kennedy's decision to put off a military response that allowed time for a deal to be done that resolved the crisis peacefully. The third lesson is that as long as nuclear weapons exist, we do need an order of some kind to reduce the dangers of nuclear war and manage relations among states with respect to nuclear issues. The nuclear order built up since the 1950s is far from perfect, but it has been a crucial element in the management of international security. Even if one objects to the inequitable character of the present order, the question of an order that can deal with the danger of nuclear war needs to be borne in mind.

In 1922 the Russian mineralogist Vladimir Vernadsky, who had a great interest in radium, wrote of atomic energy, "Will humanity be able to use this power, direct it towards good, and not towards self-destruction? Is it mature enough to be able to use the power that science must inevitably give it?"[2] Seventy-two years later Yulii Khariton, who was scientific director of the Soviet equivalent of Los Alamos from 1946 to 1992, provided an answer to this question. Khariton probably had a closer connection with nuclear weapons over a longer period than anyone else in history. In 1994 at the age of ninety, he was invited to the United States to deliver the J. Robert Oppenheimer Memorial Lecture. Khariton wanted to go, but ill health prevented him from traveling. He sent a long letter to the lecture committee, in the final paragraph of which he gave what can be read as an answer to Vernadsky's question. After years of being involved in the remarkable scientific and engineering achievements leading to mastery of an inexhaustible source of energy, he wrote, now "at a more than mature age I am no longer convinced that the human race is mature enough to possess this energy." That judgment, though it comes from a very different perspective, coincides with Pope Francis's call for a rejection of nuclear weapons.

What is required to make the move from reliance on the false sense of security provided by nuclear weapons to a concept of integral disarmament? Nuclear weapons, in the words of Pope Francis, "exist in the service of a mentality of fear." Nuclear deterrence depends on a willingness to threaten the death of millions of people as well as on preparations to carry out that threat. The transition from nuclear deterrence to an ethics of solidarity must at the very least entail among potential adversaries a mutual recognition of their common humanity as well as a sense of empathy, a willingness to understand (or at least try to understand) the way in which others see the world. The study of nuclear history will not necessarily lead to uniform views about the role of nuclear weapons in international relations. To take one example, we have had at the boot camp different views of the Treaty on the Prohibition of Nuclear Weapons, which Pope Francis refers to in his address as "a light of hope" in "our unruly world."[3] Eighty-six states have signed the treaty, fifty-six have ratified it, and it entered into force in January 2020. Some of the participants in the boot camp have supported the treaty; others have seen it as unrealistic and dangerous. But even when there are disagreements, the joint study of nuclear history may help to move us toward an ethics of solidarity by humanizing those we previously regarded as our enemies and exploring and perhaps overcoming the "mentality of fear" that nuclear weapons serve.

There is another aspect of the boot camp that resonates with Pope Francis's call for "patience and constancy" in the search for integral disarmament. We devote one day of the boot camp to the discussion of current issues. Then, we divide the students into four groups and assign each group a hypothetical policy problem. The group has to make a proposal for dealing with the problem, drawing on history to formulate its position. Each group meets several times during the boot camp to work out the proposal it wants to make. On the last day of the camp the groups present their analyses and their recommendations to all the participants.

This has been an interesting exercise not only for the proposals advanced by the groups but also for the experience it gives the fellows of working together. I remember on one occasion watching a group consisting of a Pakistani woman, a Dutch man, an American woman, and a French man engaged in an intense discussion of some particular issue and thinking that this was one of the most important things the boot camp could do: provide young scholars, some of whom might come to occupy influential positions, the experience of working with colleagues from other countries to deal with problems that present a common danger to humanity. It is an exercise that in some small way may contribute to the "ethics of solidarity" that, in Pope Francis's words, must form "the basis for peaceful coexistence between members of the human family."

Notes

1. Address of His Holiness Pope Francis to Participants in the International Symposium "Prospects for a World Free of Nuclear Weapons and for Integral Disarmament," November 10, 2017.
2. Vladimir Vernadsky, *A Few Words about the Noosphere* (translated from Russian), ed. A. G. Gacheva and S. G. Semyonova (Moscow: Pedagogika-Press, 1993), 309. Citation found in somewhat different form, possibly because of alternative translation, in Miglena Nikolchina, *Lost Unicorns of the Velvet Revolutions: Heterotopias of the Seminar* (New York: Fordham University Press, 2013), 58.
3. Address of His Holiness Pope Francis, 2017.

23

Propaganda for Peace

Memes, Mass Moralizing, and a World Free of Nuclear Weapons

THEODORE G. DEDON

Jacques Ellul, a French Christian anarchist, said, "The individual who burns with desire for action but does not know what to do is a common type in our society. He wants to act for the sake of justice, peace, progress, but does not know how. If propaganda can show him this 'how' then it has won the game; action will surely follow."[1] Yet the word "propaganda" is often met with suspicion. It may conjure up pictures of real or imaginary state power, such as the Soviet Union, or the stories of George Orwell. Propaganda means, etymologically and neutrally, to spread about, to broadcast a message. The first official usage of the term for political purposes was in 1624 when Pope Urban VIII established the Pontificio Collegio Urbano de Propaganda Fide (Pontifical College for the Propagation of the Faith). Where indeed the institution was concerned with safeguarding correct doctrine and right thinking, the premise rested on the necessity for ensuring the quality and consistency of a message. It was, to borrow a phrase from Phil Hopkins, an early example of "mass moralizing" whereby marketing and storytelling intersect with each other.[2] Moral storytelling sustains worldviews. Since the origins of this style of moral propagandizing emerged, it has proved highly effective and has served as the foundation for rousing consciences throughout time. Today, we can use the lesson of intersecting moral storytelling with marketing to arouse the consciences of masses of people for the cause of total and complete nuclear disarmament. Following Pope Francis's condemnation of not only the use of nuclear weapons but also their possession, it is imperative that we discover new pathways to mass moralize and propagandize this message.

Ellul argued that propaganda was all-encompassing and inescapable. It was a feature of the technological society in which we all live. Whereas the traditional view of propaganda sees it as a tool of the state and delivered normally through the media, Ellul believed that propaganda is more pervasive. In the technological society information itself is omnipresent, and Ellul argued this before the internet and mass communication had developed to even a small fraction of what it is today. Therefore, the challenge of the modern day to actually influence beliefs is not to inundate people with facts and evidence but instead to appeal to their attitudes. "It is a fact that excessive data do not enlighten the reader or listener; they drown him. He cannot remember them all, or coordinate them, or understand them; if he does not want to risk losing his mind, he will merely draw a general picture from them. And the more facts a person is supplied the more simplistic the image."[3]

Beyond this, Ellul argues that people are "caught in a web of facts they have been given. They cannot even form a choice or a judgment in other areas or on other subjects. Thus the mechanisms of modern information induce a sort of hypnosis in the individual, who cannot get out of the field that has been laid out for him by the information."[4] We are not, Ellul believes, free to choose. We are subjects to propaganda laid out before us often by interested parties but also artificially through the self-replication of the technological society. And "all individual passion leads to the suppression of all critical thought with regard to the object of that passion."[5] In effect, according to his argument, the game is not to educate—it is to inundate and manipulate. And thus, it is the argument of this essay that those committed to nuclear disarmament, especially those who are in positions of influence, must learn to effectively embed the idea into every ideology permeating society. Whether or not we feel that propaganda is moral or valid is, to Ellul's framework, irrelevant. What is relevant is that propaganda is a fact, and whether we choose to use it for the goal of nuclear disarmament is up to us.

Someone who took this notion seriously in 1925, a generation before Ellul, was Richard von Coudenhove-Kalergi. In his book *Practical Idealism* he argued that the world is primarily moved by a mixture of material conditions and ideas. Practical idealism, against practical materialism, is recognizing that principles beyond pleasure and pain are fundamental to the state of world affairs. Therefore, he believed that propaganda is necessary in ordering the world toward a desirable outcome. Ideas are shaped by material conditions, and material conditions require propaganda to change, he believed. Writing from Austria at the time of Nazi ascension, Coudenhove-Kalergi argued that there needed to be sustained efforts not only to "promote the peace idea," but also to produce peace propaganda. This, he says, is to make sure that the peace idea can win against all others. "Peace propaganda alone is incapable of preventing the threat of imminent war . . . ; peace policy alone is incapable of securing permanent peace," and what is needed is "complete disarmament, [that will be] only possible after the victory of the peace idea."[6] "[Peace] propaganda is directed against war instincts," he says, and this is directed strictly against war interests.[7] Nuclear war was not even a possibility when he wrote about this. Responding to the devastation of World War I and the failure of the League of Nations to stop the rise of Nazism in Europe, Coudenhove-Kalergi believed that another world war must never occur. It was through the imagination and human conscience that we could effectively change the trajectory, achieved through peace propaganda:

> Peace propaganda must also mobilize human imaginations against a future war. It has to educate the masses about the dangers and horrors that threaten them in case of war: about the new rays and gasses that can kill entire cities, about the threat of an extermination war, which would be directed less to the front, but to the rural areas; about the political and economic consequences of such a war for victors and the defeated. This propaganda must help weak human memory and weak human imagination: for if people had more imagination—there would be no more war. The will to live would be the strongest ally of [peace].[8]

How true this is today, and how true this is to the cause of nuclear disarmament. Propaganda therefore is not only an enemy of peace but is also the greatest potential weapon in stopping war, if only the very idea of peace could win the day, that is. All power to the imagination.

Memes, Memeplexes, and the Meme Machine

In internet parlance, the word "meme" has taken on the meaning as a stand-in for that which goes viral. Commonly, it is an image with a set of words overlaid usually indicating something either apparently or seemingly relatable. Memes are the funny cat pictures you are sent in your email, the references to the latest happenings with varying commentary, and political messages designed to provoke or inspire. All memes are symbols. And they are, in effect, a form of propaganda. Meme theory was pioneered originally by Richard Dawkins who, in *The Selfish Gene*, made the case that memes are units of information that, like genes, seek to self-replicate.[9] A meme, unlike a biological gene, does not replicate for its fitness of purpose but instead replicates because it is advantageous to the passing on of its information. Dawkins, in *The God Delusion*, took this notion a step further.[10] He argued that while memes apparently self-replicate, so do the structures that capture and coordinate them. He calls these memeplexes. Most famously, he applied this theory to the study of religion, and for better or for worse, he argued that religions themselves are memeplexes. Christianity, for example, has a variety of memes. The meme of the virgin birth, the meme of the one true god, the meme of the immaculate conception, the meme of atonement, and the meme of salvation. All of these memes, Dawkins argues, are coordinated together through the greater memeplex that constitutes the Christian religion. Though he does not argue it as such in his text, this basic premise can be applied to any and all self-contained and coherent ideologies or social movements. Therefore, new social movements—such as the leftist movement for social justice and the right-wing movement for nationalist sovereignty—are indeed memeplexes. They have various memes embedded within them and a coherent metastructure that coordinates them.

Meme machines, which Dawkins describes humans as, produce and maintain memes in a sort of worldview and experiential maintenance. Memeplexes that make us into a meme machine in this way are things such as the "I" who "I am," as memeplexes are the big ideas, the worldviews, and the systems which are replicated. Nuclear disarmament, in this way, is merely one meme that can participate with a variety of memeplexes.

By this logic, nuclear disarmament could be a meme without a memeplex. Whereas it may be tempting to assume nuclear disarmament is an antiwar meme or goal, this has proved increasingly untrue. When George Shultz, William Perry, Henry Kissinger, and Sam Nunn wrote *A World Free of Nuclear Weapons*, they effectively changed the trajectory of the entire movement for nuclear disarmament.[11] These four, traditionally seen as proponents of the Cold War logic for the nuclear arms race, had a change of heart and mind. They saw it as imperative for global security to not only reduce nuclear arms possession but also eliminate their existence altogether. Their article, written in 2007, made it apparent that certain issues can make strange bedfellows. Whereas once it may have been an issue that only antiwar peace activists were champions of, nuclear disarmament was clearly made an issue free of ideology—therefore, a meme free of a memeplex. Humans, as meme machines, can spread these memes as long as they are found within memeplexes true to their experience.

The Meme War and the Symbol for Peace

It is not a well-known fact that the common symbol for peace was originally a symbol for nuclear disarmament. The international symbol for peace was designed by Gerald Holtom for the Campaign for Nuclear Disarmament, based in Britain. The CND symbol, as it is known, was presented in February 1958 to the Direct Action Committee and accepted as a symbol for its march on Trafalgar Square in London to the Atomic Weapons Research Establishment in April. The symbol is the superimposition of an "N" for nuclear and "D" for disarmament but also appears like a "V" for victory and has since been recognized generically as a universal symbol for peace. Popularized through the 1960s, the symbol can be seen embedded into virtually every political cause. Like the two-fingered "V" so famously used by Winston Churchill and later by Richard Nixon, the symbol effectively communicates the idea of peace. But since that time the CND symbol has become decoupled from the cause of nuclear disarmament. Therefore, it is a symbol with a meaning but not its original meaning. It is a meme in and of itself, but it has lost its original memeplex. Thus, it is imperative to recouple the meme to its original meaning so that nuclear disarmament is an obvious and apparent desire with its very usage. The peace sign is a symbol for nuclear disarmament, and nuclear disarmament is a symbol for peace. Every good meme is a symbol, and every good symbol is a meme.

Peace is a symbol—a meme—that can be embedded into every social movement regardless of its memeplex. On the one hand, the movement for social justice could appropriately take up the cause for nuclear disarmament and integral development on the grounds that it reduces national power differentials and increases our roles as stewards for the environment. And on the other hand, the movement for nationalist sovereignty could take up the cause for nuclear disarmament on the grounds it eliminates the imperial check against nation-states and safeguards state sovereignty against such global militarism. Further, it could reasonably be assumed that nuclear disarmament, should it be global and in total, could be a meme grafted into normal, nonideological narratives wherein people are concerned with generic global insecurity and risk. It is, in other words, the kind of meme that operates as self-replicating for its own advantage regardless of its framework. It is, in general, a universal and actionable symbol for peace.

Today, it seems unclear if the popularizers of war will heed the words of Kissinger, Shultz, Nunn, and Perry; indeed, it seems unlikely. But that said, it seems highly likely or at least plausible that nuclear disarmament could reenter the conversation through other backdoor channels. While it is easy to criticize former president Donald Trump on many fronts, at least rhetorically—symbolically and mimetically—he pursued the conversation of total disarmament with North Korea. Angela Nagle's argument on the rise of Trump asserted that central to his political campaign was the use of what she calls "meme warfare."[12] The basic assumption is that through the spreading of memes, Trump was made into a candidate who was both relatable and funny. Further, it helped spread his political platform beyond the common channels for discourse—such as the mainstream news media—and made the internet the central location for political influence. The so-called meme war therefore was the effective political propaganda that, Nagle believes, propelled him to win in places often untouched by conservatives.

Part of the postwin memetic influence of those who support Trump has been the assertion that he pursued a campaign of peace against those who seek greater nuclear armaments. This is of course contestable, but it is in effect a feature of the memeplex now existing for his supporters. Whereas the mainstream media criticized his efforts to denuclearize the Korean Peninsula, he was a committed man of peace, his supporters argued.[13] Though this is indeed debatable and not borne out by his geopolitical strategy, the meme itself is embedded into their memeplex. If the meme of peace through nuclear disarmament can permeate the culture war from the center right to the alt-right, could it not permeate all the others as well?

It seems highly probable that nuclear disarmament is an issue paramount to virtually all social movements and general causes. Black Lives Matter could support nuclear disarmament because the usage and indeed development of nuclear technology would disproportionately hurt Black and brown peoples, as would most technologies of war. The March for Our Lives, the movement that seeks to condemn the ownership of semiautomatic assault rifles and the National Rifle Association, should support nuclear disarmament for the fact it is yet another threat on children's lives. Indeed, it has been central to the threat against not only millennial and Generation Z children but also children all around the world for several generations. Further, the remnants of Occupy Wall Street and the Tea Party should support nuclear disarmament, because in the former case it disrupts the profiteering of the military-industrial complex, and in the latter case it disrupts the expansion of military-state power contributing to a bloated government. Nuclear disarmament, by this logic, is a meme that can be subsumed into virtually all memeplexes, and it should be positioned to do so. One example of how this could be achieved tangibly is that organizations committed to nuclear disarmament could propose sponsored social media from activists to reach their constituencies. This is a normative practice for advertisers and could certainly be applied to activism. Therefore, in conclusion, all who are primarily committed to global zero, to the disarmament of all nuclear weapons, should develop effective messaging strategies so this embedding can occur.

Peace Is the Way, Peace Is the Message

In 2015 a study done by Georgetown University's Center for Social Impact Communication examined the problem of slacktivism.[14] Slacktivists are those who are active through social media and nothing else. A common narrative about slacktivism is that it stops with the "like" and "share" buttons, but that is actually not true. Slacktivists are twice as likely to volunteer their time (30% vs. 15%) and to take part in a localized event. They are four times as likely to encourage others to contact political representatives (22% vs. 5%) as well as five times as likely to recruit others in their cause through petition (20% vs 4%). Further, they are equally as likely as non–social media promoters to donate money in support of such a cause (at 41%). This is particularly striking given what we are arguing here. If nuclear disarmament as a meme were to be embedded in every memeplex, would it not likely increase its exposure and support? If not already apparent, the point here is to dismiss purity tests with respect to single-cause issues. If nuclear disarmament is of paramount import—and it is—then it should be ideally located in any cause or set of causes regardless of how we see the memeplex broadly. If, for example, individuals are active members of the movement for social justice yet see themselves in antagonism with the nationalist sovereignty movement, they should be very glad that each respectively supports nuclear disarmament. This should occur regardless of how they feel about other memes in the memeplex such as abortion, state sovereignty, gun confiscation, and policing.

Pablo Barbera, a researcher on the effects of social media in political activism, determined that online discourse is largely rooted in "echo chambers of contrarian clubs."[15] They are, in effect, extremist groups separated from one another. But in an earlier study, he determined sharing political messages via social media such as Facebook with in localized networks, can actually reduce extremism and open up pathways for dialogue.[16] The point to glean here is that should strategic propagandizing of nuclear disarmament occur, should it be a meme embedded into every memeplex, political rivals may find common ground and indeed pursue peace.

Peace is the way, and peace is the message. It could be a Russian message; it could be an American, Russian, or Chinese message; and it is already a Roman Catholic message. Because of this—the message of Pope Francis that even the *possession* of nuclear arms is to be condemned—we need to discover new pathways for propagating that conviction. It is my belief that this meme, the meme of nuclear disarmament, can fit into nearly every memeplex and do so comfortably and without concession. It can become thoroughly local and global. Doing so will arouse the conscience of people online through social media but also offline in real-life activism regardless of the social movement to which they belong. If successful, it should open up pathways for dialogue and, in turn, actionable political change. To do so will be difficult and will require that every institution and individual committed to global zero sees this as a game wherein political rivalry can be an advantage, not a disadvantage. Ronald Reagan, when speaking about Mikhail Gorbachev to a group of faith leaders, said that "we may hope that *perestroika* will be accompanied by a deeper restructuring, a *metanoya* [sic], a change in heart, and that *glasnost*, which means giving voice, will also let loose a new chorus of belief, singing praise to the God that gave us life."[17] Let us propagate this message of faith so that nuclear disarmament can become a global fact. As it was once, nuclear disarmament must become the ultimate symbol of the peace idea.

Notes

1. Jacques Ellul, *Propaganda: The Formation of Men's Attitudes* (New York: Vintage, 1973), 209.
2. Phil Hopkins, *Mass Moralizing: Marketing and Moral Storytelling* (Lanham, MD: Rowman and Littlefield, 2015).
3. Ellul, *Propaganda*, 87.
4. Ellul.
5. Ellul, 170.
6. Richard von Coudenhove-Kalergi, *Practical Idealism: The Kalergi Plan to Destroy European Peoples*, 1st ed. (Omnia Veritas, 1925), 172.
7. Coudenhove-Kalergi, 173.
8. Coudenhove-Kalergi, 176.
9. Richard Dawkins, *The Selfish Gene* (New York: Oxford University Press, 2016), 342.
10. Richard Dawkins, *The God Delusion* (Boston: Houghton Mifflin, 2006).
11. George P. Shultz, William J. Perry, Henry A. Kissinger, and Sam Nunn, "A World Free of Nuclear Weapons," *Wall Street Journal*, January 4, 2007.
12. Angela Nagle, *Kill All Normies: Online Culture Wars from 4Chan and Tumblr to Trump and the Alt-Right* (London: Zer0 Books, 2017).
13. This is especially apparent on Reddit's forum. r/The_Donald, a popular meme board, focused on promoting Trump and his administration. There are hundreds of similar memes.
14. Bridget Pooley, "Slacktivism at its Finest," Georgetown Center for Social Impact Communication, https://csic.georgetown.edu/magazine/slacktivism-at-its-finest/.
15. Pablo Barbera, Cristian Vaccari, Augusto Valeriani, Richard Bonneau, John T. Jost, Jonathan Nagler, and Joshua Tucker, "Of Echo Chambers and Contrarian Clubs: Exposure to Political Disagreement among German and Italian Users of Twitter," *Social Media + Society* 2, no. 3 (2016).
16. Pablo Barbera, John T. Jost, Jonathan Nagler, Joshua Tucker, and Richard Bonneau, "Tweeting from Left to Right: Is Online Political Communication More Than an Echo Chamber?," *Psychological Science* 26, no. 10 (2015): 1531–42.
17. Andrew Preston, *Sword of the Spirit, Shield of Faith: Religion in American War and Diplomacy* (New York: Random House, 2012), 599–600.

24

A World without Nuclear Weapons

Imagine It One Step at a Time

JOHN PAUL LEDERACH

Across our globe our human family owns roughly fifteen thousand active nuclear weapons. The United States and Russia built and hold 90 percent of these weapons.

It costs about $400 million to produce a single operational missile and an estimated $70 million for it to fly toward its ultimate use. A recent study shows that if any country were to deploy more than one hundred nuclear weapons, this would effectively represent pulling the trigger to create a nuclear winter on itself and its own people.

While over the last quarter century key international actors began the slow reduction of these weapons, in the past few years the trend seems to be reversing back toward increased production. The effort of one country to stay one step ahead of and control the perceived threat of its enemy competitor has reignited a mutually functional fear. The new buildup, which is euphemistically called "modernization," begs a question: Is fear of collective suicide the best source to imagine global security and well-being?

i.

During the two decades of the 1990s into the early 2000s I traveled extensively throughout Colombia. In those years the country traversed periods of devastating violence, especially in the more rural departments. The conflict involved repeated clashes between state security forces, paramilitary groups, and various guerrilla movements, each carrying a bitter past and a *cuento*, a story that justified their armed behavior. The response of one group to the action of the others fed cycles of repeated harm. Sociologists call this "reciprocal causation": the dynamics of fear and reacting to the latest provocation from the other side drive the conflict to replicate violence independent of the originating causes. We tend to create self-generating systems of harm at great cost—to ourselves, to others, and to future generations, for trauma passes from one generation to the next. "The fathers have eaten sour grapes, and their children's teeth are set on edge" (Ezekiel 18:2).

In Colombia, careful tracking and observation of these conflict patterns would eventually show that the people who died during nearly six decades of war have numbered in the hundreds of thousands and those forced to flee in the millions. One stunning fact is that 80 percent of those who died in armed violence were civilians.

ii.

I write these pages from Colombia in 2019. Two years ago the unexpected happened. The longest and largest armed insurgency in the Western Hemisphere came to an end when a peace agreement was signed between FARC and the Colombian government. Navigating from war to peace is never easy. Difficulties and violent patterns remain a constant challenge.

Nonetheless, from today's vantage point in Colombia, an unavoidable question jumps out: How did the unexpected happen?

I think it started with imagination.

iii.

In those hard decades of war I came across some extraordinary people in Colombia. I found that the most innovative and pioneering initiatives shifting away from violence came from local communities most affected by armed conflict. I titled a book that captured the unexpected with the phrase *The Moral Imagination*. Influenced by the examples of these pioneers in Colombia, West and East Africa, and central Asia, four types of imagination seemed to consistently emerge when local communities shifted out of cycles of violence.

First, people employed an imagination about their wider web of relationships. At essence, they came to understand how intimately they were connected with those they perceived to be their enemies who had inflicted great harm on their families and communities. They came to *see,* in other words, they could *imagine,* that they themselves were connected to a web of relationships that included their enemies.

I sometimes call this the grandmothers' imagination. In the latter decades of life with grandchildren and great-grands moving playfully about, there comes a long gaze about the meaning and the gift of birth on this earth.

In this long gaze, a grandmother can have moments of penetrating insight that the well-being of her grandchildren is intimately tied to the well-being of her enemies' grandchildren.

Inevitably, with this gaze a profound inquiry rises to the surface: What legacy are we leaving the yet-to-be born?

Exploring this notion of ultimate connection and legacy, a second form of imagination emerges: the *curiosity* to explore what sits below and beyond the surface of the *cuentos* of enmity and conflict.

Curiosity creates a pause, a stop to look more carefully. In the case of these local communities, this often moved people to observe and explore the patterns that kept repeating around them and to reconsider the actors, the real-life people and their lives, who by one way or another were linked in this web of harmful action.

In one community in Medio Magdalena in Colombia, a group established a key discipline that its members would live by and into. While they deeply wished others, especially perpetrators of violence, would understand their plight and story, they committed to offering others what they most sought: *We will seek to understand those who do not understand us.* This is curiosity in action. They embodied an ethic of imagination.

Third, because they moved around the web of relationships and took up highly unusual conversations with respect, they often landed on the most unexpected ideas and initiatives. We can call this imagination itself, the innate human capacity to create. Creativity gives birth to something that at this point does not exist.

One group of women on the Somali-Kenyan border literally helped end a war. They started by asking how they could make their local market safer for anyone to buy at or sell from. In Medio Magdalena local groups established peace zones, negotiated spaces where even armed actors agreed not to bring guns. At essence, without naming themselves such, these pioneers became artists of social change.

These artisans of peace rarely had any formal conflict or peacebuilding training. What they had was the patience and discipline to listen differently to a wider range of perspectives, to sit with their growing understanding, and together propose ideas that were tested and then put into action. Often the idea would shift and grow as it adapted in a complex dynamic context.

They never stopped inventing.

Finally, in every instance where innovation shifted cycles of violence, people had the courage to take a step of risk. Imagination of risk was rarely about leaping immediately to the far-off, long-term goal. The women in Wajir did not set out to stop a war. They set out to ensure a safer market. But every step of the long journey required imagination about *what next* in this particular moment and volatile context. Risk means stepping into an action without control over what will happen.

We might call that faith.

If we know and can control the outcome, it is not a risk. Far too often the concern to control shapes the contours of the political imagination. What is possible becomes defined by what now exists. The moral imagination requires a shift, rarely seeing itself bound or paralyzed by current patterns. It asks a different question: What does not now exist but must?

In contexts of violence in places such as Colombia, even small steps could carry potential loss of life. So, risk always required courage. More often than not, risk was taken jointly. Small, innovative, mixed groups of people brought together everything they knew about their context, their network of relationships, and envisioned a potential for change one step at a time.

iv.

What might this have to do with a theme such as nuclear weapons, a challenge so massive and distant from our daily life and control that we have difficulty imagining our relevancy or connection?

Maybe, to put it lightly, *everything*!

And it starts with imagination about our web of relationships and the well-being of the yet-to-be born.

v.

In 1972 a Brazilian Presbyterian theologian, Rubem Alves, wrote a book titled *Tomorrow's Child*. Alves opened a perspective that has stayed with me since I read it as a young college student. It had to do with his view of futurologists and prophets and how they are different.

In my way of carrying forward Alves's view, he was suggesting that there are differentiated understandings of prophets that somehow easily get mixed up with the role of futurologists. Futurologists have a basic way of seeing the world and their contribution. They carefully study the patterns around us. They look back at the history feeding into the current patterns. They read the meaning of what is now and what seems emergent. Based on what they see now, they predict what is coming.

The futurologist displays an imagination that suggests that the future is the predicated outcome of what currently exists. The prophets, though often portrayed as predicting the future, have a very different ethic of time. Oddly, it starts with how they listen. As one of my professors, Elise Boulding, put it, prophets listen differently. She used to say that at times of social conflict and chaos, we find many prophets who speak but few who listen. Her phrase "prophetic listening" captures the ability to listen in a way that helps people tap their deepest wisdom and listen more clearly to what God may be speaking with and to them. Prophets have a capacity to listen, take note, and understand the nature of God's presence within and around us.

This listening essence connects to the original blessing from which we were born and toward which we journey. This kind of listening defines a life of faith. The prophet appeals to this essence to inform how we may adapt and adjust *our living now* to align with the original gift and create a future that ensures dignity of people and relationships.

In ways that are different from the futurologist, the prophet calls us to live now in ways that unfold toward the future we hope to engender, an imagination and expression of God's love.

vi.

The core question we face around the production of nuclear weapons should not orient around imagination of fear—fear specifically of collective suicide that guides the investment of our global resources.

The question should orient around how we might better imagine that our security and well-being are tied not to the size or quantity of our weapons but instead to the quality of our relationships as global children of God. The legacy we leave for the yet-to-be born depends on this imagination.

vii.

I return to the imaginative pioneers who kept finding ways to rise above the cycles of armed conflict. They would seem to offer some advice about collective fear and cycles of investment in violence. Perhaps the starting points are these.

First, imagine the original blessing. Life is precious. Life is a gift. We share this gift.

Second, imagine the wide web of our relationships. We are a global family, linked and connected. It is not possible for one part of our family to live as if they are disconnected from and unaffected by the well-being of another. The global family, part of the original blessing, supersedes the invisible lines that demarcate our boundaries and frontiers.

From the heart and eye of the Creator we are single family.

From everything we know and understand of our planetary fragility, our survival ties us together. The well-being of our grandchildren can only be ensured when the well-being of the other, even our enemy's grandchildren, has been cared for and ensured. Therein lies the inevitable and ultimate reality of our journey. We are in this together as children of the original blessing.

Third, imagine what sits behind, below, and beyond the stark projection that we are at threat and that our only recourse is to ensure an organized sustained fear of suicide in order not to use what we have created. Become curious. Find widely diverse views. Open unusual conversations. Sit and see what you know together.

Finally, imagine risk. One step at a time, reach for what seems open and possible now to offer a more dignified and safe legacy.

Worry less about whether it will somehow make the big splash that shifts the whole system. If you choose to worry, worry about taking a step together on something you find relevant, compelling, and within reach.

viii.

In the end, it is the thousands of conversations and the web of small steps together that shift harmful systems.

ix.

If people lead, leaders will follow.

PART VII

Responsible Actors

25

The Ethics of Nuclear Stewards

MARYANN CUSIMANO LOVE

What are the ethical responsibilities of military officers and enlisted personnel entrusted with the safekeeping of nuclear weapons? Presidents, political leaders, and diplomats negotiate the disarmament of nuclear weapons, as agreed to in the Nuclear Non-Proliferation Treaty. Political leaders, not soldiers, decide the size of nuclear arsenals. While military commanders and soldiers cannot commit the United States to deeper disarmament of the US nuclear arsenal, they can and do play important roles in preventing nuclear proliferation, averting nuclear accidents, and safeguarding against unintentional escalation of nuclear risk. Whether or not policymakers commit to deeper disarmament, in the meantime soldiers and military officers have critical ethical responsibilities for the safeguarding of existing nuclear weapons arsenals until the time when they can be dismantled.

The Cold War was a period of heightened risk of nuclear war. US and Soviet decision makers engaged in nuclear brinkmanship and chose to radically increase the size, deployment, delivery vehicles, dispersion, and scale of destructiveness of nuclear weapons in the name of the Cold War policies of deterrence and mutually assured destruction. The United States and the Soviet Union engaged in an arms race, escalating from a handful of weapons with fifteen-kiloton blast capabilities to over sixty-six thousand nuclear weapons by the mid-1980s, which were between 80 times to over 3,333 times more destructive than the original atomic bomb, capable of destroying Earth many times over. Numerous failures of nuclear weapons safety took place during the Cold War. The US government admits losing eleven nuclear weapons, but experts believe that the actual number is much higher. The Cold War arms race was created to maximize fear and threat to the other side, not to maximize safety and security of the weapons, the arsenals, and the extended nuclear triad and complex.

The triad's widespread deployment and constant movement of nuclear weapons creates safety hazards, as nuclear weapons are transferred on aircraft, ships, and submarines and in and out of silos. US nuclear bombs fell out of US airplanes in Spain, Canada, and Greenland and in North Carolina, Georgia, Maryland, and California. One bomb fell on a children's playhouse in North Carolina, injuring the three children playing inside as well as the parents nearby. US planes carrying nuclear bombs crashed in fiery explosions, often releasing radiation contamination, in New Mexico, Texas, Kentucky, Louisiana, Florida, Indiana, and England. US nuclear bombs mistakenly fell off US ships near Japan and sank with submarines near the Azores.

Yet, despite the decrease in the size of US and Russian nuclear arsenals since the end of the Cold War, the world is still at risk. Ironically, the complex surety and safeguarding apparatus of the nuclear enterprise in the United States (and in other nuclear weapon states) may be less safe than in the Cold War. As reliance on nuclear weapons to deter a Cold War foe receded, the attention to the nuclear complex receded as well. In time the promotions, training, and education dollars once spent on the nuclear enterprise were reallocated to new urgent priorities. The war on terror, the conventional wars in Iraq and Afghanistan, and homeland security took priority in military funding, advancement, and promotions. The safety record of securing and safeguarding our most dangerous nuclear arsenals and the means to deliver them continues to erode. This pressing and very serious situation is due to many factors, including lack of senior leader attention, debates over defense priorities, and ethical lapses of the military commanders and soldiers responsible for nuclear weapons. While attempts to improve nuclear weapons security have had some impact, the situation remains dire.

Ethical Lapses Create Nuclear Risks

Several high-profile nuclear weapons scandals over the past fifteen years brought ethical, legal, leadership, and safety problems in the nuclear forces into the public eye. Nuclear bomb parts were mistakenly sent to Taiwan. No one reported them missing in the United States, and no one in Taiwan noticed the arrival of the four nuclear bomb fuses. They remained unsecured in a foreign country for over a year and a half. Eventually Taiwan notified the United States that instead of the expected shipment of helicopter batteries, the United States had sent nuclear bomb parts. But it took the US Department of Defense over a year after Taiwan's notification to understand that it had sent nuclear bomb parts rather than helicopter batteries and respond. The Department of Defense admitted its mistake in August 2006. Given geopolitical tensions over Taiwan, the mistaken shipment of nuclear bomb components to Taiwan could have ignited a crisis, creating a nuclear escalation between the United States and China.

In another incident, US Air Force crews and pilots mistakenly loaded and flew a plane full of nuclear-armed cruise missiles across country, from North Dakota to Louisiana, on August 29, 2007. Six AGM-129 advanced cruise missiles were mistakenly armed with W80-1 variable-yield nuclear warheads and loaded on a B-52. The B-52 then took off from Minot Air Force Base, North Dakota, and flew to Barksdale Air Force Base in Louisiana. The W80-1 nuclear warheads should have been removed before the cruise missiles were loaded onto the B-52. After the flight, the nuclear warheads remained mounted on the cruise missiles, and the nuclear warheads were not reported missing. For over thirty-six hours they sat unsecured on a tarmac. The nuclear warheads were not provided the extra security measures and precautions normally given to the most dangerous and highly sophisticated weapons in the US arsenal. This was not an error made by a single individual. Multiple US Air Force crews and pilots made multiple mistakes in not noticing that the dummy training warheads they were supposed to be transporting were actually nuclear warheads. No one reported the nuclear warheads missing from North Dakota, and no one noticed the nuclear warheads sitting unsecured in Louisiana for nearly two days.

In the wake of these scandals, the Department of Defense and the Air Force conducted a series of investigations. These investigations were highly critical of the nuclear enterprise—level leadership, noting ethical and leadership failures as well as resourcing and training lapses that led to a culture of shortcuts and inefficiencies. The investigations found "a decline in the Air Force's nuclear mission focus and performance" and a failure by Air Force leaders to respond effectively to the problems revealed by these incidents. In response, President George W. Bush's secretary of defense, Robert M. Gates, requested and received the resignation of Air Force secretary Michael Wynne and chief of staff Gen. Michael Moseley, the head of civilian and military leaders of the Air Force. These unprecedented high-level firings in 2008 were meant to create a clean break from the nuclear weapons scandals and to serve as an example to deter any future incidents. It did not turn out that way.

The scandals continued. Investigators uncovered widespread cheating on nuclear weapons safety tests. Twenty percent of officers cheated on their monthly knowledge and readiness test for a nuclear weapons unit, the 341st Missile Wing at Malmstrom Air Force Base in Montana, responsible for 150 nuclear intercontinental ballistic missiles. The investigation found that in order to achieve the demanding criteria for readiness certification in which anything less than 90 percent correct answers was deemed insufficient, officers routinely texted each other the answers to questions on their knowledge of the missile launch systems. The investigation also found that other officers, including commanders, knew about the cheating and did not report it, raising questions of the ethics and legal responsibilities of leadership and calling into question the training culture. Eighty-two officers were ultimately accused of providing or accepting answers ahead of the monthly exams. To decrease the incentive to cheat, the Air Force switched to a pass/fail grading system.

Th 341st Missile Wing in Montana also failed its nuclear weapons safety test and inspection in August 2013. The unit is responsible for one-third of US intercontinental ballistic missiles.

In Minot, North Dakota, seventeen officers were stripped of their authority to launch nuclear weapons in April 2013. According to Lt. Col. Jay Folds, he took action against these officers due to widespread "rot in the crew force," including acceptance of violations of nuclear weapons safety rules and potential compromises of nuclear launch codes.[1]

Top leaders of nuclear weapons units were fired for ethical and legal breaches. US Air Force major general Michael Carey was commander of the US intercontinental ballistic missile force of the 20th Air Force at Warren Air Force Base, Wyoming, and was also in charge of three wings of nuclear-armed aircraft. Carey was relieved of duty for conduct inappropriate to an officer and a gentleman, including public drunkenness and dereliction of duty while taking part in a nuclear weapons security exercise. He was representing the US government in the US-Russian Federation Nuclear Weapons Security exercise in Moscow to improve the safeguarding of nuclear warheads. Carey abused alcohol and fraternized with women during the exercise, showing up drunk and late at the exercise in July 2013 and behaving inappropriately.[2] Deputy chief of US Strategic Command Vice Adm. Tim Giardina was demoted and relieved of his control over nuclear weapons in October 2013 after allegations surfaced about unethical and illegal behavior, including his use of counterfeit gambling chips at an Iowa casino.

In another scandal, service members in two nuclear weapons units at Warren Air Force base were disciplined and court-martialed for using and distributing LSD. Fourteen enlisted troops between the ranks of airman and airman first class were disciplined, and six were court-martialed for use and distribution of drugs, including LSD, cocaine, and marijuana. The troops served in the 790th Missile Security Forces Squadron and the 90th Security Forces Squadron and were responsible for the security and defense of the nuclear weapons and the missile complex at Warren Air Force Base, which spans the Colorado-Wyoming border.[3]

Together these incidents show a disturbing pattern of not just one or two bad apples but rather a host of ethical, legal, leadership, and safety violations among troops responsible for nuclear weapons at the enlisted, officer, and commander levels in units operating in several states, including North Dakota, Montana, New Mexico, Wyoming, South Dakota, Louisiana, and Colorado, and in foreign country operations in Taiwan and Russia.

There are many reasons for the violations. Combat experience weighs heavily in military promotions, and the wars in Iraq and Afghanistan provided paths for officers to advance. Nuclear weapons units are not seen as central or an avenue to promotion and so do not attract the military's best talent. Also, withdrawals from arms control treaties and the decline in the cooperative threat reduction program decreases the duties that troops are responsible for: inspection, exercises, reporting, and implementation activities. Units of bored young people in remote places with little to occupy them, commanded by diffident leaders, is a recipe for nuclear disaster.

Positive Cases: Ethical Leaders Protect against Nuclear Risks

Behind each of these headlines of nuclear scandals also lie unheralded military service members and civilians who reported on the ethical, legal, and nuclear safety breaches they witnessed among their colleagues. For example, the inspector general's report on the conduct of Major General Carey is full of the redacted names of people who put themselves at risk to report on the inappropriate and erratic behavior of a commanding officer. Behind every blacked-out name in the report is a person who stuck his or her neck out, who risked reprisals and negative repercussions in order to prioritize nuclear safety.

These whistleblowers follow in the footsteps of others who raised ethical concerns in the face of nuclear dangers. For example, Air Force nuclear launch officer Maj. Harold L. Hering, recipient of the Distinguished Flying Cross for his rescue efforts as a helicopter pilot in Vietnam, raised questions about the security procedures for nuclear launch while serving in a nuclear missile unit at Vandenberg Air Force Base in California in 1973. He asked what procedures were in place to ensure that the launch order was legal, that the president was sane, and that the system had not been violated by a foreign power. He raised the question during the Watergate scandal, when President Richard Nixon was known to be drinking heavily during the unraveling of his presidency. Hering was discharged from the US Air Force for asking for clarification of the launch process. This was a more complicated question than it might first appear, since the process for determining the legitimacy of an order to launch a nuclear strike is premised on verifying the identity of the president. Whether or not the president is sane or is issuing a rational order was not considered, and the same is true now. While two-part identification is required for nuclear launch, there is no oversight of the state of mind of the commander in chief issuing the order.

At times, military leaders may be called upon to prevent nuclear war, even sometimes disobeying orders to deliver a nuclear attack. While Major Hering's question was hypothetical, a more dangerous case soon arose in 1983. A single commander decided against following procedures, based on faulty information that which he believed would have led to a nuclear exchange. On September 26, 1983, Lt. Col. Stanislav Yevgrafovich Petrov of the Soviet Air Defence Forces was serving as the duty officer at a Soviet early-warning detection facility. Petrov received a warning that the United States had launched five nuclear missiles at the Soviet Union. The missiles would strike in minutes, could ultimately be the vanguard of thousands of US nuclear strikes aimed at his motherland, and could ultimately lead to the catastrophic destruction of the Soviet Union. Petrov used his training, education, intuition, and common sense. He reasoned that even in the high tensions that existed between the United States and Soviet Union, particularly in the wake of the Soviet downing of Korean Airlines flight 007 just three weeks earlier, it made no sense that the United States would send five missiles to destroy the Soviet Union. Wouldn't they send them all? Petrov disobeyed military procedure and did not immediately notify higher headquarters of the impending strike. Later, he stated that he believed that his leadership would have followed the knee-jerk protocol and launched a counterstrike, thus precipitating a nuclear war. Petrov was later proven correct, and the false alarm was determined to be caused by a malfunction in the Soviet satellite early-warning system that relayed the information to his station. Yet, since massive retaliation and deterrence relies on instant response to an attack, the Soviet command questioned his judgment as an officer. Under a cloud of suspicion, Petrov ultimately opted for early retirement.

Petrov's case highlights both the moral and practical challenges associated with serving in a leadership role in a nuclear enterprise. Is upholding the process paramount and necessary to maintaining the strategic balance? What are your ethical responsibilities when education, training, and experience tell you that the process is or could be flawed? Additionally, what are the consequences for stepping outside of the process and questioning its effectiveness and rationale? For both Hering and Petrov, the established processes were not seen as sufficient to prevent the gravest of mistakes, yet both ultimately paid a price for using their training, experience, and professional military education to either point out a process flaw or, in Petrov's case, avert bumbling into a nuclear exchange based on bad data and miscalculation. Decades later, Petrov was ultimately hailed as "the man who saved the world" and lauded in a documentary of the same name that detailed how close the world unknowingly came to Armageddon. That film premiered in 2014; his accomplishments were not generally understood or acknowledged until nearly thirty years after the fact.

These are not isolated cases. Robert Kennedy and John F. Kennedy are often hailed for their ethical leadership, asking moral questions about using nuclear weapons and deescalating the 1962 Cuban Missile Crisis when some military leaders, such as Gen. "Bombs Away" Curtis LeMay, urged immediate military action. Few appreciate the actions of others who stopped nuclear war during the crisis. In Duluth, Minnesota, a black bear had the bad timing to climb a fence in a military base, which triggered a nuclear-armed F-106A interceptor aircraft from a Wisconsin air base to respond to the "intruder." Because this happened during the Cuban Missile Crisis, when the country was at heightened Defcon 3 alert, there was no way to call off the mistaken nuclear attack response. Upon learning that it was a false alarm, someone at the Wisconsin Command Center jumped in a car and raced the nuclear-armed airplane down the runway to stop it from taking off. Had that quick-thinking soldier not put himself in harm's way on October 25, 1962, a mistaken friendly fire nuclear weapon would have been dropped during the crisis.

Other quick-thinking leaders also stopped nuclear war during the Cuban Missile Crisis, such as Vasily Arkhipov, who was second-in-command of the Soviet nuclear missile–armed submarine B-59 during the Cuban Missile Crisis. The B-59 was submerged and under depth charge attack by the Americans, and the captain of the vessel, Valentin Grigorievitch Savitsky, determined that the only reason the United States was trying to bring the Soviet submarine to the surface was that a state of war must exist and that the duty of the B-59 was to attack the American fleet with its nuclear torpedoes. Since Arkhipov was the submarine flotilla commander though not the commander of the B-59, he had a vote. To launch a nuclear strike against the Americans, a unanimous decision was required. Three had a vote: Captain Savisky, Arkhipov, and the ranking political officer, Ivan Maslennikov. Cut off and under withering pressure, Arkhipov nevertheless called on his conscience and experience, which included commanding the nuclear submarine K-19 that suffered a nuclear meltdown. Arkhipov voted "no" to launching a nuclear strike.

Moral Hazards, Literally

The concept of moral hazard usually refers to an unethical shifting of risk whereby one party engages in risky behavior because another will bear its consequences. Nuclear weapons pose such standard moral hazards, as the actions and inactions of military and civilian leaders with control over nuclear arsenals bring risks to others.

But where nuclear weapons are concerned, moral hazards are literal and pose clear and present dangers. Moral lapses are nuclear hazards. Because of the high destructiveness, speed, and escalatory characteristics of nuclear weapons, ethical and leadership failures can have catastrophic consequences, including the threat of human and planetary extinction. Ethical leadership is not a peripheral concern but is required for the survival of the planet. The high destructiveness of nuclear weapons and the low tolerance for human error are a poor match for fallen human nature. For example, the United States has the world's worst drug addiction problem, while Russia has the world's worst alcohol addiction problem. Yet together the United States and Russia control over 92 percent of the world's nuclear weapons. It is naive to think that military personnel and military and civilian leaders responsible for nuclear weapons can be insulated from these epidemics savaging their countries. Scandals among the nuclear forces provide evidence of this.

All nuclear weapons missions have ethical and moral dimensions, from those involved in safeguarding and protecting nuclear weapons to those ensuring they are mission-ready and those involved in aspects of targeting, delivery, and maintenance.

Concerns for nuclear safety, the increasing number of nuclear accidents, and threats of nuclear weapons ending up in the wrong hands have led many senior military and defense officials in the United States and around the world to urge deeper and quicker nuclear disarmament. The larger the nuclear arsenals, the larger the risks, and the smaller the nuclear arsenals, the smaller and more manageable the risks. Yet many of these elder statesmen, military and civilian leaders with deep and direct experience of the dangers of nuclear weapons, are aging out or retiring and are not being replaced by a younger generation committed to ethical nuclear stewardship. Where are the next generals like Gen. William Burns and Gen. Lee Butler and the statesmen like Senators Sam Nunn and Richard Lugar among the younger generation of leaders?

Expanding participation in nuclear threat reduction and security programs is needed to develop a growing cadre of ethical nuclear stewards. Initiatives such as the Proliferation Security Initiative, the Nuclear Security Summits, and the Cooperative Threat Reduction program expand the personnel with experience in securing nuclear materials, preventing proliferation, and cooperating with counterparts across agency and national boundaries. More of these activities will help train and expose more military and civilian leaders to practices and principles of ethical custodians of nuclear weapons. Ethical leaders are needed to faithfully secure nuclear weapons and to root out problems of corruption and ineptitude in nuclear units that make accidental nuclear use and nuclear theft more likely.

As long as nuclear weapons remain on Earth, the task of being a responsible custodian of nuclear weapons, ensuring that nuclear weapons are not used, are not involved in accidents, and are not stolen, is an often unheralded but solemn responsibility. While nuclear weapons remain, ethical leaders are essential in the military and civilian chains of command to ensure the safety and security of these arsenals while lending their voices and expertise to calls for deeper nuclear disarmament.

Notes

1. Bob Butterworth, "Change How We Test, Care, Feed Air Force ICBM Crews," Breaking Defense, March 12, 2014, https://breakingdefense.com/2014/03/change-how-we-test-care-feed-air-force-icbm-crews/.
2. Inspector General of the Air Force, "Report on Investigation SP8011P: Maj Gen Michael J. Carey," October 2013.
3. CBS News, "U.S. Troops Guarding Nuclear Weapons Took LSD, Air Force Records Show," May 24, 2018.

26

In the Chain of Command

DREW CHRISTIANSEN, SJ

It is widely assumed that to sustain a credible nuclear deterrent, those in the chain of command, whether missile personnel, submariners, or senior defense officials, must be uncritical implementers of orders from above. The chain of command, the presumption holds, must be free of dissenters; selective conscientious objectors are unwelcome. Furthermore, steps will be taken to remove unreliable individuals from the nuclear forces. What is less well known is the history of officers refusing to launch nuclear weapons and the practice of scenarios of refusal by officers at the highest level.

We now know that during the Cold War the planet was saved from destruction by courageous officers who resisted pressures to launch nuclear weapons. The best known among these have been two Soviets, Stanislas Petrov, a missile launch officer who resisted repeated computerized launch signals that later proved to be false alarms, and Vasily Arkhipov, a naval flotilla commander who refused to add his key to the two others to launch a nuclear-armed torpedo against US surface ships during the 1962 Cuban Missile Crisis, even though his submarine was under depth-charge attack from the US Navy.[1]

Furthermore, during 2017 Senate hearings on the US president's unilateral authority to launch nuclear weapons, Gen. Robert Kehler and Gen. John Hyten, two heads of the Strategic Air Command, testified that they would refuse to follow illegal orders to launch a nuclear attack.[2] Furthermore, General Hyten, then on active duty, explained that any refusal would rest on established norms of armed conflict found in international law, the US military code, and the just war tradition, norms that include noncombatant immunity and proportionality. The generals also reported that in the wake of a refusal, they would offer the commander in chief options for other courses of action.

Kehler went further, adding in a talk to an international security conference in Halifax, Nova Scotia, soon after his congressional testimony, that the US Air Force took the duty of responsible obedience, including refusal, so seriously that the high command annually reviewed just war principles and ran yearly exercises in their application.[3] So, at the highest level at least, the US military understands the role of independent human judgment for those in the chain of command and acknowledges the need to be practiced in the process of objection to illegal orders.

Catholic social teaching is hardly ambiguous on the use of weapons of mass destruction. Explaining that "actions which deliberately conflict with [the] principles [of the universal natural law], as well as orders commanding such actions, are criminal," the Second Vatican Council solemnly declared that "any act of war aimed indiscriminately at the destruction of entire cities or of extensive areas along with their population is a crime against God and man himself. It merits unequivocal and unhesitating condemnation."[4] According to solemn conciliar teaching, any strategic nuclear attack would be illegal as well as morally impermissible. For that reason, in the 1983 pastoral letter "The Challenge of Peace" the US bishops condemned nuclear war-fighting and only made conditional allowance for deterrent forces.[5]

Blind Obedience versus Selective Conscientious Objection

After the Nuremberg war crimes trials, military personnel understood that blind obedience to orders is not an acceptable defense for complying with illegal orders.[6] The Second Vatican Council allowed that in a disordered world, "governments cannot be denied the right to self-defense once every means of peaceful settlement has been exhausted."[7] The council also commended those "pledged to the service of their country as members of the armed forces," though it conditioned its approval on their "properly" fulfilling their roles as "agents of security and freedom." At the same time, the council wrote, "The courage of those who openly and fearlessly resist men who issue [illegal] commands merits supreme commendation."[8]

Clearly, Catholic teaching on responsible military leadership entails independent moral judgment with the expectation that responsible military conduct includes refusal to undertake plainly immoral actions. That is especially the case where, as in strategic nuclear attacks, there would be massive deaths and extensive destruction. The Second Vatican Council urged those in authority to understand their responsibilities toward not just their own nations but also to all humanity.[9] It encouraged "especially government officials and experts in [defense and security] matters" to join in improving agreements to curb the savagery of war, foster a culture of peace, and build the institutions of disarmament.[10]

A culture of peace requires military personnel and their civilian supervisors to be ready to oppose immoral orders. The Second Vatican Council appealed for legal provision for conscientious objection "for those who for reasons of conscience refuse to bear arms," but this recommendation applied only to blanket pacifists.[11] The council made no recommendation for legal protections for those who disobey illegal orders. The question had not yet matured. But only a few years later the US bishops, in the context of the Vietnam War, urged the adoption of selective conscientious objection that would include refusal to use weapons of mass destruction.[12]

In their 1968 pastoral letter "Human Life in Our Day," the US bishops first made the case for selective conscientious objection. They then explicitly cited employment "in branches of service (e.g., the strategic nuclear forces) which would subject them to the performance of actions contrary to deeply held moral convictions about indiscriminate killing" as a case where selective conscientious objection might be invoked.[13] In a subsequent statement, the bishops' conference affirmed that we should regard conscientious objection and selective conscientious objection as positive indicators within the Catholic Church of "a sound moral awareness and respect for human life."[14] Thus, half a century ago it was already clear to the bishops that military personnel might consider service in the nuclear forces as morally problematic.

While not reiterating their suggestion that the provision of conscientious objection would be appropriate for those serving in the strategic nuclear services, in "The Challenge of Peace," the American bishops reminded military personnel, somewhat more obliquely, that refusal to undertake "acts which inflict harm on innocent civilians ... is not an act of cowardice or treason but one of courage and patriotism."[15] The bishops also asked public officials to "be particularly attentive to the consciences of those who sincerely believe that they may not morally support warfare in general, a given war, or the exercise of a particular role within the armed forces."[16] The bishops went on to encourage political authorities to give "maximum protection" to freedom of conscience. So, while not using the term "selective conscientious objection," *The Challenge of Peace* nonetheless made the case for it.

Before moving on, I should make clear that objecting to illegal orders does not require those in the chain of command to appeal to Catholic social teaching, for it is already protected under international law and military jurisprudence.[17] It must be acknowledged, however, that within the military structures—from training to the juridical process, which may follow a claim to justified objection, to an illegal order—military officers and enlisted personnel may well meet countervailing pressures that can work to inhibit and perhaps even punish a break with military good order for reasons of conscience.[18] For Catholics ensnared by such pressures to comply with illegal orders, the words of Saint John Paul II apropos of the nonviolent activists in the revolutions of 1989 offer this sober counsel: "It is by uniting his sufferings for the sake of truth and freedom with the sufferings of Christ on the Cross that man [sic] is able to accomplish the miracle of peace and *is able to discern the often narrow path between the cowardice which gives into evil and the violence which under the illusion of fighting evil, only make it worse.*"[19]

The laws of war are sometimes best served by those who uphold them at cost to themselves. In resisting illegal orders, officers and enlisted personnel obeying the spirit as well as the letter of the law may well face personal rejection, harassment, and even in some cases unjust punishment. However, resistance to illegal orders not only protects the innocent from attack but also upholds the honor of the military and the integrity of the military justice system.[20]

Today's Challenges

At the time of *Human Life in Our Day*, the US bishops made a general case for selective conscientious objection to deployment in the nuclear forces. They only cited "deeply held moral convictions about indiscriminate killing." Over the years, however, the reasons for doubting the effectiveness of deterrence have grown.[21] These criticisms were bolstered by the findings of the Humanitarian Consequences Movement that culminated in the 2017 Treaty to Prohibit Nuclear Weapons in which the Holy See was a participant. Even before Pope Francis issued his condemnation "of the threat to use nuclear weapons, as well as their very possession," that is, deterrence,[22] the Holy See had been objecting to deterrence as an obstacle to disarmament for several years.[23]

The Failure of Conditional Acceptance

Of particular importance in the current context is the failure of contemporary deterrent realities to satisfy the moral conditions that the US bishops, following Pope John Paul II, had stipulated for the provisional acceptance of deterrence, namely

- The *sole purpose* of nuclear weapons systems is *to deter* nuclear attack by others;
- The nuclear arsenal should be *only sufficient in size to deter*; and
- A deterrent force should serve as *a step toward disarmament*.[24]

The failure of today's nuclear weapons programs to meet these moral standards means that the moral legitimacy of deterrence as envisaged by *The Challenge of Peace* no longer obtains.[25] For that reason alone, Catholics in the military services would be justified in claiming selective conscientious objection with respect to working in the nuclear forces.

In addition, since 1983 the global geopolitical situation has been greatly altered. The Cold War has ended; there is no longer a stable bilateral rivalry as assumed by deterrence strategy and Cold War–era nuclear disarmament programs. We live in a multipolar world where there are now nine nuclear powers; there is a risk of nuclear terrorism from nonstate actors. Only five of the nine nuclear weapons–possessing states are signatories (parties) to the Nuclear Non-Proliferation Treaty, and for the last decade none of them have been fulfilling their commitments under Article VI of the treaty to pursue disarmament.

Finally, a new nuclear arms race is underway in the name of "modernization," with the United States alone scheduled to spend more than a trillion dollars over the next decade for new nuclear weapons and attendant systems. An aggravating complication is that these weapons are being designed for flexible use including nuclear strikes against nonnuclear threats. Reliance on nuclear weapons has been built into the war planning of post-Soviet Russia and has been repeatedly projected as well by US officials in their quadrennial Nuclear Posture Reviews. Recent guidance from the US Joint Chiefs of Staff envisions nuclear weapons as a decisive factor in warfare. The guidance asserts that "the use of a nuclear weapon will fundamentally change the scope of a battle and create conditions that affect how commanders will prevail in conflict."[26]

Use of nuclear weapons to address nonnuclear threats portends disproportionate and indiscriminate warfare; it also risks escalating quickly from a limited war to an all-out nuclear war. Given the record of recent years, we can expect that these new weapons will be employed in a strategic environment in which arms control and disarmament agreements will have expired or will have been flouted or dismantled, so the risks of nuclear war are increased.

Together these present-day realities offer very strong reasons for conscientious military personnel to reject nuclear weapons as a legitimate means of national or collective defense and to withdraw from the nuclear services as selective conscientious objectors.

The Urgent Duty to Assess New Data

The volatile nuclear environment in which the world now finds itself was symbolized when the publication *Bulletin of the Atomic Scientists* reset the Doomsday Clock. Now set at 100 seconds before midnight (as of the final edit before publication), the clock displays the narrowest interval before midnight since Soviet Union's explosion of its first thermonuclear weapon in 1953. The reassessment of the danger of nuclear war was prompted by changes in geopolitical, scientific and technical conditions of the sort we have just reviewed. It is incumbent on those in the nuclear establishment—political leaders, policymakers, weapons scientists, defense officials, and military officers—to undertake just such a reassessment in weighing their own responsibilities with respect to nuclear weapons.

More than a decade ago due to changed circumstances, four leading American statesmen, led by former secretary of state George Shultz, abandoned their support for nuclear deterrence and advocated for the abolition of nuclear weapons.[27] A decade earlier a similar reassessment led to Gen. Lee Butler, former commander of the Strategic Air Command, becoming an advocate for nuclear abolition. In a 1996 address at the National Press Club, he reflected on the evolution of his thinking after his time with Strategic Air Command. "I came away from that experience deeply troubled by what I see as the burden of building and maintaining nuclear arsenals; the increasingly tangled web of policy and strategy as the number of weapons and delivery systems multiply; the staggering costs; the relentless pressure of advancing technology; the grotesquely destructive war plans; the daily operational risks; and the constant prospect of a crisis that would hold the fate of the entire world at risk."[28] Given that assessment, Butler grew "from a staunch advocate of deterrence to a public proponent of nuclear abolition." Citing the dramatic end of the Cold War in 1989, he argued against those who object that eliminating nuclear weapons is a utopian dream. At the same time as General Butler's speech, generals and admirals from around the world, including eighteen Russians and seventeen Americans, issued a protest against nuclear weapons, calling for the "continuous, complete and irrevocable elimination of nuclear weapons."[29]

Over the last two decades the same kind of reassessment as undertaken by General Butler, Mr. Shultz's Hoover Group, and the world's generals and admirals has quietly been underway by the Holy See in United Nations venues in Geneva and New York, culminating in its participation in the Humanitarian Consequences Movement and the conference that negotiated the Treaty to Prohibit Nuclear Weapons. The Vatican signed and ratified that treaty in September 2017. This trajectory is the background of Pope Francis's condemnation of deterrence. It is the logical conclusion of church teaching since Saint John XXIII first declared in *Pacem in terris* (1963) that abolition should be the goal of the international community.[30]

Receiving the Papal Condemnation

The Second Vatican Council declared it the duty of the whole Church (and men and women of goodwill) to scrutinize the signs of the times. In that context, the council observed that "[humanity] is becoming aware that it is [our] responsibility to guide aright the forces [we] have unleashed."[31] With the possible exception of global climate change, no force created by human hands demands more thoughtful, self-critical, and disciplined exercise of social responsibility than the disposition of nuclear weapons.

Some may worry that the papal condemnation places an unfair burden on those in the nuclear forces and national security establishments. In an earlier era, one might respond "noblesse oblige," that is, high status entails duties to others. Or as the scripture says, "From those whom much has been given, much is expected" (Luke 12:48). The nuclear forces may no longer possess the high status within the military services they did decades ago, but they still control awesome power over life on Earth, and with that power comes the duty to exercise it responsibly.

Outsiders should neither disparage nor dismiss the capacity for moral judgment possessed by the men and women in the nuclear establishment. The military, especially officers, has codes of conduct that should guide its members, and they are instilled with a sense of honor that should sensitize them to the impact of their duties on those they are commissioned to protect. Others, including policymakers, scientists, and defense intellectuals, insofar as they are professionals with a wider perspective on their technical work and its social impact, should also experience the weight of the responsibility for those they are endeavoring to protect and indeed for all humanity. Insofar as they are professionals and do not compartmentalize their work from the common life of the human family, we should be able to say of them what was said of the ancient Hebrews: what we ask of you "is not mysterious and remote from you. . . . No, it is something very near to you, always in your mouths and in your hearts, you have only to carry it out" (Deuteronomy 30:12–14). Undertaking technical tasks does not entail surrendering one's humanity, and it should not require deafness to the call of conscience.

Of course, in today's technical cultures and in the hyperrationalized field of nuclear strategy, there are ample ways to excuse that responsibility and theorists ready to justify irresponsible behavior in the name of security. Nevertheless, we should have reason to hope that some, such as General Butler, Secretary Shultz, Secretary Perry, Secretary Kissinger, and Senator Nunn, will, after searching their hearts, acquire the interior freedom to speak and act on conscience and, unlike the American statesmen, do so before retirement.

Conscience in a Learning Church

For the last fifty years, Catholic social teaching has insisted on the responsibilities of those in authority to work for the elimination of nuclear weapons. Though the Holy Father exercises exceptional religious moral authority when he teaches, he should not be regarded as a dour schoolmaster commanding nuclear specialists to do something for which they have no appreciation. As Nicholas Lash has written, when bishops teach they are "educators, not commanders." Their teaching is part of an educational process in which the faithful are invited to share in the process of spiritual and moral growth. Drawing on conversations with the fathers of Vatican II, Lash wrote, "the church exists to be, for all its members, a lifelong school of holiness and wisdom."[32]

Pope Francis himself has spoken of a "listening and learning church."[33] He explains how "the '*sensus fidei*' (sense of faith) possessed by all the baptized makes it impossible to rigidly separate the '*ecclesia docens*' (the teaching church or *magisterium*) and the '*ecclesia discens*' (the learning church) because even the flock has a 'nose' for discerning the new paths that the Lord is opening up to the church." Furthermore, following the teaching of Vatican II, the International Theological Commission has affirmed that the *sensus fidei* lies at the root of episcopal teaching.[34] It is in this spirit of a shared learning process that those in the nuclear establishment, both Catholics and men and women of goodwill, need to undertake examination of the questionable moral legitimacy of nuclear deterrence today and prepare to shoulder the challenges its illegitimacy may present to them in their work.

A New Expression of the Law of Nations

In 2017, 121 states voted with the Holy See at the United Nations to approve the Treaty on the Prohibition of Nuclear Weapons. It is incumbent upon the women and men working in nuclear weapons fields to understand this development as best they can and to assess the moral choices that development poses for them. Pope Francis is voicing a judgment he shares with numerous world leaders, a majority of governments, numerous civil society groups, and Nobel laureates.[35] Such a widely held opinion is a kind of modern *ius gentium* (universal moral law); it deserves a respectful, attentive hearing and readiness to obey. Furthermore, while Pope Francis, like Pope Paul before him, has renounced the role of pronouncing on every issue in every place, as universal pastor he bears, like popes before him, a special responsibility for addressing global problems related to the universal common good.[36]

Catholics believe, moreover, that the Spirit guides the whole church in its faith, the Holy Father in his teaching, and communities within the church when they discern the signs of the times. For Catholics working within the nuclear establishment who are committed to engaging "the living and learning church," Pope Francis's teaching carries special religious-moral weight. It deserves serious and prayerful consideration.[37] It would be mistaken to think that it could be engaged by countering it with a barren, logic-chopping just war argument. In as grave a matter as nuclear warfare, deliberation calls for more than "a moral calculus." At a minimum, responding to the pope's judgment on deterrence requires imbuing arguments about peace and war with virtues of moderation and restraint.[38] The pope's judgment, however, demands still more; it ought to be considered with religious seriousness.

In the wake of Vatican II, Catholic social thought has placed greater weight on the biblical witness in addressing world problems. As Pope Paul VI said, reading the signs of the times requires assessing issues "by light of the Gospel's unalterable words,"[39] reading contemporary history in light of "Gospel values" such as peacemaking.[40] Fulfilling universal minimal norms does not exhaust the Christian responsibility for addressing the signs of the times. Christians are called to "go the extra mile," to be "a leaven in the world."[41] In the early church, though, Christians acknowledged shared fundamental moral beliefs with Jews and Pagans; they affirmed that the Gospel demanded more from them. Thus, the Sermon on the Mount reads, "You have heard it said, 'Love your neighbor and hate your enemy, I say to you, Love your enemies and pray for those who persecute you" (Matthew 5:43–44). In the first Christian centuries, baptism entailed a radical conversion of life, including the renunciation of violence and violent ways of life.[42] Thus, in his "Dialogue with Trypho," the early apologist Justin Marty wrote of his fellow Christians that "[we] through the whole earth changed our warlike weapons—our swords into ploughshares, and our spears into implements of tillage—and we cultivate, piety, righteousness, philanthropy, faith and hope, which we have from the Father Himself through Him who was crucified."[43]

The Religious Dynamics of the Church's Teaching on Deterrence

The starting point for a reexamination of nuclear deterrence in the twenty-first century is the Second Vatican Council's exhortation that we approach war "with an entirely new attitude."⁴⁴ That plea followed a reflection that "[nuclear] weapons can inflict massive and indiscriminate destruction far exceeding the legitimate defense." Pope Francis's condemnation presents an opportunity to examine ourselves on whether the renewed and growing threat of nuclear weapons has prompted us to reexamine our attitude toward nuclear war and deterrence and join in efforts for their abolition.

In *Harvest of Justice*, the US bishops taught that though just war may guide us when successive attempts at nonviolent resolution fail, the fundamental Christian attitude toward conflict ought to be nonviolence.⁴⁵ *Harvest of Justice* envisaged a set of nonviolent conflict-resolution practices and institutions that might make that goal possible.⁴⁶ Some were then in use, for example, military training in nonviolent methods of defense. Some were never developed; others, such as hotlines and threat reduction centers, have fallen out of use; and still others, such as the Intermediate-Range Nuclear Forces Treaty, have just recently been abandoned.

For men and women in the defense establishment and especially the nuclear forces, reviving these initiatives, insisting on working with those that remain in place, and initiating new ones would be ways to fulfill the fundamental commitment to a nonviolent just peace articulated in *Harvest of Justice* and affirmed by Pope Francis in his 2017 World Day of Peace message as the fundamental Catholic response to conflict.⁴⁷ This duty weighs with special strength at a time when long-standing preventative measures are being weakened or abandoned. There is a basic obligation for the military and defense officials to utilize the nonviolent resources for the prevention of conflict, including diplomacy and arms control, and to explore and expand new tools for peacebuilding.⁴⁸

It is incumbent upon the men and women belonging to the nuclear establishment to make a sober reckoning of the greatly increased risk of nuclear war and nuclear annihilation in a multipolar world in which the tools of disarmament and threat reduction have been abandoned; strategic doctrines make the use of nuclear weapons more likely, even the cornerstone of national defense; and new weapons systems radically reduce warning time, effectively preventing antimissile defenses. The current nuclear environment poses an awful challenge with which morally serious defense professionals must engage. Responding rightly to that challenge may appear to bring them into conflict with their patriotic and professional duties, but it is a challenge in which narrower allegiances and short-sighted interests must give way to their fundamental duties to humanity and to the universal common good. A thoroughgoing and enduring engagement to peacemaking is indispensable for not only political leaders and responsible citizens but also, given their expertise and their particular responsibilities, all those in the nuclear chain of command.[49]

In conjunction with its condemnation of total war, the Second Vatican Council begged "all men [sic], especially government officials and military leaders, to give unremitting thought to the awesome responsibility which is theirs before God and the entire human race."[50] Today's geostrategic conditions are the most worrisome in three generations. They demand not just thought but also action to bring about changes "seen to be urgently necessary."[51]

Discerning Courses of Action in Communities of Faith

Military personnel, as we have seen, may rightfully refuse illegal orders, including the use of weapons of mass destruction, and resign their commissions on grounds of conscience or apply for conscientious objection and possibly seek separation from the military.[52] The new nuclear arms race, however, calls for more than an individual response, treating judgments of conscience as personal idiosyncrasies the way law and military practice seem to do. Rather, it calls for concerted action to remove a grave public evil. Sensitive consciences are good; strong, active consciences are better. Nuclear abolition will not be advanced by disengagement on a one-by-one basis. Optimally, objectors to a nuclear defense should have to act not alone but rather in concert with others who are seeking to heed the Gospel's call as they discern the signs of the times together.

The Church calls on people to discern the signs of the times as communities and to choose new courses of action together. Pastors and chaplains should show hospitality to these discernment groups in the parish and other ministries in their care. The Synod for America recognized the parish as "a community of communities and movements," thereby encouraging a variety of them to gather under the big tent of the parish for the purposes of discernment; the result does not have to be the work of the whole parish, though it may be. These discernment groups may be simple discussion circles; preferably they will be prayer or faith-sharing bodies. They may also include adult religious education groups, ad hoc gatherings of informed and interested citizens, or even chapters of movements such as Pax Christi, Pax Romana, and the Catholic Peace Fellowship. Their task is to find a way forward together to contribute to nuclear abolition and to blaze a path toward the renunciation of nuclear deterrence as a means of national security.

Military ordinaries should see that their priests are prepared to transmit the church's teaching on nuclear disarmament and are comfortable with hosting and engaging with groups in open conversations on moral issues and group discernment. They should also encourage priests and other pastoral workers to be able to engage in spiritual direction ordered toward growth in the Christian life as distinguished from confessional counseling aimed more simply at repentance and avoidance of sin.

Likewise, bishops at the diocesan, regional, and conference levels ought to be ready to engage with commanders, civilian military officials, and elected civilian authorities, communicating church teaching and encouraging their interlocutors to pursue available steps on the path to the elimination of nuclear weapons. They should likewise encourage Catholics to practice such discernment with other Christians and men and women of goodwill. The latter might include groups such as Physicians for Social Responsibility, the Union of Concerned Scientists, Parliamentarians for Nuclear Non-Proliferation and Disarmament, and the Council on Christian Approaches to Defense and Disarmament.

These same church leaders and organizations should provide venues for civilian policymakers and defense intellectuals to engage the church's contemporary teaching on peace and war and to explore "the options and commitments" required of them as a result of their discerning the signs of the times. Scrutiny of the signs of the times "is a grave responsibility," declared Pope Francis, "since present realities, if not effectively dealt with, are capable of setting off processes of dehumanization that would then be hard to reverse."[53] Reflecting on this discernment, the Holy Father writes that "we need to distinguish clearly what might be a fruit of the kingdom from what runs counter to God's plan. This involves not only recognizing and discerning spirits, but also—and this is decisive—choosing movements of the spirit of good and rejecting those of the spirit of evil." On the personal side, discernment of spirits refers to the assessment of "movements of the soul," desires and aversions that at a deeper level motivate our actions. At the public level, "choosing movements of the spirit of good and rejecting those of the spirit of evil" refers to the compatibility or incompatibility of particular social movements with the Gospel. The choice of paths of action is the invitation to be associated with and engaged in the nuclear abolition movement (or, more generally, in the work of nuclear disarmament) in any of a variety of ways.

Disassembling the architecture of nuclear disarmament, renewing the nuclear arms race, developing first-strike weapons, framing strategies of prevailing in nuclear war, and abusing the Nuclear Non-Proliferation Treaty in the service of the nuclear weapon states all contemplate and contribute to processes designed to inflict massive destruction and potentially collective annihilation wholly incompatible with God's plan. To argue that these activities in any way serve the universal common good is a perversion of rationality. It is a triumph of a narrow-minded technicism over humane reason. Worse, to suggest that these activities embody Gospel values twists the Christian proclamation beyond recognition. It is a corruption of evangelical wisdom. Rejecting engagement with them is to reject "the spirit of evil." Critiquing them, opposing them, reversing them, and building structures of peace are "movements of the spirit of good" that invite the commitment of mature Christians, who are growing in love of God and neighbor, and of men and women of conscience who are committed to humanity's well-being and the flourishing of Earth, our common home.

Notes

1. Robert Krulwich, "The Man Who Saved Your Life . . . and the World," *National Geographic,* November 1, 2017.
2. US Senate Committee on Foreign Relations, "Corker Statement at Hearing on Authority to Order the Use of Nuclear Weapons," US Senate Committee on Foreign Relations, November 14, 2017.
3. Kathryn Watson, "Top General Says He Would Resist an 'Illegal Order from Trump,'" CBS News, November 18, 2017.
4. Second Vatican Council (1965), *Gaudium et spes: Pastoral Constitution on the Church in the Modern World,* nos. 79, 80.
5. National Conference of Catholic Bishops of the United States, *The Challenge of Peace: God's Promise and Our Response* (Washington, DC: United States Catholic Conference), February 1, 1984, nos. 142–77.
6. The so-called Nuremberg defense contended that obedience to superior orders exempted offenders from accountability for war crimes. That

rationale was rejected by the Nuremberg tribunal. That judgment is confirmed by the Second Vatican Council.
7. *Gaudium et spes,* no. 79.
8. It should be noted that the Second Vatican Council, in keeping with international humanitarian law and the law of armed conflict, speak of "illegal commands" and criminality, though the council is clearly making a moral argument, demonstrating the overlap between Catholic social teaching and international law.
9. *Gaudium et spes,* no. 82.
10. *Gaudium et spes,* nos. 79 and 82.
11. *Gaudium et spes,* no. 70.
12. National Conference of Catholic Bishops, *Human Life in Our Day,* nos. 150–53.
13. *Human Life in Our Day,* no. 151.
14. See United States Conference of Catholic Bishops, "Declaration on Conscientious Objection and Selective Conscientious Objection," October 21, 1971.
15. *The Challenge of Peace,* no. 311.
16. *The Challenge of Peace,* no. 324. In the United States there is still no express legal protection for selective conscientious objection, but in practice the military services honor it by allowing conscientious individuals to shift the unit or branch of their service or in due course to separate from the service.
17. In recent guidance for those in the nuclear services, the US Joint Chiefs of Staff affirm that "the law of war governs the use of nuclear weapons, just as it governs the use of conventional weapons," including the principles of discrimination and noncombatant immunity and the involvement of judge advocates general and military attorneys in planning and targeting. See Joint Chiefs of Staff, "Nuclear Operations," *Joint Publication 3-72,* June 11, 2019, III.5.
18. *The Challenge of Peace,* no. 314. Likewise, the US bishops' tenth anniversary statement *The Harvest of Justice Is Sown in Peace,* nos. 15–16, applies just war norms in a culture without a sense of restraint.
19. John Paul II, "On the Hundredth Anniversary of *Rerum novarum* (*Centesimus Annus*)" (National Conference of Catholic Bishops, 1991), no. 25 (my emphasis).
20. For various perspectives on military professionalism, honor, and integrity, see Malham M. Wakin, *War, Morality and the Military Profession* (Boulder, CO: Westview, 1986), esp. "Part I: Ethics and the Military Profession," 3–216.
21. For arguments questioning the effectiveness of deterrence, see Eric Schlosser, *Command and Control: Nuclear Weapons, the Damascus Accident, and the Illusion of Safety* (New York: Penguin, 2013); Andrew J. Bacevich, *The Limits of Power: The End of American Exceptionalism* (New York: Metropolitan Books, 2008); and Scott D. Sagan, *The Limits of Safety:*

Organizations, Accidents, and Nuclear Weapons (Princeton, NJ: Princeton University Press, 1993). For the Holy See's view of the obsolescence of nuclear deterrence, see *Nuclear Deterrence: Time for Abolition*, 87–97.

22. Address of His Holiness Pope Francis to Participants in the International Symposium "Prospects for a World Free of Nuclear Weapons and for Integral Disarmament," November 10, 2017.
23. For example, H. E. Archbishop Dominique Mamberti, "Address to the High-Level Meeting of the 68th Session of the General Assembly on Nuclear Disarmament," New York, September 26, 2013.
24. *The Challenge of Peace*, no. 188.
25. In a 2019 report, the German Justice and Peace Commission, an arm of the German Bishops' Conference, concluded that "the conditional consent to the possession of nuclear weapons is no longer ethically justifiable." See "Outlawing Nuclear Weapons as the Start of Nuclear Disarmament: A Position Paper of the German Commission for Justice and Peace," Series *Gerechtigkeit und Frieden, Heft 138* (Berlin, 2019).
26. Joint Chiefs of Staff, "Nuclear Operations," III-4.a.
27. For a study of deterrence with statements by three of the Hoover Group principals (Shultz, Kissinger, and Nunn), see George Shultz et al., eds., *Deterrence: Its Past and Future; A Summary Report of Conference Proceedings, November, 2010* (Stanford, CA: Hoover Institution Press, 2011). For a personal account by one of the Hoover Group, see William J. Perry, *My Journey at the Nuclear Brink* (Stanford, CA: Stanford University Press, 2015).
28. General Lee Butler, "National Press Club Remarks," National Press Club, December 4, 1996.
29. See "Statement by the World's Generals and Admirals about Nuclear Weapons," Canadian Coalition for Nuclear Responsibility, December 5, 1996.
30. Pope John XXIII, *Pacem in terris*, no. 113.
31. *Gaudium et spes*, no. 9.
32. See Nicholas Lash, "Teaching or Commanding? When Bishops Instruct the Faithful," *America*, December 13, 2010.
33. Cindy Wooden, "Pope Calls for 'Synodal' Church That Listens, Learns, Shares Mission," *National Catholic Reporter*, October 17, 2015.
34. International Theological Commission, *Theology Today: Perspectives, Principles and Criteria* (Washington, DC: Catholic University of America Press, 2012), nos. 33–36.
35. See Drew Christiansen, SJ, and Carole Sargent, eds., *A World Free from Nuclear Weapons: The Vatican Conference on Disarmament* (Washington, DC: Georgetown University Press, 2020).
36. Pope Francis, *Evangelii gaudium*, no. 51.
37. Wooden, "Pope Calls for 'Synodal' Church That Listens, Learns, Shares Mission."

38. On the need for moderation and restraint in applying just war principles, see National Conference of Catholic Bishops, *The Harvest of Justice Is Sown in Peace*, no. 15.
39. Pope Paul VI, *Octogesima adveniens*, 4.
40. "Reflections by Cardinal Maurice Roy on the Occasion of the Tenth Anniversary of the Encyclical *Pacem in terris* of Pope John XXIII" (April 11, 1973), in *The Gospel of Peace and Justice: Catholic Social Teaching since Pope John*, by Joseph Gremillion, 556–58 (New York: Orbis Books, 1976).
41. *Gaudium et spes*, no. 40.
42. On the conversion of life required for baptism in the early church, see Alan Kreider, *The Change of Conversion and the Origin of Christendom* (Harrisburg, PA: Trinity Press International, 1999).
43. Michael Slusser, ed., *St. Justin Martyr, 'Dialogue with Trypho,'* translated by Thomas B. Falls, revised and with a new introduction by Thomas P. Halton (Washington, DC: Catholic University of America Press, 2003), no. 60.
44. *Gaudium et spes*, no. 80.
45. *The Harvest of Justice*, no. 10.
46. In 1993 *The Harvest of Justice* affirmed that nonviolence should now have a place "in the public order." *The Harvest of Justice*, no. 12.
47. Pope Francis, "Nonviolence: A Style of Politics for Peace," Fiftieth World Day of Peace Message, January 1, 2017.
48. *The Harvest of Justice* continued: "National leaders bear a moral obligation to see that nonviolent alternatives are seriously contemplated for dealing with conflicts. New styles of preventive diplomacy and conflict resolution ought to be explored, tried, improved and supported. As a nation we should promote research, education, and training in nonviolent means of resisting evil." *The Harvest of Justice*, no. 12.
49. *The Harvest of Justice*, no. 33.
50. *Gaudium et spes*, no. 80.
51. *Octogesima adveniens*, no. 4.
52. As noted, no legal provisions make allowance for selective conscientious objection in US law. For that reason, military personnel who are opposed to military policy or practice on reasons of conscience will often apply for conscientious objector status. But as a matter of practice, the armed forces quietly make provision for selective conscientious objectors to be reassigned to other branches of the service or to be separated from military service.
53. *Evangelii gaudium*, no. 51.

27

Profiting from the Bomb

SUSI SNYDER

Boeing, Lockheed Martin, and Northrop Grumman established the US nuclear arsenal fifty years ago. These three are now building the next generation of nuclear weapons, but the first two haven't changed much since the Cuban Missile Crisis. Northrop Grumman expanded its name (adding Aeronautics Systems, Defense Systems, Mission Systems, and Space Systems, as needed) but merely acquired other companies rather than actually innovating. All claim to be able to keep peace and stability through the production of missiles designed to annihilate cities in thirty minutes or less. These systems come with multibillion-dollar contracts, and profit is the underlying motive.

All three are well aware that nukes will not be our security focus in the future. In fact, they are not even capable of meeting the challenges of today. Thus, these companies have broadly diversified their production lines into a range of activities such as targeted weapons, drones, and even outer space warfare systems. This diversification has enabled some financiers to justify loans to the companies needed for the research and design to secure future contracts, yet they remain ineligible for many others because of their continued production of nuclear weapons.

In 2015, Pope Francis told the US Congress in a historic address that profit from the arms industry is money "drenched in blood."[1] This industry allots significant resources to make sure its names are sanitized—linked to success—and that the products it produces are seen as desirable and not destructive. In 2019, he told the people of Hiroshima that "The use of atomic energy for purposes of war is immoral, just as the possession of atomic weapons is immoral."[2] So too are profits made from the manufacture of nuclear weapons. Then in 2020, Francis's encyclical *Fratelli tutti* recognized that the arms industry has a vested interest in continuing conflict and perpetuating discord among populations. It describes the industry as "a buildup of arms and ammunition in a global context dominated by uncertainty, disillusionment, fear of the future, and controlled by narrow economic interests."[3] Now, with near-universal condemnation of the possession of nuclear weapons, what can secular and faith communities do to encourage them to finally and completely end production?

First, we can focus on the reputation. Just as the tobacco industry invested in studies to demonstrate no ill effects from smoking, arms industries use devious tactics that are now coming to light. The International Campaign to Abolish Nuclear Weapons (my organization, winner of the Nobel Peace Prize in 2017) shows how the nuclear industry feigns the necessity of its weapons, spending millions lobbying officials and elected representatives each year. The lobbyists are rarely so vulgar as to defend the bombs outright, but they promote the vague, unproven concept of deterrence, which means maintaining and even increasing military power to discourage attack. The industry also invests heavily in think tanks, a more subtle way to influence the debate and defend nuclear deterrence. These industry investments in so-called strategic systems give decision makers a reason to authorize multidecade-long contracts for billions that then flow back to those same companies. This shadowy cycle of nuclear weapons complicity is finally starting to be unveiled.

Second, we can follow the money and cut it off at the source. To compete for lucrative nuclear weapons contracts, these companies invest significant borrowed funds on internal research and development. They must design and sell proofs of concept to be able to secure and maintain their production agreements. Instead of raising money through loan applications for specific projects, they instead ask for financing for general corporate purposes. This generates unrestricted income that they can then spend freely on even the most controversial conduct.

This financial support is classified as assistance with the production and development of nuclear weapons, however, so it has therefore been illegal since January 2021, when the Treaty on the Prohibition of Nuclear Weapons entered into force. The first of its kind in decades, it is the first legally binding international agreement to place nuclear weapons in the same off-limits category as other implements of mass destruction such as chemical and biological weapons. The treaty prohibits the production, development, manufacture, and possession of nuclear weapons as well as any effort to assist such acts.

The treaty thus provides a legal footing to strengthen moral outrage at continued profiteering from preparations for mass murder. Investors are taking note as the companies involved in nuclear weapons production become increasingly excluded from any legitimate form of investment. Through shareholder advocacy, some investors now actually cite the treaty as their reason for divestment, and informed companies understand better why nuclear weapons production is no longer considered a justifiable asset. The Treaty on the Prohibition of Nuclear Weapons also enables those who do not wish to grapple with huge ethical questions or frame investment decisions around them with the clear excuse of illegality. Further, those companies still involved in nuclear weapon production face legal risks as they continue to build weapons designed solely for genocide.

Some people of faith engage with these mass destruction manufacturers via language that's a bit more familiar to them. Advocates such as the Sisters of Charity (Elizabeth, New Jersey), the School Sisters of Notre Dame Cooperative Investment Fund, the Sisters of St. Francis of Philadelphia, the Sisters of St. Joseph (Brentwood, Ohio), and the Sisters of the Humility of Mary in Ohio, hold just enough stock to file resolutions designed to guide these companies (or their financers) toward paths that embrace human rights and human dignity while offering them a graceful exit by encouraging the conclusion or termination of any contracts not fitting these principles through a path of just transition.

Most ethical shareholder proposals originate from investors from faith communities. These proposals are important tools to educate and advocate for change from within. They demand that the weapons companies analyze the risks of nuclear weapons, including to the profitability of the defense sector, and consider the way these products are designed to deny human rights.

There is a growing shift in the analysis of risk and return, and the timing for targeted engagement with nuclear weapon producers couldn't be better. Major changes across the financial industry hinge on human rights due diligence and on assessing more than profit in considering corporate direction. Risk analysis that is solely focused on delivering the highest possible financial returns is no longer enough. In a world that is facing existential threats, other factors are part of fulfilling an institution's fiduciary duty and must be considered when making investment decisions. With trillions of dollars of wealth moving steadily into the sustainability market, investments cannot only do well; they must also do good.

Because they accept contracts to build nuclear weapons, companies such as Boeing, Lockheed Martin, and Northrop Grumman are part of the problem. Engaging with them to change and, if they don't, avoiding business with them is a way for others to become part of the solution.

Notes

1. *Congressional Record*, September 24, 2015, Issue: Vol. 161, No. 138, Pages H6191–H6194.
2. Pope Francis, "Address of the Holy Father," Peace Memorial, Hiroshima, November 24, 2019.
3. Pope Francis, *Fratelli tutti*, no. 29.

28

The Condemnation of the Possession, Threat of Use, and Use of Nuclear Weapons

Reflections for Scientists and Technologists

PIERCE S. CORDEN

One night in October 1962 during my senior year at Georgetown University in Washington, DC, I stood in the quadrangle with many other students listening to President John Kennedy on a transistor radio. He stated that the Soviet Union was stationing nuclear weapons in Cuba, and he announced an embargo on Soviet ships headed for Cuba. The next day, I found the campus eerily quiet and wondered whether the whispering sound of an airliner flying high overhead was from a missile launched at Washington. Looking back at that experience, I realize that the Cuban Missile Crisis must have been an important factor in my pursuing a career working for disarmament, nuclear in particular, building on my physics degrees at Georgetown and subsequently. This essay emerges from that career.

The position of the Catholic Church and, more broadly, Christian churches regarding the use of force has hardly been a constant since the time of Christ. At the outset Christians were not part of state structures, and Christian individuals and communities were what would today be termed "pacifist." This approach continues to be a recognizable one within both Catholicism and large parts of Christianity. The obverse, an absolute acceptance of resort to violence at any level to govern interactions between peoples, in particular nation-states as they presently exist, has never been countenanced.

However, from the time of the appearance of Christians in the armies of the Roman Empire, Christianity has accepted a role for organized military use of violent force in the interactions of states. But it has circumscribed this role substantially with the elaboration of the philosophical-theological construct of the just war tradition. How this has played out in the real world—for example, in wars where both parties were Christian, such as those between England and France, because of her actions in which one of the French military leaders, Joan of Arc, has even been made a canonized saint—is a matter left for another day. In the present, the Catholic Church, within larger movements to further constrain the use of force, has sought to elaborate approaches to the global order in which violence plays an increasingly smaller role.

The St. Petersburg Declaration of 1868 recognized that the "only legitimate object" of military action was to "weaken the military force of the enemy," that it was "sufficient to disable the greatest possible number of men," and that "this object would be exceeded by the employment of arms which uselessly aggravate the sufferings of disabled men, or render their death inevitable."[1]

The Hague Conventions of 1899 and 1907 sought to outlaw the use of weapons indiscriminate or far-reaching in their effect: poison and chemical agents and aircraft for other than observation. Following the carnage of World War I in which, despite the Hague Conventions, chemical weapons were first used, the Geneva Protocol of 1925 outlawed the use of chemical, toxin, and biological agents in war. Unfortunately, the other arms control agreements negotiated during the interwar period did not survive or prevent World War II. The aircraft and primitive cruise and ballistic missiles became a major part of that conflict, inflicting massive death and destruction on civilians of both sides. In 1945, the use of two nuclear weapons against the cities of Hiroshima and Nagasaki marked the introduction of this new weapon into warfare.

The negotiation of the United Nations (UN) Charter has put in place an international order in which resort to force is in the first instance the responsibility of the international community, acting through the UN Security Council. States nevertheless are recognized to possess the right of self-defense until the UN can reestablish order.

Aware that even greater levels of destruction were made possible by the advent of nuclear weapons, states and the UN have sought with greater or lesser degrees of success to constrain the use of force, particularly by seeking to outlaw altogether weapons of mass destruction and by imposing increasingly broad limitations on conventional weapons. In 1948, a UN commission defined weapons of mass destruction to include biological (and toxin), chemical, radiological (these, so-called dirty bombs, had not been introduced), and nuclear weapons.² Biological, toxin, and chemical weapons are outlawed altogether. There are substantial constraints on radioactive materials, although regrettably there is no treaty banning dirty bombs. Nuclear weapons and their delivery systems are subject to a wide variety of limitations.

At present, nine states possess nuclear weapons, and some thirty states are subject to arrangements under which their security is supported by the nuclear weapons of a possessing state. One hundred eighty-six states party to the Nuclear Non-Proliferation Treaty of 1970 are defined as non–nuclear weapon states, although some of these can have nuclear weapons based on their territory, to be delivered by either the aircraft of a nuclear weapon state or by their own aircraft. Five parties—China, France, the Russian Federation, the United Kingdom, and the United States—are defined as nuclear weapon states. Many non–nuclear weapon states are also party to regional agreements making their territories nuclear weapon–free zones. India, Pakistan, and North Korea are known possessors of nuclear weapons, while Israel adopts an official status of ambiguity but is typically dealt with as a possessing state.

Thus, in considering the social teaching of the Catholic Church regarding nuclear weapons, in particular as it affects Catholic scientists and technologists, these persons will come from the possessing states: the United States, the Russian Federation, the United Kingdom, France, China, India, Pakistan, North Korea, and, at least in an ambiguous way, Israel. Catholic social teaching may also affect scientists and technologists responsible for the weapons in the states where these weapons are stationed and possibly other non–nuclear weapon states in an alliance that envisions the potential combat use of nuclear weapons. Those with security responsibilities in other states would not be directly involved unless the state sought to acquire its own nuclear weapons.

What, then, should such individuals make of the statement of Pope Francis, delivered to an international symposium in Rome on November 11, 2017, dealing with nuclear weapons? The relevant part of the statement reads, "Nor can we fail to be genuinely concerned by the catastrophic humanitarian and environmental effects of any employment of nuclear devices. If we also take into account the risk of an accidental detonation as a result of error of any kind, the threat of their use, as well as their very possession, is to be firmly condemned."³ Pope Francis referred to this statement in his address in Hiroshima on November 24, 2019:

> With deep conviction I wish once more to declare that the use of atomic energy for purposes of war is today, more than ever, a crime not only against the dignity of human beings but against any possible future for our common home. The use of atomic energy for purposes of war is immoral, just as the possessing of nuclear weapons is immoral, as I already said two years ago. We will be judged on this. Future generations will rise to condemn our failure if we spoke of peace but did not act to bring it about among the peoples of the earth. How can we speak of peace even as we build terrifying new weapons of war? How can we speak about peace even as we justify illegitimate actions by speeches filled with discrimination and hate?[4]

During his press conference on the flight back to Rome on November 28, Pope Francis added that he "reaffirmed that the use of nuclear weapons is immoral—this must also be included in the Catechism of the Catholic Church—and not only its use, but also its possession because an accident [due to] possession, or the madness of some government leader, a person's madness can destroy humanity. Let us think about that quote from Einstein: 'World War IV will be fought with sticks and stones.'"[5]

These statements build on increasingly specific and categorical rejections of nuclear weapons. Popes from the time of World War II have spoken out against nuclear weapons. Pope John XXIII, in his pastoral letter *Pacem in terris*, issued in April 1963 with the frightening events of the Cuban Missile Crisis in mind, called for progressive steps to eliminate nuclear weapons entirely. Pope Paul VI, in his address to the UN on October 4, 1965, clearly with the threat of nuclear war in mind, called for the end of war altogether:

> Was not this the very end for which the United Nations came into existence: to be against war and for peace? Listen to the clear words of a great man who is no longer with us, John Kennedy, who proclaimed four years ago: "Mankind must put an end to war, or war will put an end to mankind." There is no need for a long talk to proclaim the main purpose of your Institution. It is enough to recall that the blood of millions, countless unheard-of sufferings, useless massacres and frightening ruins have sanctioned the agreement that unites you with an oath that ought to change the future history of the world:

never again war, never again war! It is peace, peace, that has to guide the destiny of the nations of all mankind![6]

On the other hand, Pope John Paul II, in his statement sent to the Second Special Session of the United Nations on Disarmament in 1982, allowed for a temporary acceptance of nuclear deterrence while efforts were made to achieve nuclear disarmament. His message reads, "In current conditions 'deterrence' based on balance, certainly not as an end in itself but as a step on the way toward a progressive disarmament, may still be judged morally acceptable. Nonetheless in order to ensure peace, it is indispensable not to be satisfied with this minimum which is always susceptible to the real danger of explosion."[7] Subsequent statements by a number of national conferences of bishops built on this one.

In the 1983 United States Catholic Bishops' pastoral letter *The Challenge of Peace: God's Promise and Our Response*, its statement on deterrence is as follows:

> In current conditions "deterrence" based on balance, certainly not as an end in itself but as a step on the way toward a progressive disarmament, may still be judged morally acceptable. Nonetheless, in order to ensure peace, it is indispensable not to be satisfied with this minimum which is always susceptible to the real danger of explosion. (Pope John Paul II, Message to U.N. Special Session on Disarmament, #8, June 1982)
>
> No use of nuclear weapons which would violate the principles of discrimination or proportionality may be intended in a strategy of deterrence. The moral demands of Catholic teaching require resolute willingness not to intend or to do moral evil even to save our own lives or the lives of those we love.
>
> Deterrence is not an adequate strategy as a long-term basis for peace; it is a transitional strategy justifiable only in conjunction with resolute determination to pursue arms control and disarmament. We are convinced that "the fundamental principle on which our present peace depends must be replaced by another, which declares the true and solid peace of nations consists not in equality of arms but in mutual trust alone." (Pope John XXIII, Peace on Earth, #113)[8]

European Bishops' conferences statements were issued in the United Kingdom, France, Germany, the Netherlands, and Belgium. They were followed by a statement in 1983 by the Holy See's secretary of state, Agostino Cardinal Casaroli, laying out the elements in these statements common to the views of the Vatican.[9]

In more recent statements of the Holy See, any use of nuclear weapons has been characterized as unacceptable, and the temporary acceptance of deterrence has as well been increasingly qualified.[10,11]

The Holy See also joined some 120 states at the UN in 2017 to negotiate the Treaty on the Prohibition of Nuclear Weapons (the so-called Ban Treaty), which outlaws nuclear weapons completely for its parties. (In this respect it broadens the Nuclear Non-Proliferation Treaty, which does not prohibit nuclear weapons to its five nuclear weapon state parties, to cover all its parties equally.)[12]

Thus, within the framework of international law, there are already substantial constraints on nuclear weapons and on where they may be playing a role in international security. Given the Church's general support and respect for the present international order, these constraints have moral as well as legal force.

The key part of the statement in Pope Francis's address dealing with nuclear weapons, referred to above, is as follows: "the threat of their use, as well as their very possession, is to be firmly condemned."[13]

A scientist or technologist, then, working with nuclear weapons or their delivery systems in a state where nuclear weapons are not prohibited by the existing reach of international or domestic law would in his or her moral evaluation of such work undoubtedly seek to reflect carefully on what Church officials, to include Pope Francis, have said about the use of, the threat to use, and the possession of nuclear weapons.

How might a physicist working at a nuclear weapon laboratory, for example, deal with a research and development program to introduce new features into a nuclear warhead, features that had the purpose of making the warhead more survivable to attack by an adversary? What about a research and development program to modify the yield of an existing warhead to support a use doctrine that envisions an early use of the warhead, perhaps against conventional forces? How might a technologist employed by a shipbuilding company view the construction of a submarine for launching nuclear-armed missiles in support of a new generation of such ships having envisioned lifetimes of decades? The same applies for technologists developing and testing new aircraft and missiles for delivery of nuclear warheads, systems that also have long lifetimes. What about scientists and engineers working to develop new nonnuclear components of nuclear weapon systems with a view to making the weapon more "usable"?

Further, how do we consider the situation of a physicist working on a nuclear-powered and nuclear-armed torpedo with essentially unlimited range? Or the situation of engineers engaged in developing for deployment nonstandard delivery systems, such as boost-glide vehicles?

On the other hand, if the scientist or technologist was working on a program to develop protective measures against cyberattack on the command-and-control systems of the nuclear weapons force, would this materially contribute to the continued possession of nuclear weapons? The same applies with regard to work on technologies to prevent the theft of nuclear weapons or their fissile material components.

It seems clear that the moral choices facing scientists and technologists are profound. In particular, Roman Catholics faced with situations such as these will surely need to give careful consideration to the social teaching of the Church on the use of nuclear weapons, the threat to use nuclear weapons, and the possession of nuclear weapons as outlined above. He or she will need to take into consideration ongoing diplomatic efforts to secure the elimination of nuclear weapons globally, an outcome essentially globally endorsed by the community of nations in Article VI of the Nuclear Non-Proliferation Treaty, which lacks only India, Pakistan, Israel, and North Korea, which withdrew, as relevant parties. This outcome is not an outcome to be achieved in a day, a week, a month, or a year. But the person will want to consider the importance and necessity of such diplomatic nuclear disarmament efforts and ask how his or her work is impacting those efforts.

An argument can be made that the scientist or technologist would be acting consistent with Church social teaching if the decision were to move to a related effort, for example developing technologies that support the verifiable reduction and dismantling of nuclear warheads and their delivery systems. Another option is moving into what is currently termed "science diplomacy" and working in government, nongovernmental, or industrial settings to advance negotiated constraints on nuclear weapons with the objective of their elimination as soon as agreement can be achieved.

Individuals presently involved in science and technology supporting a continued reliance on nuclear weapons in a basic deterrence stance or, even more an increased salience to potential use in war might reflect on parallel situations involving other defined weapons of mass destruction, biological, toxin, and chemical weapons in particular. States have not, at least since the time of World War II, carried out any hostile uses of biological and toxin weapons. Since the entry into force of the Biological and Toxin Weapons Convention in 1975, states seem to have operated on the premise that no use or incorporation of biological or toxin weapons, defined as weapons of mass destruction, into military planning is acceptable. Unfortunately, this has not carried over into the use of chemical weapons since the entry into force of the Chemical Weapons Convention in 1997, with attacks in Syria and Iraq, the attack in Malaysia on a North Korean citizen, and the recent attacks involving the relatively new type of nerve agent "novichuks" in Salisbury, England, and Omsk, Russia. It is not known what the involvement of scientists has been regarding any development of this agent since the Chemical Weapons Convention entered into force or what the involvement of technologists has been in the packaging and distribution of this agent and of those agents used in the Middle East and Malaysia. If use, threat to use, or possession of biological, toxin, and chemical weapons in any degree is arguably counter to the social teaching of the Church, individuals in states party to the Biological and Toxin Weapons Convention or to the Chemical Weapons Convention supporting these ends will have the added consideration of whether their involvement in the use of, threat to use, or possession of biological, toxin, and chemical weapons is contrary to domestic or international law. And within this context, individuals will need to reach for themselves considered judgments about the moral implications of their roles.

In nuclear weapon–possessing states, research, development, deployment, and use have not been outlawed by domestic law. With regard to international law, the Geneva Conventions of 1949, with the Additional Protocol of 1977, apply.[14] States possessing nuclear weapons are either parties to or, arguably, are bound by customary international law to these agreements. In particular, the Additional Protocol is aimed at protection of civilian populations. Scientists and technologists should thus be cognizant of how their work on nuclear weapons might impact potential uses of nuclear weapons. In the case of the United States, the Department of Defense has stated that were nuclear weapons to be detonated in war, this use would be guided by the relevant laws of war.[15] Presumably this would be the case for other possessor states were they to detonate nuclear weapons in war. But generally speaking, the legal situation is not so clear-cut as it is for biological, toxin, and chemical weapons.

Accordingly, individuals considering the morality of their involvement in the development and production of nuclear weapons will be dealing with a perhaps somewhat less clear overall situation in which to come to decisions as to that involvement. Nevertheless, in reflecting on the evolution of the position of the Church, as currently reflected in the statements of Pope Francis, individuals can approach their decisions supported by a realization that as both international law and the Church's social teaching can evolve with increased understanding of the issues involved, so too individuals can modify how they practice their professional lives.

Notes

1. "Declaration Renouncing the Use, in Time of War, of Explosive Projectiles under 400 Grammes Weight," International Committee of the Red Cross, November 29 and December 11, 1868, https://ihl-databases.icrc.org/ihl/full/declaration1868.
2. See United Nations Security Council, S/C.3/32/Rev.1, 18 August 1948: Resolutions Adopted by the Committee on Conventional Weapons at its thirteen meeting, August 12, 1948, and a second progress report of the commission.
3. Address of His Holiness Pope Francis to Participants in the International Symposium "Prospects for a World Free of Nuclear Weapons and for Integral Disarmament," Vatican City, November 10, 2017. For a wide-ranging discussion of nuclear-weapon issues, see George P. Shultz and James E. Goodby, eds., *The War that Must Never be Fought: Dilemmas of Nuclear Deterrence* (Stanford, CA: Hoover Institution Press, 2015).
4. Pope Francis, "Address of the Holy Father, Peace Memorial," Apostolic Journey of His Holiness Pope Francis to Thailand and Japan, Hiroshima, Sunday, November 24, 2019.
5. Pope Francis, "Press Conference on the Return Flight to Rome," Apostolic Journey of His Holiness Pope Francis to Thailand and Japan, November 26, 2019.
6. Pope Paul VI, "Address of the Holy Father to the United Nations Organization," October 4, 1965.
7. John Paul II, "Message of His Holiness to the General Assembly of the United Nations," June 7, 1982.

8. National Conference of Catholic Bishops of the United States, *The Challenge of Peace: God's Promise and Our Response* (Washington, DC: United States Catholic Conference, 1984), b3.
9. These statements are discussed in detail, particularly regarding the question of the ethics of threatening an action itself condemned as immoral, by Francis Winters, "After Tension, Détente: A Continuing Chronicle of European Episcopal Views on Nuclear Deterrence," *Theological Studies* 45 (1984): 343–51.
10. On the condemnation of the use of nuclear weapons and related issues of deterrence, see, for example, the address by Archbishop Francis Chullikatt, Permanent Observer of the Holy See to the United Nations, to the Catholic Center of the Diocese of Kansas City–St. Joseph on July 1, 2011, "The Nuclear Question: The Church's Teachings and the Current State of Affairs." See also Archbishop Edwin O'Brien, "Moral Reflections on U.S. Nuclear Weapons Policy," delivered at the Institute for Policy Research & Catholic Studies Panel Symposium "The Ethics of the Obama Administration's Nuclear Weapons Policy: Catholic Perspectives," Catholic University of America, April 26, 2010.
11. For a description of how experts view the role of nuclear weapons in international "stability," see Robert E. Berls Jr., Leon Ratz, and Brian Rose, "Rising Nuclear Dangers: Diverging Views of Strategic Stability," NTI Paper, Nuclear Threat Initiative, October 23, 2018. The authors discuss strategic stability as "a state of relations between nuclear powers that includes three key conditions. First, it minimizes incentives for one side to initiate nuclear use (first strike stability). Second, it reduces incentives for competition in the development and deployment of nuclear forces (arms race stability). Third, it provides a degree of predictability and transparency during periods of heightened tension (crisis stability)."
12. United Nations, Office for Disarmament Affairs, "Treaty on the Prohibition of Nuclear Weapons," adopted July 7, 2017, entered into force January 22, 2021.
13. Pope Francis, "Prospects for a World Free of Nuclear Weapons and for Integral Disarmament."
14. International Committee of the Red Cross, "Protocols I and II Additional to the Geneva Conventions," June 8, 1977, https://ihl-databases.icrc.org/applic/ihl/ihl.nsf/INTRO/475.
15. United States Department of Defense, Report on Nuclear Employment Strategy of the United States, Specified in Section 491 of 10 U.S.C., June 12, 2013.

29

Morality Matters

A Parliamentarian Reflects on Nuclear Disarmament

DAVID LAMMY

The nuclear dilemma is something with which I have grappled for many years. Not many people know that before I joined the Labour Party, I had joined the Campaign for Nuclear Disarmament alongside the Anti-Apartheid Movement. I remember growing up in the 1980s hugely disturbed by the idea of nuclear annihilation, which was played out all the time in films and on TV. I remember watching the film *Threads*, which depicted the immediate destruction of a nuclear holocaust on the working-class city of Sheffield and the longer-term catastrophic effects of nuclear war on civilization.

Hiroshima and Nagasaki will forever be known as the sites where hundreds of thousands of innocent people were killed and maimed. For the purpose of comparison, studies show that even a limited nuclear war between India and Pakistan could lead to two billion deaths and effectively end human civilization.[1] Each of the four submarines that make up Britain's nuclear weapons system, Trident, carries up to forty nuclear warheads, each of which is eight times as destructive as the bomb that flattened Hiroshima in 1945.

I am not in the same place that I was as an eighteen-, nineteen-, or twenty-year-old. Historically, the Campaign for Nuclear Disarmament has been unilateralist, but I have shifted towards a more multilateralist view. Nowadays, my aim is to show how it is possible to come to a multilateralist view and still have concerns about the cost of nuclear deterrence and the risks of long-term reliance on mutually assured destruction. In fact, as a multilateralist I've been determined to show that having these concerns is *required*. Multilateralism cannot be used as an excuse to shirk our responsibility to take steps towards disarmament. That's why in October 2016 during the debate in Parliament over Trident's renewal, I could not in good conscience vote for what was effectively a blank cheque for nuclear weapons.

During that debate, I noted that "one of the great traditions of [the House of Commons] is that on matters of conscience, such as that before us today, Members draw on a wide range of different experiences and viewpoints in coming to their conclusions." To borrow the title from a 2004 book by Professor Roger Trigg, *Morality Matters*, morality matters in public policy debates, especially when these debates touch on human rights, human dignity, and, in this case, human survival. It is not widely referenced, but my morality is informed a lot by my Christian faith. As I said during the debate, the idea of loving thy neighbour and protecting our world for future generations simply cannot hold if we have stockpiles of weapons that can destroy our neighbours and our world.

I declared that I stood there united with Pope Benedict XVI, who had said, "In a nuclear war there would be no victors, only victims."[2] In truth, I stood alongside all the world's faiths, relaying the words of the UK multifaith statement on nuclear weapons: "Any use of nuclear weapons would have devastating humanitarian consequences... and violate the principle of dignity for every human being that is common to each of our faith traditions."[3]

The year following the renewal of the Trident program, I spoke during the opening ceremony of St. Francis at the Engine Room, a community centre in my constituency of Tottenham. At the opening ceremony, I declared that "someone at No. 10 once said, 'We don't do God.' I've always been very clear that here in Tottenham we do do God." But God is not confined to local parish centers in Tottenham or any other local place. The faiths that move local communities to embrace moral commitments to justice and peace, to racial equality and inclusion, can also help move national governments and international institutions to embrace nuclear disarmament with renewed vigor.

In terms of global nuclear disarmament, the Catholic Church has taken a leading role in promoting the moral vision of a nuclear weapon–free world. The global reach of the Church uniquely equips it to address the moral dimensions of international issues, and few issues are of such existential importance to humanity as are nuclear questions. In a message to the December 2014 Vienna Conference on the Humanitarian

Impact of Nuclear Weapons, Pope Francis wrote, "Nuclear deterrence and the threat of mutually assured destruction cannot be the basis for an ethics of fraternity and peaceful coexistence among peoples and states.... Now is the time to counter the logic of fear with the ethic of responsibility, and so foster a climate of trust and sincere dialogue."[4] He continued to declare passionately that "spending on nuclear weapons squanders the wealth of nations. To prioritize such spending is a mistake and a misallocation of resources which would be far better invested in the areas of integral human development, education, health and the fight against extreme poverty. When these resources are squandered, the poor and the weak living on the margins of society pay the price."

This squandering of resources was right at the core of my opposition to Trident renewal. My constituency has seen two riots in a generation, the closure of residential care homes and youth centres, an unemployment rate that is double the national average, and life expectancy that is five years below the national average. Haringey, a borough of London, is home to twelve of the most deprived districts in the country, and 47 percent of children in a district on the Tottenham Hotspur Football Club's doorstep live in poverty.

Of course, there are fewer things worth spending public finance on than deterring nuclear war. But to make the case for Trident on this basis is to have misguided faith in its power as a necessary deterrent in the first place. Back in the 2016 debate I quoted Field Marshal Lord Bramall, General Lord Ramsbotham, and General Sir Hugh Beach who have said, "Nuclear weapons have shown themselves to be completely useless as a deterrent to the threats and scale of the violence we currently face, or are likely to face—particularly international terrorism."[5] These men are no pacifists or unilateralists. They are simply responding to a changing international context, characterized by the proliferation of nuclear armed nations and the prospects of nuclear terrorism or accidental launches. It is this shift from a bipolar to a multipolar world that requires a reassessment of our reliance on nuclear deterrence. To name a few, as Pope Francis did in his address at a 2017 United Nations (UN) conference, the real threats we face are cybersecurity, environmental problems, and poverty. Nuclear deterrence is at best inadequate and, more accurately, simply not applicable to these challenges.[6]

Underpinning the Catholic Church's powerful rhetoric is the refusal to choose between defense and disarmament. This is something that

Lord Desmond Browne of Ladyton, former secretary of state for defence, makes clear, arguing that this is simply a false choice:

> Many would have us believe that one can either be hard-headed and committed to defence and national security, on the one hand, or be committed to disarmament on the other, and that it is not credible or possible to be seriously committed to both. I reject that absolutely. The time has come for multilateral disarmament to be a centrepiece of the national and international security strategies of all nations and for parliamentarians to play a more sustained and better-informed role in bringing this change about.[7]

Lord Browne makes clear that we cannot rely solely on the recommendations of those charged with implementing nuclear deterrence programs. As he explains, "judgements about the role of these weapons in national security strategy and relevance of nuclear deterrence to current threats are essentially political judgements" that cannot be left to "operational and technical experts" alone. It is the role of *parliamentarians*, ultimately, to draw on a wide range of independent expertise in order to make decisions about welfare of the people whom they serve. Above all, we should draw on our own sense of morality to take practical steps toward mutually verifiable nuclear disarmament.

That's why I resist the claim that not replacing our nuclear weapons would diminish our international standing and be an abdication of our role as a permanent member of the UN Security Council. I look at it differently. As a parliamentarian in a robust democracy, I believe I have a responsibility to help my nation to exercise global leadership for disarmament. Continuing to modernize our nuclear deterrent is to abandon nuclear disarmament. *That's* an abdication of our responsibility as a permanent member of the UN Security Council. We cannot continue to mimic the behavior of the other nuclear powers and expect them to embark on a different path.

At the very least, we parliamentarians in the United Kingdom should be asking some pretty hard questions, such as why we vote against nuclear disarmament at the UN. Some argue that the failure of nuclear disarmament efforts is due to inertia. And perhaps that is part of the explanation. But today, I think it is more than inertia. I think we are dealing with momentum. The modernization plans of the various nuclear powers undercut the "grand bargain" of the Nuclear Non-Proliferation Treaty, which envisioned nonnuclear states refraining from developing nuclear weapons (nonproliferation) in exchange for the nuclear powers divesting themselves of such weapons (disarmament). And they reveal an insidious momentum toward indefinite possession of nuclear weapons.

To counter this momentum, parliamentarians need to work with civil society to inform the general public of the terrible dangers of a continued reliance on nuclear deterrence. Without public support, it will be difficult to hold governments accountable. A shining example of the effectiveness of partnerships between government leaders and civil society actors is the International Campaign to Abolish Nuclear Weapons. The organization unites nongovernmental organizations across the globe, including many religious groups, and received the 2017 Nobel Peace Prize for its work in promoting adoption of the Treaty on the Prohibition of Nuclear Weapons.

Of course, the ability of parliamentarians, even with public support, to influence their respective governments varies greatly from one state to another. I suspect the road to nuclear disarmament will be a steep climb with many roadblocks along the way. But if parliamentarians such as myself don't at least try to rid this country of weapons that can wipe out civilization, I'm not sure what we're doing here.

Thus far, nuclear disarmament has proven a difficult topic for parliamentarians to discuss with honesty and maturity. We are too often pigeonholed as either warmongers or pacifists, leaving behind an uncharted space in between that is screaming out for some nuanced discussion. It should not be the case that by raising issues surrounding the cost and morality of nuclear weapons one is caricatured as a pacifist who rejects the need for any kind of military action in any kind of circumstance. These people exist, but I am not one of them. There is a growing need for a group of people who are determined to reduce nuclear arsenals but firmly reject the smears labelling us as weak on issues of foreign policy and defense. In other words, we need more multilateralists.

In an address to participants in the international symposium Prospects for a World Free of Nuclear Weapons and for Integral Disarmament, Pope Francis countered pessimism and argued that "a healthy realism continues to shine a light of hope on our unruly world." He pointed out that "in a historic vote at the United Nations, the majority of the members of the international community determined that nuclear weapons are not only immoral, but must also be considered an illegal means of warfare." He noted that the victory "was mainly the result of a 'humanitarian initiative' sponsored by a significant alliance between civil society, states, international organizations, churches, academies and groups of experts."[8] And in 2018, the General Synod of the Church of England overwhelmingly adopted a motion declaring "that nuclear weapons, through their indiscriminate and destructive potential, present a distinct category of weaponry that requires Christians to work tirelessly for their elimination across the world."[9]

I am proud to stand with Pope Francis and the Church of England and with people of many faiths and no faith at all in seeking nuclear disarmament because morality matters.

Notes

1. "India-Pakistan Nuclear War Could 'End Human Civilisation,'" *The Telegraph*, December 10, 2013; see also Dave Mosher, "If India and Pakistan Have a 'Limited' Nuclear War, Scientists Say It Could Wreck Earth's Climate and Trigger Global Famine," *Business Insider*, February 28, 2019.
2. Pope Benedict XVI, Message for World Day of Peace, No. 13, January 1, 2006.
3. "UK Multi-Faith Statement on Nuclear Weapons—2015," An End to Nuclear Weapons, n.d., http://www.endnuclearweapons.org.uk/index.htm.
4. Pope Francis, Message to Vienna Conference on the Humanitarian Impact of Nuclear Weapons, December 7, 2014.
5. Helen Pidd, "Trident Nuclear Missiles Are £20bn Waste of Money, Say Generals," *The Guardian*, January 15, 2009.
6. Message of Pope Francis to the UN Conference to Negotiate a Legally Binding Instrument to Prohibit Nuclear Weapons, Leading towards Their Total Elimination, March 23, 2017.
7. "The Role of Parliaments in Arms Control, Disarmament, and the Nonproliferation of Weapons of Mass Destruction (WMD)," *Geneva Papers*, Geneva Centre for Security Policy, 2011.
8. Pope Francis, Address to Participants in the International Symposium "Prospects for a World Free of Nuclear Weapons and for Integral Disarmament," November 10, 2017.
9. Hattie Williams, "General Synod Calls for 'Elimination' of Nuclear Weapons," *Church Times*, July 9, 2018.

30

The Ethics of Manufacturing Nuclear Weapons

RAMÓN LUZÁRRAGA

The opening decades of the twenty-first century witnessed a resurgence of nuclear power.[1] This extended to nuclear weapons. Britain, China, France, India, North Korea, Pakistan, Russia, and the United States are the countries confirmed to possess nuclear arsenals of different sizes with regard to the number of weapons built, their destructive power, and their means of deployment. Israel has long been suspected of possessing its own nuclear arsenal, but that has never been confirmed by its government or an independent third party.[2] Despite official pledges to disarm, including those nuclear powers that signed the 1968 Nuclear Non-Proliferation Treaty, the governments and militaries of each and every nuclear weapon–possessing country have been working to upgrade their respective arsenals and weapons delivery systems.[3] Consistently, the motive cited by each of these governments is the maintenance of an independent deterrent capability. The reasons vary. Maintaining this capability can be used to check a regional rival, as in the case of China, India, and Pakistan; check a global rival, as Britain, France, and the United States have done with Russia, with China becoming a global rival in its own right; or serve as a safeguard against global powers to preserve one's own ruling regime, as in the case of North Korea.[4]

Corporations participating in the research and manufacturing of nuclear weapons keep a low profile. In the United States, the facilities used to manufacture nuclear weapons are under the direct control of the Department of Energy or the Department of Defense. Private companies participate in the management and the operations of many of these federal facilities under contract.[5] This contractual relationship does not mean, however, that these companies simply follow the directives of the government. Defense contractors have a history of lobbying the federal government to fund and construct weapons systems. For example, during the Cold War each branch of the US military wanted its own nuclear missile system. Private corporations participated in this lobbying effort.[6] Today, corporations still lobby the federal government to renew, update, and advance the development of nuclear weapons systems.[7]

When corporations speak of their work in nuclear weapons manufacturing, the language employed is matter-of-fact and utilitarian. Specifics concerning the actual manufacturing operations and the weapons procurement contracts being fulfilled by these companies for government defense ministries are few. Given the classified nature of much nuclear weapons work, the companies are limited to the most general of descriptions. Idealistic rhetoric is limited to employee safety, integrity in the fulfillment of government contracts, and helping maintain the defense of the country.[8] Corporate executives and employees do not ask ethical questions surrounding whether they should be participating in the development and manufacture of nuclear weapons at all.

This corporate silence is a change from the 1980s, when public debates about the development, possession, and deployment of nuclear weapons often included corporations and their executives. Edson W. Spencer, the longtime chairman and chief executive officer of the Honeywell Corporation, was notable for leading his company's efforts to sponsor public debates concerning nuclear weapons, investing $125,000 in such debates as well as research on questions concerning arms control and disarmament.[9] These efforts drew controversy. Some thought Spencer's efforts to be a cynical public relations ploy to build support for nuclear weapons, while others, including Spencer's executive peers in other corporations, welcomed the effort to have constructive public debate. The debates themselves featured a spectrum of views ranging from possession to disarmament.[10] These same manufacturers found themselves in the public eye when they participated in the trials of protesters who engaged in direct action to destroy the technology used for nuclear weapons, such as the Plowshares movement.[11] These public efforts by corporations were motivated as a response to national and global protests against the possession and deployment of nuclear weapons, which made their manufacturers as much an object of protests as the military and the government agencies that managed their use. For example, Honeywell's efforts were a direct response to its Minneapolis headquarters being a target of regular antinuclear protests.[12]

The drive to renew nuclear arsenals and the potential of the proliferation of the means to manufacture and deploy nuclear weapons is an about-face from the early 1990s. Then, the United States and the Soviet Union, and later Russia, agreed to a series of treaties to reduce the number of nuclear weapons and de-target each other's countries.[13] The former Soviet republics of Belarus, Kazakhstan, and Ukraine as well as South Africa each divested themselves of their nuclear arsenals and became signatories to the Nuclear Non-Proliferation Treaty.[14] The hope then was that these agreements would lead eventually to a permanent global nuclear disarmament, with nuclear weapons coming under a permanent international ban on their manufacture and deployment similar to the global ban applied to chemical weapons. Today, nuclear arms treaties, such as the 1987 Intermediate-Range Nuclear Forces Treaty, are being suspended or abrogated altogether. Nuclear powers are turning to defense contractors to renew, update, and expand their arsenals while casting a wary eye toward countries and extranational groups that want to take possession of nuclear technology as a means of political leverage.[15]

Notes

1. Andrei Adrianov, Victor Kanke, Ilya Kuptsov, and Viktor Murogov, "Re-examining the Ethics of Nuclear Technology," *Science and Engineering Ethics* 21, no. 2 (August 2015): 999–1018.
2. Hans M. Kristensen and Robert S. Norris, "Status of World Nuclear Forces, Federation of American Scientists," Federation of American Scientists, February 23, 2022, https://fas.org/issues/nuclear-weapons/status-world-nuclear-forces.
3. Jonathan Granoff, "Nuclear Weapons, Ethics, Morals, and Law," *Brigham Young University Law Review*, no. 4 (2000): 1413–42.
4. Farhad Rezaei, "Shopping for Armageddon: Islamist Groups and Nuclear Terror," *Middle East Policy* 33, no. 3 (Fall 2016): 112–32.
5. Paul Bracken, *The Second Nuclear Age: Strategy, Danger, and the New Power Politics* (New York: Times Books, 2012); and Jerry Miller, *Stockpile: The Story behind 10,000 Strategic Nuclear Weapons* (Annapolis, MD: Naval Institute Press, 2010).
6. Bracken, *Second Nuclear Age*.

7. Arnie Alpert, *Who Profits from Nuclear Weapons?*, American Friends Service Committee, August 11, 2015.
8. Jennifer J. Salopek, "Keeping Knowledge Safe and Sound," *TD Magazine*, October 2010, 64–66.
9. David A. Vise, "Honeywell-Backed Debates on Arms Control Issues Fail to Appease Protesters," *Washington Post*, October 14, 1984.
10. Vise.
11. Kristen Tobey, *Plowshares: Protest, Performance, and Religious Identity in the Nuclear Age* (University Park: Penn State University Press, 2016).
12. Vise, "Honeywell-Backed Debates on Arms Control Issues."
13. Anastasia Malygina, Sven-Eric Fikenscher, and Jenny Nielsen, "Amid High Tensions, an Urgent Need for Nuclear Restraint," *Bulletin of the Atomic Scientists* 73, no. 4, (2017): 279–83.
14. J. W. de Villiers, Roger Jardine, and Mitchell Reiss, "Why South Africa Gave Up the Bomb," *Foreign Affairs* 72, no. 5 (November–December 1993): 98–109.
15. Michael D. Beck, Richard T. Cupitt, Seema Gahlaut, and Scott A. Jones, *To Supply or to Deny: Comparing Nonproliferation Export Controls in Five Key Countries* (The Hague: Kluwer Law International, 2003); and Robert F. Mozley, *The Politics and Technology of Nuclear Proliferation* (Seattle: University of Washington Press, 1998).

31

The Responsibilities of "Enabled" Citizens for Integral Disarmament and Sustainable Human Development

JAMES P. O'SULLIVAN

In exploring the responsibilities of citizens of nuclear states to work for nuclear disarmament, this chapter will utilize Catholic social teaching, and yet necessarily, the hope is that it will also be understandable from and applicable to those holding other perspectives in our pluralistic world. My case is as follows. All societies of the world have a responsibility not to harm the flourishing of other persons and the planet itself. Going beyond this negative duty, all have the responsibility to properly use the resources of Earth toward the greater realization of flourishing for all its inhabitants. A failure in both duties is occurring through the mere possession, let alone use, of nuclear weapons. While the primary responsibility for a redirection of policy falls on governments, citizens have an essential role in this responsibility. Their responsibilities are necessarily proportionate to both their governments' role in the crisis and their capability to exercise their rights as citizens. Moreover, because many policies of nuclear nations, chief among them the United States and Russia, are failing to live up to the negative and positive duties to the global common good, there is a more urgent need for capable citizens, as part of and enabled by civil society, to assume varying degrees of moral responsibility to change these policies. In short, then, citizens truly possessed of rights and able to influence the pertinent policies have the responsibility to exercise these rights in various ways to overcome governments' abrogation of responsibility to the global common good.

This essay first examines the responsibilities of governments for integral disarmament and sustainable human development and the way in which these are not being met and the responsibility that consequently falls on citizens to correct the immoral misdirection in policy. Subsequently, the essay will examine ethically significant differences in citizens, both within and between nations; here it shall argue that citizens of some nations bear special responsibility and that in order for citizens to exercise their rights, they must first have them promoted and protected. The essay will then explicate an understanding of the role of citizens as part of civil society, which has a particular responsibility for enabling a critical mass of citizens to foment change. Finally, the essay will briefly outline some specific actions that would be effective realizations of this moral responsibility concomitant to fully realized rights.

Responsibilities for Integral Disarmament and Development as Part of Fostering the Global Common Good

In order to determine the responsibilities of citizens, it is important to briefly give a more general account of responsibilities for integral disarmament and development before identifying the failures of some actors, in particular public authorities, to fulfill these responsibilities.

Catholic social teaching has for many decades cast nuclear disarmament as necessarily connected to the wider responsibility for fostering a just and lasting peace through the promotion of integral and sustainable human development and human rights. As Pope Francis recently summarized, the enormous cost of "modernizing and developing weaponry, not only nuclear weapons," diverts urgently needed resources from "the real priorities facing our human family, such as the fight against poverty, the promotion of peace, the undertaking of educational, ecological and healthcare projects, and the development of human rights."[1] This fundamental failure in priorities, combined with the "catastrophic humanitarian and environmental effects of any employment of nuclear devices" as well as "the risk of an accidental detonation as a result of error of any kind," has led him to the conclusion that both "the threat of their use, *as well as their very possession*, is to be firmly condemned." In light of this, there is an urgent moral responsibility for a "thoroughgoing and complete" process of disarmament and a fundamental redirection of resources and policy toward fostering sustainable and integral human development.

The assumption of this responsibility falls first and particularly on the governments of the world, working together in mutual collaboration and solidarity with both one another and global civil society. For nuclear disarmament in particular, it is clear, as Scott Sagan argues, that the "major responsibility for reducing the roles and missions that nuclear weapons play in the doctrine of the nuclear powers clearly falls on the governments of those nations."[2] Again, from the perspective of Catholic social teaching, this responsibility is part of the wider responsibility of governments, in particular the wealthy and powerful nations of the world, to undertake mutual assistance toward sustainable human development and the securing of the full spectrum of rights for all peoples.

Importantly, many governments have assumed elements of this responsibility in regard to both nuclear disarmament and fostering sustainable human development through the formation of structures of solidarity. These are the result of several significant overlapping ethical consensuses that have developed in recent decades. First, even amid the undeniable pluralism of the global stage, a fairly robust consensus has developed on the connections between human rights, economic development, and sustainability, one imbued with a lens of "looking to the most vulnerable" and "leaving no one behind."[3] Further, this consensus has been translated into near-universal accords on a global action agenda in the form of the United Nations Millennium Development Goals and the subsequent Sustainable Development Goals. Second, regarding disarmament more particularly, there have been many significant treaties reducing the number of nuclear weapons and preventing their spread as well as the passing of a United Nations General Assembly resolution "banning" nuclear weapons altogether.[4]

There are, however, very substantial problems that exist both in implementation of the established ethical consensus on human rights and development and in the establishment of a full consensus on disarmament as an integral part of this global ethical agenda. First, while the ethical consensus on development and human rights and its translation into a global agenda has succeeded in many ways, there are also many flaws that plague the agenda and threaten its achievement, in particular a fundamental lack of accountability and follow-through in the goals—particularly on the necessary pledges of various forms of foreign aid—and lack of global governance mechanisms to implement the overall vision. Simply put, then, the Sustainable Development Goals agenda faces the same fundamental issues in implementation as did the Millennium Development Goals and nuclear disarmament: lack of adequate funding and failure to undertake the reform of the global order necessary to achieve them.[5] Moreover, threats exist in the nationalistic tendencies emerging in the West and in an ascendant model of development particularly coming from China, which does not see human rights and development as necessary concomitants. Second and necessarily related to funding of sustainable human development, many nations are undertaking large nuclear modernization programs, with the United States alone set to spend over $1 trillion in the next thirty years.[6] With large gaps in funding for the Sustainable Development Goals agenda alone, these policies are immoral moves in the wrong direction. Further, there are very serious concerns regarding the present state of landmark disarmament and nonproliferation treaties, and it seems clear to many analysts that such regimes face serious challenges in the years ahead, particularly with persistent tensions between nuclear weapon states and non–nuclear weapon states. Finally, while the recent Treaty on the Prohibition of Nuclear Weapons was indeed significant, it also met a wall of resistance from the nuclear weapon states. Overall, then, as Cardinal Robert McElroy has articulated, there has been a failure on the part of the most powerful nations to "embrace an ethic of the universal common good in the very issue area where such an ethic was most cogent and most necessary."[7]

Citizens therefore have responsibilities for fostering integral disarmament, most urgently because of the present state of policies but also more fundamentally because of the rights that they—at least ostensibly—enjoy. In the vision of Catholic social teaching, rights are "the fundamental requirements for a dignified life in community" and necessarily exist in both the socioeconomic and civil-political realms of social existence. Such rights are necessarily interdependent with one another and come with responsibilities to the common good.[8] In particular, as John XXIII makes clear, it is "in keeping with their dignity as human persons that human beings should take an active part in government," and it is precisely in their contact with the citizens that public officials can better learn "what is really necessary for the common good."[9] Thus, citizens have a responsibility to demand that their governments follow through on grave moral commitments. In other words, they have a responsibility to insist on an ethical global public policy agenda generally and, more specifically, on the reduction and eventual elimination of nuclear weapons and a redirection of resources to integral and sustainable human development. So, while the chief responsibility falls on governments, citizens necessarily have the responsibility to help shape the policies of governments, especially when there is such an urgent need to correct policy for the benefit of the global common good.

Gradations of Responsibility Based on Complicity and Capability

An essential element of adjudicating responsibility entails recognizing ethically significant differences between citizens. There are necessarily gradations of responsibility among citizens of global society based on both complicity and capability.[10] First, regarding complicity, while there may be a "shared responsibility" between states that possess nuclear weapons and those that do not, it is nevertheless true, as Sri Lankan ambassador Jayantha Dhanapala has argued, "shared responsibility does not mean equal responsibility."[11] Indeed, a special responsibility exists for those nations whose policies are perpetuating the nuclear threat and that are simultaneously failing to live up to their commitments to fund sustainable human development; therefore, citizens of nuclear armed states that shirk their duties of aid to the world's poor have a special responsibility to change these policies. This is not to say that citizens in non–nuclear weapon states have no responsibility; instead, this is an acknowledgment that citizens of wealthy nuclear weapon states bear a particular responsibility to push for the proper use of their abundant resources in fostering the global common good.

Within such nations, though, differences in capabilities to exercise core rights also mean further delineations of responsibility. In order for citizens to exercise their rights to influence public policy, these rights must be secured in both the civil-political and socioeconomic realms. Only insofar as citizens' rights have been promoted and protected in both of these realms can they be reasonably expected to exercise the responsibilities that are concomitant to these rights. First, it is manifestly not the case that all nuclear weapon states have successfully institutionalized civil and political structures that enable citizens to assume civil and political responsibility. Second, because of the reality of interdependence, in order to exercise key civil-political rights, other key socioeconomic rights must be promoted and protected. Citizens cannot effectively influence public policy if they are experiencing significant deprivations in levels of nutrition, education, health care, etc. There are thus special responsibilities for citizens in highly functioning democracies that are also wealthy nuclear weapon states. And even within these states, differences in the functioning levels of core rights mean distinctions in levels of responsibility. The more capability, the more responsibility.

In short, then, the responsibilities of citizens for nuclear disarmament and promoting the global common good accrue differently both between and within nations. Indeed, ethically significant differences place responsibilities in proportion to both complicity and capability. The strongest moral responsibility exists for citizens of privilege in nuclear weapon states, those who have had the full spectrum of rights promoted and protected and who experience little or no impediments in exercising these rights. Put plainly, those citizens who are most enabled to influence policy have a greater responsibility to ensure that policies are fostering the common good.

This responsibility will necessarily be assumed by citizens acting in various areas of civil society, and action on the part of a significant mass of citizens will be required to truly shift policy. Indeed, research has shown that popular mobilization has been an essential element in historical limitations to nuclear weapons. A fundamental shift toward integral disarmament, then, will most certainly require a critical mass of concerned citizens.[12]

Responsibilities of Citizens as Part of and Enabled by Civil Society

For citizens to assemble a critical mass to bring about real change—to assert moral agency and exercise their rights to promote the global common good—they must be informed and organized, and this requires building further capability. Enabling citizens to exercise their rights is in many ways the responsibility of governments, whose chief concern, as Saint John XXIII explained, ought to be to ensure that rights "are acknowledged, respected, coordinated with other rights, defended and promoted," so that citizens can fulfill their responsibilities to the common good.[13] Beyond this minimum responsibility, governments must also ensure that citizens are aware of the policies being pursued in their name; this is manifestly not being met by many governments that continue to espouse an ethic of deterrence and are far from transparent in sharing information on nuclear policy and the lack of follow-through on promoting sustainable human development. This results in a situation in which many citizens are "disengaged" from these issues and no critical mass exists to bring about the necessary change.[14]

Faced with the public's lack of full and accurate information on nuclear weapons policy, it becomes imperative that civil society assume the role of educating and engaging citizens on the urgent moral and empirical realities of nuclear weapons policy and on the losses to sustainable human development created by spending on nuclear weapons. Of course, civil society is made up of citizens, many of whom have taken up the responsibility of educating, advocating, organizing, and galvanizing other citizens and the public authorities of the world. As Susi Snyder, a leader of the PAX Nuclear Disarmament Program, explains, "Civil society is an amplification of the moral compass, needed to guide decision-making to put the collective good at the forefront" and to "amplify the moral imperative to act with urgency for development and disarmament."[15] The goal must be to inform and organize a sufficient number of citizens, and this will require civil society to undertake the following forms of enablement, with the Church, academia, and free press all having significant roles to play.

First, civil society must educate citizens to understand the urgency of the issues and the way in which many policies are moving in the wrong direction. Part of this education will involve exposing the "myth of nuclear deterrence"[16] that security supposedly comes with nuclear weapons. It will also involve stimulating a greater realization of the persistent danger these weapons pose, the resources currently being misdirected, and the ways in which these resources could be better directed.

Second, it will be necessary to show citizens that nuclear disarmament and integral development are indeed achievable policy goals, not utopian dreams, and real possibilities for success. With regard to disarmament, over the past decade an abundance of experts and former policymakers have made the case; now it must reach a greater number of citizens.[17] Greater awareness can also be fostered about the substantial consensus that exists on human rights and development needs and the issues that exist in follow-through and accountability for implementing this consensus agenda.

Third, there must be education on the wider moral vision of the interconnected reality of disarmament and development; in other words, the issue must be placed within the wider context of what is necessary for a real and lasting peace. A particular role for the Church, then, is to continue to clarify and educate citizens on the need for a shift from an ethic of deterrence to robust disarmament and peacebuilding. Finally, it will be necessary to organize and channel the energies of citizens; indeed, even the most enabled citizens cannot be expected to foment change if there is no clear and achievable agenda.

While many citizen activists have been taking up these responsibilities, a critical mass of citizens will be required to bring about such a significant shift in policy. There is much work yet to be done in building that critical mass, and so it is the responsibility of those citizens who have taken up roles in civil society to persist and reach more of their fellow citizens, clarify the ethical agenda, and continue gathering momentum for change. For the many fully enabled citizens who are not yet engaged, there is at minimum the responsibility to be willing to hear the case being put forward by many of their fellow citizens. Of course, this does not mean that most citizens must become experts on nuclear and development policy, but insofar as they are capable, they do have the responsibility to be aware of what is occurring and to insist in various ways that policymakers undertake efforts to surmount the obstacles to disarmament and to prioritize sustainable human development.

There are two ways that informed and enabled citizens can influence policy, both focusing on holding public officials accountable to the needs of the global common good. First, responsibilities exist in voting, in particular paying attention to politicians' positions on arms reduction, counterproliferation, the modernization of nuclear arsenals, and commitments to foreign aid and improved structures of global governance.

Second, enabled citizens must be persistent in advocacy: against modernization, against the withdrawal from established regimes of nonproliferation, for sustained diplomacy in reducing weapons, and for follow-through on the pledges made to the Sustainable Development Goals agenda and the myriad commitments to human development, climate change, and global governance. Political leaders must come to understand, in short, that a critical mass of citizens supports disarmament and the redirection of resources toward the consensus agenda of sustainable human development. This will mean advocacy for both continued commitment to sustaining and improving those structures of solidarity that already exist in the global order and the creation of new institutions that can achieve integral disarmament and sustainable development.

Conclusion

If the goal of a world free of nuclear weapons is "like the top of a very tall mountain," then the goal of integral disarmament and sustainable human development is like a mountain range.[18] This essay has argued that citizens have a vital role in scaling these mountains, a role that exists as part of a set of ethical responsibilities to the global common good necessarily entailed in having fully realized rights as citizens in a global society. It has also argued, though, that while these responsibilities exist in gradations based on both complicity and capability, they will only be effectively exercised insofar as citizens continue to enable one another to assume, together and in varying degrees, the role of "moral compass" guiding global society toward greater realization of the global common good.

Notes

1. Address of His Holiness Pope Francis to Participants in the International Symposium "Prospects for a World Free of Nuclear Weapons and for Integral Disarmament," November 10, 2017.
2. Scott D. Sagan, "Shared Responsibilities for Nuclear Disarmament," *Daedalus* 138:4 (Cambridge, MA: MIT Press on behalf of American Academy of Arts & Sciences, Fall, 2009), 164.
3. See further United Nations, *Transforming Our World: The 2030 Agenda for Sustainable Development,* October 21, 2015, A/RES/70/1; and *United Nations Millennium Declaration, Resolution Adopted by the General Assembly,* September 18, 2000, A/RES/55/2.
4. Chief examples include the Nuclear Non-Proliferation Treaty and the two Strategic Arms Reduction treaties between the United States and Russia.
5. See further Thomas Pogge and Arjun Sengupta, "The Sustainable Development Goals: Nice Idea, Poor Execution," *Washington Law Journal* 24 (2015): 571–87.
6. See further Arms Control Association, "US Nuclear Modernization Programs," January 2022, https://www.armscontrol.org/factsheets/USNuclearModernization.
7. Cardinal Robert M. McElroy, "We Must Do No Less," 2017 address to the Vatican conference "Prospects for a World Free of Nuclear Weapons and for Integral Disarmament," November 10, 2017.

8. United States Catholic Bishops, *Economic Justice for All: Pastoral Letter on Catholic Social Teaching and the U.S. Economy*, 1986, nos. 79–84.
9. John XXIII, *Pacem in terris*, no. 73.
10. The language of capabilities utilized here is not identical to and yet also not separate from the discussion of the "Capabilities Approach" of Martha Nussbaum, Amartya Sen, and others. See further Martha C. Nussbaum, *Creating Capabilities: The Human Development Approach* (Cambridge MA: Belknap, 2011).
11. Quoted in Karla Mae G. Pabeliña, "Shared yet Different Responsibilities in Nuclear Disarmament," *Philippines Foreign Service Institute Insights*, 5, no. 2 (February, 2015): 2.
12. See further David Cortright, *Peace Works: The Citizen's Role in Ending the Cold War* (Boulder, CO: Praeger, 1990); and Jeffrey W. Knopf, *Domestic Society and International Cooperation: The Impact of Protest on US Arms Control Policy* (New York: Cambridge University Press, 1998).
13. John XXIII, *Pacem in terris*, no. 60.
14. See further John Kultgen, *Abolition of Nuclear Weapons as Moral Imperative* (Lanham, MD: Lexington Books, 2015).
15. Susi Snyder, "The Role of Civil Society," 2017 address to the Vatican conference "Prospects for a World Free of Nuclear Weapons and for Integral Disarmament," November 10, 2017.
16. See further Ward Wilson, "The Myth of Nuclear Deterrence," *Nonproliferation Review* 15, no. 3 (2008).
17. Perhaps the most prominent example of this case can be seen in the public arguments made by the so-called Gang of Four, former secretaries of state George Shultz and Henry Kissinger, former defense secretary William Perry, and former senator Sam Nunn, in a series of *Wall Street Journal* op-eds published since 2007.
18. George Shultz et al., "A World Free of Nuclear Weapons," *Wall Street Journal*, January 4, 2007.

PART VIII

The Role of Lay Catholic Movements

32

Organizing the Church for a World without Nuclear Weapons

KEVIN AHERN

The Christian scriptures speak frequently of the responsibility that comes with power, knowledge, and influence. In the synoptic gospels, for instance, Jesus invites his followers not to hide their light but instead to let it "shine before others, so that they may see your good works and give glory to God" (Matthew 5:16). Elsewhere, followers of Christ are called to become the "salt of the earth" and the "light of the world" (Matthew 5:13–14), to respond to Jesus's teaching through action and not only words (Matthew 7:24–27), and to not bury their resources in the ground (Matthew 25:14–30). In short, the gifts and potential that one has must be actualized in the world.

In the campaign to abolish nuclear weapons, the Roman Catholic Church has a unique potential to mobilize people and institutions on multiple continents. The essays in this volume demonstrate both the range and depth of the Church's engagement on this issue. Despite many significant statements, campaigns, and programs, however, this potential has yet to be realized. Looking forward, a central question must be how the Church can better actualize its potential for disarmament. This essay examines this question by pointing to the valuable role of mediating groups that operate in the Church and in civil society.

The Catholic Potential for Disarmament

The Roman Catholic Church is arguably one of the largest and complex institutions worldwide. With a global reach and robust doctrine of peace and social justice, Catholicism has an enormous potential to transform individual worldviews and political policies for the better. Already, the power of the Catholic potential can be seen in a range of social policies, including immigration, human trafficking, democracy, and labor justice.

Despite the negative role that religion plays as a source of conflict, faith-based agents can also be powerful "forces for peace and conflict transformation."[1] Religious agents, including Catholic communities and structures, have a unique ability to both form individual consciences and influence public discourse on social issues.[2] The resources offered by Catholicism and other religious actors, however, are often overlooked for several reasons, including a Westphalian bias that both focuses on sovereign states as the main players in global politics and plays down the public role of religious actors.[3]

In recent years, scholars from different disciplines have sought to draw attention to the role of religion and other nonstate actors in the global public square.[4] Nongovernmental organizations (NGOs) have been described as the "third" United Nations (UN), a complement to international relations scholar Inis Claude's distinction between the "first UN" of sovereign member states and the "second UN" of international civil servants.[5] Religious agents could also be described as agents of "soft power," in contrast to the "hard" coercive power of states with military and criminal justice systems.[6] They might also be seen as agents of two-track or multitrack diplomacy through their direct engagement in peacebuilding and diplomatic negotiations, spaces usually reserved for sovereign powers.[7] The oft-cited example here is the work of the Community of Sant'Egidio, an international Catholic movement that successfully facilitated and hosted the peace talks that ended the brutal Mozambican Civil War (1977–92).[8]

With his peacebuilding pyramid, this book's contributor John Paul Lederach offers another model applicable to the work of religious agents and Catholicism in particular.[9] Looking primarily at national peacebuilding efforts, Lederach presents a three-tiered pyramid, with each level representing a different location for peacebuilding action. Applying this model to the Roman Catholic Church, it is possible to highlight the Catholic potential for nuclear disarmament by considering three levels in which the Church, as a complex global agent, operates.

Top-Level Engagement

At the apex of Lederach's pyramid are those top-level leaders, including senior government officials, political figures, high-ranking military officers, and the leadership of intergovernmental systems. This level is often the principal focus for scholars and the wider public when considering policies of war and peace. Applying the pyramid model to the Catholic community, those in the Church hierarchy stand at the top of the pyramid. Like political figures, bishops, the pope, and groups of bishops often dominate scholarly and popular attention on the Church's role in international public policy.

The hierarchical structure of Catholicism and its long history of political engagement make it well positioned to call for disarmament. At the global level, the pope and the curia, including the recently created Dicastery for Promoting Integral Human Development (formerly the Pontifical Council for Justice and Peace), offer a symbolic and substantive moral voice on issues of social concern. This voice is expressed in a number of ways, including through official magisterial teachings such as papal encyclicals, lobbying efforts by bishops' conferences, bilateral diplomatic action with over 183 states, and multilateral action with over forty intergovernmental organizations.[10]

In this top-level (Track I) engagement, the Holy See has been a remarkable voice for nuclear disarmament. It was, for example, one of the first three state parties to sign and ratify the Treaty on the Prohibition of Nuclear Weapons in September 2017.[11] High-level Church leadership has used its convening power to bring together voices to address the cause of nuclear disarmament, including the November 2017 International Symposium on Prospects for a World Free of Nuclear Weapons and for Integral Disarmament that occasioned this book. With this particular event, Pope Francis made international headlines by condemning both the use and the possession of nuclear weapons.[12] Weeks later, the pope again used the power of his global pulpit during a Sunday Angelus to praise the work of the International Campaign to Abolish Nuclear Arms (ICAN), which had just been awarded the Nobel Prize for Peace.[13]

Grassroots Engagement

The power and potential of the Catholic Church in nuclear disarmament extends far beyond the work of the pope and bishops. While top-level engagement—the apex of Lederach's pyramid—receives most of the attention, the base level offers opportunities that may not be fully appreciated. At the grass roots, Catholicism has an enormous capacity for ethical formation of the individual conscience. The Church, for example, operates 222,514 parishes, 96,573 elementary schools, and 47,862 secondary schools.[14] What is more, Catholics have created well over 1,000 colleges and universities and sponsor a wide range of local newspapers, radio stations, and television networks.

If coordinated effectively, schools, courses, weekly homilies, local media sources, and grassroots community groups can play an effective role in changing public opinion on the moral and legal legitimacy of nuclear arms. In some places, the Church's grassroots potential for peacebuilding is already being actualized in profound ways. Far too often, however, many at this level seem unaware of the official disarmament positions taken by the Church in international forums and the growing body of social doctrine on the immorality of the use and possession of nuclear weapons. To expect all these groups to take action on nuclear weapons would be nothing short of miraculous. However, it is reasonable and possible that more groups at the grass roots can be mobilized more than at present. But how can this happen?

Middle-Range Actors

The two ends of Lederach's pyramid, the top level and the grassroots base, offer different roles in any processes of social transformation. Each brings with it its own possibilities, and each demands distinct strategies. A space that is often overlooked, however, is the middle range. In his work, Lederach highlights the transformative potential of civil society agents that occupy a mediating position between the grassroots and top-level political leadership. Mediating agents, including national and international NGOs, and social movements and networks have enormous potential for shaping both ends of the pyramid.

Applying this to the Catholic Church worldwide, this middle-range position would include a broad assortment of actors including thousands of religious congregations of women and men (e.g., Sisters of Charity, Jesuits), lay movements (e.g., International Movement of Catholic Students, Young Catholic Workers), new ecclesial movements (e.g., Sant'Egidio, Focolare), Catholic development agencies (e.g., Catholic Relief Services), and a growing number of networks of local institutions (e.g., International Federation of Catholic Universities).

As middle-range agents, these structures mediate in several distinct ways. First, as Lederach's model illustrates well, middle-range agents mediate between the top level and the grass roots. A number of Catholic structures do this through advocacy and partnerships with governmental and intergovernmental bodies. For instance, over one hundred Catholic organizations have formal consultative status with the UN Economic and Social Council. This enables them to both attend and advocate at UN meetings and grants them access to information that they can diffuse and share with their members on the ground. Pax Christi International, for example, engages the top-level leadership on themes of disarmament at the UN as an accredited NGO and a partner in the ICAN network. At the same time, this Catholic peace movement also seeks to educate and mobilize Catholics in parishes and schools on the deeper themes and the teachings of the Church.

Protests and organized acts of civil disobedience are other ways in which arbitration forces mediate between individuals and top-level leadership. In contrast to a more "public style" of formal engagement with governments and the UN, some Catholic movements adopt a more "prophetic style" in calling for nuclear disarmament.[15] Consider the controversial tactics of the Plowshares movement, which organizes real and symbolic acts of disarmament at military and corporate facilities related to nuclear weapons.[16]

Second, these agents can play a similar mediating role within the Church. For example, the Catholic Nonviolence Initiative, a project of Pax Christi, organized the April 2016 conference at the Vatican. The event and its media coverage influenced both public and scholarly discourse on the ground as well as the official teaching of top-level Church leadership, including the 2017 World Day of Peace Message on nonviolence. It is precisely groups at this level that can then take those top-level commitments and exert pressure in parishes, schools, and universities to better share the Church's teachings on this issue.

Third, middle-range actors also mediate among peoples at the grass roots, empowering them by "giving the individuals who work together in the movement greater power to bring about social change than they could have alone."[17] For example, international networks, religious congregations, and movements often share perspectives and best practices of activists in one country with those in another through social media, newsletters, and visits. Alternative perspectives from peers on the legitimacy of nuclear arms can be transformative for people in countries where such weapons are often uncritically accepted.

Finally, social movements and other organizations mediate between faith and politics. Communities and movements can provide spaces for reflection and faith formation that go beyond traditional catechetical and pastoral education. The *Compendium of the Social Doctrine of the Church*, in fact, explicitly recognizes the special role of *"various specialized associations"* in the formation of *"mature Christians"* and in the education on the Church's social teaching.[18]

Actualizing the Catholic Potential for Disarmament

In short, Catholic middle-range agents, from lay groups to religious congregations, are a critical component in the Catholic potential for disarmament. Unfortunately, much more is needed to actualize these efforts at Catholic organizing. Catholic movements and organizations concerned with disarmament are hampered by a number of challenges, including limited financial resources, competition and tensions among groups with different priorities and styles, a lack of coordination, and polarized ecclesial contexts that inhibit bold action. The full actualization of this potential for disarmament will demand scaling up existing structures, leadership, and coordinated efforts that bring together a range of actors within and outside Catholicism.

One possible model to consider is the Jubilee 2000 debt forgiveness campaign.[19] Here, middle-range actors actualized the Catholic potential for social change in a profound way. In partnership with other organizations, Catholic middle-range groups, including European development agencies, lay movements, and religious congregations, organized global campaigns for debt forgiveness. Middle-range actors with various styles and missions educated their membership and the wider public on the realities facing highly indebted poor countries and the exploitative practices of lending countries, engaged Pope John Paul II and other Church leaders in top-level positions, used relationships with governments and intergovernmental bodies to lobby and advocate specific policy changes, mobilized celebrities to take up the cause, and coordinated an international grassroots campaign with a clear and direct message.

Like the debt forgiveness campaign, the movement to abolish nuclear weapons offers a relatively clear and achievable goal that is both reasonable and grounded in Catholic moral teaching. It is also a goal that could be shared by many non-Catholic partners and expressed in a variety of ways. Encouraging more international and national Catholic groups to join the ICAN network would be an important step.

The existence of nuclear weapons represents a disturbing threat for destruction and devastation. As a unique global community, the Catholic Church is well positioned to be a force for nuclear disarmament. While it is unrealistic to imagine that all Catholics or even all middle-range Catholic groups would take up nuclear abolition as a major issue, much more can be done to better actualize the Catholic potential. This will not be easy. It will require leadership, strategy, and a scaling up of the human and financial resources of existing mediating groups working for a nuclear-free world.

Notes

1. Cynthia Sampson, "Religion and Peacebuilding," in *Peacemaking in International Conflict: Methods and Techniques*, ed. I. William Zartman and J. Lewis Rasmussen (Washington, DC: United States Institute of Peace, 1997), 275.
2. J. Bryan Hehir, "Overview," in *Religion in World Affairs: The Findings of a Conference Organized by the DACOR Bacon House Foundation*, ed. Robert T. Hennemeyer (Washington, DC: DACOR Bacon House Foundation, 1995), 15.
3. Douglas M. Johnston and Cynthia Sampson, eds., *Religion: The Missing Dimension of Statecraft* (New York: Oxford University Press, 1994).
4. See José Casanova, *Public Religions in the Modern World* (Chicago: University of Chicago Press, 1994); and Monica Duffy Toft, Daniel Philpott, and Timothy Samuel Shah, *God's Century: Resurgent Religion and Global Politics* (New York: Norton, 2011).
5. Thomas G. Weiss, Tatiana Carayannis, and Richard Jolly, "The 'Third' United Nations," *Global Governance* 15 (2009): 123–42; and Inis L. Claude, "Peace and Security: Prospective Roles for the Two United Nations," *Global Governance* 2, no. 3 (1996): 289–98.
6. See Joseph S. Nye, *Soft Power: The Means to Success in World Politics* (New York: PublicAffairs, 2004).
7. See M. J. Zuckerman, "Track II Diplomacy: Can 'Unofficial' Talks Avert Disaster?," *Carnegie Reporter* 3, no. 3 (2005): 2–11; and Louise Diamond and John McDonald, *Multi-Track Diplomacy: A Systems Approach to Peace*, 3rd ed. (West Hartford, CT: Kumarian Press, 1996).
8. See Régis Ladous, Andrea Riccardi, and Jean-Dominique Durand, *Sant'Egidio: Rome and the World* (Maynooth, Ireland: St. Paul's Press, 1999).
9. John Paul Lederach, *Building Peace: Sustainable Reconciliation in Divided Societies* (Washington, DC: United States Institute of Peace, 1997).

10. Holy See Press Office, "Note on the Diplomatic Relations of the Holy See," *Daily Bulletin*, January 8, 2018; and "Bilateral and Multilateral Relations of the Holy See," Holy See Press Office, October 22, 2009, https://www.vatican.va/news_services/press/documentazione/documents/corpo-diplomatico_index_en.html.
11. For an excellent analysis, see Drew Christiansen, SJ, "The Vatican and the Ban Treaty," *Journal of Catholic Social Thought* 15, no. 1 (2018): 89–108.
12. Pope Francis, "Address of His Holiness Pope Francis to Participants in the International Symposium 'Prospects for a World Free of Nuclear Weapons and for Integral Disarmament,'" November 10, 2017.
13. Gerard O'Connell, "Pope Francis Calls for Abolition of Nuclear Arms as ICAN Formally Receives Nobel Peace Prize," *America*, December 10, 2017.
14. The Center for Applied Research in the Apostolate, "Frequently Requested Church Statistics," 2017.
15. Kristin E. Heyer, *Prophetic & Public: The Social Witness of U.S. Catholicism* (Washington, DC: Georgetown University Press, 2006).
16. See Kevin Ahern, *Structures of Grace: Catholic Organizations Serving the Global Common Good* (Maryknoll, NY: Orbis Books, 2015), chap. 4.
17. David Hollenbach, "Sustaining Catholic Social Engagement: A Key Role for Movements in the Church Today," ed. Cheryl Handel and Kathleen Shields, *Journal of Catholic Social Thought* 10, no. 2 (2013): 434.
18. Pontificium Consilium de Iustitia et Pace, *Compendium of the Social Doctrine of the Church* (Washington, DC: United States Conference of Catholic Bishops, 2004), nos. 549–550.
19. Elizabeth A. Donnelly, "Making the Case for Jubilee: The Catholic Church and the Poor-Country Debt Movement," *Ethics & International Affairs* 21, no. S1 (November 2007): 189–218.

Index

ABM (Anti-Ballistic Missile), 148; Treaty, 157
abolition, xii, 8–11, 25, 33–36, 59–64, 69, 71, 75, 128–29, 163, 195, 239–40, 242, 244, 258, 302–3, 353; abolitionism, 62–63; abolitionist cause, 64; abolitionists, 11; nuclear, 11, 69, 71, 242
above-ground tests, 214
accidents, nuclear, 23, 35, 177, 181, 191, 287, 295
accompaniment, 20, 240, 242, 244, 246
Acheson, Ray, 236
activism, 38, 95–96, 99, 275–76
actors, international, 123, 137, 278, middle-range, 354–56; midlevel, 27; nonstate, 14, 139, 142, 154, 173, 301, 352; religious, 352, 386
Adelphi Papers, 56, 191
advanced conventional weapons, 114
adversary nations/states, 16, 112
advocacy, 79, 80, 84, 86, 231, 316; of deterrence, 22; of nonviolence, 16
AEC (Atomic Energy Commission), 210–11, 213–14, 219
Aegis Ashore, 148
Affronté, 201
Afghanistan, 109, 156, 258, 288, 291
Africa, 15, 149, 386
aggression, 47, 49, 56, 155

agreements, 70, 84, 87, 113, 115, 129, 138, 146–49, 175, 233, 299, 320
Ahern, Kevin, 26–28, 351–58, 381
Akiyama, Nobumasa, 170
Allied Forces Occupation Authority, 82
allies, xii, 8, 19, 46, 49, 108, 134, 137, 144
Allman, Mark, 387
allowance, 54, 313; conditional, 298
Almighty: Courage, Resistance, and Existential Peril in the Nuclear Age, Dan Zak book, 100
Alves, Rubem, 282
American Catholic Philosophical Association, 57
American Constitution Society, 127
American Friends Service Committee, 337
American University, 2, 27; College of Law, 385; Kennedy address, 241
Amoris laetitia, papal encyclical, 6, 19, 246
Annan, Kofi, 251
annihilation, 37, 181, 196, 215, 307, 310, 328
Anti-Ballistic Missile (ABM), 148; Treaty, 157
antipersonnel land mines, 134, 174
Anscombe, Elizabeth, 42, 45, 184–85, 188, 192, 196–97

359

Anthropocene, 66
apocalypse, 11, 28, 52, 124, 190, 212
Appleby, Scott, 169, 179, 191, 386
Aquinas, Saint Thomas, 53, 56, 238, 241, 244, 246
archbishops, 3; Gabriele Giordano Caccia, 57–58; Francis Chullikatt, 327; Richard Paul Gallagher, 3; Dominique Mamberti, 312; Edwin O'Brien, 327; Fulton J. Sheen, 187, 192
Arkhipov, Vasili, 294, 297
Armageddon, 8, 121, 172, 293, 336; apocalypse, 52, 124, 190, 212; nuclear, 11, 28
arms control, 12, 129–30, 137, 144, 162, 232; agreements, 14, 120, 146, 150, 153, 157, 159, 171, 264, 291, 302, 319, 337
Arms Control Association, 20, 126, 210, 218, 235, 382–83, 385
arms race, 13, 17, 23, 85, 97, 157, 159, 163, 178, 301, 308, 327
arms reduction, 71, 74, 233, 236, 345
arms trade, 13, 133–34
Arrupe SJ, Pedro, 212, 218
artificial intelligence, 163, 170, 386
Association of Los Alamos Scientists, 217
Atlantic Life Community, 93
Atomic Energy Commission, Atomic Energy Act, 210. *See also* AEC
Atomic Heritage Foundation, 262
atomic scientists, 18, 109, 117, 171, 219, 260, 302
Augustine of Hippo, Saint, 230
Auschwitz, 217, 219

Bacevich, Andrew J., 311
Baker, James E., 126
Baker, Lauren, 66
ballistic missiles, 108, 110, 131, 195, 319; intercontinental, 110, 290
Baltimore, Maryland, 92, 99, 101, 179; Baltimore Four, 92

Bamat, Tom, 179
Bangladesh, 149
Ban Treaty, 83, 116, 169, 174, 214, 323, 358
baptism, 7, 306, 313
Barbera, Pablo, 276–77
Barbieri, William, 8, 10, 59–68, 187, 381
Basel Peace Office, 260
BBC, 91, 143
Beach, General Sir Hugh, 330
Beck, Michael D., 337
Beckley, Michael, 55
Beijing, 107, 112
Belarus, 174, 336
Belgium, 322
Benedictine University, 385
Benedict XV. *See under* Pope
Benedict XVI. *See under* Pope
Benevento, Maria, 100
Bergant, Dianne, 43
Berkley Center for Religion, Peace, and World Affairs, xv, xvi, 100, 237, 382
Berls, Robert E., Jr., 327
Berrigan, Daniel, 12, 91, 200
Berrigan, Philip, 99, 100, 200
Berrigans, 101, 193
Bichsel SJ, William ("Bix"), 94, 100
Biden, Joseph, 136, 147, 195, 383
Bikini Atoll nuclear testing, 84
bishops. *See* United States Conference of Catholic Bishops
Blair, Bruce, 235
Bleul, Burkhard, 127
blood, 90, 133, 321; drenched in, 314; innocent, 46, 133
Boertje-Obed, Gregory, 12, 28, 91, 98–99, 387
Boff, Leonardo, xiii
Bok, Sissela, 206, 217
Bolton, John R., 145
bombers, 108, 110, 224; B-52, 289; B-59, 294
bombs, 11, 17, 22, 42, 73, 77–78, 169, 211, 225, 294; atomic, 77, 84, 87, 90, 92, 190, 207, 211, 214, 287; dirty,

175, 258, 320; Hiroshima and Nagasaki, 76, 81, 84, 88, 264
Bonneau, Richard, 277
boot camp, nuclear, 264–65, 267
Boston College, 381, 385
Boylan, Kathy, 93
Boyle, Francis, 95
Boyle, Joseph M., Jr., 57, 183, 191, 201
Bracken, Paul, 336
Bradley, Curtis A., 126
Bramall, Field Marshal Lord, 330
Brands, Hal, 55
Braziller, George, 218
Brezhnev, Leonid, 148
Brinkmann, Svend, 66
Broken Arrow incidents, 256, 262
Brookings Institution, 218, 235
Browne, Lord Desmond, 331
Bull, Hedley, 56
Bundy, McGeorge, 158, 165, 168, 170
Burke, Kevin, 218
Burns, William, 295
Burr, William, 74
Bush, George H. W., 188, 213
Bush, George W., 14, 136–38, 148, 188, 200, 290
Butler, Lee, 71–72, 74, 295, 302–3, 312
Butler, Nilak, 218
Butterworth, Bob, 296
Byelorussia, 129

Cafardi, Nicholas P., 236
Cahill, Lisa Sowle, 19, 24, 229–37, 381
Caldicott, Helen, 211, 214, 218–19
Cameron, Prime Minister David, 384
Campaign for Nuclear Disarmament (CND), 273, 328
Canberra Commission report, 71–72, 74
cancer, 1, 213–14
capabilities, nuclear, 107, 109 114, 158, 163, 197, 207, 211, 287, 347
Carayannis, Tatiana, 357
Carey, Michael J., 290–92, 296
Caritas, xiii, 55, 179, 200, 235–36

Carver, Michael, 71
Casanova, José, 357
Casey-Maslen, Stuart, 57
casuistry, 5, 10, 19, 26, 240, 244
casus belli, 164, 170
Catechism, 5, 321, 356
Catholic Church, xiii, 3, 5, 7, 38–39, 43, 59, 160, 225–26, 318–21, 329–30, 353, 357–58; Église catholique, 201
Catholic Nonviolence Initiative, 43, 355
Catholic perspectives, 169, 236, 327; teaching, 5, 17, 40, 60, 94, 221, 223–24, 226–27; theology, 169, 179, 191, 381, 386–87
Catholic University of America, 167, 312–13, 327, 354, 381, 385
Catholic Worker, 92–93, 99–100; Dorothy Day Catholic Worker, 93; Houston Catholic Worker, 45; St. Peter Claver Catholic Worker, 386
Catonsville Nine, 92, 96–99, 101, 200
Central Intelligence Agency, 70, 73
chain of command, 24, 107, 120, 297–313
Chambésy, 200, 235
chemical weapons, 85, 131, 134, 160, 319–20, 325–26, 336
Chile, 236
China, xiii, 13–14, 25, 105–12, 114, 117, 128, 130, 143, 183, 276, 320, 334
Christ. *See* Jesus Christ
Christiansen SJ, Rev. Drew, xi–xiv, 1–29, 100, 163, 169–70, 193, 200, 238–49, 297–312, 358, 382, 387
Churchill, Winston, 181, 273
Church of England, 333
Citizens for Integral Disarmament and Sustainable Human Development, 338
civil disobedience, 96, 124, 355
civil society, xiii, 25, 26, 79, 80–81, 83–84, 86, 150, 181, 227, 233–34, 305, 332–33, 338–40, 343–45, 347, 351, 354
Civiltà Cattolica, La, 193, 200

Clamshell Alliance, 92
Clark, Ramsey, 96–97
Claude, Inis, 352, 357
climate, 2, 8, 34, 97, 258, 303, 330
Clinton, William J., 188
Cluff Lake, 212
cluster bombing, 40, 46; Cluster Munitions Treaty, 13
CND. *See* Campaign for Nuclear Disarmament
CODEPINK, 100
coercive force, 46; diplomacy, 56; forms of disarmament intervention, 156
Colangelo, Anthony J., 127
Cold War, 14, 16–17, 23, 34, 56–57, 72–74, 106–7, 149–50, 153–54, 158–62, 172–74, 185–87, 251–52, 256, 258, 287–88, 301; educational propaganda, 261
Coleman-Haseldine, Sue, 83, 88
collaboration, 16; cross-sector, 255; mutual, 339; transnational, 1
Colombia, 21, 278–81, 279, 385
Colorado, 291, 385
Columbia Center for Nuclear Studies, 260
Commission on International Religious Freedom, 385
compellence, compellent threat, 48, 55
complicity, 125, 186, 210, 231, 236, 238, 342–43, 346
Comprehensive Nuclear-Test-Ban Treaty, 73, 134, 147, 214, 382
condemnation, 4–5, 31, 42, 55, 86, 182–83, 184, 188, 195, 226–27, 232, 240–46, 298, 315, 353
conditional acceptance of deterrence, 8–9, 42–43, 241; conditions of strategic deterrence, 56
conscience, 7, 9, 17–18, 20, 27, 32, 79, 94, 96, 98–99, 164, 203, 205–19, 224–27, 269, 236, 239, 271, 276, 294, 299–300, 304, 308, 310, 329, 352–53

conscientious objection, xi, xiv, 35, 92, 124, 197, 221–22, 299, 302, 308, 311, 313
contracts, 314, 315–17, 334–35
Conventional Armed Forces, war, 14, 52, 55, 129, 133–34, 148, 150, 163–64, 166, 170, 215, 288; disarmament, 14, 154, 163–65
conversion, 192, 234, 313; apparent, 70; conversion of life, 313; moral, 64; radical, 306
Cooke, Stephanie, 207, 209, 217–18
Cooperative Threat Reduction (CTR), 154, 174, 176, 178, 291, 295, 383
Corden, Pierce S., 14, 24, 128–35, 165, 318–27, 382
Cornell, Tom, 200
Cortright, David, 11, 69–75, 168–70, 347, 382
Corrigan-Maguire, Mairead, 38, 43
cosmic common good, 66
Costa Rica, 126
Coudenhove-Kalergi, Richard von, 270–71, 277
Council on Christian Approaches to Defense and Disarmament, 309
courage, 87, 100, 226, 281, 298–99
Coyle, Philip E., 168
criteria of right relationship and restoration, 63
Croatia, 382
Crowe, William, 70
cruise missiles, 289
CTR. *See* Cooperative Threat Reduction
Cuban Missile Crisis, 1–2, 115, 118, 160, 164, 264–66, 294, 297, 314, 318, 321
Cummins, John, 243
Cupitt, Richard T., 337
Cusimano Love, Maryann, 16, 22–23, 162, 170, 172, 179, 186, 236–37
cybersecurity, 162, 252, 330; cyberattack, 107, 111, 114, 324; cyber

weapons, warfare, 8, 107, 156–57, 159
Czech Republic, 148

damage, 32, 53, 78, 83, 111, 173, 184; collateral, 36, 52; environmental, 177
Damascus Accident, 179, 191, 311
Davenport, Kelsey, 20, 251–62, 382
Dawkins, Richard, 272, 277
Declaration on Selective Conscientious Objection, xiv, 311
Dedon, Theodore G., xvi, 21, 269–77, 383
defense, 3, 15, 57, 97, 106, 108, 110, 124, 154, 176, 183, 187, 198, 225–26, 245, 288, 298, 302, 307–8, 335–36, 384; defence (UK), 46, 145, 331; strategies, 8, 95, 160; systems, 148, 314; teams, 95
DeMott, Peter, 100
Dennis, Marie, 237
DeRosa, Mary B., 127
Desch, Michael C., 170, 191, 201
deterrence, 2, 8, 10, 12, 17, 19, 31, 33, 36, 48–51, 54–59, 65, 69, 72–73, 86, 106, 110, 114, 157–58, 163–68, 170, 184, 188–89, 198, 201, 216, 230, 298, 301, 330, 334
detonation, 47, 111, 128, 326; accidental, 40, 55, 182, 223, 256, 320, 339; actual, 47; inadvertent, 256; nuclear, 81, 256
development, economic, 39, 177, 259, 340; and deployment of nuclear forces, 206, 326–27, 335; integral, 26, 63–64, 240, 273, 344; policy, 345; spiritual, 239, 263; technological, 154, 157, 164, 167
Dhanapala, Jayantha 342
dialogue, 7, 73, 215, 330; "Dialogue with Trypho," 306
Diamond, Louise, 357
Dicastery for Integral Human Development, xv, 3, 39, 353, 386

dignity, fundamental, 173; human, 62, 66, 173–74, 316, 329
dilemmas, 71, 180; moral, 240; of nuclear deterrence, 71, 118, 169, 326
diplomacy, 4, 112, 163, 175, 177, 181, 194, 226, 234, 277, 307, 313, 345, 352, 358, 384; nuclear diplomats, 11, 72
Direct Action Committee, 273
disarmament, 12, 14, 16, 20, 25, 26, 34, 36, 48, 55, 71–72, 84, 85, 89, 100, 128–29, 132, 135–36, 154–62, 167, 173–76, 184–86, 197, 210, 217, 223, 236, 242, 251–61, 274, 287, 302, 307, 322, 324, 327, 331, 340–45, 382–87
disaster, 74, 291; relief, 149, 175
discernment, xiii, 99, 205, 217, 241, 243, 247, 308; communal, 206, 216, 246
disciples, 20, 199; discipleship, 32, 242
discourse, 76, 85–86, 274; international, 76; online, 276; public, 352; scholarly, 355
disobedience, 124, 127, 242, 299; Disobey Illegal Nuclear Strike Orders, 127
disproportionate force, 52, 83, 88, 159
disputed areas, 108, 116, 181
divestment, 217, 316
doctrines, 269, 351; of deterrence, 82, 182; disarmament intervention, 155; *Doctrine sociale*, 201; military, 11, 76; Roman Catholic, 31; strategic, 34, 307
Dominicans, Grand Rapids, 94, 96
Donnelly, Elizabeth A., 358
Doomsday Machine, 196, 201, 302
Day, Dorothy, 12, 91, 93, 96, 98–100; Dorothy Day Catholic Worker, 93
Drell, Sidney D., 158, 167–68, 200
Dresden, 212, 225
drones, 107, 314
Duke University, 126; Duke Divinity School, 44
Dunlap, Charlie, 126

Durand, Jean-Dominique, 357
Dworkin, Gerald, 201
Dwyer, Anabel, 95

Earth, 110, 190; salt of the, 351
East-West conflict, 129; context, 134
ecclesia discens vs. *docens*, 305
ecclesial movements, 26; new, 354
ecology, ecological, 10, 19, 27, 39, 60–66, 198, 215–16, 247, 339, 386; ecocide, 206, 215
economy, 166, 235, 315, 347; political, 60
ecosystems, 35, 61, 212, 215–16; biological, 64
education, 251, 255, 260, 288, pastoral, 356; professional military, 293; public, 72, 177, 234; educators, 3, 20, 227, 305
Edwards, Kathryn A., 261
Edwards-Levy, Ariel, 235
Efron, Sonni, 261
Egeland, Kjølv, 57
Eichstaedt, Peter H., 218
Einstein, Albert, 207, 321
Eisenhower, Dwight D., 209–10, 218
electricity, 176; electronic communications, 134
elimination of nuclear weapons, of war, 2, 20, 43, 87, 134, 156, 165, 168, 303, 383
Ellsberg, Daniel, 196–97, 201
Ellul, Jacques, 207, 269–70, 277
El Salvador, 190
energy, nuclear, 120, 212
engineers, 24, 211, 323–24, 336
Eniwetok Pacific testing zone, 92
environment, natural, 60–63, 177–78, 187, 212, 215, 218, 257–58, 330; nuclear, 302, 307
equality, 32, 322; racial, 329
equilibrium, 65, 198; moral, 10, 60; stable, 197

Erikson, Erik, 242, 246
error, 40, 55, 111, 223, 233, 289, 295, 320, 339
escalation, 33, 36, 39, 57, 111, 255, 295; nuclear, 33, 289; unintentional, 287
ethics, xiii, 5, 16–17, 22–28, 52–64, 115, 127, 153–79, 191, 198, 200–217, 232, 235, 238–39 240–45, 265, 280–82, 287–88, 290–96, 316, 330–37, 340–66, 358, 381–87; bioethics, 385; peace, 63, 169; Roman Catholic, 31, 60, 66, 154, 196, 244
Eucharist, 182, 246
Europe, 11, 14, 70–71, 129, 148–49, 164, 383–84; European, 106, 135, 174, 213, 322–27, 356, 383
Evangelii gaudium, 6, 19, 27, 246, 312–13
evil, 17, 20, 35, 85, 183–88, 196, 231–38, 240, 244, 300, 308–13, 322
examen, 216
existential, 37, 154, 158, 168, 241; ecosystems, 65; peril, 100

Faber, Saint Peter (Pierre Favre), 238, 244
Facebook, 265, 276
Factor, Regis, 38, 43
Fahey, Joseph J., 18–19, 220–28, 383
faith communities, 86, 315–16, 383; formation, 356; interfaith statement, 89; in international affairs, 382; leaders, 86, 276; traditions, 329
fallout, 11, 83, 214, 264; shelters, 252
Falls, Thomas B., 313
FARC, 279
Fasching, Darrell J., 208, 217, 219
Feaver, Peter, 127
Fiat iustitia, ruat caelum, 240
Fikenscher, Sven-Eric, 337
Finn, Daniel R., 66
Finnis, John, 57, 183–85, 191–92, 201, 245
first strike, nuclear, 48–49, 52, 327, 310

first use of nuclear weapons, 108, 115, 259
Fisher, Anthony, 236
fission, 128, 263
Focolare, 354
Folds, Jay, 290
Fonzone, Christopher, 127
Ford, John C., 188, 192
foreign policy, 38, 74, 245, 332, 385
Forest, Jim, 200
France, 71, 105–6, 108, 128, 130, 145, 319–20, 322, 334
Francis of Assisi, xiii, 221, 316, 329
Francis, Pope. *See under* Pope
Frankena, William K., 245
fraternity, 243, 330
Freedman, Lawrence, 169
freedom, interior, 304; religious, 382, 386; spiritual, 243; of conscience, 300
Futter, Andrew, 163, 170

G8, 174, 178
Gaddis, John Lewis, 55, 115, 191
Gaetan, Victor, xiii
Gagner la paix, 55–56, 196, 201
Gahlaut, Seema, 337
Gandhi, Mohandas (Mahatma), 38, 91, 238, 246
Ganss, George E., 244
Gates, Robert M., 290
Gaudium et spes, xiv, 27–28, 31, 33, 36, 38, 191–92, 222, 247, 310–13
Gauthier, David, 51, 57
Geach, Mary, 192
general disarmament, 128–29, 131, 133–35, 163
General Dynamics Electric Boat, 100
General Electric, 211
Geneva, xiii, 2, 55, 83, 87–89, 136, 141, 333; Conventions, 325, 327; Diplomatic Corps, 87; P-papers, 333; Protocol, 319
genocide, 172, 206, 215, 316

Gensuikyo, 83
geopolitical landscape, altered, 65; strategy, 212, 274; geopolitics, contemporary, 40, 302
Georgetown University, 275, 318, 382–83, 386–87; Law Center, 125, 384
Germany, 71, 91, 138, 143, 188, 206–7, 265, 312, 381
Giangravè, Claire, 43
Giardina, Tim, 291
Gilbert OP, Carol, 96, 99
Gillis Long Poverty Law Center, 95
Gilson, Etienne, 6, 28
Girard, René, 207
Glaser, Charles L., 167–68
glasnost, 277
global agenda, xiii, 73, 174, 178, 236, 258, 334, 340–46, 352–53; common good, 26, 28, 234, 338–39, 358, 381; community, 15, 147, 149; governance, 227, 340; issues, 170, 179, 385; justice, 381; militarism, 274; problems, addressing, 1, 305; security, 75, 134, 165, 273, 278
Global Security Institute, 260
God Delusion, The, 272, 277
Gods of Metal Plowshares, 94
Goodby, James, 12–13, 70, 105–18, 158, 162, 167–69, 200, 245, 247, 326, 383
Goodpaster, Andrew J., 11, 74
Gopin, Ruth, xv
Gorbachev, Mikhail, 70, 113, 276
Gormally, Luke, 192
gradations of responsibility based on complicity, 342, 346
Graham, Thomas, Jr., 70
Granoff, Jonathan, 336
grassroots, 21, 353–55
Gremillion, Joseph, 245, 313
Griffin, Taylor, 127
Grimsrud, Ted, 42, 45
Grisez, Germain, 57, 183, 191, 201
Groves, Leslie, 207

growth, moral, 99, 239, 242, 305
guilt, 18–19; guilty of cooperation, 224–25; guilty of evil, 224; guilty verdict, 95
Gula, Richard, 205, 217
Guterres, António, 258
Gustafson, James M., 244

Hague, 141, 319, 337
Haiti, 382
Hall, Daniel, 11, 76–89, 383
Halton, Thomas P., 313
Handel, Cheryl, 358
Hanford Reservation, 178, 212
Harbaugh, Erin, 145
Hard Ground, 192
Harrell, Eben, 28
Harvard University, 127, 384, 386
Harvest of Justice is Sown in Peace, 17, 45, 167, 169, 307, 311, 313
Hasegawa, Tsuyoshi, 100
Hauerwas, Stanley, 38, 43–44
Hayashi, Nobuo, 86, 89
hazards, 117; nuclear, 23, 295
H-Bomb Sufferers Organization, 79
Hehir, Bryan, 33, 36, 158, 167–68, 357
Heinrichs, Rebeccah, 127
Hennemeyer, Robert T., 357
Hennessy, Martha, 96, 100, 200
Hering, Harold L., 292–93
Hersh, Seymour, 245
Hey, Nigel, 261
Heyer, Kristin E., 358
Hibakusha, 76, 78–88, 193
Himes, Kenneth, 169
Hiroshima, 12, 77, 88, 90, 117, 189, 191–94, 217, 219, 314, 317, 320, 328; Hiroshima and Nagasaki, 76, 78–82, 84, 86–88, 115, 187–89, 193, 212, 263–64
Hollenbach, David, 41–45, 358
Hollis, Duncan B., 126
Holloway, David, 20–21, 263–68, 384
Holtom, Gerald, 273

Holy See, 2, 3, 55, 57–59, 132, 153, 159, 170, 200, 301, 303, 323, 358, 382
Holy Spirit, 6, 94, 206, 239
Honeywell Corporation, 25, 335–37
Hoover Institution, 28, 71, 312, 383
Hope, Claire, 261
Hopkins, Phil, 269, 277
Hsiao, James, 95
Hudson OP, Jackie, 96
Humanae vitae, 188
humanitarian, 11, 40, 55, 59, 63, 76, 80–82, 84–89, 97, 116, 156, 174, 198, 222, 320, 329, 333, 339, 383; Humanitarian Consequences Movement, 10, 19, 301, 303
human rights, 122, 180, 186, 188, 316, 329, 339–41, 344, 381, 385
Hyten, General John, 125, 231, 234, 297

ICAN. *See* International Campaign to Abolish Nuclear Weapons
ICRC. *See* International Committee of the Red Cross
Ideh, Julie, 179
Ignatius of Loyola, Saint, 238, 244–45
illegal orders, 23, 124–25, 127, 231, 236, 297–300, 308, 311; illegality of nuclear weapons, 81, 96, 97, 316
immigration, 235, 352
immorality, 19, 50, 154, 186, 188, 224–25, 229, 232, 299, 339
implementation, 49, 132, 291, 297, 340, 384
implications, 80, 135, 153, 200, 210, 223, 325
India, 106, 108–9, 112, 125, 128, 131, 260, 262, 320, 334; and China, 108; and Pakistan, 107–8, 131, 174, 264, 328, 333
Indigenous, 83, 88, 212–18, 216
indiscriminate warfare, 17, 182, 188, 299–300, 302
inspections, 114, 146, 165

Index 367

Institute for Policy Research and Catholic Studies, 381
integral, disarmament, 26, 38–39, 44, 56–57, 63–66, 112–13, 115–17, 164, 263–68, 326–27, 332–33, 338–39, 341–47; ecology, 10, 59–64, 66, human development, xv, 39, 44, 330, 339, 386
Intermediate-Range Nuclear Forces Treaty, 114, 136, 144, 149, 178, 186, 195
International Atomic Energy Agency, 73, 130, 134, 154, 165
International Campaign to Abolish Nuclear Weapons (ICAN), 81, 84, 260, 353, 355, 357–58
International Committee of the Red Cross (ICRC), 26, 80–81, 326–27
International Court, 85, 89, 121, 124, 126
International Federation of Catholic Universities, 354
International Fellowship of Reconciliation, 92
international humanitarian law, 13, 80–81, 85, 127, 156, 222, 311
international law, 80, 85, 89, 96, 123–24, 126, 139, 141, 163, 227, 297, 300, 319, 323, 325–26, 384; peace and security, 132–33, 139, 156
International Peace Studies, 382–86
International Red Cross, 80–81, 88
international security, 3, 55, 82, 105, 145, 169, 263, 266, 298, 383
International Theological Commission, 28, 305, 312
intersectionality, 257–58
Iran, 108, 147–48, 167, 195, 382
Iraq, xi, 148, 155–56, 164, 167, 175, 288, 291
Ireland, 95, 265, 357, 384
Islam, xi, xiii, 383, 386
Israel, 106, 108, 117, 125, 128, 131, 185, 245, 262, 265, 320, 324, 382

Italy, 91, 138, 143, 265, 277
ius gentium, 305

Japan, 17, 79, 81, 83, 86–87, 92, 100, 106, 115, 188, 190, 194, 229, 235, 326
Jardine, Roger, 337
Jesuits (Society of Jesus), 6, 94, 188, 239, 244–45, 354, 382
Jesus Christ, 6–7, 20, 44, 91, 94, 199, 220, 226, 242, 246, 300, 318, 351; Christendom, 313
Jinping, Xi, 109
Joan of Arc, 91, 319
John Paul II. *See under* Pope
John XXIII. *See under* Pope
Johnston, Douglas M., 357
Johnston, Laurie, 44
Joint Chiefs of Staff, 137, 311–12
Jolly, Richard, 357
Jonah House, 92
Jonas, David S., 126
Jones, Scott A., 337
Jong-un, Kim, 110
Jonsen, Albert R., 244
Joseph, Saint, 316, 327
Jost, John T., 277
judgments, 22, 33, 41, 65, 94, 124, 155, 183–84, 298, 306–8, 331
Junod, Marcel, 77
jurors, 95, 97; jury nullification, 12, 96
jus in bello, 33–34, 40–41, 44
Justenhoven, Heinz-Gerhard, 169, 381
justice, economic, 347, 385–87; global, 247; justice studies, 227, 381; labor, 352; postconflict, 16; social, 99, 272–73, 276, 351, 387
justification, 51, 53–54, 232, 240, 257
Justin, Saint, 313
just peace, 44, 62, 172
just war, 38–39, 42–45, 381

Kahn, Herman, 245
Kampelman, Max, 28, 71, 166, 169
Kanke, Victor, 336

Karl, Kristyn, 253, 261
Kashmir, 108, 386
Kaurin, Pauline Shanks, 127
Kavanagh, Jennifer, 261
Kaveny, Cathleen, 28, 194, 198, 200, 236
Kavka, Gregory, 49, 51–52, 56, 201
Kawada, Kazuko, 78
Kazakhstan, 174, 336
Kehler, Robert, 297–98
Kellenberger, Jakob, 87
Kellogg-Briand Pact, 14
Kelly SJ, Steve, 93, 98, 100–101
Kennedy, John F., 1–2, 14, 27, 116, 118, 241, 246, 265–66, 294, 318, 321
Kennedy, Robert F., 118, 294
Kenny, Anthony, 200
Kershner, Isabel, 117
Khan, A. Q., 15, 143
Khariton, Yulii, 266
Khrushchev, Nikita, 1
Kim, Ji Eun, 192
King, Martin Luther, Jr., 91, 238
Kingdom, 184, 192, 242, 309; Kingdom of God, 8, 243
Kings Bay Plowshares, 12, 96, 101
Kissinger, Henry A., 8, 70, 74, 162, 169, 191, 272, 274, 277, 304, 312, 347
Knopf, Jeffrey W., 347
knowledge, 11, 22, 141, 252, 254, 290; workers, 28, 169
Koch, Susan J., 145
Koplow, David A., 13, 119–27, 384
Korb, Lawrence J., 15, 146–52, 384
Korea (South or North), 25, 74, 106, 162, 175, 265, 274, 293
Kreider, Alan, 313
Krepon, Michael, 171
Kristensen, Hans M., 117, 336
Kroc Institute for International Peace Studies, 382–84, 385–86
Krulwich, Robert, 310
Kultgen, John, 347
Kuptsov, Ilya, 336
Kwan, Judy, 95

Labour Party, 24, 328, 384
LaDuke, Winona, 44, 213, 218
Laffin, Arthur (Art), 99–100
LaForge, John, 100
Laggner, Benno, 87
Lammy, David, 24, 328–33, 384
Lash, Nicholas, 6, 27, 305, 312
László, Ervin, 208, 215, 218
Latiff, Robert H., 170
Laudato sì, 59–66, 164, 170, 215, 219, 230, 234, 236
launches, accidental, 73, 292, 330; launch order, 292; launch system, 230
law, 13, 25, 95, 119, 122, 124, 126, 143, 178, 220, 227, 325, 384–85; of armed conflict, 127, 300, 311; enforcement, 38, 46, 143–44; of nations, 222, 305
Lawyers Committee on Nuclear Policy, 95
Lay Catholic Movements, 9, 26, 349; laypeople, 12, 221
League of Nations, 271
Lederach, John Paul, 21–22, 26, 28, 191, 278–86, 352–54, 357, 384
Lee, Patrick J., 94, 100
legalism, 6; moral, 239
legality, 96, 121, 126, 137
legally binding instrument, 2, 87–89, 237, 333
legal obligations, 120, 123, 125; legal protections, 299, 311
legislation, 178, 259; legislators, 18, 22, 24
legitimacy, 48–49, 70, 305, 354; in principle of deterrence, 17
legitimate form, 316; legitimate use, 41
Leipold, Andrew D., 101
Lenten Desert Experience, 93
Leroy, David, 213
Lester, Karina, 83, 88
lethal force, 45
Lettow, Paul, 71, 74
Lewis, Tom, 43, 90, 98–99

Liber pastoralis, 244
libido dominandi, 230
Libya, 143, 156
Liffey, Kevin, 89
Lieber, Keir, 167, 192
Linacre Centre, 236
Lind, Jennifer, 192
Linhart, Michael, 88
Little Boy, 90
Livermore, Lawrence, National Laboratory, 243
Lockheed Martin, 314, 317
Lord, Miles, 95
Los Alamos Laboratory, 207, 213, 217, 266
love, 6, 220, 246; love of God and neighbor, 238, 245, 310
Love, Maryann Cusimano, 162, 170, 172–79, 186, 192, 236–37, 385
Love, Richard A., 14, 136–45, 270, 277, 385
Loyola University New Orleans, 95
LSD, 291, 296
Lugar, Richard, 174, 295
Luke, Gospel, 246, 304
Luther, Martin, 239
Luzárraga, Ramón, 25, 334–37, 385
Lytle, Ashley, 253, 261

Magill, Gerard, 231, 236
magis, 7, 239, 247
magisterium, 37, 41, 48, 305
Magna Carta, 178
Mahoney, John, 244
Makhijani, Arjun, 210–11, 214, 218–19
Malaysia, 143, 325
Malygina, Anastasia, 337
Manhattan College, 381, 383
Manhattan Project, 206–9, 211, 214
manufacture of nuclear weapons, 25, 131, 315, 334–35, 337
man who saved the world. *See* Petrov, Stanislav, Lt. Col.
Marbury v. Madison, 126

Marquette University, 385
Marshall, Katherine, xvi
Marty, Justin, 306
Maryknoll Seminary, 383
Maslennikov, Ivan, 294
massacres, 185, 196, 321
mass destruction, 35, 95, 128, 174, 262, 316; defined weapons of, 319, 325; manufacturers, 316; use of weapons of, 298, 308
material conditions, 270–71; creation, 212
materialism, 270
materials, constituent, 130; educational, 256; fissile, 130, 154, 162, 176, 206, 210; of mass destruction, 174; radioactive, 258, 320; toxic, 211
Matthew, Gospel, 199, 306, 351
Maurin, Peter, 93
May, Rollo, 246
McDevitt, Robert L. and Catherine H., 387
McDonald, John, 357
McElroy, Cardinal Robert M., 193, 341, 346
McGowan Center for Ethics and Social Responsibility, 386
McLaughlin, John, 70
McMahan, Jeff, 201
McNamara, Robert, 56, 71–74, 162, 169, 266
medicine, 22; consequences of Hiroshima and Nagasaki, 264; interventions, 177; nuclear, 120; and law, 22
memes, 21, 269, 271–77, 276; memeplexes, 271–76; original, 273
Mennonites, 21, 92, 221
Merton, Thomas, 12, 91, 101, 193, 199
Mexico, 59, 81, 87–88, 382
Micah, prophet, 90
microproportionality, 44
Middle East, 108, 116, 131, 134, 137, 325, 382; Christians, 382

military action, xii, 4, 9, 15, 22, 52–53, 71, 74, 126, 130, 150, 153, 155–56, 170, 216, 226, 233, 287–88, 291, 294, 299–309, 311–19, 325, 332; commanders, 11, 25, 71, 91, 184, 227, 287–88; doctrine, 82–83, 108, 313; ethics, 127, 311, 386; forces, 52, 124, 220, 223, 227, 307, 319; illegal orders, 126–27; jurisprudence, 124, 127, 227, 300; spending, 198, 225; structures, 124, 300; targets, 33, 52–54, 184
millennials, 252, 261, 275
Miller, Jerry, 336
ministers, defense, xiii, 19, 71, 97, 190, 220, 308, 335; foreign, 3
miscalculation, 105, 108, 114, 265, 293
Mische, George, 100
missile defenses, 56, 70, 114, 148–49, 154, 157–58, 160, 163, 165–66, 168; personnel, xi, 22–23, 297
missiles, 14, 108, 110–11, 136–37, 178, 206, 224, 252, 278, 290–91, 293–94, 314, 318, 323
mobilization, 27, 92, 172, 271; broad-based political, 230; popular, 343, 351, 356
Monan, Donald, 381
Montgomery RSCJ, Anne, 100
morality, moral, 5, 10, 60–63, 157, 183, 191–92, 200–201, 231, 328–29, 331, 333, absolutes, 187; argument, xii, xiii, 5–7, 18, 34, 36, 41, 49, 55, 60–66, 72, 86, 111–12, 154–56, 166, 194–95, 206, 230–40, 299–300, 305–11, 322–29, 339–41, 386; assessment of deterrence, 34, 56, 159, 168; calculus, 32, 34, 155, 167, 306; compass, 23, 232, 236, 344, 346; ecology, 8, 9, 10, 20, 49, 59–66, 160, 187–88, 249, 323; hazards, 164, 217, 214, 294–95; imagination, 21, 28, 279, 281; imperative, 53, 55, 194, 200, 269, 344, 347; judgments, 299, 41; justification, 8, 10, 34, 36, 41, 301, 305; law, 190, 305; life, 17, 31, 32, 199, 239, 244–45; limits, 32, 56–57, 184, 194, 240; norms, 183, 187–88, 239; of nuclear deterrence, 54, 166, 197, 201, 235; of nuclear war, 43, 167, 192, 216; quandaries, 156, 232; reasoning, 10, 38, 117, 244, 269, 277; teaching, 18, 59, 183, 238, 356; theology, 239, 381; theories, 8, 60–65, 197; vision, 153, 162, 329, 344
Morita, Setsuko, 78
Moseley, Michael, 290
Mosher, Dave, 333
Mosul University, 175
motu proprios, 4
Mozley, Robert F., 337
MSNBC, 91
Mulligan, Stephen P., 126
multilateralism, 137, 143, 328, 332, 358, 383
murder, 31, 33, 42, 182, 184, 188, 195; mass, 42, 316; normalizing, 187
Murogov, Viktor, 336
Murray SJ, John Courtney, 31, 33–34, 36, 42, 45, 155, 167, 230, 235

Nagasaki, xiv, 76, 78–87, 115, 187–89, 193–94, 212, 263–64. *See also* Hiroshima
Nagle, Angela, 274, 277
Nagler, Jonathan, 277
Nakamitsu, Izumi, 84, 89
National Catholic Reporter, 44, 100, 312
National Defense University, 385
National Education Association, 261
National Environmental Protection Act, 178
nationalism, 190, 229, 341
National Press Club, 303, 312
National Rifle Association, 275
national security, 4, 35, 70, 74, 137, 241, 304, 331; National Security Council, 137
nation-states, 227, 232, 234, 274, 318

Native Americans, 176, 212–14, 218, 221; Mescalero Apache Indian Reservation, 213; Navajos, 212–13
NATO (North Atlantic Treaty Organization), 11, 13, 25, 37, 72, 106, 108, 128–29, 148, 383
natural law, 5, 187, 238, 245, 298
Nayarit conference, 81–82, 87–88
Nazis, 124, 188, 207, 221, 271
Nebel, Mathias, xiii, 55, 200, 235
negotiation, 16, 20, 70, 79, 88–89, 113–14, 116, 121, 123, 126, 129, 132, 167, 169, 174, 232–34, 352, 384
Nepstad, Sharon Erickson, 100
Netherlands, 91, 138, 265, 322
Nevada, 214, 219; Nevada Desert Experience, 93; Test Site, 93, 213–14
New Delhi, India, 107, 109
New Mexico, 288, 291
new world order, 161, 233, 236
Newman, Saint John Henry, 3, 184
NGO (nongovernmental organization), 26, 80–81, 63, 254, 261, 332, 352, 354
Nicolas, Ashley, 127
Nielsen, Jenny, 337
Nihon Hidankyo, 79, 83, 87, 88
Nikolchina, Miglena, 268
Nitze, Paul H., 11, 28, 72, 74
Nixon, Richard, 148, 273, 292
Njølstad, Olav, 167
Nobel Peace Prize, 3, 38, 43, 84, 89, 99, 181, 210, 305, 315, 353, 358, 387
noncombatants, 33, 35, 42, 54, 231, 233, 298, 311
nongovernmental organization. *See* NGO
nonnuclear states/forces, 84, 107, 126, 134, 147, 175, 245, 302, 332; weapons, 13, 108, 134
nonproliferation, 34, 80, 120, 125–26, 132–37, 143–44, 154, 159, 179, 261, 332–33, 341, 345, 347, 383–84; Non-Proliferation Treaty (*see* NPT)

nonviolence, 16, 18, 32, 35, 38, 41, 43–45, 97–99, 221, 234, 236, 300, 307, 313
Norris, Robert S., 117, 336
North Atlantic Treaty Organization. *See* NATO
North Carolina, 256, 288
North Dakota, 289–91
Northeast Asia, 116, 134, 195
Northern Ireland, 38, 190, 382
North Korea, 13–14, 105–7, 110, 120, 123, 125, 131, 137, 147–48, 195, 200, 252, 320, 325, 334
Northrop Grumman, 314, 317
Norway, 59, 71, 81, 89
NPT (Non-Proliferation Treaty), 13–14, 80–82, 86, 89, 105–6, 119–20, 123–24, 130–33, 147, 175–76, 262, 323–24; Article VI, 2, 13, 119–23, 125–26, 130, 132–33, 262; Article VIII, 126
NTI (Nuclear Threat Initiative), 127, 192, 260, 327
Nuclear Age Peace Foundation, 74, 260–61
nuclear-armed airplane, 294; missiles, 111, 323; torpedo, 297, 324
nuclear arms race, 107, 111, 116, 121, 129–30, 225, 230; arsenals, 23–24, 65, 111, 131, 288, 303; attack, 34, 52, 56, 73, 294, 298–99; blackmail, 48, 196–97; breakout, 73, 155, 163; brink, 287, 312; danger, 72–74, 165, 168, 292; issues, 2, 161, 190, 252, 254–55, 266; launch codes or "button," 235, 290, 292, 294; reductions, 72, 178
Nuclear Claims Tribunal, 176
nuclear deterrence, 11, 31–32, 46–49, 51–57, 64–69, 74, 105–7, 114–16, 170, 179–83, 185–91, 195–98, 199–201, 235, 239–42, 252, 297, 330–32; moral acceptability of, 36, 55, 159; morality of, 183, 191–92, 201; myth of, 344

nuclear disarmament, 12, 16, 19–21, 87, 153–55, 160–75, 177–79, 198–200, 253, 259–62, 269–77, 295–96, 309–10, 328–29, 331–33, 336, 338–40, 352–53, 357, 387; mutual, 44, 182, 191, 198; skeptics, 163–64
nuclear ethics, 38, 44–45, 167, 169, 172, 240–41. *See also* ethics
nuclear, exchange, 33, 41, 146, 257, 292–93; facilities, 12, 90, 99, 108, 130; forces, 17, 114, 117, 135, 149, 299, 336
Nuclear History Boot Camp, 20–21, 263–65, 267
nuclear holocaust, 215, 328. *See also* Armageddon
Nuclear Information and Resource Services, 218
nuclear materials, 24, 165, 175, 177, 296
Nuclear Modernization Programs, 148–49, 218
Nuclear Navy Plowshares, 94
Nuclear Non-Proliferation, 126, 168, 214, 309; treaty (NPT), 13–14, 88, 119–20, 147, 175–76, 262, 264, 323–24, 332, 334, 336
Nuclear Notebook, 109–10, 260
nuclear posture review, 107, 148, 191
nuclear powers, 12–15, 146, 162–65, 195, 197, 199, 331–34, 336
nuclear proliferation, 34, 167, 170, 176, 192, 195, 232, 235, 263, 287
nuclear stewards, 22–23, 287, 289, 291, 293, 295
nuclear strategy, 10, 41, 215, 240, 245, 304
nuclear taboo, 117, 166, 233
nuclear tests, 16, 83, 88, 92, 130, 264
Nuclear Threat Initiative. *See* NTI
nuclear umbrella, 85, 106
nuclear war, xii, 8–9, 21–22, 34, 37, 41, 59, 111, 117, 178, 195, 199, 201, 223, 240–41, 298, 302, 306, 321, 328, 333

nuclear warheads, 73, 107–8, 109–10, 289, 291, 323–24, 328
nuclear waste, 76, 81, 210–11, 213, 218
nuclear winter, 278
nuclear zero, 168, 170, 382
Nunn, Sam, 8, 11, 70, 74, 162, 169, 174, 191, 272, 274, 277, 295, 304, 312; Nunn-Lugar program, 383
Nuremberg tribunals, 96, 124, 298, 310–11
Nussbaum, Martha C., 347
Nuti, Leopoldo, 264
Nye, Joseph S., 357

Oak Ridge, Tennessee, 12, 90, 178, 212
Obama, Barack, 73, 112–13, 117, 146–48, 189–92, 327
O'Brien, William, 42
O'Connell, Gerard, 200, 358
O'Connor, John, 223
Octogesima adveniens, xiv, 27, 246–47, 313
Oka, Yoshie, 79
Oppenheimer, J. Robert, 207–8, 217; memorial lecture, 266
Orange is the New Black, 96
orders (military, launch), 38, 96, 124–27, 208, 228, 266, 292, 298, 310, 319, 341, 345
Orwell, George, 269
Oslo, Norway, 81, 89, 170
Oslo Peace Research Institute, 170
O'Sullivan, James P., 25–26, 338–50, 385
Oughourlian, Jean-Michel, 207, 217
Outrider Foundation, 255, 257, 260–61

Pabeliña, Karla Mae G., 347
Pacem in terris, 1–2, 27, 60, 63, 91, 132, 135, 160–61, 163, 169–71, 220, 312–13, 347
pacifism, 8–10, 32, 38, 41–45, 63, 92, 220, 299, 318, 332, 381
Pakistan, 14–15, 106–9, 125, 128, 131, 260, 262, 264–65, 267, 320, 333–34

papacy, xii, xiii–xiv, 4, 43, 59, 153, 303, 353; condemnation of deterrence, 66, 168, 191
parliament (UK), 24, 329, 333, 384; parliamentarians, 309, 328, 331–32
pastoral care, xii, 6, 19–20, 97, 182, 238–39, 228, 238, 241–44, 305, 308; pastoral constitution, xiv, 27, 36, 150, 188, 191–92, 245; letter, xiv, 8–9, 17, 25, 33, 36–38, 298–99, 321–22
Patrick, Stewart, 236
PAX (Netherlands), 260, 344, 387
Pax Christi, 26, 199, 309, 355; Pax Christi International, 38, 355; Pax Christi USA, 18, 383
Pax Romana, 26, 309
Payne, Keith B., 57, 168
peace, 2–3, 16, 21, 55, 63, 72, 97, 100, 131–33, 139, 155–56, 172–73, 176, 178, 179, 181, 183, 191, 195, 200, 217, 234, 240, 247, 271–73, 322, 384; medieval, 221; memorial, 167, 199, 317, 326; message, 150, 236, 313, 355; movements, 11, 99, 221; of a sort, 34, 36, 161, 164; studies, 163, 381, 383
Peace Research Institute, Oslo, 386
peacebuilding, 16–17, 39, 63, 99, 153, 159, 161, 169, 172, 179–88, 180–91, 281, 312, 352, 354, 381, 385–86
peacekeeping, 92, 99, 385
peacemaking, 21, 227, 242, 306, 308, 357, 381
Pearl Harbor, 115
Pecorario, Alessio, xv
Pelopidas, Benoit, 170
Pentagon, 93; Pentagon Papers, 196
perestroika, 277
Perry, William J., 8, 70, 74, 162–71, 191, 272, 274, 277, 304, 312
Pershing Plowshares, 94
Petrov, Stanislav, Lt. Col., 292–93, 297
Pew Research Center, 189

Pfeil, Margaret R., 18, 205–19, 385
philosophy, 192, 201, 383, 386; deterrence, 10, 47–57, 235, 245; moral, 385
Philpott, Daniel, 16–17, 28, 179, 180–92, 357, 386
Pidd, Helen, 333
Pifer, Steven, 162, 169–70
Platte, Ardeth, 99
plowshares, 12, 28, 90–101, 193, 335, 337, 355, 387; Ploughshares (UK), 306
pluralism, 5, 62, 340, 383
plutonium, 128, 174, 212
Pogge, Thomas, 346
Poland, 71, 138, 145, 148–49, 265
Polanyi, Michael, 246
Pontifical, 26, 38, 59, 255, 269, 353
Pontificio Collegio Urbano, 269
Pooley, Bridget, 277
Pope, 165, 312; Benedict XV, 182; Benedict XVI, 26, 159, 329, 333; Francis, xi–xiii, 1–4, 6–7, 10, 12, 27, 39–44, 57, 59–64, 66, 111–12, 115–17, 135, 161, 167, 169, 181–83, 181, 193, 198, 205, 234–46, 266–68, 305–6, 309, 315, 326–27, 332–33, 358; Francis, condemnation of nuclear weapons, xii–xiii, 3, 9–10, 17, 20–26, 39, 41, 60, 133, 158, 242–43, 263, 269, 303, 306–7, 323; St. Gregory the Great, 238, 244; St. John XXIII, xii, 1, 27, 63, 112, 117, 132–35, 169–70, 221, 227, 245, 303, 312–13, 321–22, 343, 347; St. John Paul II, 5, 27, 36, 159, 168–69, 182, 191–93, 195, 200, 223, 229–30, 235–36, 300, 311, 322; St. Paul VI, xiv, 5–6, 27, 62, 239, 243, 246, 305, 321, 326; Urban VIII, 269
Populorum progressio, 62
possession, 31, 85, 111, 125, 155, 199, 205, 215–16, 232, 314, 319–20, 332, 335–36
poverty, 15, 39, 63, 183, 198, 213, 330, 339

Powers, Gerard F., xvi, 15, 44, 65–66, 153–71, 179, 191, 195, 198–99, 201, 235, 386
prayer, 90, 94–95, 234, 243, 306; praise, 45, 221, 277, 353
Press, Daryl G., 167
Preston, Andrew, 277
presumption, 32, 44, 125, 172, 297
principle, 1, 5, 10, 14, 23, 45, 60, 91, 133, 138, 156, 222, 238, 312, 322; of cooperation, 231–32; of dignity, 329; of discrimination, 184, 311, 322; of discrimination and noncombatant immunity, 311; of double effect, 53, 236
prison, 91, 93, 95, 97–99
privilege, 32, 86, 156, 214, 343; white, 97, 99–100
profitability, 97, 210, 314–15, 316–17; profiteering, 275, 316
progress of souls, 245, 238–39
prohibition of nuclear weapons, xi, 10–11, 13, 81–82, 84, 121, 236–37, 387; chemical weapons, 134
proliferation, 138–40, 142–45, 139, 165, 174, 252, 296
Proliferation Security Initiative. *See* PSI
propaganda, 21, 84, 269–72, 269, 271, 274, 276–77
propagation, 3, 258, 269, 276
prophecy, 17, 28, 193–94, 197, 199, 200, 282, 355, 358
proportionality, 52, 54, 183
protestants, 91, 244
protesters, 93, 335, 336, 347
provisions, constitutional, 13; humane, 222; legal, 299, 313
provocation, 109, 279
Prusak, Bernard, 17, 193–204, 386
PSI (Proliferation Security Initiative), 14, 136–45, 295
psychology, 66, 173, 253
Pugwash Conferences on Science and World Affairs, 74

punishment, 48, 65, 98, 177, 220, 300
Putin, Vladimir, 136, 146, 195

Qadhafi, Muammar, 143
Quadragesimo anno, 60
Quakers, 92, 221
Quigley, Bill, 95
Quinlan, Michael, 53, 57

racism, 218
radiation, 77, 82, 212; exposure, 35, 176, 213, 214
Radio Free Europe, 384
raising consciousness, 21
Ramsbotham, David John, 330
Ramsey, Paul, 52–54, 57, 201
RAND Corporation, 252, 261
Rasmussen, Lewis, 357
rationality, 9, 52, 57, 193, 206, 212, 215, 241, 310
Ratz, Leon, 327
readiness, 35, 50, 56, 86, 111, 290, 305
Reagan, Ronald W., 15, 28, 70–71, 74, 157, 276; Reagan-Gorbachev era, 70, 74, 113
realism, realists, 43, 69–70, 161, 162, 168, 170, 234, 332; realities, 6, 8, 126, 207, 241, 301–2, 309, 339, 344, 356
reason, reasoning, 19, 39, 53–54, 65, 217
recommendations, 72, 93, 267, 299, 331
reconciliation, 62, 177, 386
recourse, 16, 32, 222, 283
Red Crescent, 80–81, 88
reductions, 72–73, 110, 112, 114, 117, 126, 167, 175, 278, 324
regimes, 35, 45, 132, 138, 156, 162, 341, 345,
Reichberg, Gregory M., xiii, 10, 47–58, 170, 196–97, 200–201, 230, 235, 245, 386
Reid, Charles, 36
Reif, Kingston, 210, 218
Reinhold, Steven, 126
Reiss, Mitchell, 337

relations, bilateral, 16, 174–75; cooperative, 73; ethical, 64; hostile, 110; interstate, 12, 49, 107
religion, 66, 97, 173, 179, 337, 381, 383; education, 5; and international affairs, 28, 194, 200, 306, 357, 383–84; and peace, 260, 352; and war, 277, 357
renewal, 8, 15, 1, 25, 147, 187, 236, 310, 329, 335–36
Rerum novarum, 60, 311
Rescher, Nicholas, 245
resistance, 23, 66, 100, 207, 238, 240, 243, 300, 341; civil, 96; to illegal orders, 23, 222, 300
responsibility, 1, 3, 124, 164, 243, 290, 296, 305, 308, 338–43, 347; for evil, 232; military leadership, 299; responsible actors, 9, 22, 228, 285
ressourcement, 8
Reykjavik, 69–71, 74
Riccardi, Andrea, 357
Rice SHCJ, Megan, 12, 28, 91, 99–100, 387
Riegle, Rosalie, 100–101
rights, 26, 120, 140, 154, 165, 167, 194, 221, 339–40, 342–43, 346
risk, 35, 57, 108, 114, 190, 206, 213–14, 260, 287, 292, 302–3, 307, 316
rivalries, 16, 133, 264, 276, 301, 383
Roberts, Brad, 167, 169
Robledo, Juan Manuel Gomez, 88
robotics, 170
Rocard, Michel, 71
Rocky Flats, 212
Rogers, Mark, 179
Rogoff, Martin A., 126
Romero, Saint Óscar, 12, 91
Rose, Brian, 327
Rotblat, Joseph, 207–9, 217
Rousselot, Pierre, 246
Roy, Maurice, 245, 313
RSCJ (Society of the Sacred Heart), 94, 96, 99–100

rule of law, 13, 119, 125, 180; international, 85
Russia, 13–14, 92, 105–8, 111–14, 116–17, 120–22, 135–36, 146–47, 176–78, 181, 185–86, 266, 295, 334; and China, 114; Federation, 14–15, 126, 128–29, 149, 186, 320, 383; Moscow, 73, 112–14, 129, 174, 268, 291; post-Soviet, 302; Russians, 72, 113, 148–49, 207, 268, 276, 288, 303; violations, 195. *See also* Soviet Union

Sachs, Jeffrey, 246
safety, 175, 256, 288, 291–92, 295, 335
Sagan, Scott D., 56, 170, 311, 340, 346
Saint Joseph's University, 385
Saint Patrick's Pontifical University, 387
Salopek, Jennifer J., 337
Sampson, Cynthia, 357
Samson Option, 240, 245
Sanchez, Virginia, 214, 218
sanctions, 147, 156, 165
Sane Nuclear Policy, 11, 92, 382
Sant'Egidio, 352, 354, 357
Sargent, Carole, xv, 12, 27–28, 90–101, 169–70, 312, 386
Sauer, Tom, 168
Savitsky, Valentin Grigorievitch, 294
Schaffer, Marvin, 168
Scheid, Daniel, 66
Schell, Jonathan, 74–75, 157–58, 161, 166, 168–69, 171, 215, 219
Schelling, Thomas, 55, 115
Schlosser, Eric, 179, 191, 311
Schreiter, Robert, 169, 179, 191, 386
Schultz, George P., 191
Schwartz, Stephen I., 210–11, 218–19
Scoville Jr., Herbert, 382
scripture, 8, 90, 205, 304
Seabed Treaty, 130; sea, 14, 84, 137–38, 140, 146, 176
Second Vatican Council. *See* Vatican: Vatican II
secrecy, 17, 206–7, 209, 217

secular, 315, 385; peacebuilders, 173; responses, 8; way, 112
security, 11, 23–25, 32, 40, 69, 114, 126, 143, 161, 170, 207, 252, 291–95, 314, 320, 383–84; collective, 9, 36; guards, 90, 98; homeland, 288; policy, 59, 127, 333, 382; studies, 385; threats, 129, 252, 258; UN Security Council, 134, 139, 144, 156, 319, 331
selective conscientious objection, xiv, 17, 227, 298–301, 311, 313
self-defense, 165, 298, 319
Selfish Gene, The, 272, 277
sensus fidei, 7, 28, 305
sentences, jail and prison, 94–95, 97, 120, 242
Seventh Decade, 74, 168–69, 171
Shafer, Elizabeth J., 126
Shah, Timothy Samuel, 357
SHCJ (Society of the Holy Child Jesus), 91, 94, 99–100
Sheen, Archbishop Fulton J., 187, 192
Sherwin, Martin, 264
Shield, Kathleen, 277, 358
Shultz, George P., 8, 11, 22, 28, 69–74, 113, 118, 162, 169, 272, 274, 277, 302–4, 312, 326, 347
signs of the times, 5, 195, 243, 246, 303, 306, 308–9
silence, 77, 216; corporate, 335; culpable, 133
Silo Pruning Hooks Plowshares, 94; silos, 257, 288
sin, 184, 192, 224, 239; *simul iustus et peccator* (at once justified and a sinner) 239
sisters, Catholic, xv, 12, 91, 94, 99, 316, 354
skepticism, xi, 33, 41, 164
slacktivism, 275, 277
Slaughter, Anne-Marie, 236
slavery, 161, 182, 242
Slusser, Michael, 313
Snyder, Susi, 314–17, 344, 347, 387

social change, 5, 230, 281, 355–56; cohesion, 172; democrats, 71; movements, 272, 310
Society of the Holy Child Jesus. *See* SHCJ
Society of Jesus. *See* Jesuits
Soka Gakkai International, 11, 87, 383
Sokolsky, Richard, 135
Solis, Gary D., 127
Sollicitudo rei socialis, 200
Somali-Kenyan border, 280
Sonne, Paul, 201
Sorondo, Marcelo Sánchez, 170
South Africa, 147, 175, 190, 265, 336–37
South Asia, 108–9, 116, 134, 162
South Korea. *See* Korea
Soviet Union, 1–2, 14, 49, 129–30, 146, 148, 172, 174, 183–84, 287, 292–93, 302, 383–84; Soviets, 37, 150, 207, 214, 266, 293–94, 297. *See also* Russia
space, 12, 62, 130, 157, 231, 352, 354, 356, 384; systems, 107, 314
Spadaro, Antonio, 239, 244–45
Spain, 137–38, 288
spiritual directors, xii, 19, 244; spirituality, 6, 97; spiritual writings, 244
Spiritual Exercises of Saint Ignatius of Loyola, 244, 238
stability, 55, 157, 161, 217, 385
Stalin, Joseph, 97, 100, 384
Starmer, Keir, 384
START treaties, 70; extended, 178; New START treaty, 13, 114, 136, 146–48, 175, 195
states (nations), xi, 14, 16, 40, 49, 54, 59, 97, 106, 109, 111–12, 138–39, 140–41, 143–44, 148, 156, 177, 181, 189, 233, 278, 341, 353; nuclear-armed, xii, 8, 12, 17, 86, 105, 123, 188, 301, 320, 325; party, 320, 325; rogue, 154, 163; sovereignty, 276
status quo, 138, 153, 157, 167–68, 255

Staudt, Jared, 192
Steele, David, 179
Stein, Walter, 42, 45–46, 192
Steinfels, Peter, 45, 201
stockpiles, 14, 42, 121, 214, 119
Stowe-Thurston, Abigail, 117
Strategic Air Command, 231, 297, 302–3
Strategic Arms Reduction, 186, 346
strategic (defense, deterrence, weapons), 39, 56, 126–27, 145, 148, 157, 183–85, 195, 336; studies, 56, 168, 191, 385
strike, nuclear, 254–57, 292, 294; retaliatory, 110; second, 33, 48, 114
structures, 35–36, 61, 120, 134, 158, 173, 176–78, 215, 342, 345, 353; of grace, 26, 28, 358, 381; of solidarity, 340, 345
submarines, 108, 130, 226, 288, 294, 297, 323, 328
sufferings, 300, 319, 321
suicide, 283; collective, 278, 282
Summa Theologiae, 244
superiority, 35, 159, 185; nuclear, 34, 252; superiors, 94, 124, 222
superpowers, 15, 106; nuclear, 14
survival, survivors, 35, 82, 88, 115, 189, 329; atomic bomb, 79, 81, 212
sustainability, 60, 317, 340, 358; development, 15, 25, 149, 338–42, 344–46; reconciliation, 191, 357
Swaine, Edward T., 126
Switzerland, 80, 87–88, 200, 235
symbol, 273–74, 277; symbolic strategies, 234
synod, 5, 28, 308, 312; general 333
Syria, 108, 131, 325
Syse, Henrik, 56
system, 1, 5, 20, 24, 61–62, 65, 106, 111, 114, 158, 160, 209, 211, 258, 279, 290, 301, 324, 352–53; early-warning, 293; international, 35, 130, 160; military justice, 23, 300; missile launch, 148, 230, 290, 335; of nuclear deterrence, 36, 48, 106; philosopher, 208; social, 209, 214; space warfare, 314; strategic, 34, 315, 357; view, 218; of violence, 85
Szilard, Leo, 207, 209

Taiwan, 109, 289, 291
Takemura, Hitomi, 127
Taliban, 109
Tannenwald, Nina, 115, 117
targets, 49, 53, 82, 111, 200
Taubman, Philip, 169
taxes, 98, 210, 216, 224–25, 226
Taylor, Maxwell, 266
teaching (papal, church), 3, 5, 7, 48, 181–82, 185, 225–26, 227, 229, 232, 298, 303, 305–6, 309, 353, 355; teaching profession, 227
technologies, 8, 163–64, 147, 243, 324; students, 265
tensions, 14, 23, 71, 73, 131, 149, 289, 293, 327, 341
territory, 11, 108–10, 131–32, 138, 212, 320
terror, 74, 86, 137, 181, 251, 288, 336
terrorism, 40, 111, 164, 175, 200, 252, 258, 330; nuclear, 35, 154, 162, 301, 330
Test Ban Treaty, 129
test explosions, 84, 106, 108, 111, 128, 213
testimonies, 11, 76, 84–85, 87, 96, 298
theology, theologians, 3–4, 8–10, 43, 243, 382–83, 385–86
thermonuclear weapon, 302
thought experiment, 17, 196–97
threat, 3, 23, 31, 56, 86, 116, 133, 137, 139, 154–55, 181, 185, 198, 210, 252–53, 257, 278, 295, 307, 317, 330, 383
Thurlow, Setsuko, 77, 79, 81–82, 83–85, 87–89
Tobey, Kristen, 337

378   Index

Toft, Monica Duffy, 357
Tokyo, 87, 212, 225
Tomasi, Cardinal Silvano, xv, 3
Tomonaga, Masao, 78
torture, 98, 182
Toshogu Shrine, 78
Tottenham, 24, 329–30, 384
Toulmin, Stephen, 244
Tours, Saint Martin of, 220
TPNW (Treaty on the Prohibition of Nuclear Weapons), 11, 13, 57, 76, 84–86, 88, 153, 156, 165–66, 171, 315–16
trafficking, 138, 143, 352
tranquilitas ordinis, 160
transformation, 27, 160, 191, 214, 346, 354
treaty, 3, 14, 70, 73, 83, 88, 112, 123, 126, 129, 132, 136–37, 144, 147–48, 162, 164, 174, 176, 195, 214, 233, 253, 320, 340–41
Treaty on the Prohibition of Nuclear Weapons. *See* TPNW
trident submarine, 12, 25, 94, 100, 108, 328–30, 333; Trident Nein Plowshares, 94
Trigg, Roger, 329
Truman, Harry, 74, 100, 207
Trump, Donald, 107, 110, 144, 148, 127, 178, 195, 235, 274, 277, 310
Tsuchida, Yayoi, 83
Tucker, Joshua, 277; Robert W., 200
Turkson, Cardinal Peter, xv, 3
Turner, Stansfield, 73, 75
Tylenda, Joseph N., 245

U-2 plane, 266
Uganda, 190
Ukraine, 129, 174, 265, 336
United Kingdom, 120, 128, 130, 138, 188, 320, 322; multifaith statement, 329, 333
United Nations, xi, 57–59, 105, 116, 120, 131–36, 137, 145, 227, 261, 303, 305, 319, 321–22, 326–27, 340, 346, 382–83; general assembly, 2–3, 14, 28, 33, 36, 80, 83, 87, 89, 133, 135, 168–69, 191, 259, 261–62, 312, 326, 340, 346; member states, 81, 141
United States, 12–15, 71, 95–96, 105–7, 117, 119–20, 122–23, 128–30, 136–38, 148–49, 185–86, 188–91, 287–89, 293–95; and China, 110–11, 289; and Russia, 41, 107, 111–13, 116, 121–22, 136, 146–47, 149, 159, 176–78, 181, 186, 264, 287, 291, 293, 295
United States Conference of Catholic Bishops (USCCB), xiii, 45, 36, 157, 169, 236, 311, 322, 347, 358, 382, 386; National Conference of Catholic Bishops, 3–28, 38–48, 52–60, 69–76, 79–90, 103–35, 160–72, 220–27, 229–37, 251–69, 294–97, 309–27, 329–44; US bishops, 9–10, 24, 25, 38, 161–62, 193, 223, 241, 243, 298–301; US Catholic bishops, 2, 8, 35, 37, 41–42, 45, 199, 229–30, 385; USCC, 28, 36, 43, 168–69, 191, 199, 235, 246
unjust wars, 57, 236
uranium, 128, 175–76, 212–13, 218, 255; enriched, 90, 174
US Air Force, 289–90, 292, 296, 298
US arms control policy, 347, 382, 384
US Army, 38; War College, 385
US Congress, 133, 135, 260, 314; US Constitution, 13, 119, 122, 125–26; US courts, 119, 122, 126
US Department of State, 137, 145, 382
use, first, 25, 33, 41–42, 107, 150; indiscriminate, 159; of force in international affairs, 16; policy, 108, 299; use and possession of nuclear weapons, 354; use doctrine, 108, 323; of violence, 41, 45, 221
US Joint Chiefs, 302, 311
US military, 124, 298, 335; code, 297; Navy, 70, 143, 297, 385

US policy, 74, 157, 184–85, 196–97, 199; makers, 183–84, 187
US Senate, 147, 214, 310
US Strategic Command, 71, 125, 291
utility, 47, 51, 114, 335; perceived military, 85–86
utopia, 1, 27, 69, 74, 153, 166, 244, 303, 344

vademecum, xiii
Valente, Judith, 200
values, intrinsic, 61–62
Vatican, xi, xiii, 3, 7, 34–35, 38–39, 43, 59, 63, 163–64, 179, 193–95, 228, 234, 263, 355, 382; Vatican City, 170, 179, 326; Vatican II, xii, xiv, 5, 7, 8, 15, 17, 23, 38, 149–50, 191–92, 221, 230, 298–99, 305–6, 310–11
Väyrynen, Raimo, 168, 170, 382
Vazquez, Carlos M., 126
Veritate Foundation, xiii, 55, 200, 235
Vernadsky, Vladimir, 268
veterans, 91, 93, 176
victims of nuclear weapons, 83, 176; of the bomb, 218
Vienna, 81, 88–89; conference, 55, 82, 86, 88, 329, 333; document, 129, 135
Vietnam, 92, 292, 299
violence, 44, 62, 85, 98, 180, 191, 212, 256, 279, 306, 318
Vise, David A., 337
vision, church's, 165; collective, 36, 164; ethical, 60; idealistic, 160; positive, 161; and moral imperative, 166; Vision Campaign, 260
vocations, 240, 244; moral, 6, 20
von Braun, Joachim, 170

Wada, Masako, 83, 88
Wall Street Journal, 11, 70, 74, 169, 191, 277, 347
Walli, Michael, 12, 28, 91, 99, 387
Waltz, Kenneth L., 56, 170, 191
Walzer, Michael, 10, 54, 57, 236

Wampler, Robert, 74
war, 2, 5, 8–10, 15–16, 31–32, 39, 41–45, 49, 56, 74, 98, 106, 137, 155, 164, 167, 170, 181, 185, 192, 227–28, 231, 236, 240, 274, 302, 306–8, 352; crimes, 156, 190, 310; -fighting strategies, 184; games, 37; instincts, 271; norms, 32, 311; planning, 302; principles, 42, 298, 313; reasoning, 39–40, 42–43, 59; resistance, 92, 100; theories, thinkers, 8–10, 16, 38–39, 41–46, 54, 163, 244; tradition, 8, 35, 38–39, 165, 167, 297, 319; victims, 16, 176; zones, 172, 178
warfare, asymmetric, 40; conventional, 198; counterpopulation, 41
warheads, 24, 110, 128, 137, 214, 256, 323
Warsaw Pact, 129; uprising, 188
waste, contaminated, 211, 333; hazardous, 176, 210
Watergate scandal, 292
Watson, Kathryn, 310
Watt, Helen, 236
weapons, 15–16, 23–25, 39, 41, 73, 97, 111, 120, 128, 133, 149, 172, 174–76, 196, 215, 220, 225, 240, 253, 262, 302, 306, 316, 319, 321, 325, 333–34, 339; antisatellite, 110; atomic, 177, 262, 314; conventional, 129, 131, 133–34, 225–26, 311, 319, 326; labs, 24; nonnuclear, 134; nuclear, 15, 32, 116, 149, 210, 224, 251; reducing, 345; scientists, xii, 24, 176, 243, 302; space, 114; systems, 33, 109–11, 176, 178, 301, 307, 324, 328, 335
weapons of mass destruction (WMD), 13–14, 40, 58, 128, 131, 134, 136–43, 155, 223, 225–26, 298–99, 319, 325, 333
Webb, Eugene, 217
Weida, William J., 210–11, 218
Weigel, George, 167
Weiner, Charles, 217

Weiss, Thomas G., 357
Wellerstein, Alex, 253, 261
Werpehowski, William, 9, 31–36, 387
West Africa, 385
Western Shoshone, 213–14
whistle blowers, 292
White, Mark, 118
Wieland, Paki, 100
Williams, Hattie, 333
Williams, Ian, 145
Williams, Jody, 210
Wilson, Carroll L., 211
Wilson, Ward, 55, 179, 347
Winright, Tobias, 10, 37–46, 387
Winters, Francis, 327
wisdom, 226, 241, 282, 310
witnesses, 11, 69, 76–89, 220, 306
WMD. *See* weapons of mass destruction
women, 173, 176, 238–39, 242–43, 280–81, 304–5, 307; International League, 92, 387
Wooden, Cindy, 312
Woodrow Wilson International Center for Scholars, 21, 263
workers, 177, 210, 212–13, 216; Catholic (*see* Catholic Worker); pastoral, xii, 3–4, 9, 19, 242, 309

world, 16, 133, 178, 199, 226, 298, 306, 319, 338; free, 82, 134, 166, 251, 329; nuclear forces, 336; peace, 2, 355; politics, 15, 357; security, 74
worldviews, 19, 269, 272; individual, 352
world war, 93, 225, 271; World War I, 182, 221, 271, 319; World War II, 128, 134, 186, 188, 190, 221, 319, 321, 325; World War IV, 321
Wynne, Michael, 290

Y-12 National Security Complex, 12, 90–91, 96, 98
Yanchar, Stephen C., 66
Yemen, 137
Yoder, John Howard, 41–46

Zak, Dan (*Washington Post* reporter, author of *Almighty: Courage, Resistance, and Existential Peril in the Nuclear Age*), 100
Zala, Benjamin, 163, 170
Zamagni, Stefano, 170
Zartman, William, 357
Zinn, Howard, 96
Zizola, Giancarlo, 1, 27

About the Contributors

KEVIN AHERN, Manhattan College, associate professor of religious studies. Catholic theologian, ethics of church movements and structures. Past director, Peace and Justice Studies and Labor Studies. Past president, International Movement of Catholic Students. Selected books: *Structures of Grace: Catholic Organizations Serving the Global Common Good* (Orbis, 2015) and *God's Quad: Small Faith Communities on Campus and Beyond* (Orbis, 2019).

WILLIAM BARBIERI, Catholic University of America, professor of ethics, research on historicity of morals. Religion and Culture and Moral Theology/Ethics programs, School of Theology and Religious Studies. Director, Peace and Justice Studies Program. Fellow, Institute for Policy Research and Catholic Studies, Center for the Study of Culture and Values. Selected books: *Constitutive Justice* (Palgrave, 2015); *From Just War to Modern Peace Ethics* (DeGruyter, 2012, with Heinz-Gerhard Justenhoven). Articles on human rights, comparative ethics, peace studies, Catholic social teaching, and German studies.

LISA SOWLE CAHILL, Boston College, J. Donald Monan, SJ Professor of Theology. Past president, Catholic Theological Society of America; Society of Christian Ethics. Board member, *Journal of Religious Ethics; Theology; Asian Horizons*. Selected books: *Global Justice, Christology and Christian Ethics* (Cambridge, 2013); *Blessed Are the Peacemakers: Pacifism, Just War and Peacebuilding* (Fortress, 2019).

DREW CHRISTIANSEN, SJ, Georgetown University, Distinguished Professor, Ethics and Human Development, School of Foreign Service. Senior Fellow, Berkley Center for Religion, Peace, and World Affairs. Previously faculty at Jesuit School of Theology/Graduate Theological Union–Berkeley. University of Notre Dame, founding member of the Kroc Institute for International Peace Studies. Past director, United States Conference of Catholic Bishops Office of International Justice and Peace. Past editor, *America*, the Jesuit weekly journal of opinion. Selected book (of four): *A World Free from Nuclear Weapons: The Vatican Conference on Disarmament* (Georgetown University Press, 2020), lead editor. Second place, Catholic Media Association awards, theology/ethics. Contributing editor, *Journal of Catholic Social Thought* and the *Review of Faith in International Affairs.* Director, United States Conference of Catholic Bishops Foreign Affairs Office, working in global trouble spots including Guatemala, Haiti, Mexico, Northern Ireland, Croatia and Bosnia, Israel-Palestine, Jordan, and Lebanon. Consultant to the Holy See (Vatican) on the Middle East and Middle East Christians, religious freedom, and nuclear disarmament.

PIERCE S. CORDEN, Holy See Mission to the United Nations, New York, expert adviser. American Association for the Advancement of Science-Center for Science, Technology and Security Policy, visiting scholar (2009–16). Provisional Technical Secretariat, Comprehensive Nuclear-Test-Ban Treaty, director of administration (2002–7). US Department of State, office director (1999–2002). US Arms Control and Disarmament Agency (1971–99), division chief 1989–99. PhD, University of Pennsylvania; BS, Georgetown University.

DAVID CORTRIGHT, University of Notre Dame, professor emeritus, Kroc Institute for International Peace Studies. Selected books: *Truth Seekers: Voices of Peace and Nonviolence* (Orbis, 2020); *Towards Nuclear Zero* (Routledge, 2010, with Raimo Väyrynen); *Peace: A History of Movements and Ideas* (Cambridge University Press, 2008). Executive director of SANE, the Committee for a Sane Nuclear Policy (1978–88).

KELSEY DAVENPORT, Arms Control Association (Herbert Scoville Jr. Peace Fellow), director for nonproliferation policy, focusing on the nuclear and missile programs in Iran, North Korea, India, and Pakistan.

Reports for *Arms Control Today* and runs the Arms Control Association's project assessing the effectiveness of multilateral voluntary initiatives that contribute to nonproliferation efforts. MA, peace studies, Kroc Institute for International Peace Studies; BA summa cum laude, international studies and political science, Butler University.

THEODORE G. DEDON, Georgetown University, Department of Theological and Religious Studies, PhD 2022. Research focuses on religion and international affairs, religious nationalism, countering violent extremism, and comparative, theological approaches to religious pluralism and religious rivalries (especially Muslim-Christian and Orthodox-Catholic relations). 2020 Teacher of the Year in Humanities, Graduate School of Arts and Sciences, Georgetown University.

JOSEPH J. FAHEY, Manhattan College, professor of religious studies (retired); former director of the BA in peace studies. Past general secretary, Pax Christi USA. *War and the Christian Conscience: Where Do You Stand?* (Orbis, 2014). PhD, New York University, Christian social ethics; MA, BA, Maryknoll Seminary, philosophy and theology.

JAMES E. GOODBY (ambassador, retired). Hoover Institution, Annenberg Distinguished Visiting Fellow. US Foreign Service, career minister. International security negotiations, the Soviet Union, and later the Russian Federation. Past head, US delegation to the Conference on Confidence- and Security-Building Measures and Disarmament in Europe. Chief negotiator, the Helsinki Process, Cooperative Threat Reduction (the Nunn-Lugar program). Service: US Missions to the European Community, NATO, later deputy assistant secretary of state for European affairs, and ambassador to Finland. Worked with George Shultz at Stanford University's Hoover Institution (2007–21).

DANIEL HALL, Soka Gakkai International–USA, director, public affairs. US Institute of Peace, conference organizer, "Making a Difference: Faith Communities and the Humanitarian Impact of Nuclear Weapons"; United States Capitol Visitor Center, "Toward a Fundamental Change in Nuclear Weapons Policy"; and "Eliminating Nuclear Weapons before They Eliminate US: Opportunities under the Biden Administration to Take Action." Citizen lobbyist, 2017 United Nations preparatory meetings, Treaty on the Prohibition of Nuclear Weapons. Book chapter: "Pope John Paul II, Radio Free Europe and Faith Diplomacy," *Religion and Public Diplomacy* (Palgrave MacMillan, 2013).

DAVID HOLLOWAY, Stanford University, professor emeritus of history and political science. PhD, social and political sciences, and MA, modern languages, Cambridge University. Selected books: *The Soviet Union and the Arms Race* (Yale, 1983) and *Stalin and the Bomb: The Soviet Union and Atomic Energy, 1939–1955* (Yale, 1994). Book in progress on the international history of nuclear weapons. Born and raised in Ireland.

DAVID A. KOPLOW, Georgetown University Law Center, is a professor of law, teaching public international law and national security law, with an emphasis on arms control, nonproliferation, outer space, and counterterrorism. He is the author of five books and multiple law review articles on treaty negotiation, verification, and implementation. Koplow has served as US Arms Control and Disarmament Agency attorney-adviser and special assistant to the director (1978–81) and as US Department of Defense deputy general counsel for international affairs (1997–99) and special counsel for arms control to the general counsel (2009–11).

LAWRENCE J. KORB, Center for American Progress, senior fellow. Previous senior fellow and director of national security studies, Council on Foreign Relations. Council vice president, director of studies, and holder of the Maurice Greenberg Chair (1998–2002).

DAVID LAMMY, Member of Parliament. LLB (Hons), SOAS School of Law, University of London. First Black Briton at Harvard Law. Member of Parliament for Tottenham, the most ethnically diverse constituency in Europe. Ministerial posts (Labour) include Culture and Higher Education. Commissioned by Prime Minister David Cameron to lead an independent probe into Black, Asian, and minority ethnic criminal justice outcomes (2017). Shadow justice secretary in Labour leader Keir Starmer's first team (2020). Delivered first School of Law Annual Inception Lecture at SOAS, University of London (2011).

JOHN PAUL LEDERACH, University of Notre Dame, professor emeritus; director of the Peace Accords Matrix, Kroc Institute for International Peace Studies. Known for pioneering work in conflict transformation, especially in Colombia, the Philippines, and Nepal plus East and West Africa and globally. Twenty-two books on peace and conflict resolution. PhD, sociology, University of Colorado.

MARYANN CUSIMANO LOVE, Catholic University of America, associate professor, politics. PhD, Johns Hopkins. Service: Pope Francis Security Task Force; Arms Control Association, Board of Directors; US Catholic Bishops' International Justice and Peace Committee; and Catholic Peacebuilding Network, Advisory Board. Previous work: Core Group, Department of State's working group on Religion and Foreign Policy; fellow, Commission on International Religious Freedom; ethics fellow, US Naval Academy. Selected book (of thirteen best-selling): *Global Issues beyond Sovereignty* (Rowman & Littlefield, 2020).

RICHARD A. LOVE, National Defense University, professor of cyber law and strategy. Catholic University of America, teaches courses in law and politics. Past professor of strategic studies, United States Army War College; assistant director and professor of the Irregular Warfare, Peacekeeping and Stability Operations Institute. PhD, international relations and security studies, University of New South Wales; LLM, American University College of Law; JD, George Mason University School of Law.

RAMÓN LUZÁRRAGA, Benedictine University, assistant professor and founding faculty member of theology. PhD, systematic theology and ethics, Marquette University; MAR, Yale Divinity School; and BA, Fordham University, political science and theology. Research on Catholic faith, doctrine, and practice; political theology; and Hispanic and Caribbean theology.

JAMES P. O'SULLIVAN, St. Joseph's University, assistant professor, social ethics; advisory board member, Faith Justice Institute and Institute for Clinical Bioethics. PhD, Boston College, theological and philosophical ethics. Studies social and economic justice, human rights, human development, and the relationship between Catholic social thought and secular political and moral philosophy.

MARGARET R. PFEIL, Notre Dame, joint appointment in Theology and the Center for Social Concerns. Faculty fellow, Kroc Institute for International Peace Studies and Klau Institute for Civil and Human

Rights. Founder and resident, St. Peter Claver Catholic Worker Community, South Bend, Indiana.

DANIEL PHILPOTT, Notre Dame, professor of political science. PhD, Harvard University, studies religion and global politics, religious freedom, reconciliation, political behavior of religious actors, and Christian political theology. Selected books: *Just and Unjust Peace: An Ethic of Political Reconciliation* (Oxford University Press, 2012); and *Religious Freedom in Islam: The Fate of a Universal Human Right in the Muslim World* (Oxford University Press, 2019). Reconciliation activist, Kashmir and the Great Lakes Region of Africa.

GERARD F. POWERS, University of Notre Dame, director, Catholic peacebuilding studies, Kroc Institute for International Peace Studies (2004–present). Coordinator, Catholic Peacebuilding Network, Revitalizing Catholic Engagement on Nuclear Disarmament. Past director, Office of International Justice and Peace, US Conference of Catholic Bishops (1998–2004), and policy adviser (1987–98). Selected books: *Catholic Peacebuilding and Mining: Integral Peace, Development, and Ecology* (Routledge, 2022, with Caesar Montevecchio); and *Peacebuilding: Catholic Theology, Ethics and Praxis* (Orbis, 2010, with Robert Schreiter and R. Scott Appleby).

BERNARD G. PRUSAK, King's College, Wilkes-Barre, Pennsylvania, professor of philosophy. Director, McGowan Center for Ethics and Social Responsibility. Moral and social philosophy, bioethics, theories and cases of conscience. Selected book: *Catholic Moral Philosophy in Practice and Theory: An Introduction* (Paulist Press, 2016); his criticism and public scholarship appear often in *Commonweal*.

GREGORY M. REICHBERG, Peace Research Institute Oslo, research professor. Works on military ethics and is currently researching how use of artificial intelligence is changing the nature of warfare. Consultor to the Holy See's Dicastery on Promoting Integral Human Development.

CAROLE SARGENT, Georgetown University, literary historian, founding director, Office of Scholarly Publications. Selected books: *A World Free from Nuclear Weapons: The Vatican Conference on Disarmament*

(Georgetown University Press, 2020, with lead editor Drew Christiansen, SJ); and *Transform Now Plowshares: Megan Rice, Gregory Boertje-Obed, and Michael Walli* (Liturgical Press, 2022). RSCJ Associate (Society of the Sacred Heart).

SUSI SNYDER, past president, International Campaign to Abolish Nuclear Weapons during negotiations on the Treaty for the Prohibition of Nuclear Weapons and when the organization won the Nobel Peace Prize (2017). Coordinator, Don't Bank on the Bomb. Nuclear Free Future Award colaureate, 2016. Previously, secretary-general of the Women's International League for Peace and Freedom, Geneva; manager, nuclear disarmament efforts, PAX (Dutch NGO).

WILLIAM WERPEHOWSKI, Georgetown University, Robert L. McDevitt, K.S.G., K.C.H.S. and Catherine H. McDevitt L.C.H.S. Chair in Catholic Theology. Selected books: *Karl Barth and Christian Ethics: Living in Truth* (Ashgate, 2014); and *American Protestant Ethics and the Legacy of H. Richard Niebuhr* (Georgetown, 2002). Former president, Society of Christian Ethics. Previously at Villanova University for over three decades; director, Center for Peace and Justice Education (1999–2010).

TOBIAS WINRIGHT, Saint Patrick's Pontifical University, Maynooth, professor of moral theology. Associate member, Las Casas Institute for Social Justice, Blackfriars Hall, University of Oxford. Selected books: *Can War Be Just in the 21st Century? Ethicists Engage the Tradition* (Orbis, 2015); and *After the Smoke Clears: The Just War Tradition and Post War Justice* (Orbis, 2010, with Mark Allman). Coeditor, *Journal of the Society of Christian Ethics* (2012–17). Vice president, College Theology Society (2019–21).